NOAH'S ARK

NOAH'S ARK

AN ANNOTATED ENCYCLOPEDIA OF EVERY ANIMAL SPECIES IN THE HEBREW BIBLE

DONALD RAY SCHWARTZ

JASON ARONSON INC.
Northvale, New Jersey
Jerusalem

This book was set in 11 pt. Cheltenham Book by Alabama Book Composition of Deatsville, AL and printed and bound by Book-mart Press, of North Bergen, NJ.

Library of Congress Cataloging-in-Publication Data

Ray Schwartz, Donald.
   Noah's ark : an annotated encyclopedia of every animal species in the Hebrew bible / by Donald Ray Schwartz.
     p.   cm.
   Includes bibliographical references and index.
   ISBN 0-7657-6110-6
   1. Animals in the Bible. 2. Animals in rabbinical literature.
   3. Noah's ark. I. title.
BS663.R39   2000
220.8'59—dc21

99-28887
CIP

Printed in the United States of America on acid-free paper. For information and catalog write to Jason Aronson Inc., 230 Livingston Street, Northvale, NJ 07647-1726, or visit our website: www.aronson.com

Wherein is described their scientific designation, their behaviors, their significance to the ancients of biblical times, sundry rabbinical and other commentaries, and selected stories of interest and intent.

CONTENTS

Contents

FOREWORD

In the early 1860s H. B. Tristram, a renowned explorer, geographer, and churchman, traversed the entire Middle East area, to survey the "Physical Geography, Geology, and Meteorology of the Holy Land." Tristram's expedition was financed by the American Tract Society, a theological group expressing interest, as was not uncommon in that era, in combining the rational with the theological: that is, of locating the natural sites of the events and miracles described in the biblical text—a sort of physical proof of the true faith.

Although the parameters of the journey had been largely to map out the physical biblical terrain, Tristram soon realized he was observing the animal and plant life mentioned in the text as well. Compelled to set these down, his landmark study of practically every living species mentioned in the text has to this day to be outdone in its exhaustive exploration. There are errors, of course, based on some poor translations, several of which still afflict us (I have attempted to correct as many of these as I can). Nonetheless, overall, his persistence resulted in a benchmark achievement that will probably serve as the standard even into the next century. All biblical animal scholars who have tracked his spoor have properly relied upon it. Therefore, in this fashion, it forms the basis for the current study. A somewhat charming attribute was, again, the rationalist approach that led him, for example, to perceive Behemoth as a hippopotamus rather than the mythical creature of lore, as is the case with Leviathan being reduced to the great blue whale or the crocodile (pp. 50–51; 151f; pp. 257–259).

Tristram was Christian and had little access to the talmudic and midrashic references (although he did know Hebrew, Greek, and Latin and could relate from the ancient works found in those languages in the original). His translation of KoaCH in Leviticus 11:30 as "chameleon" provides an insight into his astute scholarship and the indication that he may still be correct: ". . . There is no certainty as to the exact animal designated . . . The root signifies 'strength'; and the best critics refer it to another lizard . . . The Chameleon itself (*Chamaeleo vulgaris*). . . . From the context it is pretty certain that some lizard is intended, and from the etymology 'to breathe' it is believed to be the Chameleon, which the ancients supposed to live upon air. . . ."

Latter-day scholars in Jewish theology and Judaica in general, such as Toperoff and Schochet, have attempted to fill in these etymological and other relative gaps.

Whether with a zoological background, a Christian theological background, or a Jewish theological background, I am indebted to all these scholars and the works they produced.

Tristram was not the first. That designation must go to the biblical writers themselves, and, following them, the Rabbis, especially of the *tannaim* period. Their contemporaries, the Hellenists, also attempted these observations. Aristotle's treatise is the one we have most complete; it also demonstrates the scientific technique of its day, in some cases reading as if it were written in the second half of the twentieth century, in other cases, seeming to us in our time as quaint and naive.

ACKNOWLEDGMENTS

Other than these scholars who went before me, I would like to give the following acknowledgments—to the fine library and librarians at the Jewish Community Center Library in Omaha, one of the Jewish world's best kept local secrets (soon to be known as The Meyer and Dorothy Kripke Library). To the fine reference librarian staff at Peru State College, especially James Mulder; this is the third resource he has assisted me in, locating material I thought I might not be able to locate. The University of Nebraska at Omaha Library and the Omaha Public Library deserve mention. To the following rabbis at Temple Israel in Omaha, who lent me or gave me access to their volumes without complaint—Sidney Brooks z"l, Aryeh Azriel, and Debbie Stiel. To my son, Mordecai Schwartz, and his wife, Esther Reed, rabbinical students at the Jewish Theological Seminary in New York, who steered me toward some resources I might otherwise have ignored; and whose insights into tracts of *Mishnah* that were difficult for me, provided me with, at once, enlightenment. To my teachers of the past decade, especially Dr. Richard Freund, Rabbi Meyer Kripke, Rabbi Mendel Katzman, Rabbi Joseph Friedman, Rabbi Paul Drazan, Rabbi Sidney Brooks, Rabbi Isaac Nadoff (z"l), Cantor Leo Fettman, and to my students and friends in "Beyond Midrash."

Of course, Arthur Kurzweil of Jason Aronson Inc., whose patience was remarkable and who encouraged me to go forward with the project, even as it developed into a conceptualization neither of us at first envisioned. And, as always, to Ann, who somehow finds a way to put up with me.

Ultimately, however, to those wondrous creatures we share this planet, our world, with. We should be gentler and kinder with them than we are; and we should watch and listen to them. They have much to teach us, if only we would go and learn it.

IN THE BEGINNING:
LIMITATIONS UPON THE
CREATION OF THE WORK

It would be only too easy to fall into the trap of beginning, working through, and ending with the mention of any animal or animals in the text. However, that would result in a Herculean task and one that must ultimately prove redundant.

For the scope of this work, therefore, I have limited the entries to specific species. Thus, for example, in the Flood story, I shall not bother with the animals that entered two by two; rather, only the specific species mentioned will attain sufficient notoriety to be included in this work. Thus, again, in the Flood story, only the raven and the dove receive specific species mention; ergo, they have the honor of being the only ones from that story to be included.

At the same time, however, virtually no singular species of animal will be excluded. In this, I have relied on the purely scientific definition and understanding of the term *animal*; that is, any living creature that is neither a plant nor a fungus, which, at some point in its career, reproduces and experiences locomotion. Thus, a very high order of animal, such as the loyal and dutiful camel, is included; and a very low order of animal, such as the despicable but functional maggot (or worm) is included.

The other process that will be adhered to is the listing methodology. The listing and discussion of the creatures will occur chronologically and by text citation. Thus, the first specific animal, disregarding man and woman, mentioned is the serpent (Genesis 3:1—"Now the serpent was more subtle than any beast of the field which the Lord God had made. And he said unto the woman: 'Yea, hath God said: Ye shall not eat of any tree of the garden?'"); the *serpent* therefore is listed immediately following man and woman. There are a few exceptions, especially toward the end, when it seems a later biblical passage is more significant. By and large, though, the pattern holds.

However, to avoid redundancy in the listings and to provide opportunity for expansion about any place in the text that that animal appears, a *concordance* is included with each listing.

Ultimately, I hope that my readers and I can set about to learn valuable lessons from the creatures that share this vale of tears and laughter, and that share this text, with us. Up to now, we have given them quite short shrift. It is time to pay them their due.

PRELUDE AT CREATION

Three enormously significant creatures are alluded to during the Creation story, albeit they are not, at this point, mentioned literally. We shall not deal with the leviathan, ziz, and behemoth at this point. In any case, one of them is mentioned specifically later in the biblical text. We shall be sure to include them all. They are most significant in Jewish mystical thought. Many stories have been circulated concerning them. (See Genesis 1:21.)

Animals of the biblical text in chronological sequence, with a concordance for each species first named, with divers interesting facts and myths, parables and lessons, commentaries and reports.

1

HUMANITY

What a piece of work is a man! . . . in action how
like an angel! In apprehension how like a
god! . . . the paragon of animals!
I might call him a thing divine . . . Hamlet, II, 2;
The Tempest, I, 2
He has told you O man, what is good.
—Micah 6:8 1.

The first specific animal mentioned in the biblical text is Man, *Homo sapiens* (Genesis 1:26). To avoid rational-theological controversy, at least temporarily, we will deal with this strange creature, as the only one considered a little lower than the angels.

"And God said, 'Let us make man in our image, after our likeness. They shall rule the fish of the sea, the birds of the sky, the cattle, the whole earth, and all the creeping things that creep on earth.'" (See also Genesis 2:7, 2:22, and 5:1.) Fundamentalist theologians will perceive three or four continuing versions of the same story; a more academic version perceives three or four different writers of the same ancient Mesopotamian legend, "Judaized," of course, and connected by a common strand woven together by the Redactor of the text.

1

The Rabbis said that God, the Master Architect, worked with a master plan of creation before Him. This plan was the Torah, which provided that His world would exist not merely for the sake of existing but for a moral purpose bound up with the creation of man. The creature called man is formed in the image of God, in His likeness. These words reflect the Torah's abiding wonder over man's special stature in creation, over his unique intellectual capacity, which bears the imprint of the Creator. This likeness also describes man's moral potential. Man's *nature* is radically different from God's, but man is capable of approaching God's *actions*: His love, His mercy, His justice. Man becomes truly human as he attempts to do the *mitzvot*, the obligations, the God-like deeds. Six times the Bible says that God found His creation "good"; after man was created, He found it "very good." Being is better than nothingness, order superior to chaos, and man's existence—with all its difficulties—a blessing. But creation is never called perfect; it will in fact be man's task to assist the Creator in perfecting His creation, to become His co-worker.

It says that God found His creation to be "very good," which implies a comparison. From this, it may be inferred that God had created and destroyed previous worlds. (*Midrash*, in Plaut, p. 24)

Every man should know that since creation no other man ever was like him. Had there been such another, there would be no need for him to be. Each is called on to perfect his unique qualities. And it is his failure to heed this call which delays the Messiah. (Baal Shem Tov, in Plaut, p. 24)

Humanity is commanded to master or to take dominion over the earth. The nations, and even, to some extent, *b'nai yisrael* (the children [or *ahm*, people] of Israel), have at times interpreted this passage to mean that all other animal and plant life exists on earth only for humanity to take and use for humanity's benefit. Now, it is most certainly true in the traditional view (and may very well be true in any case) that the *korbanim*, the Temple sacrifices, not only elevated the individual engaging in the ritual but elevated the animal as well. In fact, even today, chasidic and fully Orthodox communities perform the customary ritual of *kipporah* during the Days of Awe (which became known as *shlepping kipporah*, although it is a misnomer—i.e., the animal is *not* [and certainly never should be] hurled or twirled about). The live chicken is held above the head of the celebrant, to expiate for the year's sins. Following this solemn part of the ritual, the bird is given a ritual slaughter. Again, it is believed by those observing this rabbinic precept that the animal is indeed elevated to a higher plane of existence. Of course, the celebrant is also elevated. It is a rare remnant memory of the practice of the *korban* as it existed in Temple times. It should not be dismissed in so cavalier a fashion and scoffed at by the modern world, as often happens.

In any event, however, the precept of the sacrificial ceremonies presents no indication that unadulterated exploitation of animal life and its habitat is in any way defensible. Indeed, the Jewish calendar, which still operates based upon the lunar cycle, and holidays such as Succot recall an affinity for the natural world, for preserving its beauty, and for the preservation of wildlife. When one first comes upon a fruit tree, one is obligated to recite a blessing. When one engages in war, such trees are, nearly at all cost, to be spared.

The sacrificial offerings that occurred during the Jerusalem Temple rituals were immersed in blood, incense, and the rising of the smoke through the earthly realms up unto the heavenly realms. It must have been a highly emotional and spiritual encounter for the individual to see his or her animal or crop sacrifice with all good intent of the guilt-offering or the sin-offering to rise and ascend unto the first portal of the seven portals of heaven. And there was a practical matter as well. The priests and the Levites who performed and tended the rituals consumed the burnt portions along with their families. There was no waste. There was mastery. There was no exploitation of resources.

Plaut, on page 25, quotes directly from Robert Gordis regarding this passage.

> To claim that (Genesis 1:28, master [the earth]) provides "justification" for the exploitation of the environment, leading to the poisoning of the atmo-

sphere, the pollution of our water, and the exploitation of natural resources is . . . a complete distortion
of the truth. On the contrary, the Hebrew Bible and
the Jewish interpreters *prohibit* such exploitation.
Judaism goes much further and insists that man has
an obligation not only to conserve the world of
nature but to enhance it because man is the co-
partner of God in the work of creation. . . . All animal
life and all growing and life-giving things have rights
in the cosmos that man must consider, even as he
strives to ensure his own survival. The war against
the spoilation of nature and the pollution of the
environment is therefore the command of the hour
and the call of the ages.

Hertz, on pages 4 and 5, includes the traditional theological
viewpoint.

Mankind is described as in a special sense created by
God Himself. To enhance the dignity of this last work
and to mark the fact that man differs in kind from the
animals, Scripture represents God as deliberating
over the making of the human species. Man is made
in the "image" and "likeness" of God: his character is
potentially Divine. . . . Because man is endowed with
Reason, he can subdue his impulses in the service of
moral and religious ideals, and is born to bear rule
over Nature.

Male and female. A general statement: man and
woman, both alike, are in their spiritual nature akin
to God.

And God blessed them. Here the words "And God
said unto them" are added, indicating a more inti-
mate relationship between Him and human beings.

Be fruitful and multiply. This is the first precept
(*mitzvah*) given to man. The duty of building a home
and rearing a family figures in the rabbinic Codes as
the first of the 613 *Mitzvot* . . . of the Torah.

R. Jeremiah b. Leazar said: When the Holy One,
blessed be He, created Adam, He created him a
hermaphrodite (not androgynous, but here it means
two bodies, male and female, joined together), for it
is said, *Male and female created He them and called
their name Adam.* . . . R. Samuel b. Nachman said:

When the Lord created Adam He created him double-faced, then He split him and made him of two backs, one back on this side and one back on the other side. To this it is objected: But it is written, *And He took one of his ribs* . . . R. Tanchuma, in the name of R. Banayah, and R. Berekiah, in the name of R. Leazar, said: He created him as a lifeless mass extending from one end of the world to the other; thus it is written, *Thine eyes did see mine unformed substance* (Psalms 129:16). R. Joshua b. R. Nehemiah and R. Judah b. R. Simon, in R. Leazar's name, said: He created him filling the whole world . . . [that he stretched] from east to west . . .

R. Berekiah said: When the Holy One, blessed be He, came to create Adam, He saw righteous and wicked arising from him. Said He: "If I create him, wicked men will spring from him; if I do not create him, how are the righteous to spring from him?" What then did the Lord do? He removed the way of the wicked out of His sight and associated the quality of mercy with Himself and created him . . .

R. Samuel b. Nachman said, in R. Jonathan's name: When Moses was engaged in writing the Torah, he had to write the work of each day. When he came to the verse, *And God said: Let us make man . . . ,* he said: "Sovereign of the Universe! Why dost Thou furnish an excuse to heretics?" [Herein concerning the plural form in Hebrew, i.e., *elohim.*] "Write," replied He; "whoever wishes to err may err." "Moses," said the Lord to him, "This man that I have created—do I not cause men both great and small to spring from him?"

R. Joshua b. R. Nehebiah said, in the name of R. Chanina b. R. Isaac, and the Rabbis, in the name of R. Leazar, said: He created him with four attributes of the higher beings [i.e., angels] and four attributes of the lower beings [i.e., beasts]. [The four attributes of] the higher beings are: he stands upright, like the ministering angels; he speaks, like the ministering angels; he understands, like the ministering angels; and he sees, like the ministering angels. Yet does not a dumb animal see! But this one [man] can see from the side. He has four attributes of the lower beings: he eats and drinks, like an animal; procreates, like an

animal; excretes, like an animal; and dies, like an
animal. R. Tifdai said in R. Acha's name: The celestial
beings were created in the image and likeness [of
God] and do not procreate, while the terrestrial
creatures [dumb animals] procreate but were not
created in [His] image and likeness. Said the Holy
One, blessed be He: "Behold, I will create him [man]
in [My] image and likeness [so that he will partake]
of the [character of the] celestial beings, while he
will procreate, [after the nature] of the terrestrial
beings." (*Midrash Rabbah* 1:8, *Bereshith* pp. 54–63)

In the following selection of commentary upon the creation
story, Ginzberg alludes to the three Creation stories of humanity. In *Bereshith*: "And God created man in His own image, in the
image of God created He him"; "Male and female created He
them"; "The Lord God formed man of the dust of the ground,
and breathed into his nostrils the breath of life; and man
became a living soul" (2:7); "This is the book of the generations
of Adam. In the day that God created man, in the likeness of
God made He him; male and female created He them, and
blessed them, and called their name Adam, in the day when
they were created" (5:1–2). The author then continues his
discourse concerning their holy and magical union.

When Adam was barely an hour old, God assembled
the whole world of animals before him and the
angels. The latter were called upon to name the
different kinds, but they were not equal to the task.
Adam, however, spoke without hesitation.

The Divine resolution to bestow a companion on
Adam met the wishes of man, who had been over-
come by a feeling of isolation when the animals came
to him in pairs to be named. To banish his loneliness . . . in all her surprising beauty and grace, he
exclaimed, "This is she . . ."

The wedding of the first couple was celebrated
with pomp never repeated in the whole course of
history since. God Himself, before presenting her to
Adam, attired and adorned Eve as a bride. Yea, He
appealed to the angels . . . The angels accordingly
surrounded the marriage canopy, and God pronounced the blessings upon the bridal couple, as the

Hazan does under the *Huppah* (sic). The angels then danced and played upon musical instruments before Adam and Eve in their ten bridal chambers of gold, pearls, and precious stones, which God had prepared for them. . . . as long as they walked in the ways of God and observed His commandments, His name would shield them against all harm. But if they went astray . . . (pp. 59–69).

When I look back, the Garden is a dream to me. It was beautiful, surpassingly beautiful, enchantingly beautiful; and now it is lost, and I shall not see it any more.

The Garden is lost, but I have found *him*, and am content. He *loves* me as well as he can; I love him with all the strength of my passionate nature, and this, I think, is proper to my youth and sex. If I ask myself why I love him, I find I do not know, and do not really much care to know . . . this kind of love is not a product of reasonings and statistics. It just *comes* . . .

It is my prayer, it is my longing, that we may pass from this life together . . .

But if one of us must go first, it is my prayer that it shall be I; for he is strong, I am weak, I am not so necessary to him as he is to me—life without him would not be life; how could I endure it? . . .

(Later, Adam, at Eve's grave): Wheresoever she was, *there* was Eden. (Mark Twain, "The Diary of Adam and Eve")

Noah's Ark

". . . two of each, male and female, came to Noah into the ark, as God had commanded Noah."

Genesis 7:9

"But ask the beasts, and they will teach you;
The birds of the sky, they will tell you,
Or speak to the earth, it will teach you;
The fish of the sea, they will inform you."

Job 12:7–8

2

S E R P E N T

SERPENT (Snake, Viper, Asp . . .)
Hebrew *NaCHaSH*

> *Now the serpent was more subtle than any beast*
> *of the field which the Lord God had made.*
> *And he said unto the woman: "Yea, hath God said:*
> *Ye shall not eat of any tree of the garden?"*
>
> —Genesis 3:1

Elaphe logissima: Elaphes, Greek, a deer (obscure rationale); longus, Latin, long.

Its common name is Aesculapian Snake. In ancient times, this snake was (and is still considered by some to be) associated with Aesclepius, the Greek god of medicine (Aesculapius, Roman) and may be seen as medicine's symbol today. It appears in mysterious and sympathetic healing aspects under the hand of Moses (Exodus 4:3; Numbers 21:9—"And Moses made a *serpent* of brass, and set it upon the pole; and it came to pass, that if a *serpent* had bitten any man, when he looked unto the serpent of brass, he lived"). For this reason and because it is the only large snake with a range throughout the Middle East, I have selected it. An argument could be made for *Naja Naja* since Kipling uses it as the paradigm of his talking snake. But "Nag's" habitat extends from India east through the Philippines, not in any westerly direction.

E. logissima attains a length of up to seven feet; and it has been known, on occasion, to wrap itself in spiral fashion around a straight rod to attain what seems to be a half "standing" position. Most scientists dispute and disclaim this trait. However, folk legends persist concerning this unique ability of the animal. In such a position, it would resemble somewhat a "standing" cobra, sans the hood.

CONCORDANCE

Genesis 49:17.
Exodus 4:3, 4; 7:9, 10, 12, 15.
Numbers 21:6, 8–9.
Deuteronomy 8:15.
2 Kings 18:4 ([Hezekiah] broke in pieces the brazen serpent).
Isaiah 11:8 (. . . Sucking child shall play on the hole of the a[sp]); 14:29; 30:6; 34:15 (arrowsnake); 59:5; 65:25 (and dust shall be the snake's food).
Jeremiah 8:17; 46:22; 48:28 (and be like the dove [see number 5] that maketh her nest in the *pit's* mouth).
Amos 5:19 (see number 16, 60).
Micah 7:17 (they shall lick the dust like a snake).
Psalms II–58:5 (s . . . asp); IV–91:13 (Thou shalt tread upon the lion and *asp*; the young lion and the snake . . .) (See number 16); V–140:4 (They have sharpened their tongues like a snake;/Vipers' venom is under their lips).
Proverbs 30:19 (See number 26) (The way of an eagle in the air; the way of a snake upon a rock).
Job 20:14, 16 (He shall suck the poison of asps;/The *viper's* tongue shall slay him).
Ecclesiastes 10:8, 11 (If the snake bites before it is charmed,/Then the charmer hath no advantage).

The image of the serpent or the snake is one of the most ingrained of icons in Western and Near-Eastern culture. Even a person who has had little or no introduction to the biblical text recognizes the Serpent and Eve story. In medieval and Renaissance art, it is often pictured curled about a tree, hissing its forked tongue at a shamed first couple fleeing the Garden at the aggressive urging of the avenging angel. However, the image of the snake appears in other contexts throughout Scripture.

Some conceptualizations of especial interest concerning the serpent may be pointed out: the concept of atrophied appendages; a talking animal; an animal trained in the Hellenistic rhetorical methodology of persuasion; as a tempter of woman; as an object of fear; as an object of assistance; as a symbol of Dan, the tribe of judges; and, as already indicated, a symbol of the healing arts.

The curious nature of the story also makes it seem almost childlike, like a folk tale; an animal speaks. Of course, all is possible before the expulsion from Eden. However, far later on, after the redemption from slavery and following the revelation at Sinai, there is another case of a talking animal, the donkey or ass of Balaam (Numbers 22:28—"And the Lord opened the mouth of the ass, and she said unto Balaam: 'What have I done unto thee, that thou hast smitten me these three times?'"). Nor is this the only parallel or analogous attributive to these two stories, both at once charming and profound. Indeed, it almost strikes one that a pre-deluvian story somehow found its way by the writers and the Redactor into a later story concerning a renowned heathen prophet who comes to curse and winds up blessing the escaping Israelites.

There is an angel holding a flaming torch or sword in both stories. There is argument and dispute, in the form of dialogue, between the animal and the main person involved in making a critical life decision. In both stories, the animal, not the person, is persuasive; Eve and Balaam are convinced.

The contrast is also obvious. In Eve's case, although her eyes and Adam's are opened, husband and wife now think and behave in ways that were forbidden; ultimately, they must leave Paradise. Balaam, however, convinced in his turn, proceeds to his mission, turned now from evil to good.

Graves describes a cult of moon-priestesses who relied upon Athene for patronage and the half-serpent half-man Aesclepius for their renowned healing abilities. The cult was apparently attacked by followers of Apollo, to ensure a more patriarchal, or masculine, leadership to the gods than an earlier matriarchal, or feminine, one.

Aesclepius apparently had the ability to engage in metamorphosis, changing from half of one species and half of another to that of a complete man or serpent, at least for a temporary time period. As we shall soon see, snake metamorphosis changes history in biblical Egypt as well. Graves's discussion details the complex relationship of the Aesclepiun myth; the reader may uncover certain biblical parallels, in particular the penultimate development of the symbol for healing.

In rabbinic tradition, the serpent was at one time a walking and upright animal, as well as devious yet wise. Apparently, throughout the Mediterranean cultures, the snake was not always an object of fear nor loathing; in fact, it apparently had, or was thought to have, significant healing powers.

> An anonymous Sumerian physician, who lived toward the end of the third millennium B.C., decided to collect and record, for his colleagues and students, his more valuable medical prescriptions. He prepared a tablet of moist clay . . . and wrote down, in the cuneiform script of his day, more than a dozen of his favorite remedies . . . (including) milk, snake skin, and turtle shell. (Kramer, pp. 60–61)

A Rashi commentary: "At first the serpent pushed Eve gently until her hand touched the tree. Then he said: 'You see, nothing happened when you touched the tree. Neither will you die if you eat of the fruit!' ""

The second most famous story concerning snakes in Scripture occurs in Exodus 7:5–13.

> So Moses and Aaron went to Pharaoh and did as the Lord commanded; Aaron cast down his rod before Pharaoh and his servants, and it became a serpent. Then Pharaoh summoned the wise men and the sorcerers; and they also, the magicians of Egypt, did the same by their secret arts. For every man cast down his rod, and they became serpents. But Aaron's rod swallowed up their rods.

In this passage, the Hebrew word employed by the writer is *TaNY(i)N/*, not the *NaCHaSH* of the serpent's first employ. The New Bantam-Megiddo dictionary translates *TaNYN/* as "Crocodile." *The Interpreter's Bible*, however, translates the word as "a dragon or primeval monster." Referring to the increase from "mere" serpent to a lizard-monstrosity, this resource continues: "The element of wonder has grown."

That the rod of Aaron could change or appear to be changed into a serpent-like grotesque was of little or no consequence to Pharaoh and his courtiers. Such magical incantations, such production of wonders, such dramatic visual manifestations were well known to the accomplished court magicians and their sophisticated audiences. The astonishing element that occurred was that Aaron's metamorphosis devoured their metamorphoses. Furthermore, *Midrash Rabbah* comments that the rod neither grew in length nor width with the other rods inside it. Any amateur or would-be observer of herpetology knows that a snake may consume in its diet a hapless victim exceeding the dimensions of its own width; but the outline of the digesting prey will be visible through the girth of the predator for some time. This was all something beyond mere magic.

It was not the first time that Hebrew magic, divinely inspired, had "consumed" Egyptian incantation. Several generations earlier, Moses', Miriam's, and Aaron's ancestor, Joseph, had interpreted dreams for the ruler of Egypt. Again, Egypt had its quite competent coterie of dream interpreters; but that Joseph, a "Hebrew" (not an Egyptian), a "slave" (not a noble free man), and a "youth" (not a wizened elder) should be able to interpret them and do so with validation indicated that a Divine presence ruled over these actions, a Divinity perhaps stronger than the Egyptian gods and Pharaoh. That, in faith so burning, so strong as to be considered absolute, without question, was, of course, known to Joseph, Judah, Benjamin, Jacob (Israel), and later to Moses, his brother, and his sister.

Thus, Joseph's interpretations of his Pharaoh's dreams, personal interpretations that he foresaw but did not tell Pharaoh, were also, like the seven years of plenty and famine, coming to pass. The ugly lean cows ate up the fat cows. The sickly grain ate up the good grain. The rod charged with YHVH's holy direction shape-shifted into a serpent-like creature and ate up the rods of the Egyptian sorcerers, changed in their turn by mere magical arts. Soon, nine plagues would come to eat up the entire land of Egypt. And then, by Pharaoh's own evil decree, firstborn male children—not of the Hebrews, but of the Egyptians—would be taken by Divine retribution; and the children of dreamers would go free

From *Midrash Rabbah*:

> But Aaron's *rod* swallowed up their rods (What is the meaning?) R. Eleazar said: To teach us that a double wonder occurred; the rod resuming its original form and then swallowing up their serpents. When Pharaoh beheld this, he was amazed and said: "What will happen if he now says to his rod: 'Swallow up Pharaoh and his throne'?" R. Jose b. Chanina said: . . . still the rod did not all become any thicker, and all who saw it recognised (sic) it as Aaron's rod. On this account, Aaron's rod became a good symbol for all the miracles and wonders which were to be performed for Israel throughout the generations. (9:7–8)

In 3–4, the *Midrash* inserts this seemingly strange commentary: (in reference to 7:9, And cast it down before pharaoh, that it become a serpent) "We have learnt: One who is praying must not return the greeting even of a king; and even if a serpent has entwined itself round his heel, he must not cease." Now, before continuing with the midrashic commentary at this point, the commentary will be clearer if the cross-reference is indicated.

The *Midrash* is referring to a talmudic reference, specifically, *Berachot* 30B. The *Mishnah* reads as follows:

> One should not stand up to say *tefillah* save "with heaviness of lead" (i.e., in a reverent frame of mind). The pious men of old used to wait an hour before prayers. Even if a king greets him . . . he should not answer him: Even if a snake is wound round his heel, he should not break off.

The *Gemarah* takes about four pages to reach its commentary about the snake-heel part of this *Mishnah*.

> R. Shesheth said: This applies only in the case of a serpent, but if it is a *scorpion* [see number 35], he breaks off (the argument is, a scorpion is more certain to sting). An objection was raised: If a man

fell into a den of *lions* [see number 16] . . . one
cannot testify . . . that he is dead, but if he fell into a
trench full of serpents or scorpions one can testify
concerning him that he is dead! The case there is
different, because on account of his crushing them
[in falling] they turn and bite him. R. Isaac said: If he
sees *oxen* [see number 13] [coming towards him] he
may break off: For R. Oshaia taught: One should
remove from a *tam* (i.e., an ox which has not been
known to gore) fifty cubits, and from a *mu'ad* (i.e., an
ox which has been known to gore three times) out of
sight. It was taught in the name of R. Meir: If an ox's
head is in a [fodder] basket (i.e., even if it is busy
eating) go up to a roof and kick the ladder away
(Soncino indicates this to be a humorous exaggera-
tion). Samuel said: This applies only to a black ox
and in the month of Nissan, because then Satan is
dancing between his horns.

At this point, the *Gemarah* digresses into a fascinating
story concerning one of the miracle rabbis, R. Channia b. Dosa.
It seems that in a certain community, there was a feared
creature. Soncino translates the word *YaRoD* as "lizard." Perhaps this is a similar creature to Aaron's rod-serpent; or, since
it is clearly evil, a Satan-manifested lizard-snake. The story
reminds one of the Greek myth of Oedipus. The once and
future king, already guilty, albeit at this point unwittingly, of
patricide, solves the riddle of the Sphinx, a half-woman,
half-lion monster, and relieves the community of its oppression. It is interesting that Oedipus, a very physically strong
man, solves this immediate problem by his wits; R. Dosa solves
his by his wits and, like his Egyptian ancestors, by his faith.

R. Channia b. Dosa . . . said: Show me its hole. . . .
he put his heel over the hole, and the (creature) bit
him, and it died. He put it on his shoulder and
brought it to the Beth ha-Midrash and said to them:
See, my sons, it is not the lizard that kills, it is sin that
kills!

The *Gemarah* here ends with a warning to all evil creatures.
"Woe to the man whom a lizard meets, but woe to the lizard

which R. Channia b. Dosa meets!" An additional commentary
indicates that a spring of water had miraculously opened at
the feet of R. Channia and that was what "sealed" the fate of
the lizard.

In a different *Gemarah* (62a–62b), in response to this
Mishnah (54a): "If one sees a place where miracles have been
wrought for Israel, he should say, 'Blessed be He who wrought
miracles for our ancestors in this place (and the same for a
place where idolatry has been extirpated)'": "It has been
taught: Ben 'Azzai says: Lie on anything but not on the
ground . . .' (i.e., for fear of serpents)."

The implication is obvious; this decree would not have
been placed here by the Rabbis had not a reference or a story
been indicated somewhere that such a tragedy occurred to
some one. Pilgrimages have been known to Jews for centuries.
Since the expulsion, many in each generation ventured to see
the holy land and the Temple Mount. Tombs and graves of
revered rabbis and sages were and still are visited. Considering the dangers inherent in all of these travels, Ben 'Azzi's
advice is no doubt most sound.

On a less pragmatic level, *Gemarah* 55b indicates the evil
manifestation of the serpent. ". . . Four died through the serpent's machinations, viz Benjamin b. Jacob; Amram, the father
of Moses; Jesse the father of David; and Caleb b. David."

Now, to return to *Midrash Rabbah* 9:3, based on Exodus 8:9
(again, *And cast it down before Pharaoh that it become a
serpent*), the phrase "We have learnt One (sic) who is praying
must not return the greeting even of a king; and even if a
serpent has entwined itself round his heel, he must not cease"
is, in consideration of the cross-reference to *Berachot* 30b,
clearer. The *Midrash* now asks what made the Sages compare
the twining of a snake to the kingdom of Egypt, and why did
God compare the kingdom of Egypt to a serpent.

> Just as a serpent is twisted, so does the kingdom of
> Egypt pervert her ways. Hence God said to Moses:
> "Just as a serpent is crooked, so is Pharaoh; and
> when he begins being crooked, just tell Aaron to
> raise the rod in front of him, as if to say: 'By this wilt
> thou be smitten.'"

There may be a subtext understanding here as well. In the *Midrash*'s own language, we have learned that one of Egypt's gods and symbol of power was the snake, in its erect aspect.

That the hapless snake was perceived as a representative of Satan, or even an aspect of Satan himself, is a very old tradition that can be perceived in several ancient writings, including *The Book of the Secrets of Enoch*. It is considered by the scholars to be a pristine example of pseudepigrapha. Barnstone states: "It was probably written by a Hellenistic Jew from Alexandria in the first century. There may have been a Hebrew original for parts of the book, but the present versions, two texts surviving in Old Church Slavonic, are translations from the Greek." That it represents a Jewish viewpoint, and not a Christian one, is strongly indicated. Here is an excerpt (page 6 in Barnstone); the Rabbis, in indicating the evil nature of Egypt and of Pharaoh, would have been quite aware of this tradition.

> (Satan) is the evil spirit of the lower places, a fugitive. . . . He entered his world and seduced Eve (sic) but did not touch Adam. . . . I said to him, "You are earth, and into the earth from which I took you, you shall go, and I shall not destroy you but send you away from where I placed you."

Preuss's lengthiest discourse concerning this matter occurs on pages 196–199, under the heading of "Snakebites." Preuss points out that snakes are "by far" the most dangerous animals for people throughout the Middle East. As we have seen earlier, the scorpion (number 35) was regarded even more so, but Preuss seems to place the two animals in a singular category.

From *Pirke Avot* 5:8, Preuss finds that an animal such as an ox that gores may be put away only after an orderly court-proceeding, but a snake should be dealt death whenever one finds it. The story of R. Dosa again wiggles to mind. "The danger from snakes existed everywhere: a thirsty maiden descended to a well to drink. When she placed her hand on the stone wall, a snake emerged and bit her, and she died of the bite."

At this point, Preuss sheds some light upon the *seraph*

snakes, the so-called fiery serpents that bit many Israelites, who subsequently died. This is the passage in Numbers 21:4–9 where Moses constructs his brass snake pole, perhaps resembling a modern-day caduceus, the symbol of medicine. Once again, the Aesclepian Snake was the species chosen for this very entry. The sympathetic magic-mystery-medicine phenomenon worked in this way: Whoever was bitten would look upon the brass staff; this victim would remain alive and would be healed. We shall not dwell at this point in the matter of the power of faith healing and of mind and fervent belief over science. However, that the technique had deteriorated into plain idol worship under the monarchy is obvious. The Israelites had come to worship the brass staff not as a source from where their true strength comes, but as an idol. Hezekiah destroyed the object (2 Kings 18:10).

> The *Mishnah* (*Rosh Hoshana* 3:8) categorically asserts: the brass snake neither killed nor brought back to life; rather, if those bitten were reminded to serve God by looking at the (brass) snake, they would remain alive. So, too, in the Wisdom of Solomon, it states: "They saw a picture of deliverance which reminded them of the judgement (sic) of God, for if someone turned to Him, he is not saved by the looking at the picture but by the Savior and Redeemer of all mankind."

Preuss also points out some interesting *kashrut* indications: it was forbidden to eat an animal (presumably, no matter how kosher it was otherwise) that was known to have been bitten by a snake. This prohibition extended to meat that had already passed previous inspection, even had been cooked and prepared. This admonition extended to suspicious-looking fruits and vegetables.

> It once happened in a place called Zalmon that a certain man called out: "I was bitten by a snake and I am about to die"; when they reached him, they could no longer recognize him (from his swelling up).
> During the time of the *Tosefta*, a physician was called for a man who was bitten by a snake; . . . a hen was dismembered for him and a leek was cut

for him, obviously the well-known medicine. The physician's duty was "to heal the patient with his tongue," i.e., to suck out the wound, a method known since antiquity. Plinius relates that the Ophiogenites "healed snake bites with their spittle."

Nebuchadnezzar had a snake . . . which swallowed up everything thrown to it. He was very proud of it and thought it invincible. Daniel hid nails in straw and threw it to the snake. The snake swallowed the nails and they lacerated its bowels (*Genesis Rabbah* 68:13). (In "Bel and the Dragon," the food projectile by Daniel was made of a cake of pitch, fat, and hair.)

Preuss has some additional entries throughout the work.

AN ADDITIONAL TALMUD TAIL (*Avodah Zorah* 29b–30b)

The *Mishnah* deals with forbidden objects (or any benefit derived from them) belonging to heathens, such as wine, animal skin pierced at the heart (perhaps the heart was used for an idol sacrifice), and hadrianic earthenware.

The *Gemarah* derives how an inspector is to recognize the age of a serpent by the avoirdupois characteristic of the venom. "R. Safra said in the name of R. Joshua of the South: There are three kinds of venoms: that of a young one sinks to the bottom, that of one not quite young drops to about the middle; while that of an old one floats to the top."

The discussion then attempts to refute that as a serpent ages, its strength diminishes, with a reference to *Shabbat* 77b (There are three whose strength increases as their age advances ". . . a fish, a serpent, and a swine!"). The reconciliation is: "Its strength may indeed increase, but its venom becomes weaker." R. Jeremiah then relates the story of the ten who drank from the same barrel. The first nine were fine; the tenth died, for the "venom" had sunk to the bottom. The story can be seen as a metaphor, of course.

3

SHEEP

SHEEP (Ewe, Lamb; but Ram Separate—See number 8)
Hebrew *Tso'N*

> *She then bore his brother Abel. Abel became a
> keeper of sheep, and Cain became a tiller of the soil.*
> —Genesis 4:2

Ovis aries: *Ovis*, Latin, a sheep; *aries*, Latin, a ram.

There are today over four hundred breeds of this ancient, fully domesticated species. Its actual ancestry is unknown or uncertain to science. (See also number 8.)

CONCORDANCE

Genesis 20:14; 21:27, 28, 29, 30; 22:7, 8; 24:35; 29:2–3; 6–10; 30:32–33, 35, 40;
    31:19, 38; 33:14; 47:17.
Exodus 9:3; 12:3–5, 21; 13:13; 20:24; 22:1, 4, 9, 10, 30; 29:38, 40; 34:20.
Leviticus 1:10; 3:7; 4:32, 35; 5:6–7; 7:23; 12:6, 8; 14:10, 12–13, 21, 24–25; 17:3;
    22:19, 23, 26, 28; 23:12, 18–20; 27:26.
Numbers 6:14; 7:15, 17, 21, 23, 27–28, 33, 35, 39, 41, 45, 47, 51, 53, 57, 59, 63,
    65, 69, 71, 75, 77, 81, 83, 87–88; 15:5, 11; 18:17; 22:40; 28:3–4, 7-9, 11, 13,
    19, 21, 27, 29; 29:2, 4, 8, 10, 13, 15, 17–18, 20–21, 23–24, 26–27, 29–30,
    32–33, 36–37; 31:32, 36–37, 43; 32:24, 36.
Deuteronomy 14:4; 17:1; 18:3–4; 22:1; 28:31; 32:14.
Joshua 6:21; 7:24.

Judges 6:4.

1 Samuel 7:9; 14:32, 34; 15:3, 9, 14–15, 21; 16:11 (he [David] keepeth the sheep [or, flock]), 19; 17:15, 20, 28, 34 (and flock); 22:19 (Slaughter of the Priests of Nob); 24:3 (cotes); 25:2, 4, 16, 18; 27:9.

2 Samuel 7:8; 12:2, 4, 6; 13:23 (Absalom had sheep shearers)–24; 17:29; 24:17.

1 Kings 1:9, 19, 25; 5:3; 8:5, 63; 22:17.

2 Kings 3:4; 5:26.

Isaiah 1:11; 5:17; 7:21, 25; 11:6 (and the wolf [number 18] shall dwell with the l[amb]); 13:14; 16:1; 22:13; 34:6; 40:11; 53:6 (are we like sheep did go astray)–7 (as a lamb that is led to the slaughter, and as a sheep . . .); 65:25 (the wolf [number 18] and the lamb shall feed together); 66:3.

Jeremiah 11:19 (But I was like a docile lamb that is led to the slaughter); 12:3; 23:1; 50:6 (my people have been lost sheep), 17 (see numbers 16); 51:40 (see numbers 7, 8).

Ezekiel 27:21 (see numbers 7, 8); 34:2, 6–12, 15, 19; 39:18 (see numbers 7, 8, and 27); 45:15; 46:4–7, 11, 13, 15.

Hosea 4:16 (see number 6); 12:13.

Joel 1:18; 6:4 (see number 11).

Micah 5:7 (see number 16).

Zechariah 10:2; 13:7 (smite the shepherd, and the sheep shall be scattered).

Psalms I–8:8 (see number 15); 37:20 (And the enemies of the Lord shall be as the fat of lambs); II-44:23 (Nay, but for thy sake are we killed . . . accounted as sheep for the slaughter); III–78:52, 71 (From following the eyes that give suck He brought him [David]); 104:4 (The hills like young sheep) (see number 8), 6: V–114:4 [and again]), 6 (see number 8); 144:13.

Proverbs 27:26 (see number 7).

Job 1:3 (see numbers 10, 13, 15), 16 (. . . A fire of God . . . hath burned up the sheep); 31:20; 42:12 (see numbers 10, 13, 15).

Song of Songs 4:2 (Thy teeth are like a flock of ewes/All shaped alike . . .); 6:6.

Ezra 6:17 (see also numbers 7, 8, 27), 20; 7:17 (see also numbers 8, 27); 8:35 (see also 7, 8, 27).

Nehemiah 3:1 (Then Eliashib the high priest and his fellow priests . . . rebuilt the sheep gate; . . .), 32; 5:18 (see number 15); 12:39.

1 Chronicles 5:21 (see numbers 10, 12, 13); 12:41 (see numbers 10, 13, 15); 17:7 (. . . I took thee . . . from following the sheep, that thou shouldest be prince over my people Israel); 21:17; 29:21 (see also numbers 8, 27).

2 Chronicles 5:6 (see number 15); 7:4 (see number 15); 14:14 (see numbers 12, 14), 32 (see also numbers 8, 27)–33 (see also number 15); 30:15 (Then they killed the Passover lamb on the fourteenth day of the second month; . . .), 17, 24 (see also number 27); 31:6 (see also number 15); 35:1 (And Josiah kept a passover unto the Lord in Jerusalem; and

they killed the passover lamb on the fourteenth day of the first month),
6–7, 11.

One of the most numerous of the creature images in the
Hebrew Bible, the significance of this docile and fully domesticated animal to the Israelite writers of the text was pervasive.
It is significant in its historicity; it is significant in the quality of
its metaphor. Albeit Christianity developed even to a greater
extent the concept of the Lord as a Shepherd, and the people
as a flock—still, the verse from David's Twenty-Third Psalm
rings out across the ages: To reflect our bittersweet joy and
sorrow at the close of *Shabbat*; to comfort us at every mourning and memorial service: "The Lord is my Shepherd, . . . He
maketh me to lie down in green pastures . . . I will fear no evil."
What evil could a shepherd fear? In biblical days, there
were very real fears of wolves, lions, sudden storms, and,
perhaps the worst of all, loneliness. Yet this same solitary
existence could lead to a contemplative solitude, resulting in
nothing less than the concepts that led to actions that redeemed the people. The primary concern of those who cared
for sheep was their economy; but the majestic thoughts that
developed from the life they led gave humanity nothing less
than the survival of the people chosen to disseminate God's
Own Word, and the survival of the ethics and justice Israel
believes it gave to the world.
Through tending this most gentle of creatures, Amos, the
competent businessman, changed into the reluctant and astonished prophet for simple justice.
"I am no prophet nor son of prophets. YHVH took me as I
followed the flock and . . . said to me, 'Go prophecy against
thy people Israel.'" Amos was a Judahite, but his trade was in
that religious and commercial center of Israel, Bethel. Here
the prophet saw the deterioration from the heady days of
Jeroboam's reign. In the time of King Jehu, licentiousness,
drunkenness, bribery favoring the wealthy over the poor in
judgment cases—these ruled the land, and all centered from
the corruption of YHVH worship reflected by the golden
calves, pillars of the temple and the throne, a Baal cult that
had usurped the theology of the land. To Amos, it may have
been that he saw himself as a modern-day Moses, also a
shepherd, hurtling the Tablets of Law to the revelers at the

foot of Mount Sinai. He would also recall Moses' injunction to follow always justice, righteousness. Worship of YHVH was deteriorating in Israel. Justice was deteriorating in Israel. Amos soon opened his mouth and spoke the words he had been contemplating as he developed his trade in the little town of Tekoa, just outside of Bethlehem.

Here we can see that in the Hebrew Scriptures, although the concept of God as Shepherd and the people as flock clearly exists, it is from being a shepherd by trade that one is able to develop fully his or her conceptualizations of something great, something finer, something good.

Something evil occurs early in the Bible. The first entry in this category tells of the murder of Abel, a keeper of sheep, by Cain, a tiller of the ground. Shepherds, however, do very well in the subsequent stories; perhaps, then, this early allegory may be a warning to the inheritors of the Davidic kingdom (Amos, the shepherd in Judah, prophecies against the traditionally agrarian northern nation of Israel, brothers and sisters, after all).

Following Abel's tragic demise, the heroes and heroines of the text tend sheep. Much of Israelite history, in fact, occurs around the flocks. Indeed, Israelite history could not have occurred were it not for those who, like Abel and Amos, were keepers of sheep.

In the second entry, a full sixteen chapters later, Abraham acquires wealth through the gift of flocks from Abimelech. Isaac's matchmaker meets Rebecca, a shepherdess, at the well, where she comes to water the flock. Jacob meets Rachel at the well, whence she comes to water the flock. Jacob acquires his own wealth through being an expert ovine husbandman in the fields of his father-in-law, Laban. Joseph is sent to see how his brothers are doing with the flocks. By so doing, the cycle of descent into Egypt and redemption as a nation is set in motion. The Israelites take up residence in Goshen, for two reasons: the Egyptians are cattle ranchers and hate sheep and the land is good for the flocks (there is a *Midrash* that one of the Egyptians' god was a lamb, thus, the Passover offering particularly leaves a terrible stench in their nostrils, but the validity of this cult is weak at best).

There is the famous *Midrash* of Moses tracking down the wayward lamb, and only then, as a compassionate shepherd, is he deemed worthy to perceive the revelation of the bush that burns and is not consumed, to accept his calling as a shepherd of the flock of Israel. And, of course, there is David, a simple shepherd boy, who receives Samuel's call to unite the tribes. It may not be too presumptuous to ponder if David, like Citizen Kane—after years as a boy-warrior, an exile, a King and King restored, a man slayer, a husband with marital difficulties, a father bereft, decades of palace intrigue—longed for his Rosebud, his days as a youthful shepherd, guarding his flock against enemies he could see or sense.

> And (Jesse) said: "There remaineth yet the youngest, and, behold, he keepeth the sheep." . . . And he sent and brought him in. Now he was ruddy, and withal of beautiful eyes, and goodly to look upon. And the Lord said: "Arise, anoint him; for this is he." . . . And the spirit of the Lord came mightily upon David from that day forward.

Hertz (3:1) recalls the popular *Midrash*:

> When feeding the flocks of Jethro, . . . Moses saw a little lamb escape from the flock, and when he followed it, he overtook it at a brook quenching its thirst. "Had I known that thou wast thirsty, I would have taken thee in my arms and carried thee thither," he said. "As thou livest," a Heavenly Voice resounded, "thou are fit to shepherd Israel."

From this, the Rabbis infer, "God never gives an exalted office to a man unless He has first tested him in small things."

Another version of the midrashic tale has Moses going through many desert and mountain hardships (always moving up, of course) in concerned pursuit for the welfare of the little lamb; when he at last discovers the young sheep, that is the moment he discerns the burning bush. It was always burning. It burns even now—and it is we who are not prepared to see it, is the lesson of the Rabbis.

> When Josiah celebrated the Passover festival in Jerusalem to his Lord, he sacrificed the Passover on the fourteenth day of (the) first month . . . And he

ordered the Levites . . . put the holy chest of the
Lord in the house of the Lord, which Solomon the
king (sic) the son of David, had built; . . .

And Josiah gave the people that were present
thirty thousand lambs and kids, and three thousand
calves; these were given out of the king's revenues,
as he promised, to the people and the priests and
Levites. And Hilkiah and Zechariah and Jehiel, the
temple (sic) gave the priests for the Passover two
thousand, six hundred sheep . . . And Jeconiah and
Shemaiah and Nathanael, his brother, and Assabiah
and Ociel and Joram, colonels of regiments, gave the
Levites for the Passover five thousand sheep . . .
And it was done . . .

. . . And in the castle of Ecbatana, in the land of
Media, was found a roll in which this was recorded:

"In the first year of the reign of Cyrus, King Cyrus
ordered the rebuilding of the house of the Lord in
Jerusalem, where they sacrifice with perpetual
fire . . . and that a grant from the tribute of Coele-
syria and Phoenicia be particularly given these men
for sacrifices to the Lord, that is, to Zerubabel, the
governor, for bulls and rams and lambs . . . so that
libations may be offered to the Most High God for the
king and his children, and that they may pray for
their lives." (*The First Book of Esdra*, which is Ezra, in
The Apocrypha [Goodspeed], pp. 1, 25, 11–15)

(The main departure from the biblical texts of Ezra and
Nehemiah is the rhetorical contest won by Zerubabel, who
then implores the king to remember his promise to rebuild
Jerusalem and restore the captives. Zerubabel was appointed
governor of the restored theocracy.)

In *B. Pesahim* 66A and *Y. Pesahim* 33A, the text relates the
appointment of Hillel to the honored position of Nasi, the
leader (literally, the "Prince") of the Academy. The discussion
then proceeds to a dispute concerning the observance of the
Passover sacrifice when it occurred on the Sabbath Day. One
of the halakhic injunctions of the oral commentary was that
one cannot carry on the Sabbath; the problem, therefore, is
how can the people bring their *shechit* knives to the altar?

Afterward (after answering the Halachic question, receiv-

ing the appointment, and sitting in the honored position), . . .
they asked him:

> "Master, what is the law if a man forgot to bring the
> slaughtering knife in advance to the Temple Court on
> Friday before the Sabbath? [Interestingly, one is
> reminded of the American custom of driving to the
> synagogue on Friday or another *eruv*, leaving the car
> in place, walking Friday night and Saturday morning,
> and retrieving the vehicle for the ride home immedi-
> ately following *Havdalah*; or of bringing one's *tallit* on
> Friday afternoon and leaving it at the synagogue for
> the service in the morning.] May he bring it on the
> Sabbath or is that carrying prohibited as work?"
>
> He said to them: "I know that I've heard this
> *halakhah*, but I've forgotten it. Leave this to the
> people of Israel themselves, for although they are not
> prophets they are sons of prophets and will surely
> know in practice what to do."
>
> The next day (some persons did forget and)
> those who were bringing a lamb as their Passover
> sacrifice and leading the animal along had the knife
> entangled in the thick wool of its neck . . . Thus they
> did not have to carry the knife on the Sabbath day,
> for the animal itself carried it. When Hillel saw what
> they had done, he recollected the *halakhah*, which
> taught just that, and said, "Such is the tradition that
> I received from Shemaya and Avtalyon" (his own
> teachers). This, then, is a relatively strong proof text
> that, indeed, the oral tradition was exactly that and
> could even be temporarily forgotten by a mind as
> magnificent as that of our great sage Hillel. (See also
> Buxbaum, pp. 22–25)

In *Chullin* 3:2, the *Mishnah* declares an animal with both
kidneys removed to be viable. Preuss states that the explanation of this obvious error most likely lies in the fact that the
ancients had little knowledge concerning the function of the
kidneys. Thus, Preuss continues, (for example), the followers
of Asklepiades of Bithynia disregard the connection between
the kidneys and the bladder; many things in nature, they
taught, such as the kidneys, were created without a function.
The *Gemarah* (55a–b), however, teaches that viability of an

animal may be denied by illnesses of the kidneys. Thus, for example, if a very small kidney is found—the size of a bean, in the case of goats and sheep . . . the animal is considered to be nonviable (p. 217).

Now, only animals whose bodies are free of blemishes are suitable to be sacrificed in the Temple. Therefore, a lamb with a double ear may not be sacrificed. However, the *Tosefta*, in *Becharot* 6:9, adds that "an animal whose ears are rolled together over a single cartilage [a medical or veterinary condition known as *meguphaphoth bechasisa*] may be sacrificed . . ."

A priest who is to offer a sacrifice must also be without a blemish. Noticeable abnormalities of the ears render the priest unfit for Temple service. At least four such abnormalities are indicated, including small ears, ears that resemble a "sponge," ears "obstructed" or nonexistent, ears that are pierced by an awl, and—a person whose ears are pendulous, as seen in some sheep (also see Preuss, p. 289).

The iconography of Moses as the Expected Child, surviving a harrowing experience and being cast on the waters to be saved, has several parallels in Middle Eastern mythology and history. In all of these stories, shepherds play key roles in the first or second rescue. Moses, it will be recalled, is "rescued" a second time by Midianite shepherds. Oedipus, for example, as a child, is rescued by a shepherd.

Graves indicates there is a tract of the Oedipus legend that Sophocles chose to eliminate—of Oedipus also being cast out upon the cradle-ark and being discovered by a Queen or Princess who raises him as her own; in fact, the etymology of the name *Oedipus*, according to Graves, may be traced to a root meaning "son of the swelling sea," as opposed to "swollen foot." Graves points out that in one version of the story, the piercing of the feet occurs at the end. Sophocles, of course, used the piercing of the eyes for dramatic effect (it looked quite stunning upon the mask when the protagonist returned from behind the skene).

Other mythological and historical figures that reflect this imagery are: Perseus, Hippothous, Pelias, Aegisthus, Cyrus, and Romulus (v. 2, pp. 12–13; see also Lind, pp. 111–154 [or any contemporary translation]).

Oedipus

If I may guess, although I never met him,
I think, elders, I see that shepherd coming
Whom we have long sought, as in the measure
Of lengthy age he accords with him we wait for.
Besides, the men who lead him I recognize
As servants of my house. You may perhaps
Know better than I if you have seen him before.

Chorus

Be assured, I know him as a shepherd
As trusted as any other in Laius's service.

Servant (Shepherd)

. . . If you are he
Whom this man speaks of, you were born curst by fate.
(Lines 1110–1115, 1178–1180)

According to Bradbury, humanity's oldest friend "must certainly" be the sheep. Evidence exists to show that sheep and goats were herded and used for skins and wool since at least the Stone Age. Bradbury discards the rabbinic flaw concerning the sheep as an Egyptian god. "The ancient Egyptians used them to tramp in newly sown grain."

The origin of the first sheep is confused, Bradbury continues. Some of the early ancestors closely resembled goats, and even today the two species are similar in many respects. Domestic sheep are believed to be descended from two wild sheep species, the Asiatic Urial and the Mouflons. Mouflons are still found in Asia Minor and the Caucasus, in Sardinia and Corsica.

> While the Urial lives on grassy plains in large flocks, the Mouflons are independent and daring, able to withstand harsh mountain weather conditions and leap nimbly over the roughest terrain. Mouflon-like short-tailed domestic sheep are still found in northern Europe and on the uninhabited island of Soay, northwest of Scotland. These latter sheep see man only once a year, when the people of St. Kilda come to round them up and shear them.

> The Romans . . . developed sheep with fine lus-
> trous wool from which their togas were made.
> Roman . . . flocks . . . produced the finest wool in
> the world. . . .
>   As a farm animal, the sheep is unsurpassed in its
> adaptability. . . . Sheep graze and do well both on
> land that is unfit for or inaccessible to plowing and
> on grasses not suitable for grazing other animals. . . .
> sheep need very little grain. . . .
>   A few factors on the debit side . . . Sheep are
> defenseless animals, and their tendency to scatter in
> panic makes them easy prey to dogs and coyotes.
> (Pp. 10-6)

In various legends concerning King Solomon, his downfall is portrayed in metaphorical and highly mystical overtones, especially his departure from the lush garden (viz, *PaRDes/* Eden) to the desert sans vegetation (the emptiness). Based on the historicity of the text, where, with great promise and devotion, eventually he succumbs to the high places of the idols of his wives, the stories generally share the theme of his attempting to return to the faith and life he knew, sometimes successfully, sometimes not. In one version, the turning point for Solomon is when he encounters kindhearted shepherds.

King Solomon ruled over all animals and birds and over the demons. Once, however, Asmodeus, King of the Demons, outwitted him and tricked the king into handing over his magic ring upon which was inscribed the ineffable Name. At once, Solomon's powers dissipated and he found himself cast into a great desert.

Several attempts were made by the king to find his way back to his country and his throne. But the people in this place had never heard of Solomon, of Jerusalem, or of Israel.

At length, nearly exhausted from thirst, sun, and despair, he espied an oasis in the distance. He ran to it as best he could. There he found shepherds grazing their flocks. The shepherds showed compassion. They gave him water, food, and a place to rest in the shade.

(Following this turning point of the progression, Solomon, now with renewed vigor, begins to find people who know of him, then people who believe him, and, finally, re-discovers his way to Jerusalem. [Ausubel, pp. 366–369].)

Solomon's father—King David, of course—began his career, as we have indicated, as a shepherd. The symbology to the people was quite clear—like Moses, from a shepherd herding his flocks, to one who shepherds his people Israel. In an original *Midrash*, this journey of lives and loves and ethics lost and gained is told quite well:

> Come and see how even the mighty are brought low and then exalted at the dignified position and career of shepherd. Did it not come to pass in those days that King David rose from a simple shepherd boy to a great warrior and the king of all the tribes of Israel? And in that time, the king became the favorite of the Lord our God; and David worshiped the Lord our God and promised to build a house for Him wherein the *Shechinah* might dwell.
>
> But, alas, it came to pass in those days that David went out to stroll on the rooftops one night, and gazed upon the rooftops, and beheld the beauty of the wife of Uriah the Hittite, and her name was BathSheba. And the king admired her beauty from a distance, and his heart was moved with love for her, and he coveted her. And David strayed from the *mitzvot* of the Lord our God, and in this matter the Lord's anger waxed mightily against David. For David sent the soldier, Uriah the Hittite, into the battle in the front charge of the line, so that he would receive a mortal wound. And so it was. And David made it so that BathSheba would be his wife.
>
> Now in those days, the prophet Nathan prophesied mightily; and Nathan approached the king. And he said unto the king: "Oh Lord King, let me tell you a case in this land, wherein a certain man has taken a sheepfold from another man, and sent the man out to look for the lambs, in a place where the lions dwell, and the man was slaughtered by the lions, and the man has the sheepfold and all the wealth wherein the sheepfold is attached. Now, Lord King, in your wisdom and judgment, the man's fate is in your own

hands, and by your words you will tell what should be done unto him."

And the king said, "This is in violation of our law. That man should be found and brought before the king to receive his just punishment."

And Nathan pointed his finger at the king, and he said, "Thou art the man!" And King David knew at once that the matter of Uriah the Hittite and Bath-Sheba was known. And he knew that the anger of the Lord was against him on that day.

And this is what David did. The king came off his throne, and he mourned the death of the man for three days. And he put on sackcloth and rent his clothes, he removed his crown and he went out from the City of Zion, and he went out from Jerusalem and he went out into the countryside. And he came at last after some days' journey to the home of Uriah the Hittite. And the man's mother and father were there, and they were sore aggrieved for the loss of their son.

And David came unto them, and he said: "I am David, once and future King of Israel. And in the matter of your son's death I am to blame and only I. And it was for the coveting of his wife, BathSheba, that I am to blame. I confess this my sin to you with all my heart and soul. And whatever you wish for me to do, so I will do."

Now the parents of Uriah the Hittite were shepherds, and kept a mighty flock. And they said unto David, "Stay and keep our sheep, for our son was to come to keep our sheep and now he is no more, and thus we will live, lest we go hungry and perish from off the good land which our god and the Lord your God hath seen fit to give unto us; for we know that the Lord your God is the most powerful of all the gods."

And King David said: "By your own words will it be done."

Now David had been a shepherd in his youth, and, like his father Jacob, he knew the ways of sheep. And David set about to keep the sheep of the mother and father of Uriah the Hittite and so to honor the man's father and mother.

And the sheep became a mighty flock again, even

mightier than before. And the wealth and good
fortune of the mother and father of Uriah the Hittite
waxed great. And the husband came in unto his wife
and they knew each other and the wife conceived
and bore another son. And this son grew to live a life
as a fine and decent man and lived the length of his
days.

And, at the end of seven years, the parents of
Uriah the Hittite came out into the fields where the
sheep lay, and they approached King David, and they
said: "Now for seven years you have been in our
service and we have waxed great for the shepherding
wherefore you shepherd; and do we not have a fine
son besides? Surely if you wish to return to your
throne, you may do so."

And David said unto them: "The time is not yet
arrived for the end of my *tsuvah*, my repentance."
And David served the parents of Uriah the Hittite for
seven more years, and their flocks waxed even more
mighty than before, with great wealth.

And all the years were but as a day to David, so
great was the matter of his study and his praying,
and his repentance. And the lad grew, a fine and
strong lad.

Now at the end of fourteen years, the lad wished
to go out to the wars, to be a great warrior as was his
brother. And David spoke to the lad, and told him
that he must beat his sword into a pruning hook, his
spear into a plow, and that he must dedicate himself
to the ways of the One True God and study Torah and
perform good deeds. And the lad did so, and taught
many of the way in his turn, and became a great sage
and honored the memory of his brother, and it was
because of David's wisdom and his teaching of the
lad Torah that it came to pass. And again God loved
David as His favorite.

And the parents of the lad came out to David in
the fields, and said unto the king: "Surely now the
time of your repentance is over and it is time for you
to return to your throne." And the king knew that,
indeed, the time had arrived.

And David left the land of Uriah the Hittite, and
he returned to Jerusalem, and he danced before the
gates, and the people came out to meet him and to

greet their king, and the women danced with timbrels and with song and King David entered Zion and
sat upon his throne. And this is the *Midrash* in the
story of King David in the matter of Uriah the Hittite.
And David was the Lord's own favorite but for the
matter of Uriah the Hittite when David sent him in
the front lines of the battle so that he might covet the
man's wife, the same is BathSheba.

And King David performed the necessary ablutions, and so repented the deed he had done, and
was restored as King of all Israel. And David was a
shepherd from the hill country of Judah. (Rosstein)

It is a curious matter that in modern times, those who find
the sacrificial cult a mystery and an exponent of cruelty will
proceed to dine on flesh without any consideration of the
ultimate sacrifice the animal has given to become part of our
physical and spiritual being. Only a vegetarian, it would seem,
is vested with any right to be critical of the ancient rite of ritual
slaughter upon the perpetually burning altar. In fact, the
highest order of *gilgul*, the cycle of reincarnation as indicated
by the kabbalists, is a woman who is a vegetarian. Rather than
being cruel, the sacrificial cult in actuality is far less cruel than
the manner in which we herd and slaughter largely bovine and
ovine creatures for consumption upon our dinner tables and
tables of restaurants.

When one sacrifices his or her own known animal, it truly
is a sacrifice and can be a difficult matter. I once visited a farm
for the weekend. In the morning, I came to "know" the cow that
would later be sacrificed for our benefit that evening. In
mid-morning, the farmer went out to the slaughtering shed. By
afternoon, the fresh meat was being butchered. And, by
evening, we sat down to dine on steaks. There was a certain
mystical feeling to it all, as if the creature had been elevated
and had become part of us.

When one saw one's own sacrifice rise in wisps of incense-
infused smoke up into the heavenly spheres, climbing the
s'ferot to the *merkavah* and, ultimately, to the *keter*, to the
crown of the Godhead, both animal and person were spiritu-
ally enhanced.

The animal that was sacrificed at least as often as any

other was the sheep or lamb. And especially was this the case at the great pilgrimage festival of Passover, called, in fact, the *Paschal* lamb, the only time the sacrificial animal is the name of the holy day. Even unto today, the Samaritans continue this annual practice at their mountain altar.

How was the animal slaughtered? Although the exact technique is recorded in the Talmud, we may also presume that it was quite similar to the way kosher animals are slaughtered today under the laws of *shechitah*. Although it is a very complex and sophisticated activity, with a large order of *halakhah* apportioned to its practice, a reduction to five aspects may also illustrate how Temple sacrifices may have been conducted:

1. The *shechitah* must be performed in one continuous act; there must be no hesitation.
2. The special knife must be clean and clear: it may not be covered with skin, feathers, wool, or cloth.
3. The *shechitah* must be accomplished by the sharpness of the knife itself; the *shochet*, the ritual slaughterer, must perform the act with no undue or extra consideration of pressure.
4. There is a proscribed area; cutting outside this area is forbidden.
5. The trachea and esophagus must remain in their place. If they are "uprooted," the *shechitah* is invalid.

In addition, the *shochet* is a highly trained and vigorously tested individual. He must past the muster of skill, dedication, ethical behavior, and be *shomer*, one who fully guards and keeps the written and oral Torah *halakhah* (refer to Forst, 36–37).

> And those priests that were pure and without any blemish went up to the altar and sanctuary clothed in fine linen, and abstained from wine chiefly from the fear that otherwise they should make some mistake in their ministration. The high priest also went up with them, not always indeed, but on the sabbath (sic) days and new moons. (Josephus, *The Jewish War*, rev. Shilleto, 28)

The final entry in this section describing the creature that has shared its destiny with ours for so long and served us so well, is from the Silverman *Haggadah* (p. 26). It is interesting that the inclusion maintains the tradition of the sheep or lamb as an Egyptian god.

> QUESTION
> What is the meaning of the PASCHAL LAMB which our ancestors used to eat at the time when the Temple was still in existence?
>
> ANSWER
> *(Point to the shank bone of the lamb and answer)*
> The PASCHAL LAMB is to remind us that the Holy One, praised be He, passed over the houses of our ancestors in Egypt, as it is written in the Bible: "You shall say that it is the sacrifice of the Lord's passover, for He passed over the houses of the Children of Israel in Egypt when He smote the Egyptians, but spared our houses. The people bowed their heads and worshiped." (Exodus 12:27)

Scholars maintain that, because the Egyptians worshiped the lamb, that animal was deliberately chosen to be sacrificed for Passover, to emphasize the fact that the Israelites rejected the worship of animals. Before the destruction of the Temple, a lamb, offered as a sacrifice, was roasted and eaten at the *Seder*. Later, when animal sacrifices were abolished, other meat was substituted. However, the meat served at the *Seder* was not to be roasted on an open flame because the lamb of the *Paschal* sacrifice had been roasted.

It is significant that the first ordinance of the Jewish religion concerns a family festival to celebrate the birth of freedom. "They shall take every man a lamb, according to their fathers' houses, a lamb for each household" (Exodus 12:13).

What an impressive sight it must have been when, from all parts of the land, people gathered in Jerusalem, and the head of each household brought a lamb to observe Passover with his family! Just as in the past, the *Seder* in our day is the family festival par excellence for it brings together members of family and friends. . . . May the *Seder* each year be a means of drawing us ever closer to our family and friends, and may it help to keep each Jewish home a miniature sanctuary where God's spirit shall dwell, and where reverence, love, and peace shall prevail.

AN ADDITIONAL TALMUD TAIL (*Rosh Hoshanah* 16a)

The Mishnah states: "At four seasons [Divine] Judgment is passed on the world. At Passover (for produce), at (Shavuot for fruit), at New Year all creatures pass before (God) like children of Maron . . . and on Tabernacles . . ."

Gemarah 18a explains the curious *Mishnah* of "Maron." In Aramaic *MR'ah* derived from sheep. "Resh Lakish said: As [in] the ascent of Beth Maron" (alternately, Horon—a narrow pass known in ancient days requiring sojourners to proceed in single file); thus, the *Gemarah* states: "In Babylon it was translated, 'like a flock of sheep.'"

Gemarah 8a details the heralding of the new year seasons by the mating and parturition behavior of sheep (expl. Soncino, p. 72).

4

RAVEN

RAVEN
Hebrew *(O)Reb*

> *. . . and sent out the raven; it went to and fro until*
> *the waters had dried up from the earth.*
>
> —Genesis 8:7

Corvus corax: *Corvus*, Latin, a raven; *korax*, Greek, a raven. Widespread throughout the world's northern hemisphere.

CONCORDANCE

Deuteronomy 14:14.
1 Kings 17:4, 6.
Isaiah 34:11.
Proverbs 30:17 (see number 47).
Job 38:41 (Who provideth for the raven his prey . . .).
Song of Songs 5:11 (. . . His locks are curled/And black as a raven).

Ravens, crows, magpies, and jays, all considered corvids, are among the most intelligent of birds, and to some extent, of animals in general. They have a far range. They are highly adaptable, making themselves at home in civilization or in the wild. They construct and use tools. They solve problems.

Perhaps most significant, they engage in play. It is not uncommon for ravens and crows in particular to initiate contact with and to make human friends.

I recall once we lived in a small apartment over a bicycle shop. The kitchen in the rear had a large window overlooking the roof of a tool shed. This roof abutted up to the sill, and so formed a long platform leading away from the window. The kitchen was so arranged that we prepared meals next to this window. Soon, morning and evening, we attracted the attention of a curious and opportunistic raven or crow. He began by strutting on the platform at a distance, turning his head to get a better view of us and our activity. Day by day, he approached closer to the window. By sight, or by aroma, he intuited that food was within. Finally, seemingly impatient that we had not yet figured out he was begging for a meal, he began to peck at the window, then step back a bit. We were conned saps for his antics. We soon had another mouth to feed and were taking him into consideration when we undertook our grocery shopping. Eventually, he even became our alarm clock, letting us know without fail and with incessant pecking that it was time for us to rise and to provide his daily sustenance.

It is the dove in the Noah story that always seems to receive the best press. The raven never returned. The dove returned with an olive branch in its beak. Perhaps it is time to re-examine the flight of the raven. A creature so intelligent, adaptable, and opportunistic may have found just the right place for himself, perhaps a little bit of the garden, until humanity returned to begin destroying it all over again.

Friedman, in his landmark book, uses the Noah story as one of his prime examples of the Documentary Hypothesis, especially, in this case, the differences in the J and E author, and how the Redactor wove them together. Pritchard, Ferry, and many other scholars have shown clearly that the Flood story had been around quite some time before the Israelite or Judahite version was reduced to text. Its main exponent is found in the ancient Sumarian hero-myth epic, *Gilgamesh*. The translation is Ferry's (pp. 70–72, viz., tablet 11, verse 3, lines 37–66):

I looked outside. Nothing was moving at all. It looked
as flat as a flat clay roof looks flat; and all the human
beings had turned to clay. I fell to my knees and wept.
The tears ran down the sides of my nose. I wept in
the total silence. I looked outside and looked as far as
I could, trying to find, looking across the world,
something. And then, far off, something was there.
What looked like signs of an island could faintly be
seen; and then the boat was caught and held from
under by the peak rock of a mountain under the
water. It was Mount Nisir the boat was grounded on.
A first day it was held, . . . a sixth day, and then on
the seventh day I freed a dove. The dove flew free
and flew away from the boat. Seeking a place for its
little feet to alight, and finding none, it flew back to
the boat to perch. I freed a swallow then and it flew
free and flew away from the boat, seeking a place for
its little feet to alight, and finding none, flew back
to the boat to find a place to alight. I freed a raven
then and it flew free and flew away from the boat,
and never returned. It had found a place to alight,
and circled about the place, and alighted, and settled
itself, and ate. And never after that returned to the
boat. Then I set free all the other birds in the boat
and they flew free, scattering to the winds.

Pritchard (vol. 1, p. 40) comments on this epic poem:

All but a few of the Akkadian texts come from the
library of Ashurbanipal at Nineveh . . . (and) is
known also from versions which antedate the first
millennium B.C. (sic). From the middle of the second
millennium have come down fragments of a Hittite
translation, as well as a fragment of a Hurrian rendering of the epic. From the first half of the second
millennium we possess representative portions of
the Old Babylonian version of the epic. . . . That this
version was itself a copy of an earlier text is suggested by the internal evidence of the material. . . .

Clearly, this text and its several stories were well known to
the Israelite storytellers and, later, to those who reduced the
stories to the canon.

Several *Midrashim* about both the raven and the dove exist, of course. Some are well known; others not so well known. It is interesting that the story-tellers and exegetical expansionists seem to favor the more interesting raven in the telling of their interpretative and expansion texts. Gellman has done a masterful job of redacting some of these *midrashim* into his own charming, almost fairy tale–like storytelling talent.

> But when Noah opened the window, a cold blast of wind howled in from the black sky. . . .
> Noah decided that a bird should go out and explore. So he asked the parrot next to the window, but the parrot just ruffled her feathers and squawked, "Don't be ridiculous! My feathers are much too beautiful to be messed up that awful wind . . ." The flamingo . . . stood up and sneered. . . . And so it went, right down the bird beam . . . until . . . the raven flew out the window.
> When the raven did not return after several days, Noah asked the birds if one of them would go out and try to find the raven. But all the birds found new reasons why they could not go. All except the dove, that is, who whooshed out the window to try and find her friend the raven in the black and windy sky.
> After a long flight, the dove found the raven perched in an olive tree on a tiny island in the great flood sea. After munching on a few fresh olives, the dove said, "Let's go back and tell our friends the birds that there is land out here."
> "Our *friends?*" laughed the raven. "Those birds don't care if we ever return. Why don't you just stay here with me, and no bird with colored feathers will ever make fun of us again."
> But the dove said, "I don't think it's fair for us to sit here munching olives while everyone else is cooped up in the ark." And off she flew.
> Meanwhile, back at the ark, Noah stood at the little window, staring out into the cold night for some sign of either the raven or the dove.
> The dove was lost . . . [the dove's tale will continue in the listing following].

AN ADDITIONAL TALMUD TAIL (*Chullin* 59a)

The *Mishnah* attempts to clarify the characteristics of birds for dietary acceptance.

Gemarah 63a shows the identification for the Raven to be simple. "Our Rabbis taught: Raven signifies the Raven, *every raven* includes the Raven of the valley, *after its kind* includes the raven that moves ahead of the doves."

. . . AND A MIDRASH (Leviticus 19:1)

> R. Assi was of an inquiring turn. He once saw a raven making a nest, laying eggs, and hatching fledglings. He took the young and put them in a new pot and pasted over its top. After three days he opened its top to find out what they were doing, and found they had been secreting excrement, which produced gnats, and the fledglings were swooping over them and devouring them. R. Assi applied to them the verse from Job 38:41.

Elijah was said to be served by the raven from the ark (and other ravens).

5

DOVE

DOVE
Hebrew *Yo(V)NaH*

> *Then he sent out the dove to see whether the waters had decreased from the surface of the ground.*
>
> —Genesis 8:8.

Oena capensis: *Oinas*, Greek, the vine (may refer to the color); *capensis*, of the Cape (locus).

CONCORDANCE

Leviticus 12:6, 8; 14:22, 30; 15:14, 29.
2 Kings 6:25.
Isaiah 38:14; 59:11; 60:8.
Jeremiah 48:28 (see number 2).
Psalms II—68:14 (The wings of the dove are covered with silver).
Job 42:14 (i.e., *J'MiMaH*).
Song of Songs 2:14; 4:1 (see number 7); 5:2, 12 (His eyes are like doves).

Though named from South Africa, it inhabits the Gulf and Red Sea area. Pigeons and doves are basically the same bird. This species, however, is still wild. For that romantic notion, I have accorded it this place of honor.

Pigeons and doves frequent all land habitats, this one desert and grassy areas (more reason for its choice). Its preferred diet is seeds, berries, insects, and worms. It has a wing span slightly longer than a large urban pigeon and tends a bit more toward maroon, especially on its top side. (Refer to number 9.)

One of the possible reasons the dove is "favored" in the Flood story is revealed later in the text, when it becomes clear it is elevated in the sacrificial cult. Various references in the Talmud, and "as taught by our tradition," state that the *kohanim*, the priests in the Second Commonwealth (and presumably in the First as well) had long, sharp fingernails, purposefully grown so as to enact the sacrifice of these birds as they were held in the hand.

In several talmudic tractates, the story of Titus's final days are related, clearly suffering for the sin of destroying the *Kadosh Kadoshim*, the Holy of Holies. *Gittin* 56b is a particularly well-indicated reference for the story. *Genesis Rabbah* 10:7, however, relates an alternate version. Preuss (pp. 204–205) gives the popular story and the alternate version:

> When Titus landed on dry land after the destruction of the Temple in Jerusalem, a gnat [number 20] flew into his nose, ascended into his head and knocked against his brain for seven years. One day as he was passing by a smithy, the gnat heard the noise of the hammer and stopped knocking. After thirty days, however, it became accustomed to the noise and again began to knock. . . . at the request of the pain-plagued Titus, his skull was split open and something like a dove was drawn forth. When the latter changed, he also changed; and when it flew away his soul also flew away.

One of the fascinating side issues concerning this story is that Titus may have had a brain tumor, and his surgeons may have tried brain surgery. Preuss continues: ". . . it is well known that trepanning was a very common operation in antiquity, even though Galen's assertion that he observed myriads of trepanned patients is probably one of his beloved exaggerations. . . . Talmudic sources also describe . . . a skull borer (*Oholoth* 2:3) (and) the case of a trepanation on a person . . . the skull defect . . . later covered with the dried shell of a pumpkin . . . (*Tosefta, Oholoth* 2:4)."

Perhaps more curious is that Trachtenberg traced dove sacrifices occurring in the Middle Ages, albeit obviously with improper intent. It was, after all, a very superstitious age.

> Still another type of magical action comprised in essence an offering to the spirits, to gain their good-will and their aid, though its character was not perceived, or at least admitted, despite the recognition that "it is the custom of magicians to offer sacrifices and to burn incense to the spirits." One such prescription required that two white doves be slaughtered in a special manner, and their entrails mixed with old wine, pure incense, and clear honey, and the whole burned on the hearth; the smoke rising from this would induce a divinatory dream. (Pp. 130–131)

Plaut (p. 113) and other scholars relate that the strange ritual when Abraham used the dove, heifer, she-goat, and ram (Genesis 15), was, or likely was, a contract arrangement, in which one walked through the middle of the torn sacrificial parts, thus signifying that one agreed to both sides of the contract; the presumption is that the other party, in this case, God, also walked through and agreed to both sides.

[We now continue Gellman's version of the raven's and dove's tale.]

> The dove was lost. Her white wings were dipping closer and closer to the churning black waves, and she felt she could not flap her tired wings another flap. Then, through the roaring wind, the dove heard a *ha-choo*! Following the sound, she came to Noah's outstretched hand, and he brought her into the warm ark.
>
> When the dove reported that there was land out there, none of the birds believed her. The next morning, when they woke up, the dove was gone. Her

little nest at the end of the bird beam was soaked with tears.

"I knew they wouldn't believe you," said the raven to the dove when she returned to the olive tree, which was now on the top of a hill on a large island in the great flood sea. "Stay with me and forget about them. Here, have an olive."

"I don't want an olive, but I will take an olive leaf," said the dove. "This will show them that there really *is* land out here."

. . . Soon the dove was lost at sea and straining her ears for Noah's *ha-choo* or a flicker of light from the ark. But all the dove heard was wind and waves, wind and waves.

Then, suddenly, up ahead the dove saw something very strange. Rising out of the sea was a rainbow! Flying closer she saw that the rainbow was fluttering in the wind. And it was chirping!

In fact, the beautiful rainbow was a tower of birds flapping their wings against the strong wind. The parrot was flying up and down the bird-feather rainbow, squawking orders: ". . . our friend the dove is lost at sea, just because we were too dumb to believe her. . . ."

When the two great doors of the ark swung open and all the animals were let out at last, they were greeted by a wondrous sight. A real rainbow was shining in the sky, stretching from the ark at one end to an olive tree on top of a mountain at the other.

That night, before all the birds flew off to their new homes in the new world, they nested together in the olive tree. And on the very top branch were the raven and the dove. (Pp. 36–39)

An Additional Talmud Tail (*Bezah* 10b)

The *Gemarah* refers to the *Mishnah* as self-evident. Nonetheless, as we might expect, the *Gemarah* continues a discussion about the derivation of the logical process (why two but three, three but two, etc.)

Bezah ("egg") is a tractate dealing with proper foods and eating and their preparations for festivals.

Mishnah: If he designated black [doves] but found white, white but found black, two but found three, they are [all] forbidden. Three but found two, they are permitted. [If he designated doves] inside the nest and found them in front of the nest, they are forbidden; but if none except these were there, they are permitted.

6

HEIFER

HEIFER

Hebrew *'ehGLaH*

He answered,
"Bring Me a three-year-old heifer, . . ."

—Genesis 15:9

CONCORDANCE

Numbers 19 (see number 12).
Deuteronomy 21:3–4, 6.
Judges 14:8 (metaphorical—see notation at number 12).
1 Samuel 16:2.
Jeremiah 46:20 (see number 28); 48:34; 50:11 (because ye gambol as a heifer at grass) (see number 15).
Hosea 4:16 (for Israel is stubborn like a stubborn heifer) (see number 3); 10:11 (and Ephraim is a heifer well broken).

Heifer, bull, and calf are treated separately, but for the cumulative total of listings in the biblical text, see the Appendix, where the total number is considered to be under "cattle."

The bovine species has been as significant a part of humanity's time on earth as the ovine, canine, and equine species, or nearly so. A fuller treatment of the evolution of these once proud and fierce animals is found under the other three listings (numbers 11, 12, and 28). I chose to isolate the heifer listing largely because of the mystery of the ritual that occurs in Numbers 19, an ancient rite that possibly "Judaizes" an even more ancient sympathetic heathen magic cultic ritual. Even Hertz spends an unusual amount of space in his commentary on this very curious rite.

> . . . provides for the removal of defilement resulting from contact with the dead. A red heifer, free from blemish, and one that had not yet been broken to the yoke, was to be slain outside the camp. It was then to be burned, cedar-wood, hyssop, and scarlet being cast upon the pyre. The gathered ashes, dissolved in fresh water, were to be sprinkled on those who had become contaminated through contact with a dead body.

So far, Hertz basically recounts the textual indications as stated in Chapter 19. He goes on, however, to relate a very good summary of the feeling the Rabbis had concerning the ritual throughout the generations.

This ordinance is the most mysterious rite in Scripture, the strange features of which are fully enumerated by the Rabbis. Thus, its aim was to purify the defiled, and yet it defiled all those who were in any way connected with the preparations of the ashes and water of purification. . . . So inscrutable was its nature—they said—that even King Solomon in his wisdom despaired of learning the secret meaning of the Red Heifer regulations.

Now, Hertz recounts the story of the Roman who approached R. Johanan ben Zakkai concerning the strange ritual. After R. Zakkai had dismissed the heathen with a simple albeit false analogy, his students request of him the true answer. R. Hertz quotes directly the passage.

> "By your lives, said the Master, "The dead man doth not make impure, neither do the ashes dissolved in water make pure; but the law concerning the Red Heifer is a decree of the All-holy, Whose reasons for issuing that decree it behooves not mortals to question."

Hertz then makes a case that we shall never know and it will always remain a mystery to us. Still, he cannot help providing some of the symbol answers that have been attempted in the past; and he concludes in a predictable yet lofty manner: " . . . the ceremony, therefore, is a powerful object-lesson, teaching the eternal truth that a holy God can be served only by a holy People."

The expiation of sin through the sympathetic slaying of a perfect or near perfect animal is not uncommon in pagan rituals (the famous diatribe of Elijah mocking the priests of Baal and calling down the fire from heaven, 1 Kings 18, for example), and is recounted in numerous incidences in Scripture. What seems to be unique here is that the creature must be red, and must be a heifer; that is, it must be of a certain color and of a certain gender. Red may signify blood, for, in both ancient Israelite cultic ritual and rabbinic Judaism, the blood is considered to be the life. The conceptualization of a ritual involving an animal so proscribed to symbolize life concerning a ritual where one is to be purified (i.e., from death to life) would represent a powerful and dramatic motif.

It is interesting that Graves enumerates Hercules's tenth labor concerning herding not just cattle but cattle of a certain color.

> Heracles's Tenth Labour was to fetch the famous cattle of Geryon from Erytheia, an island near the Ocean stream, without either demand or payment. Geryon . . . was the King of Tartessus in Spain, and reportedly the strongest man alive. He had been born with three heads, six hands, and three bodies joined together at the waist. Geryon's shambling red cattle, beasts of marvelous beauty, were guarded by the herdsman Eurytion son of Ares . . . (also, Erytheia, Eurytion, refer to red in a similar fashion).

An entire tractate of Talmud is devoted to the mystery of the red heifer and its ceremony. As we would expect, the main part of the discussion involves disputations and legalistic procedures. *Mishnah 1*, for example, opens with what seems a dispute between R. Eliezer, "The Sages," and R. Meir. R. Joshua gives support to one of the views.

> R. Eliezer ruled: The . . . Red Cow (must be) no more than two years old. But the Sages ruled: . . . even

> three or four years old. R. Meir ruled: Even five years
> old. One that is older (may be) valid, but they did not
> wait with it so long since it might in the meantime
> grow some black hairs and become invalid.

The reference to the hairs relates the indication to deem
the animal free of any yoke; that is, the two hairs on the back
of the neck were inspected carefully to determine if the hairs
had been bent under the yoke or if they grew in a pattern that
indicated the neck had not yet received the yoke. Here, the
Rabbis intuit that if the animal were older, it could conceivably
grow out two new hairs, and the inspection would be difficult
at best and probably suspect. Another way to inspect was to
see if the animal rolled its eyes heavenward when a person
approached it; that is, if it had known the yoke previously and
was therefore looking for it. Those who have ridden horses or
have had dogs for pets know it is much the same when one
approaches with the bridle or the leash—the animal will reach
for it in anticipation to go running or walking, or, in some
cases, attempt to avoid it (most horses, in particular, as is
understandable, do not like to take the bit).

The dispute between R. Eliezer and his adversaries continues in *Mishnah* 2:1:

> R. Eliezer ruled: A [Red] Cow for the sin-offering that
> is with young is valid. But the Sages rule that it is
> invalid. R. Eliezer ruled it may not be bought from
> idolaters. But the sages rule that such a one is
> valid. . . .

In *Mishnah* 2:3, the disputations continue. There is an
indication of R. Eliezer's brilliance by the particular proof text
he chooses, turning an *a priori* argument on its side. There
follows the proposition of a Talmudic principle.

> One that is born from the side (i.e., Caesarean), the
> hire of a harlot or the price of a dog is invalid. R.
> Eliezer rules that it is valid, for it is written, Thou
> shalt not bring the hire of a harlot or the price of a
> dog into the House of the Lord thy God. While (the
> Red Heifer) was not brought into the House.

The quote is from the Torah, viz. Deuteronomy 18:19. R. Eliezer's retort is one of those that seems complicated at first glance, but upon introspection is realized as simple and obvious: Since the Red Heifer is not brought into the House of the Lord, and since one is prohibited from bringing other offerings derived from the sources indicated, therefore, one may purchase the Red Heifer from those sources since there is never any concern that it will be brought into the Temple. Now one of the general rules for validity is established

> . . . (Nonetheless), all blemishes that cause consecrated animals to be invalid cause also the Red Cow to be invalid. If one had ridden on it, leaned on it, hung on its tail, crossed a river by its help, doubled on its leading rope, or put one's cloak on it, it is invalid. But if one had only fastened it by its leading rope or made for it a sandal to prevent it from slipping or spread one's cloak on it because of flies, it remains valid. This is the general rule: Wherever anything is done for its own sake, it remains valid; but if for sake of any other, it becomes invalid.

It is easy to perceive that if one had insulted the Red Heifer with any of the majority of the actions indicated, it most likely would have received the yoke, again, one of the Torah proscriptions. One or both of the other prohibitions (the blemish [derived from Torah] or the hairs [usually translated in text as "faultless," i.e., the hairs also must be red]) is pronounced in *Mishnah* 5: "If it had two black or white hairs growing with one follicle, it is invalid . . ."

Mishnah 3:1 turns toward the actual ritual itself, particularly that concerning the ablutions of the *Kohen*.

> Seven days before the burning of the [red] cow the priest who was to burn the cow was removed from his house to a chamber that was facing the northeastern corner of the Birah, and which was called the stone chamber. Throughout the seven days he was sprinkled upon with . . . the sin-offerings that were there. . . .

Cross references in *Yoma* 2a relate that the "Birah" was the name of a certain spot on the Temple Mount. From this, we learn that during the time of festivals and during Yom Kippur, there was much ritual and ceremony occurring all about the Temple Mount, as well as within the Temple courtyards themselves. It was a colorful, noisy, smelly, full-bodied, and lusty place, indeed. Also in *Yoma*, we learn that stone was considered to be free of susceptibility to impurity.

There is a tradition that R. Eliezer was a lineal descendant of Moses. R. Jose the Gallilean recounts a proof text from Exodus 18:4: "And the other was named Eliezer"; that is, because it says "the other one" the reference is to R. Eliezer. R. Jose claims that because Parah opens with R. Eliezer's opinion about the age of the Red Heifer, that this was his opening instruction upon assuming his chair. Nadich (vol. 2, pp. 32–33, 148–149) has tracked this tradition and other *midrashim* from *Pesikta de Rav Kahana* (4:7), *Peshita Rabbati* (14:13), *Numbers Rabbah* (19:7), *Midrash Tanhuma* on *Hukkat* (8). From these sources, the author notes that Moses considered this ritual to be an expiation for all of Israel for the sin of the Golden Calf, and used the ashes of the Calf in the ritual ceremony itself.

> Rabbi Aha taught in the name of Rabbi Jose bar Hanina that when Moses went up to heaven, he heard the voice of the Holy One, blessed be He, as He sat studying the section dealing with the Red Heifer, quoting the law in the name of its author: "Rabbi Eliezer says that the . . . Red Heifer (must not be) more than two years old." Moses then said to the Holy One, blessed be He, "Master of all worlds, the worlds above and the worlds below are in your domain, yet You sit and quote a law taught by a mere mortal human being!"
>
> The Holy One, blessed be He, replied, "Moses, there will arise in My world a righteous man who [in his concern for the purification of Israel] will begin his instruction in the Oral Law and so I . . . say, 'Rabbi Eliezer taught . . .'"
>
> Moses said, "Master of universes, may it please You to decree that Eliezer be my descendant."

Nadich relies upon Rabbi William G. Braude for an exegetical teaching of the matter.

> (It) seems intended to indicate God's comforting of
> Moses for his disappointment in his immediate de-
> scendants. Moses, like God Himself, is understood to
> have meditated deeply on the Red Heifer as a means
> of purifying Israel. Thus, after Israel had defiled
> themselves with idolatry, Moses used the powder of
> the Golden Calf, an anticipation, as it were, of the use
> of the ash of the Red Heifer, to begin Israel's puri-
> fication . . . His remote descendant, R. Eliezer, like-
> wise concerned, began his instruction in the Oral
> Law with regulations pertaining to the ash of the
> Red Heifer, in striking contrast to Moses' own chil-
> dren who, in their lack of concern for God's prohibi-
> tion of idolatry, were a grievous disappointment to
> Moses. . . .

Braude, in his turn, relies heavily upon R. Jose bar R. Hanina's exegeses in *Pesikta*. Nadich proceeds to relate that the honor accorded R. Eliezer extends even further. R. Judah ha-Nasi, in his redaction of the *Mishnah*, placed the teaching of R. Eliezer concerning the recitation of the *Shema* as the opening entry in the Talmud (*Berachot* 1:1), "so to please Moses, the putative ancestor of Eliezer."

Further, in *Sanhedrin* 11a and in the *Yerushalmi* (*Yerushalami, Sotah*), R. Eliezer is deemed worthy of being endowed with the Holy Spirit (which would oddly seem to indicate his ancestry from David, rather than Moses).

In Volume 1, Nadich relates a story that places the mishnaic references into the context of an occurrence well known at the time.

> It once happened that a red heifer was needed for
> the ritual purification ceremony and none could be
> found. At long last one was found at a heathen's.
> Some Jews went to him and said, "Sell us the heifer
> you have for we need one." He replied, "Give me my
> price for her and take her." (And what was the going
> price for a heifer? Three or four gold coins.)

There ensues a scene of Middle-East bargaining and haggling. However, the heathen perceives he has the advantage. He knows what the sale of the heifer is for, and he knows the

Jews must have it. So, in the end, he will only sell it to them for an outrageous fortune. Still they agree, for indeed the ceremony must occur. But his attempt to fool the purchasers even more becomes the means of his undoing. Wishing to make a parody of the Jews and their ritual, he places a yoke upon the neck of the animal.

> When they came with all the gold to take the heifer from the heathen and showed him the gold, he went in and, first removing the yoke from the heifer, led her out to them. When he led her out, they proceeded to examine her for the two signs of her never having borne a yoke, but the two particular hairs that should have been straight were bent down, and in addition her eyes were rolling back (i.e., heavenward, expecting the yoke) . . . They said to him, "Take your heifer. We can do without her. Fool around with your own mother!" When the wicked heathen saw that they were returning the heifer to him and that he had come out with hands empty . . . his mouth, which had said, "I will have some fun at their expense," proceeded to say, "Blessed is He Who chose His people." Then he went into his house, strung up a rope, and hanged himself.

The midrashic source material ends with a quote from Judges 5:31: "So may all Your enemies perish, O Lord!"

Like all good stories, this one has many layers. There is the teaching of the *mitzvah* and ritual itself, especially how significant it was that, indeed, the heifer be without blemish and without having suffered a yoke. Beyond this, the metaphor (not even so much a metaphor) of the heathen representing Rome and its evil ways, of Rome's yoke upon the Israelite people, of Rome's theft of the treasury of the Jewish people, and Rome's ultimate demise while the Jewish people continue on their eternal journey with the guidance of the Rabbis may be indicated.

A final insight provides a glimpse into the mystical realm. The ritual itself is a mystery. The *Zohar* uses terminology such as cleansing the soul of its impurities, impurities gained while one engaged in sin. From Vol. II, 129b: " . . . according to man's strivings in this world is his habitation in the next world; hence such a man is polluted by the spirits of uncleanness and cast into Gehinnom."

Gehenna or Gehinnom was (is) one of the places of the lower depths. It was a place of purgatory. The purification process took up to twelve months. It consisted of special fires to burn the soul of its impurities. From Vol. III, 64b: . . . seven rivers of fire issue forth and descend on the heads of the wicked, along with burning coals of fire, generally in the evening, when God Himself judges the sinners.

Might the Red Heifer have been a symbol of the fires raging in Gehenna, a warning of what awaits the soul that does not purify itself in this world? In actuality, the question posits a rather weak argument, since the oral legends of Torah, and the redaction by the writers and its editor, begs the issue that they were little aware or were unaware of the sophisticated conceptions of the afterlife and *gilgul* (reincarnation), divined later by the Rabbis, and more fully expiated by Moses de Leon in the fourteenth century as he compiled the *Zohar*. Still, albeit perhaps an anachronistic supposition, the ritual was clearly performed in the latter days of the Second Commonwealth; as the period of messianic fervor grew, it may have taken on, to a degree at least, some of this implication (see especially Raphael, pp. 301–308.)

What remains, then, is what existed at the beginning of this listing. In our time of prayer and study, we have before us a ritual strange and seemingly hidden. It has been for some time. It likely will remain so. To our ancestors, however, once again, an animal, in a certain proscribed ritual format, sacrifices her life for the benefit of expunging defilement from the individual and from the community. I doubt that anyone who ever experienced the rite or who observed it ever forgot it. I suspect they lived better lives after it.

Fox (p. 748, his translation follows) points out that the *mitzvah* occurs "Apparently to close out the Korah story (the major rebellion in the desert), in which(,) and in the subsequent plague of punishment(,) perhaps more than 15,000 persons perished (Chapters 16 and 17)." With the tasks of the Levites clear in Chapter 18, this intense purification ceremony can be instructed. Note again that the ceremony seems to be indicating that it is a ritual purification for the entire community of Israel. Perhaps that is its point, after all, that it is a pivotal moment, a *Havdalah*, a separation from death—as a pure living animal dies—to rebirth and life renewed, a life of the individual and the community toward righteousness.

Or, perhaps, as T. S. Eliot once said, sometimes the best questions are those that lead to additional questions.

> 1 YHWH spoke to Moshe, saying:
> 2 This is the law of the instructed-ritual that YHWH has commanded, saying: Speak to the Children of Israel, that they may take you a red cow, wholly sound, that has in it no defect, that has not yet yielded to a yoke;
> 3 you are to give it to El'azar the priest, it is to be brought forth, outside the camp, and it is to be slain in his presence.
> 4 El'azar the priest is to take (some) of its blood with his finger and is to sprinkle toward the face of the Tent of Appointment, some of its blood, seven times.
> 5 Then the cow is to be burned before his eyes; . . .
> 9 And a (ritually) pure man shall collect the ashes of the cow, depositing them outside the camp in a pure place. It shall be for the community of the Children of Israel in safekeeping as Waters Kept-Apart, it is for decontamination
> 10 . . . It shall be for the Children of Israel and for the sojourner that sojourns in their midst as a law for the ages; . . .

An Additional Talmud Tail (*Kiddushin* 56b)

The *Mishnah* indicates an interesting procedure for the betrothal bride-price. "If he betroths [a woman] with . . . the heifer which is to be beheaded . . . she is not betrothed. If he sells [it] and betroths [her] with the proceeds (i.e., their money), she is betrothed."

. . . AND A *MIDRASH* (*Numbers Rabbah* 19:4–5)

The *Midrash* gives the explanation to Moses to deal with a priest who is defiled, the mode of purification to be the ritual of the red heifer.

7

GOAT

GOAT
Hebrew *'AiTS*

> . . . *a three-year-old she-goat,* . . .
> —Genesis 15:9

Capra aegagrus: *Capra*, a she-goat; *aix*, a goat. The only nomenclature I find, although it describes a still wild goat, as well as the domesticated variety, of which it is thought to be its direct ancestor.

CONCORDANCE

Genesis 27:9, 16; 30:32, 35; 31:10, 12, 38; 32:5, 14; 37:31; 38:17, 20; 47:17.

Exodus 9:3; 12:5; 20:24; 23:19; 25:4; 26:7; 34:26 (this is the passage upon which the Rabbis expanded the dairy-meat exclusion in the dietary law); 35:6, 23, 26; 36:14.

Leviticus 1:10; 3:12; 4:23-24, 28; 5:6; 7:23; 9:3, 15; 10:16; 16:5, 7–10, 15, 18, 20–22, 26–27; 17:3,7; 22:19, 26; 23:19.

Numbers 7:16–17, 22–23, 28–29, 34–35, 40–41, 45, 46–47, 52–53, 58–59, 64, 65, 70–71, 76–77, 82–83; 87–88; 15:11, 27; 18:17; 28:15, 22, 30; 29:5, 11, 16, 19, 22, 25, 28, 31, 34, 38; 31:20.

Deuteronomy 14:4–5, 21; 32:14.

Judges 6:19 (kid); 13:15, 19; 14:6 (kid); 15:1 (kid); 13:15, 19; 14:6 (kid); 15:1 (kid).

57

1 Samuel 10:3 (kids); 16:20 (kid); 19:13 (Michal's quilt of goat . . . hair), 16;
24:2; 25:2.

1 Kings 20:27 (kids).

Isaiah 1:11; 11:6 (and the leopard [number 72] with the kid); 13:21 [reference
to "satyrs"]; 34:6.

Jeremiah 50:8; 51:40 (see numbers 3, 8).

Ezekiel 27:21 (see numbers 3, 8); 34:17 (see numbers 8, 12); 39:18 (see
numbers 3, 8, 28); 45:23.

Zechariah 10:3 (and I will punish the he-goat).

Psalms II–50:9, 13 (see number 28); 66:15 (see numbers 8, 27); IV–104:18
(The high mountains are for the wild goat).

Proverbs 27:26 (see number 3) (The lambs will be for thy clothing and the
goat the price for a field), 27 (And there will be goat milk enough for thy
food . . .); 30:31.

Job 39:1 (see number 17).

Song of Songs 4:1 (see number 5) (. . . thine eyes are as *doves* behind thy
veil;/Thy hair is as a flock of goats,/That trail down from Mount Gilead);
6:5.

Daniel 8:5, 8.

Ezra 6:17 (see also numbers 3, 8, 28); 8:35 (see also numbers 3, 8, 28).

2 Chronicles 17:11 (see also number 8); 29:21 (see also numbers 3, 8, 28), 23;
35:7 (see also #3, 27).

Goats can be identified, along with a wide variety of
species, as hollow-horned ruminants. Among the (generally
large) group of "upon the hoof" animals, these are the most
abundant and most widely distributed. The other species include cattle, bison, buffalo, antelope, and sheep. Deer and elk
are considered to be solid-horned. Australia, Central America,
and South America appear to be the only areas where these
creatures are not native. Typically, animals in this wide category are either very swift or very sure-footed in difficult
terrain.

Wild goats and sheep have been sharing this terrain with
people for a very long time. Goats are another one of those
types of domesticated animals, such as sheep, horses, dogs,
that have ingratiated themselves with humans in a symbiotic
relationship. Their lives are sometimes easier, sometimes
harsher as a result. They are certainly more secure, but they
have sacrificed much, that sense of being untamed, wild, free.
For their part, goats provide much. It is not true that they will

eat anything, but they do enjoy a variety in their eating habits. They provide milk and cheese, and for many cultures, these results are the only manifestation of dairy goods. They are generally strong and wiry, characteristics to their benefit, as this usually renders them unfit for use as meat. (See especially Clark, pp. 94, 173.)

There are two central passages concerning goats, both of them in the Torah. Leviticus, Chapter 16, *Acharey Mot*, details the Temple cultic ritual for Yom Kippur, especially that explaining the rite of the Goat-To-Be-Sent-Away, the two goats, one determined by lot for the Lord, and the other to be sent into the desert or the surrounding cliffs for Azazel. In time, this second goat, the one sent away, to carry the sins of the people upon it, became known as the scapegoat. The second passage is found in Exodus 34:26. It indicates that the kid shall not be boiled in the milk of its mother. From this, the Rabbis developed the entire series of regulations concerning the separation of dairy products and meat products.

Several entries in *Midrash Rabbah* give an explanation of Azazel as a particular high-ranking demon, perhaps even one created on the sixth day for just this purpose. There is much dispute among scholars in this regard, the more rational including, as we shall see, Rashi's, that it was a particular place in the countryside known for its high cliffs. Brown, following Gesenius, traces the derivation of the word to *AZZ-EL*, Desert Demon (sent away from) God.

Disagreement exists also concerning whether the goat led away was cast off the cliff, or whether it was left to wander off the cliff. I have seen goats on cliffs in the Sinai, and it has always been a curious matter to me why it would be presumed the goat would fall of its own accord. Even the domesticated variety is nimble-footed and resourceful. According to the resources generating the entry in the *Encyclopedia Judaica* (Vol. 3), there is little or no question that in the days of the Second Commonwealth, the goat was cast off the cliffs to be hurled to its death. The article also traces the ritual as perhaps influenced by Babylonian, Akkadian, Hittite, and Hellenistic rituals.

> During plagues, the Hittites used to send a goat into
> enemy territory in order that it should carry the
> plague there. On the head of the goat they would
> bind a crown made of colored wool, comparable
> perhaps to the thread of crimson wool which was
> tied to the head of the goat in the Second Temple
> period.

The crimson (or scarlet) cord is discussed in the *Mishnah*
(*Yoma* 4:2). Some attempts in the legends have been made to
trace this cord to the one tied around the hand of Perez's twin
brother, Zerah (Genesis 38:27–30), the same used by Rahab
(Joshua 2) of Jericho to let down the spies from her house
preceding Joshua's invasion. In the Genesis story, it is interesting that one of Judah's exchanges for the services of the
disguised Tamar was a kid from his flock, and one of his
sureties for his promise was his signet cord.

The article continues with an attempt to derive the various
meanings of the word *Azazel*. The sources refer to the place, a
place in the land that is inaccessible, strong, or hardiest of the
mountains, and, albeit it has been reduced in the emphasis
toward rationality, the original supernatural demonic power,
the desert demon. Ibn Ezra and Nachmanides are quite clear in
their viewpoint: "The school of Rabbi Ishmael explained it is
called Azazel because it atones for the acts of the fallen angels
Uzza and Azael." A remnant of this legend can be found in
Genesis 6:1–4:

> And it came to pass, when men began to increase
> upon the earth, and daughters were born unto them,
> that the sons of God saw the daughters of men that
> they were fair; and they took them wives, whomso-
> ever they chose. . . . The Nephilim were in the earth
> in those days, and also after that, when the sons of
> God came in unto the daughters of men, and they
> bore children to them; the same were the mighty
> men that were of old, the men of renown. (JPS, 10)

One is immediately reminded of the several Near East
mythologies recounting desired and compelled visits of fair
maidens by the gods, demigods, and demi-urges, the most
famous perhaps being that of Zeus and Europe (variant,

Europa) (Graves 1:58, p. 194). Interestingly, although Zeus's manifestation assumes the aspect of a bull, not a goat, Europe dallies with the animal by placing garlands among its horns.

Graves (1:27, pp. 103–111) also derives the detailed biography of the god Dionysus, sometimes called the goat god and associated with satyrs (goat-men) and maenads (wild women reveling in drunken heterosexual and lesbian orgies). Dionysus was killed and resurrected; the Jesus resurrection cult may trace its origins to Dionysus and other Middle East god resurrection mythologies.

One of Dionysus's several aspects is that of a goat. The origins of theater and drama, especially tragedy, have always been traced to the cult of Dionysus, since it was his pagan ritual celebrations that gave birth to the dithyramb antiphonal art that quickly evolved into scenario and dialogue. As Graves points out, this scholarly viewpoint has always followed Virgil's supposition. The Greek word for goat is *tragos*, thus tragedy; however, Graves further indicates that J. E. Harrison

> . . . suggests that *tragedy* may be derived . . . from *tragos*, "spelt"—a grain used (around) Athens for beer-brewing (since) . . . in early vase-paintings, horse-men, not goat-men, are pictured as Dionysus's companions. . . . In fact the Libyan or Cretan goat was associated with wine; the Helladic horse with beer and nectar . . .

Whatever the several Middle East cultic influences, it seems a curious matter that the Redactor would leave even a remnant of the story of heavenly visitors violating or merely impregnating earthly women in the text, albeit it remains clear that God is still the ruler over all. The *midrashic* interpretations follow the view that these were angels cast out, probably from the revolt of the adversary, generally referred to as Satan (Job 1:6: "Now it fell upon a day, that the sons of God came to present themselves before the Lord, and Satan came also among them").

The Books of Enoch, pseudepigrapha from about the time of the Dead Sea Scrolls (indeed, one of the scrolls is a remnant of the resource), give perhaps the most coherent view. From 2 Enoch:

> And one of the angels, having turned away with
> the order that was under him, conceived an impos-
> sible thought: to place his throne higher than the
> clouds above the earth that he might become equal
> in rank to my power. And I threw him out from the
> height. . . . (Barnstone, p. 5).

The Encyclopedia Judaica article summarizes best the
events in 1 Enoch.

> . . . Azazel (or Azael) is one of the leaders of angels
> who desired the daughters of men and it was he who
> taught human beings how to manufacture weapons
> and ornaments. . . . (Soon,) the angel Raphael is
> commanded to "bind the hands and feet of Azazel
> and cast him into the darkness. Make an opening to
> the wilderness which is Dudael and cast him there.
> Put upon him hard sharp rocks." Dudael is the
> (place) mentioned in the *Mishnah* and the associa-
> tion is certainly with the cliff from which the goat
> was cast.

It is in *Yoma* 62a that the main *Mishnah* concerning the
regulations in which the ritual was to be carried out is found.
"The two he-goats of the Day of Atonement are required to be
alike in appearance, in size, in value, to have been bought at
the same time. But even if they are not alike they are valid."
　　There follows a discussion in the *Mishnah* concerning if
one or the other or both of the goats should happen to die
before the ceremony occurs. The *Mishnah* then continues with
a dispute concerning whether the Goat-To-Be-Sent-Away should
be put to death or not.

> The other one is left to pasture until it becomes
> blemished, when it is to be sold and its value goes to
> the Temple fund. For the sin-offering of the congre-
> gation must not be left to die. R. Judah says: It is left
> to die. Furthermore . . . the blood (of the Goat-for-
> the-Lord?) is poured away.

A later *Mishnah* (66a) relates the actual ritual by the *Kohen*.
It is included here in its entirety.

Note that the verse from *Achery Mot* (Leviticus 16:30), "For on this day shall Atonement be made for you . . ." is spoken by the priest, with attribution to "the Torah of Moses, Thy servant."

The Causeway of Arsela appears occasionally in legend as one of the secret passageways to the Temple Mount, and thus to the *Kadosh Kadeshim*, the Holy of Holies. Occasionally, throughout the centuries of the Diaspora, rabbis or learned persons would attempt to locate it. Archaeologists search for it today and may have located it.

The term *Israelite* is generally understood by the Rabbis to mean a non-priest. Such an indication is interesting, because in traditional synagogues, the *Alleyot* (the calling up to the Torah for its public reading) is usually divided into *Kohen*, Levi, and Israelite (i.e., non-*Kohen* or -Levi). In the *Gemarah*, Abaye asks, "You might even say that it is in accord with R. Judah: Are the priests not included in 'Thy people Israel?'" (Today, of course, in Reform, liberal Conservative, and most Reconstructionist and Renewal synagogues, this custom has waned or been eliminated; all are called up "equally.")

The Rabbis understood that the Babylonians (or any non-Jew) shouting and pulling at the goat were attempting to cast their own sins upon the animal. Perhaps some of them fell into that large category of neither heathen nor Jew called God-fearers, which grew during the Second Commonwealth. Many from this group may have turned to the new messianic movement and formed a coterie of the early Christian sect.

One of the miracles of the *Beit Hamikdash* was that, even though the people stood shoulder to shoulder in the Temple courts, when they heard the Ineffable Name and bowed to the ground, albeit there should not have been room for them, there was always room.

> He then came to the scapegoat and laid his two hands upon it and he made confession and thus would he say, I beseech thee, O Lord, Thy people, the House of Israel, have failed, committed iniquity, and transgressed before thee. I beseech thee, O Lord, atone the failures, the iniquities and the transgressions which Thy people, the House of Israel, have failed, committed, and transgressed before Thee, as

it is written in the Torah of Moses, Thy servant, to
say for on this Day shall atonement be made for you,
to cleanse you, from all your sins shall ye be clean
before the Lord.

And when the priests and the people standing in
the Temple court heard the fully pronounced Name
come forth from the mouth of the High Priest, they
bent their knees, bowed down, fell on their faces, and
called out: Blessed be the Name of His Glorious
Kingdom for ever and ever.

They handed it over to him who was to lead it
away. All were permitted to lead it away. But the
Priests made it a definite rule not to permit an
Israelite to lead it away. R. Jose said: It once happened that Arsella of Sepphoris led it away, although
he was an Israelite, and they made a causeway for
him because of the Babylonians, who would pull its
hair, shouting to it: "Take and go forth, take and go
forth."

From Rashi:

> . . . He places one goat at his right and the other at
> his left. He then puts both his hands into an urn and
> takes one lot in his right and the other in his left.
> Then he places upon them . . . "For the Lord" . . .
> and "For Azazel" (which) was afterwards sent forth
> to the Azazel . . . a precipitous and flinty rock—a
> towering peak (*Yoma* 67b, into a craggy land). (Sil-
> bermann, *Vayikra*, p. 73)

The Yom Kippur service that developed over the centuries
demonstrates how fully it (the traditional service, at least)
recalls the haunting rituals of our ancestors. Notice how the
Rabbis clearly identify Azazel as a location. Through the ages
they fought what they considered to be superstitious elements, and perhaps wished to avoid any recollection of the
demon mythology. Bokser's *machzor* serves well; from *Shachrit*
(p. 322) and *Musaph* (p. 420):

> Our God and God of our fathers, pardon our sins on
> this Day of Atonement. Let our sins and transgres-
> sions be removed from thy sight, as Thou didst

promise: It is I who erases your transgressions, for Mine own sake, . . . On this day shall atonement be made for you to cleanse you; of all your sins shall you be cleansed . . .

And the High Priest in awe prolonged the utterance of the divine name until the worshipers had completed their response. Then he turned to them and added: "You shall be purified." And Thou didst forgive Thy faithful High Priest.

He then proceeded to the eastern court, where two goats alike in form and size stood ready for the sin-offering of the whole community of Israel. By the drawing of lots he assigned one as an offering to the Lord and the other to be banished into the wilderness, to a place called Azazel, as a token of the renunciation of sin. . . . He tied a crimson thread on the head of the goat selected for banishment and placed it in the direction to which it was to be sent away; and he returned to the bullock which was his own sin-offering.

In the last Yom Kippur of his life, Shimon Hatzaddik, the *Kohen Gadol* [High Priest], predicted to the people that he would die the coming year. They asked him, "How do you know?" To which he replied, "Every year, when entering the Holy of Holies on Yom Kippur, I was accustomed to see an old man clothed in white garments who accompanied me as I entered and exited. However, this year, he only accompanied me when I entered but not when I left."

The *Medrash* (sic) concludes: Rav Avihu commented, "Who says that was a person? Why, it was the Holy One, blessed be He, Himself in the form of an old man accompanying him for protection.(")
(Kahan, p. 132 *Mitzvah* 185, Leviticus 16:3: "Thus shall Aaron come into the holy place," derived from *Vayikra Rabbah* 21:12])

The *Kapparah* rite is an interesting version of the famous "scapegoat" offering, which occurs in various forms among many peoples. It was first mentioned in early Geonic (sic) times, and probably originated toward the end of the Talmudic period. The following account, . . . describes a form of the rite which was no longer practiced during the Middle Ages: . . . the head of the family planted beans in little baskets, one for each member of the family; when these sprouted on the eve of the New Year he would circle the head of each individual with his basket seven times, saying, "This is in place of this person, this is his surrogate, this is a substitute for him," and throw it into the river.

The procedure that prevailed in the Middle Ages, also mentioned in Geonic writings, differed. It involved the slaughter of a cock . . . (in Geonic times, a ram, or lamb, or goat might also be used), after . . . (it was) passed three times around the head of the subject, while various Biblical passages were recited. . . . (Trachtenberg, p. 163)

Preuss located two medieval treatments for disease extracts from goats:

The use of goats' milk was considered highly efficacious in antiquity, and milk cures for chronic cough were always held in high esteem since the time of the Knidisch school (8th–9th century?) (p. 174).

The juice of the kidney of a goat was recommended by the physician Minyami for earache (p. 436).

Berachot 44b points out that the price for a fat kid was no small amount, two *zuz* (*zuzim*, as found in the ditty at the finale of the Passover *Seder*).

One only kid, one only kid, which my father bought for two *zuzim*; one only kid, one only kid.

And a cat came . . .

. . . Then came the Most Holy, blessed be He, and slew the angel of death, who had slain the slaughterer, who had slaughtered the ox, which had drunk the water, which had extinguished the fire, which had burnt the staff, which had smitten the dog, which had bitten the cat, which had devoured the kid, which my father bought for two *zuzim*; one only kid, one only kid.

An Additional Talmud Tail (*Sheba'oth* (Oaths), *Mishnah* 1

"R. Meir says all the goats have equal powers of atonement."
The *Gemarah* explains that in a *Baraitha* it was taught:

> For a case where there is no knowledge either at the
> beginning or at the end, and for a case where there is
> no knowledge at the beginning but knowledge at the
> end and for a (pure) man who ate unclean holy food,
> the festival goats and the goat offered outside [the
> veil on the Day of Atonement] bring atonement. This
> is the opinion of R. Meir.

This *Mishnah* is very complex, detailing many holidays and
goat offerings. The *Gemarah* attempts to explain the logical
processes and rationale as well as the opinion of the Rabbis. R.
Meir's opinion, albeit not in agreement with that of others,
clearly carries considerable weight.

8

R A M

RAM (See number 3)
Hebrew *'ahYiL*

> *. . . a three-year-old ram . . .*
>
> —Genesis 15:9

Ovis aries: Like the Bull, his biblical heritage is as distinct as its sexual dichotomy, and so receives his special reference.

CONCORDANCE

Genesis 22:13; 31:38; 32:14, 23.

Exodus 19:13; 25:5; 26:14; 29:1, 3, 15, 17–19, 22, 26–27, 31–32, 34; 35:6, 23; 36:19; 39:34.

Leviticus 5:15–16, 18, 25; 8:2, 18, 20–22, 29; 9:2, 4, 18; 16:3, 5; 19:21-22; 22:28; 23:18.

Numbers 5:8; 6:14, 17, 19; 7:15, 17, 21, 23, 27, 29, 33, 35, 39, 41, 47, 51, 53, 57, 59, 63, 65, 69, 71, 75, 77, 81, 83, 87-88; 15:6, 11; 23:1–2, 4, 29–30; 28:11, 14, 19–20; 27–28; 29:2–3, 8–9, 13–14, 17–18, 20–21, 23–24, 26–27, 29–30, 32–33, 36–37.

Joshua 6:4–6, 8, 13 (ram's horn).

1 Samuel 15:22.

1 Kings 1:39 (ram's horn).

Isaiah 1:11; 34:6; 60:7.

Jeremiah 51:40 (see numbers 3, 7).

Ezekiel 27:21 (see numbers 3, 7); 34:17 (see number 7); 39:18 (see numbers 3, 7, 28); 45:23–24; 46:4–7, 11.
Micah 6:7.
Psalms II–66:15 (see numbers 7, 28); V–114:4 (The mountains skipped like rams [see number 3]), 6.
Job 42:8 (see number 28).
Daniel 8:3–4, 6–7.
Ezra 6:17 (see also numbers 3, 7, 28); 7:17 (see also numbers 3, 28); 8:35 (see also numbers 3, 7, 27); 10:19.
1 Chronicles 15:26 (see number 28); 29:21 (see also numbers 3, 28).
2 Chronicles 13:9 (see number 28); 17:11 (see number 7); 29:21 (see also numbers 3, 7, 28)–22 (see also number 28), 32 (see also numbers 3, 28).

Much of the species indication has already been given under the *Sheep* (number 3) entry, which see.

Rams are tough. They are hardy. Like most horned ungulates, they are sure-footed. The psalmist gave us one of the most enduring images of the graceful and nimble style of rams, comparing the quaking or shuddering mountains to their lissome skip. Clearly, the male of the species was known for these admirable attributes three thousand years ago; not much has changed in his genetic heritage.

One story stands out above all others in the Bible. Again, it is in Torah. Again, it is in Genesis. It is, perhaps, along with Joseph's coat and his dreams, the Passover destruction of the firstborn in Egypt, the crossing of the sea, the revelation on Mount Sinai, Joshua's defeat of Jericho (which also involves a ram, at least ram's horns), David's defeat of Goliath, and Solomon's wisdom stories, one of the most famous stories of the Bible. I'm not sure that it is one of the most endearing. It is a story that befuddled Rabbis and Sages. It is as perplexing to us today as it was to them in their days. Still, it is a story so ingrained in the Israelite consciousness, so unique, so much a benchmark of the separation between Judaism and the heathen faiths, that it is given its own name, "Akedah."

Also, to the ram's glory, or to his despair, his horn is singled out as the one to develop into the *shofar*, the singular horn producing its distinctive sound. Although Rosh Hashana and the end of Yom Kippur are not the only times the *shofar* is to be blown, it is these sacred times that most Jews are familiar with, look forward to, and are inspired by.

*   *   *

Gesenius (p. 785) derives the word *Akedah* (*AHKeD[ah]*) from the verb "to bind," with the implication of twisting, as in arms being twisted behind one's back. In its adjective form, it is the word used when Jacob marked his flock of sheep to separate them from Laban's flock. Thus, a better translation now becomes "striped with bands," and ties together the patriarchs, father and son, in yet another fashion. One is reminded also of the straps that wrap the arm when one dons *tefillin*, and the impressions left upon the skin when the phylacteries are removed at the end of the prayer service; however, this is admittedly a thin scholarly strand, since the vocabulary connection works better in English than in Hebrew (where Gesenius [p. 905] indicates the derivation of KSHR, to bind in this sense); nonetheless, even a slender thread of connection is compelling and may advocate a gentler situation. Thus, in Judah's magnificent plea to Joseph for the life of his brother Benjamin, and his father, Jacob, Genesis 44:30— "Now therefore when I come to thy servant my father, and the lad is not with us; seeing that his soul is bound up with the lad's soul"; and, again, in 1 Samuel 18:1—"And it came to pass, when he had made an end of speaking unto Saul, that the soul of Jonathan was (bound) with the soul of David, and Jonathan loved him as his own soul" (Tanakh, Jewish Publication Society). The translation is from Hertz (22:9, 13; 30:39; Deuteronomy 6:8):

> And they came to the place which God had told him of, and Abraham built the altar there, and laid the wood in order, and bound Isaac his son and laid him upon the altar, upon the wood. . . .
>
> And Abraham lifted up his eyes, and looked, and behold behind a ram caught in the thicket by his horns. And Abraham went and took the ram, and offered him up for a burnt-offering in the stead of his son.
>
> And the flocks conceived at the sight of the rods, and the flocks brought forth streaked, speckled, and spotted.
>
> And thou shalt bind them for a sign upon thy hand, and they shall be for frontlets between thine eyes.

Fox's translation captures more vividly and intently the drama of the moment.

> They came to the place that God had told him of; there Avraham built the slaughter-site and arranged the wood and bound Yitzhak his son and placed him on the slaughter-site atop the wood. . . . Avraham lifted up his eyes and saw; there, a ram caught behind in the thicket by its horns! Avraham went, he took the ram and offered it up as an offering—up in place of his son.

We are so accustomed to the image of this scene that it seems burned into our vision. Yitzchak, a mere lad, whose name means "laugh" or "laughter," lies placidly, as if in a daze, gazing up to the heavenly spheres, willing to die for the glory of the Lord. But with the word derivation of *AH[ayin]KD* made clear, perhaps the fact that it is a ram becomes most significant. This is not a lamb or even a goat, animals far more easy to deal with. The ram is not brought up. It is caught, depending on one's point of view, gloriously, or tragically for the creature, in an entanglement of vines, in a thicket. This is a very sure-footed animal. It could only have been captured by its horns, which had probably grown very large. At that point, it would have taken at least two strong men to deal with it. Therefore, one needs to ask, what's wrong with this imagery?

First, Isaac was no lad. He was an adult. He would have been strong enough to ward off the attempts to bind, or at least to make a fight of it. Also, he would have been bound with his hands behind him, face down, probably his neck on the edge of the altar. Finally, Abraham would have had a time with the ram, albeit it may have been exhausted from struggling to get free. Obviously, as in all Judaic interpretations, there is considerable room for dispute (but Isaac's age is textual).

What is easy to interpret and difficult to dispute is the passage's, and thus the Israelite faith's, decry of human sacrifice, especially child sacrifice. There are several references, direct and inferred, to child sacrifice in the text (Leviticus 18:21, Deuteronomy 18:10, from the Fox translation):

> Your seed-offspring you are not to give-over for bringing-across to the Molekh that you not profane

the name of your God, I am YHWH! There is not to be
found among you one having his son or his daughter
cross through fire, . . .

Judges (11:30–31, 33–35, 39) relates a story seemingly in
violation of the Torah text. It is a story that clearly had
variants throughout the Near East. One is reminded of the
Agamemnon-Iphegenia story.

There also seems to have been a cultural memory of a tribe
or a cult that sacrificed virgins.

> And Jephtah vowed a vow unto the Lord, and said: "If
> Thou wilt indeed deliver the children of Ammon into
> my hand, then it shall be that whatsoever cometh
> forth of the doors of my house to meet me, when I
> return in peace from the children of Ammon, it shall
> be the Lord's and I will offer it up for a burnt-
> offering."
>
> And he smote them from Aroer until thou come
> to Minnith, even twenty cities, and unto Abel-
> cheramim, with a very great slaughter. So the chil-
> dren of Ammon were subdued before the children of
> Israel. And Jephtah came to Mizpah unto his house,
> and, behold, his daughter came out to meet him with
> timbrels and with dances; and she was his only child;
> beside her he had neither son nor daughter. And it
> came to pass, when he saw her, that he rent his
> clothes, and said: "Alas, my daughter! thou hast me
> very low, and thou are become my troubler; for I
> have opened my mouth unto the Lord, and I cannot
> go back."

At this point the girl requests two months to prepare
herself before the sacrificial ritual is carried out: "And it came
to pass at the end of two months, that she returned unto her
father, who did with her according to his vow which he had
vowed; and she had not known man. . . ."

There is also a famous *Midrash* concerning Ruth. That is,
she was to be a sacrificial maiden, but God caused boils to
appear on her skin. With this blemish, she was rejected by the
Moabite priests and cast out of the temple cult (probably the
Ashera cult) altogether. She marries Naomi's son, is widowed
(the *Midrash* suggests Naomi's sons, Mahlon and Chillion,

protested the cultic beliefs and were executed for it, perhaps in the hapless role of the offering in the sacrificial ritual). She then proceeds to accompany Naomi, eventually marrying Boaz and beginning the line that will lead to King David.

But are there outside resources?

It is a difficult question. Scholars have been frustrated with the paucity of discovered ancient Near East texts outside the biblical text that overtly or even subtly indicate child sacrifice. In the history portion of Scripture, that part of the biblical text that tends to be validated by the accumulating evidence of archaeological research, there are two interesting indications. Both are from 2 Kings. In 3:27, in this particular war, the King of Israel, Jehoram, has united with the King of Judah, Jehoshaphat, and the King of Edom against Mesha, King of Moab: "Then he [the King of Moab] took his eldest son that should have reigned in his stead, and offered him for a burnt-offering upon the wall. And there came great wrath upon Israel; and they departed from him, and returned to their own land."

The second (23:10) recounts an act by the king during the all-important YHVH revival under Josiah. The king destroys a pagan high place apparently used by some Israelites: "And he defiled Topheth, which is in the valley of the son of Hinnom, that no man might make his son or his daughter to pass through the fire to Molech." Gesenius (p. 574) traces the derivation of Molech to the same root as MLCH, that of the word *king*.

Pritchard (Vol. 2, the ellipses are those of the ANET, Ancient Near East Texts) has two interesting entries. But even from these sources, one is pressed to confirm child sacrifice and can only infer it.

> *"Never has a sinless child been born to its mother,*
> (Line deleted)
> *My god, the . . . of destruction which I have*
>   *. . . against you,*
> *The . . . of . . . which I have prepared before you*
> (p. 140, "Man and His God," Sumerian)

> *Worship your god every day.*
> *Sacrifice and (pious) utterance are the proper*
>   *accompaniment of incense*
> (p. 147, "Counsels of Wisdom," Akkadian)

The problem is obvious: There is little or no outside evidence of the human sacrificial cult. Yet that it must have occurred is also obvious. A theologian, or a society, doesn't include a prohibition in his, or its, law code against an abhorrent activity unless the activity exists.

What, then, does all this imply? Hertz, Telushkin (pp. 36–39), and other scholars indicate the main thesis: That Abraham was told to leave a land (where, presumably, these horrific cult rituals occurred) and go to another land; That the Akedah stands not as the sacrifice of Isaac, but as the non-sacrifice of Isaac, the clarion call that no longer will there be child or human sacrifice; that if the people must sacrifice, they will only sacrifice healthy, strong, perfect animals to stand in the place of human beings. Plaut (pp. 149–150) also concurs with this view, although he does point out the fascinating Greek legend of Phrixus.

It is a cogent thesis. It resonates with validity throughout all generations. It is an enduring, lasting monument and tribute to the patriarch writers of the text, and to those who comment upon and study the text. It is a thesis that determines one of the defining moments between Judaism and the faiths that surrounded it then, and some that surround it now. After all, in our own time, and perhaps not so metaphorically, it is all too easy to perceive of our children being sacrificed in some fashion upon the altars of false deities.

Nonetheless, having said all of that, and accepting all of that, still we have a problem.

This, after all, is Abraham. This is the Middle East dissembler who manipulated his wife, Sarah, to appear as his sister before Pharaoh. This is the Middle East businessman who negotiates the division of grazing land for his herds and Lot's herds. This is the Middle East rhetor who persuaded God to let the evil cities of Sodom and Gomorrah stand but for ten righteous persons. This is the Middle East haggler who dickered over a few sheckels of silver for a burial plot for his wife. And this arbitrator, this manipulator, this rhetor, this bargainer, is silent and immediately obedient when it regards his own son!

There is, of course, the view that both men had complete faith—they knew that the worst would not occur. After all, Abraham even states (22:8), " . . . God will see to the sheep for his burnt offering . . ." (Plaut; Fox, "lamb," which raises another issue concerning that it came to be neither a sheep nor a lamb, but a ram).

But there is also the view, told in some of the traditions, that Isaac was de facto sacrificed, that he went to study in heaven with Enoch (or Shem), and that he tumbled back to earth (resurrected!) when Rebecca approached, and that this is the reason she "fell" off her camel, from the shock of this strange sight. According to this view, this is what is meant when she espies Isaac for the first time and says: "Who is the man over there that is walking in the field to meet us?" The textual defense of this view is found in Verse 9, where Abraham and Isaac go up together, and in Verse 19, where Abraham comes down alone. The academic explanation is simple— clearly there were two legends or traditions that the Redactor wove together in a near perfect rendition.

Nonetheless, it is interesting that we may in fact have a vestigial clue of child sacrifice as an Israelite cultic practice. (The verses concerning Rebecca are: 24:62–65.)

Fox (p. 92) probably indicates the mysterious nature of this story best:

> . . . The fact (of) . . . Israel's rejection of local and widely practiced ideas of child sacrifice . . . may be quite beside the point. Coming just one chapter after the birth of the long-awaited son, the story completely turns around the tension of the whole cycle and creates a new, frightening tension of its own. The real horror of the story lies in this threatened contradiction to what has gone before.
>
> Most noticeable in the narrative is Avraham's silence, his mute acceptance of, and acting on, God's command. We are told of no sleepless night, nor does he ever say a word to God. Instead he is described with a series of verbs: hurrying, saddling, taking, splitting, arising, going . . . After this God will never speak with him again.

Fox continues for a bit, pointing out that the story is the midpoint of Genesis in that certain Aristotelian tensions are now released, since we now know God will come to the rescue of His chosen ones (the author points out also that to be chosen altogether means to be subjected to an extraordinary test).

Ultimately, no easy answer exists. Only an increase in the mystery lies before us in the text. The answer does exist, however. It is we who may not discern it. For my part, I believe the answer lies tangled in the thicket, deep in the heart and out upon the horns of the ram. A ram doesn't just get tangled up. He was running toward the area, either in rutting or, more likely, attempting to evade a predator; or, perhaps, he had sensed, somehow, that his time had come.

Rashi also clearly faced the same or similar dilemma. Using in the main *Sanhedrin* 89b, the commentary he provides recalls the opening of the Book of Job. According to the Rabbis, Rashi informs us, Satan again came forward to taunt God in testing one of His most righteous.

> AFTER THESE WORDS (usual trans., THINGS, 22:1) . . . means after the words of Satan who denounced Abraham, saying: " . . . not a single . . . ram did he bring as a sacrifice to You." God replied to him, "Does he do anything at all except for his son's sake? Yet if I were to bid him, 'Sacrifice him to Me,' he would not refuse."

As this *Midrash* unfolds, the bargaining-haggling-dickering character of Abraham we are familiar with previously expressed in the text does come out. There is a rhetorical wordplay concerning which son, Ishmael or Isaac, in a more characteristic barter between God and Abraham. Later, the mountain picked to which father and son will go to perform the deed is indicated as the mount in the future city of Jerusalem where the *Beit Hamikdash*, the Great Holy Temple, will be established. This is a traditional belief that continues today. Rashi also offers a "head of a pin" rhetorical explanation for the Verse 2 statement ". . . bring him up there for a burnt offering": "He did not say, 'Slay him,' but he told him to bring him up to the mountain to prepare him . . . So when he had taken him up, God said to him, 'Bring him down.'"

The explanation now comes to its climax. Even Satan, as in Job, is compelled to assist Abraham, albeit in a manner opposite his design; once more, the trickster is tricked. And, again, Abraham's characteristic as a Middle East arbiter finds its voice: " . . . after all the words of the angel and the *Shechinah*, and after all the arguments of Abraham . . . IN A THICKET . . . BY ITS HORNS—because it was running towards Abraham, but Satan caused it to be caught and entangled among the trees" (attr. R. Eliezar).

Now, Rashi brings his argument home in his usual compelling fashion. And so we are also provided the answer why the Akedah is chosen to be read on the High Holy Days.

> At every sacrificial act he performed on it he prayed saying, "May it be Thy will that this act may be regarded as having been done to my son" . . . (but) Its real meaning is as the *Targum* renders it: The Lord will choose and select for Himself this place to make His *Shechinah* reside in it and for sacrifices to be offered there . . . (thus) The midrashic explanation is: May God see this Binding of Isaac every year to forgive Israel and to save them from punishment, so that it may be said, "in this day" (to mean) in all future generations (as Verse 17) THAT I WILL GREATLY BLESS THEE . . . THY SEED. (Silbermann, pp. 93–96)

The Agamemnon-Clytemnestra-Cassandra-Iphegenia myth cycle is one of the better-known stories from Greek mythology. The Phrixus story is not so well known, but forms the background for one of the most celebrated of all the myths. Both stories—and an attendant minor myth concerning Meaender—clearly were influenced by or had a common antecedent of the Abraham-Isaac and Jephthah's Daughter stories. The commonalties of the ram being substituted and the call from heaven's gate to cease child sacrifice are particularly striking. Throughout the Middle East, there may have been an uncomfortable tension concerning the fait accompli of child sacrifice and society's disdain of the terrible ritual by the particular society wherein some elements, for personal gain perhaps, saw it as necessary.

Again, Graves remains the most scholarly and trustworthy resource for the retelling of the myths, their variants, source material citations, and tracking to the original historical events, whether by hard evidence or brilliant supposition. Note also the possibility of an animal substitution-replacement at the last moment.

> Note 2: A version of the "Jephtah's daughter" myth . . . seems to have been confused with Agamemnon's sacrifice of a priestess at Aulis, on a charge of raising contrary winds by witchcraft . . . (and) offended conservative opinion at home, women being traditionally exempt from sacrifice. The Taurians . . . worshipped Artemis as a man-slayer. (Vol. II, pp. 290–295, viz. entry 161, esp. d., e)

We turn our attention to the lesser-known, but perhaps more striking, of the myths. Yet another biblical story is invoked here, that of Joseph and Potiphar's wife.

> This Phrixus was a handsome young man, with whom his aunt Bladice, Cretheus's wife, had fallen in love, and whom, when he rebuffed her advances, she accused of trying to ravish her. The men of Boeotia, believing Bladice's story, applauded Apollo's wise choice of a sin-offering and demanded that Phrixus should die; whereupon Athamas, loudly weeping, led Phrixus to the mountain top. He was on the point of cutting his throat when Heracles . . . came running up and wrested the sacrificial flint from his hand. "My father Zeus," Heracles exclaimed, "loathes human sacrifices!" Nevertheless, Phrixus would have perished despite this plea, had not a winged golden ram, supplied by Hermes at Hera's order—or, some say, by Zeus himself—suddenly flown down to the rescue from Olympus.
> "Climb on my back!" cried the ram, and Phrixus obeyed.
> "Take me too!" pleaded Helle. "Do not leave me to the mercy of my father."
> So Phrixus pulled her up behind him, and the ram flew eastwards, making for the land of Colchis, where Helius stables his horses. Before long, Helle . . . lost her hold; she fell into the straits between Europe and Asia, now called the Hellespont in her honour; but Phrixus reached Colchis safely, and

there sacrificed the ram to Zeus the Deliverer. Its golden fleece became famous a generation later when (Jason and) the Argonauts came in search of it.

Note 2: The myth of Athamas and Phrixus records the annual mountain sacrifice of the king, or of the king's surrogate—first a boy dressed in a ram's fleece, and later a ram—during the New Year rain inducing festival which shepherds celebrated at the Spring Equinox. Zeus's ram-sacrifice on the summit of Mount Pelion, . . . took place in April, when, according to the Zodiac, the Ram was in the ascendant . . . and the rite still survives there today in the mock-sacrifice and resurrection of an old man who wears a black sheep's mask. . . . (The Biadice–Phrixus and Potiphar's wife–Joseph story have an antecedent in an old Canaanite tale.) (Vol. I, pp. 225–231, viz. entry 70, esp. d., e.)

Graves's fascinating Note 5 to his entry No. 169, p. 352, as indicated, weaves together some of these variant strands in Near East mythology.

A vow . . . was made by Maeander . . . (to sacrifice) to the Queen of Heaven . . . (that) the first person who should congratulate him on his (victory) . . . and this proved to be his son Archelaus. . . . Maeander killed him and then remorsefully leaped into the river . . . as Jephthah doubtless did to Anatha, who required such burnt-offerings on her holy Judaean mountains. It looks, indeed, as if sacrifice of a royal prince in gratitude for a successful campaign was once common practice—Jonathan would have been after the victory near Michmash, had not the people protested . . . (all of these stories seeming to mark) the anti-matriarchal reaction characteristic of heroic saga.

The anti-matriarchal characteristic: Sarah is not consulted, and soon perishes; Clytaemnestra is duped; the mothers of Jephthah's daughter and of Jonathan appear to be nonexistent or, at least, ignored.

The Jonathan-Saul story that Graves refers to can be found in 1 Samuel, Chapters 13 and 14, especially 14:36–46. Graves states that the "people" protested, but the authoritative New JPS translation (*Tanakh: The Holy Scriptures*, p. 439), and other biblical versions, use the appropriate translation, "soldiers." Jonathan's troops, whom he had led to a great victory, supported him and defended him against the king.

This apparently brings us full circle and gives some insight into why the writers of the text found it necessary to show Abraham as apparently willing, and his twice called name to mean "No—no more will this occur" so compelling. But the ram is the focal point.

Nadich recalls another midrashic indication concerning the ram. Throughout Abraham's journeys, he sacrifices and offers three other animals, a heifer, goat, and a turtledove-pigeon. These four offerings, invoking also his military engagement against the four kings, foretell of the four empires that will conquer his descendants. In Verse 15:12, " . . . a trance fell upon Abram, and a deep dark dread descended (fell) upon him."

> *Dread* refers to the Babylonian exile; *dark* to . . . the evil days (in Persia) in the time of Haman. The word *deep* alludes to Greece, . . . and . . . *fell* to Rome . . . the three-year-old ram (refers) to Greece, which extended its dominion in three directions—westward, northward, and southward. . . .
>
> When God had thus shown Abraham the four captivities, He said to him, "As long as your descendants will study the Torah and offer sacrifices, they will be saved from these captivities. But a time will come when they will cease offering sacrifices. Choose, therefore, which your children will then suffer, Gehenna or captivity?" Abraham chose captivity, some say because God so advised him. Abraham was assured, however, that just as his descendants would be enslaved by the Egyptians, who would be punished in their turn, so too would the Four Empires be successively subjugated. (P. 10)

> Our God and God of our fathers, sound the great *shofar* to herald our freedom and lift a banner for the ingathering of our exiles. Bring together the home-

less of our peoples from among the nations, and assemble them from the farthest places of the earth, under the wings of Thy Presence. And restore us in song to Zion Thy city, and in enduring joy to Jerusalem, the site of Thy sanctuary. There may we yet perform the service of each festival, bringing to Thee our offerings, the tokens of our devotion, as prescribed for us in Thy Torah, given by Thee through Thy servant Moses:

On the day of your gladness, on your festivals and on your new moons, you shall sound the trumpets as you bring the designated offerings, and they shall be a remembrance before your God; I am the Lord.

For Thou hearest the call of the *shofar* and givest heed to its summons; none may be compared to Thee.

Footnote: The verb HRT derived from HRH has been interpreted as meaning "trembling," appropriate . . . because the Day of Judgment is a day of trembling. The more general interpretation regards it as meaning "conception," or "giving birth," a reference to the doctrine that Rosh Hoshanah celebrates the creation of the world. This usage is reflected in the word H(o)VRYM, parents, or those who give us birth. (Bokser, p. 208, H and E)

Arise from your slumber, arouse yourselves from
    lethargy,
Look well into your deeds and return in penitence.
You have lost your way pursuing vain desires,
Think of your Creator, heed the call of your souls,
Return to the Lord your God, and He will have
    mercy upon you. . . .
When the shofar is sounded in the city shall the
people not tremble?
The Lord is enthroned in judgment, tremble before
Him all the earth.

                    (p. 167)

The Rosh Hoshanah holy day(s), over the years, have taken on such an awe-inspiring cachet that it should not be surprising that the demonic hoard would attempt to disrupt the affair. Such fears and manifestations developed during the Middle Ages and on into the Enlightenment period, despite the attempts of some rabbis to quell what they consider a superstitious direction. The best resource, as usual in such matters, continues to be the classic work by Trachtenberg. Here, from pages 112–113:

> The most popular selection from the Bible . . . used (to ward off these demons) was the so-called *Shir shel Pega'im*, commonly interpreted the "anti-demonic psalm." The Talmud, in which this title was first employed, records variant opinions as to just which Psalm it designated, with the honors divided between Ps. 3 and Ps. 91. The latter was preferred. . . .
>
> . . . We have a report that during a Rosh Hoshanah service in the city of Frankfort the *shofar* refused to function; the remedy employed was to breathe the words of the *shir shel Pega'im* three times into the wide opening of the ram's horn, whereupon its hoarse notes were restored. Satan had seated himself inside the horn and had impeded its call until dislodged by the charm!

Anyone who has ever had to blow *shofar* on Rosh Hoshanah can testify how often these demonic forces enter the instrument. Now, a centuries-old defense is again revealed. Tractenberg's Talmud citation may be found in *Shabbat* 15b:

> PSALM 91:
>
> *O you who dwell in the shelter of the Most High*
> *and abide in the protection of Shaddai—*
> *I say of the Lord, my refuge and stronghold,*
> *My God in Whom I trust,*
> *that He will save you from the fowler's trap,*
> *from the destructive plague.*
> *He will cover you with His pinions;*
> *you will find refuge under His wings;*
>
> . . .
>
> *For He will order his angels*
> *to guard you wherever you go*
> (1–5, 11, Tanakh, pp. 1217–1218)

An Additional Talmud Tail (*Eruvin*, *Gemarah* 102a–b)

On a weekday, spreading a canopy may be accomplished with no consequence; on *Shabbat*, however, such an act may be considered tent-building and would be unacceptable. Since kindness to animals is of a very high order of action, the Rabbis find a way to protect the animals without being in *Shabbat* violation. The technique used is one of being incidental. That is, if the canopy is already partially in place, then . . .

> R. Huna possessed some rams that needed the shade in the daytime and the open air at night. When he came to Rab the latter said to him, "Go and roll up . . . but leave one handbreadth unrolled, and on the morrow spread it all out and you will be merely adding to an occasional tent and that is perfectly legitimate."

9

PIGEON

PIGEON (See Number 5)

> . . . *a [or turtledove, JPS,* 21] . . .
>
> —Genesis 15:9

Columba livia. *Columba*, Latin, a pigeon or dove; *livius*, Latin, beige-gray. (See Number 5.)
The common name is rock dove.

CONCORDANCE

Leviticus 1:14; 5:7, 11; 12:6, 8; 14:22, 30; 15:14, 29.
Numbers 6:10

Toperoff (pp. 53–57) classifies three of our species in one section: dove, turtledove, and pigeon. It is, in effect, an accurate choice. Doves and pigeons are indeed very close in specific description; in some cases, they mate interchangeably. Some are wild. Some are domesticated. Some hybrid species are the result of escaped domestics mating with those considered wild.
In some cases, the measure of interbreeding has occurred back and forth so often that only ornithologists can pronounce

it a dove or a pigeon. Typically, however, if only for the sake of convenience, and not necessarily true to taxonomy, doves are considered largely shaded white and fly wild, pigeons with darker coloration and either home in to domestication or adapt to urban life.

Therefore, the terms for the three ubiquitous species, perhaps, variants of one species, is "breeds" by Goodwin (p. 117): "The turtle doves are trim, shapely pigeons, mostly about half the size of the average Feral or Domestic Pigeon, although some species are rather smaller or larger than this. They can be divided into four main groups . . ." Even the biblical text uses basically the same word, when one of the differing species is indicated in the translation—*YoNAH*, although, usually the translation for "Pigeon" is preceded by *BeN* or *B'Nei*; *GoZaL* (Genesis 15:9) is also employed for "Pigeon." Toporoff traces the *shoresh* of *YoNAH* "either from *yanah*, 'to oppress or maltreat,' or from *anah*, 'to mourn.'" Gesenius doesn't emphasize this derivation as much as the similitude of return (as we saw with the valiant dove that Noah released for her mission of discovery); the lexicographer places his emphasis with the GZL root to be connected to robbery or plunder. In this, again, doves are usually perceived as white, that is, pure, and pigeons as grey or darker-striped, that is, impure.

This may explain, at least partly, why it is the pigeon that is indicated for the purification ritual when a mother gives birth (Leviticus 12).

From the Fox translation, 2, 5–8:

> . . . A woman—when she produces-seed and bears a male, she remains-*tamei* for seven days, . . . Now if (it is) a female (that) she bears, she remains-*tamei* for two-weeks, like her time of being-apart; and for sixty days and six days she is to stay for (a period of) blood purification And at the fulfilling of the days of her purification, for a son or for a daughter, she is to bring a lamb, . . . and a young pigeon or a turtle-dove, as a *hattat*-offering. to the entrance of the Tent of Appointment, to the priest. He is to bring-it-near, before the presence of YHWH, and is to effect-purgation for her, then she will be purified from her

> source of blood. . . . But if her hand does not find
> enough (means) for a sheep, she is to take two
> turtledoves or two young pigeons . . .

Toporoff and other translators refer to the pigeon or
turtledove offering as a "sin-offering"; but the word *HTT* has a
more profound meaning than this. Fox includes the original
Hebrew term; the new *JPS* (pp. 156, 171) renders the term
"purgation," and it is this that Gesenius favors for tracing the
shoresh. It makes more sense. After all, why would giving birth
to a child necessitate a *sin*-offering? But because the mother is
in her period of separation, a ritual of bringing forth is
necessary.

Fox (p. 562) indicates a succint clarification:

> . . . a new mother as *tamei*, most likely due to her
> intimate contact with the life/death boundary during
> childbirth. Her separation from and reintegration
> into the community echo similar customs in many
> societies . . . ; as often happens with life-cycle events,
> ritual here reflects what is happening psychologi-
> cally. The doubling of the separation period when it
> is a girl that is born is best explained by the concept
> that a girl potentially doubles the "life-leak" that has
> taken place . . . since she will one day be a child-
> bearing woman who will herself confront the life-
> death continuum.

Fox also points out that while men do not contract ritual
pollution through childbirth, a few chapters later (15), they are
involved in pollution from bodily discharges, albeit the discharge is involuntary (such as from a nighttime emission).
Greenstein also has an effective discussion and insight in this
regard.

Toporoff, in a gentle, beautiful syllogism, suggests that the
HTT offering "indicates that the woman was pure before
marriage and that she is always faithful to her partner. In this
manner we equate the purity of married life among humans
with the fidelity of the dove (turtledove or pigeon) toward its
mate."

This concept of separation during a woman's time of *tamei*,
often misinterpreted as "ritually unclean," is still practiced by

pious couples today. Since the year 70, there has been no sacrifice of living things. However, a bride proceeds to the *mikveh*, the ritual bath, for immersion before her wedding, and then every month until she is pregnant. The key to the matter of separating herself from her husband is if and when she detects her menses or other blood flow. Some couples merely separate twin beds. Some couples have a separate room. Those who wish to do more will not even hand household items to one another during this period of time.

The wife counts her menstrual time, generally seven days. She then counts seven days where no spot of blood is detected. At that time, she proceeds to the *mikveh*. She immerses. She recites the proscribed blessings. She is observed by an attendant, for safety reasons and to ensure she correctly prepares herself and completely immerses herself. And then, like a pigeon (or a dove) knows always to return, she returns to her husband, like a bride. The son or daughter born of such a sexual union is considered to be regarded highly in the heavenly spheres.

AN ADDITIONAL TALMUD TAIL (Sanhedrin 24b–25a, b)

The *Mishnah* states: "And these are ineligible [to be witnesses or judges]: A gambler with dice; a usurer; a pigeon-trainer . . ."

The *Gemarah* asks the logical question, "What are pigeon trainers?" From the disputation that ensues, in the main by R. Chana b. Oshaia, the clear meaning is these are "racers"; apparently, pigeon racing, as well as the racing of four-footed animals, was a common gambling activity of the time. A problem develops, however, in that the special term indicated here is *ara*, which can mean a "fowler," in effect, one who trains his birds to coax another's birds into his cote. The Rabbis clearly saw this as robbery, even though the view that since pigeons are partially wild, it could be considered otherwise (since it relies on the pigeons' abilities): "His answer is that the conduct of an *ara* [is regarded as robbery] merely from the standpoint of neighborliness."

This view seems to hold and supports the clear meaning of the *Mishnah*. The Torah verse the Rabbis point to is Exodus

23:1—"You must not carry false rumors; you shall not join hands with the guilty to act as a malicious witness."

This view is also supported in *Mishnah* 7 of the tract "Testimonies": "They declared 3 things before R. Akiba, 2 in the name of R. Eliezer and 1 in the name of R. Joshua. . . . They that fly pigeons are unfit to bear evidence. . . ."

10

DONKEY

DONKEY (Ass)
Hebrew *PeRe'*

> *He shall be a wild ass of a man;*
> *His hand against everyone,*
> *And everyone's hand against him;*
> *He shall dwell alongside of all his kinsmen.*
>
> —Genesis 16:12

Equus asinus: *Equus*, Latin, a horse; *asinus*, Latin, an ass. The domestic donkey (although the Hebrew indicates, as the initial entry relates, "a wild ass [of a man]")." *AYiR* is also used.

CONCORDANCE

Genesis 22:3, 5; 24:35; 30:43; 32:5, 15; 34:28; 42:26–27; 43:18, 24; 44:3, 13; 45:23; 47:17; 49:11, 14.
Exodus 4:20; 9:3; 13:13; 21:33; 22:4, 9, 10; 23:4, 5, 12; 34:20.
Leviticus 22:26.
Numbers 22:21–23, 25, 27–30, 32–33; 31:28, 30, 34, 39, 45.
Deuteronomy 5:14, 18; 22:3–4, 10; 28:31.
Joshua 6:21; 7:24; 9:4; 15:18.
Judges 1:14; 5:10; 6:4; 12:14; 15:15–16 (jawbone of); 19:3, 10, 19, 21, 28.
1 Samuel 8:16; 9:3, 5, 20; 10:2, 14, 16; 12:3; 15:3; 16:20; 22:19; 25:18, 20, 23, 42; 27:9.

2 Samuel 13:29; 16:1–2; 17:23; 18:9 (Absalom . . . upon his mule); 19:28.

1 Kings 1:33, 38 (Solomon . . . upon King David's mule), 44; 2:40; 10:25; 13:13, 23–24; 27–29; 18:5.

Second Kings 4:22, 24; 5:17; 6:25 (an ass's head was sold . . .); 7:7, 10.

Isaiah 1:3; 21:7; 30:6, 24; 32:14 (a joy of wild ass), 20; 66:20.

Jeremiah 2:24; 14:6; 22:19.

Ezekiel 27:14 (see number 15).

Hosea 8:9; 10:5.

Zechariah 9:9 (Behold, thy king . . . triumphant . . . riding upon an ass); 14:15 [here ass and mule are presented as distinct species] (see also numbers 13, 14).

Psalms I–32:9 (see number 15); IV–104:11 (The wild asses quench their thirst).

Proverbs 26:3 (see number 10).

Job 1:3 (see numbers 3, 13, 14) (His possessions were . . .), 14 (see number 15); 6:5 (see number 13); 1:12 (But an empty man will get understand-ing,/When a wild ass's colt is born a man); 24:3 (see number 15), 5; 39:5; 42:12 (see numbers 3, 13, 14).

Daniel 5:21 (see number 14).

Ezra 2:66–67 [here ass and mare are presented as distinct species] (see also numbers 13 and 15).

Nehemia 7:68 [here as ass; mule in next verse] (see number 14)–69.

1 Chronicles 5:21 (see numbers 3, 12, 14); 12:41 [here ass and mule are presented as distinct species] (See numbers 12, 13); 27:30 (see also number 14).

2 Chronicles 9:24 (see also number 15); 28:15.

Along with the horse, its stalwart relative, the donkey (ass, or in a variant breed, burro) has been a long-time friend, companion, hard worker, and passenger conveyer to human-ity. Perhaps it is time to recognize it as also a noble creature. Unlike their sometimes negative reputations, donkeys are friendly, loyal, eager to please, and affectionate. They have been known to warn their human comrades of danger and to rescue their human comrades from dangerous situations. On occasion, a male donkey may mate with a mare and produce a mule, an oddly hybrid creature that seems to exhibit the best characteristics of both animals, excepting perhaps the swift-ness of a horse. (Donkeys and mules also seem less inclined than horses to charge into the fray of battle; some might see the horse as more valorous; others might be inclined to accord a degree of higher intelligence to the smaller equine). However, donkeys and mules are sure-footed animals and can often traverse with confidence terrain that horses would rather shy away from. All three animals are enormously strong. I have been around horses more than the other species; but any equine-oriented person will generally concede that the animals do not even realize just how strong they are.

It is not true, as a general rule at least, that donkeys and mules are stubborn. In actuality, in most cases, they are industrious. Once they understand what is being asked of them, they will set about the task with diligence. It is also not true that mules are always sterile animals. Documentation supporting their known, albeit uncommon, fertility exists at least as far back as the 1830s (see especially Youatt, Simpson; Skinner within Youatt).

In the biblical text, all of these characteristics are exhibited. The first mention of the animal exhibits a metaphorical description of Ishmael, in which a memory or a contemporary observance recalls the creature back to its wild gamboling ancestors from which the domesticated animals have all derived.

Youatt and Simpson both mention that a herd of wild animals was observed in Ethiopia, but the one resource sports a nineteenth-century copyright date, nor is the other particularly recent.

By the second Genesis citation, the animal is now fully domesticated and, in fact, carries the burdens leading to the Akedah sequence, discussed more fully under the Ram. Later, it is used to carry individuals.

The transport of a particular individual presents one of the most curious stories of the Torah and the Bible. For, in the Bible, the donkey, only along with the serpent, is one of two animals invested with the faculty of speech, that one of God's gifts that seems more than any other to separate humans from animals.

With speech, Mosaic, Aristotelian, and rabbinic thought processes can follow. With speech, philosophers can expound great thoughts, scientists can intuit great discoveries, and all can engage in the best and the worst events of everyday commerce and intercourse. Animals think and communicate, of course, specifically as well as inter-specifically; but only humans (some evidence exists that perhaps cetaceans—whales, dolphins—to a lesser degree) can use symbolic sounds, forming words, forming syntax, forming thoughts understood by others to a greater or lesser degree.

For those familiar with the text, the story is a familiar one, and one that students of the weekly reading of Torah look forward to; anticipation builds, for the story is fairly late in the cycle, coming well along in Numbers (22–25:9). By the Book of Judges, the poor creature has died, and all that is left is her jawbone. Even at this end, however, she manages to be handled in a manner that rescues the Israelites.

The *parshah* (again, Numbers 22:2f) is called Balak, who is a Moabite king; but it is in actuality the story of Bilam (typically rendered in English as Balaam). It is one of the few Torah *parshot* in which an Aristotelian story is allowed to unfold in its entirety (although those familiar with the text know that the denouement is not in actuality complete).

To summarize, Balak has heard of the exploits of the Israelites following their escape from Egypt. He fears a conquest (probably of the One True God over idol worship, more than a military conquest). He calls upon a seer, one who is known to cause curses to rain upon those on whom he casts his spells. At first, Bilam refuses; apparently, even he begins to recognize the influence of the One God. After several diplomatic missions, however, Bilam succumbs to that which represents eternal idol worship, gold and silver. He saddles his donkey. He rides out on his way to curse the Israelites.

However, along the trail, an Angel of the Lord stands in their path. The donkey is given mystical vision and speech; the so-called prophet is blind to the truth and dumbfounded at the animal's halt. He beats the poor creature to continue. The Angel goes this way, then that way, then back again. A series of visions, halts, and beatings ensues. Finally, the donkey presses her rider's foot against a wall. This strains Bilam's foot. The donkey then turns her head to look at her cruel master. Astonishingly, she opens her mouth and speaks.

She is curious as to what she has done; after all, like others of her kind, she has served her master loyally and well. She is curious as to why the prophet cannot see the vision in front of them, a clear warning. Finally, the scales drop from Bilam's eyes, he supposedly understands the message, and is permitted to proceed on his way. Now he knows that God will be putting the words in his mouth, and not Satan.

In high comedy, Balak welcomes him and takes him out to the cursing site, only to be shocked and outraged when Bilam, finding his tongue, proceeds to bless the Israelites and their campsite. So it goes for a number of new sites, again the shock, again the blessing. Finally, the two men part company. We do not hear of the donkey again. Bilam has not learned his lesson, however. The donkey tried. But the seer continues his dastardly ways and is later killed in battle.

This completed story seems almost a Greek satyr play. It is integrated. There is a beginning, middle, and an end. There is a talking donkey and high farce. As Fox points out (p. 768), the poetry in these passages reach the highest of the biblical writers' art. The work, nearly a finished script, could be produced—and, if done well, audiences should be rolling in the aisles. Fox indicates something like that may have involved the ancients; the italics are mine.

> Most memorable, of course, is the sequence about the talking donkey, which must have been more than a little amusing to ancient *audiences*. For here we have a dumb animal who sees divine messengers and possesses the divine gift of speech, . . .

The theatricality and the farcical attributive in the image of a talking donkey was not lost on the master dramatist. Shakespeare convolutes the farcical attribute in *A Midsummer Night's Dream*.

Bilam's blessing-not-curse or curse-turned-to-blessing became one of the introit prayers designated by the rabbis to be used early in the prayer services. Hertz (p. 678) renders the translation most of us are familiar with: *Ma tovu ohalecha ya'akov . . . yisrael . . .* , "How goodly are thy tents, O Jacob, thy dwellings, O Israel!"

Some of the most popular rabbinical teachings developed out of an analysis of this typical repetition device found in Hebrew poetry. In one interpretation, tents and dwelling places represent the Temple in Jerusalem that was destroyed and the synagogues that continue to keep the faith alive. In another interpretation, tents are the synagogues, dwellings the study halls. Yet another indicates the synagogues and the study halls, and the dwellings the homes, wherein Jewish life is so important.

Overall, there is the consideration of familial respect and respect for privacy, for what Bilam actually saw was that the tents of the Hebrew clans were set at off angles, so that a person looking through the doorway of her or his tent could not look into the doorway of another's.

Toporoff examines Maimonides's *Guide for the Perplexed* to locate one of the Rabbinical dicta against cruelty to animals as one of the leitmotifs of the passage. Thus, the Angel's (Fox— Messenger's) scolding (22:32): "For what (cause) did you strike your she-ass (on) these three occasions?" gives rise to the following question posed by the Rambam.

> There is a rule laid down by our sages that it is directly prohibited in the Law to cause pain to an animal . . . the object . . . to make us perfect, that we should not assume cruel habits and that we should not uselessly cause suffering to others; on the contrary we should be prepared to show pity and mercy to all living creatures, except when necessity demands the contrary.

This moral and ethical teaching invokes the classic talmudic rhetorical device of *chol v'chomer*: thus, in this case, if one is so commanded to ease the suffering and treat well animals, how much more should one do in the case of our fellow human beings?

Rashi reminds us that Bilam is traveling with Balak's emissaries, the princes of Moab. The farce, therefore, is being played out in front of these aristocrats. This is the man, the great seer, who is going to curse the great and growing nation of Israel, and he cannot even control his own donkey. Even worse, he is talking to the donkey and believes the donkey is talking to him. And the donkey sees more than does he. What are the princes to think?

The other question Rashi asks is why three times (did the donkey get blocked this way and that, and beaten)? Here he uses a bit of hermeneutics: It is as if Bilam is being asked, So, you mean to attempt to curse a people who had three righteous patriarchs, and who observe three righteous festivals?

The Rabbis, however, involved themselves in a darker side of Bilam. Nadich (pp. 170, 366–367) recounts the legend that Pharaoh's advisers were Jethro, Job, and Bilam. Pharaoh contemplates extermination of the Israelites by killing every firstborn male child, the very decree (or curse!) that returns to haunt the Egyptian leader so terribly.

> Balaam who gave assent to the plan was killed [later, in Numbers 31:8]; Job, because he was silent, was doomed to much suffering; Jethro showed his opposition by flight and, therefore, his descendants were privileged to sit in the Chamber of Hewn Stones.

Much of this didactic is taken from *Midrash Rabbah* (Exodus 1:9, 27:3), *Sotah* 11a, and *Sanhedrin* 104, 106a.

The implications are fascinating. Here we have a clear solution to the difficulties that have vexed biblical readers concerning the Book of Job (albeit it is not fully cathartic, since Job's children seem, at least at first glance, to be innocent victims). Also, silence is perceived as tantamount to committing the crime. The Rabbis admonish us to speak out against injustice. Obviously, Job repented. The only way he could have repented would have been to speak out against injustice. The Chamber of Stones is the term used for the Sanhedrin, which judged the highest cases in the Temple courts. Jethro already had established a precursor to the Sanhedrin in Exodus 18:13–27, when he advised Moses to establish judicial review strata of courts and judges. Deuteronomy 16:18–20, *Shoftim*, establishes the system of courts leading up to the Sanhedrin as the authoritative body, quite similar today to the system of lesser courts leading up, by degrees, to the Supreme Court.

Bilam, clearly, is perceived by the Rabbis as an evil-doer from the get-go. This allows the Rabbis to snub their thumbs in his nose as turning his curse to a blessing recited in the synagogue throughout the centuries on a daily basis. The Rabbis understood Bilam to be one of the few souls consigned to Gehenna for eternity. Still, Bilam's blessing turns back upon itself as a curse nearly in the end. "How goodly are your tents

O Jacob, and your dwelling places O Israel"—both the First Temple, "tents," and the Second Temple, "dwelling places" were destroyed.

There remains, however, the oddity of a talking creature, especially since it appears far beyond the pre-diluvian mythological stories. The kabbalists, having delved into the concept of *gilgul*, reincarnation, briefly entertained the transmigration of souls into animal beings. Raphael (pp. 318–319) traces the disputation over this controversial subject through *Sefer Ha-Temunah* and *Taamei Ha-Mitzvot*, both written in the thirteenth century, when mysticism in general and mystical literature in particular experienced an explosion of revival, culminating in the *Zohar*. *Zohar* and *Sefer Ha-Bahir*, while pursuing the concept of transmigration of souls into higher forms, are silent on the matter of deceased souls entering into animal bodies. Nonetheless, Raphael has uncovered an interesting sixteenth-century story.

> . . . there was a spiritual leader of Modena, Italy, named Rabbi Barukh Abraham da Spoleto. In 1585 he caused quite an uproar in his community after delivering a Sabbath sermon on the subject . . . in which he maintained that the souls of those who sinned against God were condemned to transmigrate into the bodies of animals. When word of his teachings got out into the community, he was directly challenged by other authorities, in particular Abraham ben Hananiah Yagel, who found such a view to be heretical to the kabbalistic philosophy . . .

In the concept of *gilgul*, after all, one is to be reincarnated in the next life at a higher level, until, ultimately, one can enter the higher palaces of the heavenly spheres.

Nonetheless, we may be left with the intriguing question of whether Pharaoh wound up as a talking donkey, to be beaten by his adviser who promulgated evil, and condemned always to see God's messenger with the flaming sword.

The late sixteenth century and early seventeenth were apparently a time of the presentation of mystical concepts followed by retorts by other learned scholars. Trachtenberg (pp. 84–86) traces one of these ongoing disputes concerning the *golem*, the homunculus or animated man, created by lumps of clay and certain incantations including the Ineffable Name (stories that Mary Shelly obviously became familiar with).

The author in particular points to the retort in 1615 by Zalman Zevi of Aufenhausen:

> . . . I made the turncoat look ridiculous, for I said there that he himself must be fashioned from just such kneaded lumps of clay and loam, without any sense or intelligence . . . we call such an image a *chomer golem* . . . which may be rendered "a monstrous ass" . . . which I say is a perfect description of him.

Trachtenberg points out this is "a really good pun." The concept of a homunculus was discussed much earlier than this, in the talmudic period (*Sanhedrin* 67b), and continued throughout the centuries, culminating in its most pronounced (supposed) exponent, Rabbi Judah Loeb of Prague.

R. Loeb always disavowed any knowledge of these supernatural powers and practice of their incantation rituals, but his name somehow became identified with the *golem* that protected the Jewish communities from pograms. In actuality, R. Loeb was an excellent diplomat, and, like Joseph, whom some regarded as his ancestor, had access to the ear of the magistrates of the duchy. Trachtenberg concludes: "The remains of the Frankenstein monster which he is supposed to have brought into being are said still to be among the debris in the attic of Prague's *Altneuschule*."

What we are left with is this: that sometimes we should listen very well indeed to our animals. They may be seeing and speaking with those we cannot see and cannot speak directly with. Kindness to animals is a blessing. Who can say that it cannot lead to greater blessings?

Even when long since dead, the jawbone of the creature, lying out upon the field, is used to rescue Samson and the Israelites from the attack of the Philistine warriors. Here is an excerpt from the Masoretic text (Judges 15:9, 15–17):

> Then the Philistines went up, and pitched in Judah, and spread themselves against Lehi. . . .

> And he (Samson) found a new jawbone of an ass,
> and put forth his hand, and took it, and smote a
> thousand men therewith.
> And Samson said:
> With the jawbone of an ass, heaps upon heaps,
> With the jawbone of an ass have I smitten a
> thousand men.
> And it came to pass, when he had made an end of
> speaking, that he cast away the jawbone out of his
> hand . . .

Notice that Samson speaks his lyrical message while holding the jawbone of (Bilam's?) donkey. His casting it aside may foreshadow when he will soon cast aside all his Nazorite vows, leading to his capture and despair. But, as we can all return, Samson also returns and brings down the idol worshipers.

Veterinary medicine may be as old as human medicine. Pritchard's complete account of the Code of Hammurabi (Vol. 1, p. 138f) reveals an interesting item at list numbers 224–225. Following this indication, Preuss has also uncovered several interesting items in this regard.

> If a veterinary surgeon performed a major operation
> on either an ox or an ass and has saved (its) life, the
> owner of the ox or ass shall give to the surgeon
> one-sixth (shekel) of silver as his fee.
> If he performed a major operation on an ox or an
> ass and has caused (its) death, he shall give to the
> owner of the ox or ass one-fourth its value.
> Among animal physicians, the *Midrash* first men-
> tions the Roman institution of horse surgeons who
> took on the designation *hippiatros*. The *hippiater* . . .
> cauterized a sick she-ass. (Preuss's resource here is
> *Numbers Rabbah* 9:5, which continues with other
> indications.)

An Additional Talmud Tail (Sanhedrin 11)

In the well-known *Mishnah* of expounding who has and has not a portion in the world to come: "The following have no portion therein: he who maintains that resurrection is not a Biblical doctrine, the Torah was not divinely revealed, and an epikoros."

In addition, one who reads noncanonical texts, but possibly only in public readings, a charm-whisperer over a wound, and one who pronounces the Divine Name as it is spelt. Jeroboam, Ahab, Manasseh, Balaam (Bilam), Doeg, Ahitopel, and Gehazi are added to the list. Notice the donkey is not excluded.

In *Gemarah* 98a–b, R. Joshua b. Levi, it is told, once met Elijah standing by the entrance of R. Simeon b. Yohai's tomb. He inquires if he has a portion in the world to come. Elijah directs him to the Messiah, who waits to be called while dressing his leprous wounds and those of the other lepers. R. Joshua receives the oracle he seeks, but because he could hear his voice, it is not enough for the Messiah to come. Later, R. Joseph answers those who desire the coming of the Messiah but might be afraid or embarrassed: "Let him come, and may I be worthy of sitting in the shadow of his ass's saddle."

The commentators indicate the word *saddle* actually to have a more scatological meaning.

Some say the Messiah will come on a white horse, others state he will come on Bilam's donkey. In 105a–b, the supposition is presented that Balaam committed bestiality with his donkey, an indication that would demonstrate without question the depths to which Bilam had descended.

11

CALF

CALF (Cow, Cattle, which see number 12; Bull, which see number 27)
Hebrew *'eGehL*

> *Then Abraham ran to the herd, took a calf, tender
> and choice, and gave it to a servant-boy, who
> hastened to prepare it.*
> —Genesis 18:7–8

Bos taurus. Although an offspring of the adult (see number 12), it is included here mainly to emphasize its famous and all-important status in the story of the golden calf.

CONCORDANCE

Exodus 32:4, 5, 8, 19, 20, 24.
Leviticus 9:3, 8.
Deuteronomy 9:16, 21.
1 Samuel 6:7, 10; 14:32; 29:24 ([Witch of Endor's] fatted calf).
1 Kings 12:28, 32 (the king [Jeroboam] . . . made two . . . calves of gold).
2 Kings 10:29 (golden calf); 17:16.
Isaiah 11:6 (. . . and the calf and the lion [number 16]).
Jeremiah 31:18; 34:18–19; 46:21.
Ezekiel 1:7–11 (see numbers 11, 13, 16, 26, 88).
Hosea 8:6 (Yea, the calf of Samaria shall be broken in shivers); 13:2.

Amos 6:4 (see number 3).
Micah 6:6.
Malachi 3:20 (and ye shall . . . gambol as calves of the stall).
Psalms I–6 (see number 86) (He maketh them also to skip like a calf);
    II–68:31 (see number 28); IV–106:19 (They made a calf in Horeb).
Nehemia 9:18.
2 Chronicles 13:8 (. . . and there are with you the golden calf which
    Jeroboam made you for gods).

The Golden Calf is one of the most famous and easily recognizable stories in the biblical text. It has been as well one of the most perplexing. In actuality, it is not the behavior of the people that is so perplexing, as that of Aaron, Moses' brother, his compatriot in the telling times of witnessing before Pharaoh, and the High Priest designate. How could such a person have agreed to contribute so readily to the pursuit of the idol-worshipers? Aaron's inveterate response to Moses, "So I said to them, 'Whoever has gold, take it off! They gave it to me and I hurled it into the fire and out came this calf!'" rings hollow, and begs the question with even greater intensity.

Various *Midrashim* have presented Aaron as a man of peace, a gentle person who did not wish to create strife and so acquiesced. But, at best, this presents only a partial answer. A little-quoted talmudic reference may provide another viewpoint, and it is presented in conjunction with the building of the calves by Jeroboam, some centuries later. This occurs almost immediately following the split of the northern kingdom, which became known as Israel. The Jeroboam story in fact gives a clue.

> So the king took counsel and made two golden calves. He said to them (to the people), "You have been going up to Jerusalem long enough. This is your god, O Israel, who brought you up from the land of Egypt." He set up one in Bethel and placed the other in Dan . . . the people went to worship [the calf at Bethel and the one at Dan]. He also made cult places and appointed priests from the ranks of the people who were not of Levite descent.

Soon a prophet from the southern kingdom of Judah appears decreeing various signs and portents, declaiming against this seeming heresy. However, even after some of the portents become manifest, Jeroboam continues to maintain these shrines.

It is easy to perceive these places as locales for idol worship, and a complete turning from the YHVH God. The JPS translation in practice assumes this direction for the reader, placing the small "g" in Jeroboam's decree for G[g]od. In English a capital letter or a lower-case letter can predetermine if the writer is describing the One True God or a pagan god. In Hebrew, however, which has no capital letters, it is not so easy.

Now, if we assume one more cross-reference, if we look at Ezekiel's majestic and mysterious vision, we perceive a throne-chariot. Any [K]king needs to have a [F]footstool, a place to rest his (or, we are leading up to, His) feet. If Jeroboam is revealing to his subjects that this is (for?) their God, then these two golden calves could have been seen as the resting places for the footstool of the Heavenly Throne. After all, it was the southern Kingdom of Judah that maintained sovereignty over the Holy of Holies, the footstool of the Throne of Heaven in Jerusalem. The people of Israel needed such (a) shrine(s) to worship YHVH as well. If this is so, Jeroboam's commemoration now makes more sense: YHVH is still their God, still the One Who brought their ancestors out of Egypt.

Perhaps, then, it was this way with Aaron. That is, he was not giving in to a pagan overthrow. Rather, the Egyptian-Caananite bull god was to become merely an ornamental footstool for the One True God. The people, Aaron included, simply lost patience, and failed to wait just one more day. The *Midrash* comments that they miscalculated the day Moses began his ascent to the mountain and to the Heavenly spheres. Had they waited one more day, Moses would have brought them the Torah.

Alternate views address the issue more directly, that in actuality it was this holiest of communities in history that lost their faith and fell the hardest. No other community ever as a whole heard the Voice of God, and then within a day's time, fell so far. In this view the Children of Israel are as guilty as the mixed multitude from Egypt (another group on which some of the commentaries place nearly all the blame). In this view, Pandora's box has been opened, and the ills perpetrated upon the Jewish people throughout history, including the destruction of the Holy Temples, can be traced back to this event. In this view, we, the descendants and heirs, must continue to repent.

Again, *Mishnah* 11:

> All Israel have a portion in the world to come . . . But the following have no portion . . . who maintains resurrection is not a Biblical Doctrine, the Torah was not divinely revealed, an epikoros. R. Akiba added one who reads uncanonical books . . . (also Jeroboam, Ahab, Manesseh . . . Balaam . . .)

Gemarah:

> R. Oshaia said: Until Jeroboam, Israel imbibed (sin) from one calf; but from him onwards, from two or three calves (at) Beth-el and Dan furnishing additional incentives to sin. R. Isaac said: No retribution whatsoever upon the world which does not contain a . . . fraction of the first (i.e., golden) calf.

Mishnah 1:

> . . . A tribe, a false prophet, and a High Priest can only be tried by a court of 71. . . .

Gemarah:

> R. Simeon . . . said: The case of the High Priest on the Day of Atonement , . . propitiates even when it (gold) is not worn on his forehead [The High Priest did not officiate in the Holy of Holies on the Day of Atonement robed in garments that had gold interwoven, as that would recall the sin of the golden calf]. (*Sanhedrin*)

My rabbi once told me a story about the destruction of the Second Temple—that it was brought about by adultery, the lack of deeds of loving-kindness, and by the corruption of the priests. A certain man coveted another man's wife. One day, he saw the man come up to the ramparts for his watch. This first man deserted his post and went to cavort with the man's wife.

While they enjoyed their sinful earthly pleasures, the Roman army burst through the post the man had deserted. A man had a morsel of food. He was eating it on his way to his watch. A widow and her two daughters needed food. The man ignored them and passed them by. Before he could get to his post, in his haste, he slipped and fell. The food lodged in his throat. He choked and died. His assigned post was the second place the Roman army breached the rampart wall. And the High Priest on that day, in arrogance, wore gold fabric into the Holy of Holies. The fire of conflagration began not from the Roman army, but from the Temple Mount.

Likutei Peshatim, in its commentary on Verse 32:6 ("And they rose up early on the next day and offered burnt-offerings and brought peace-offerings and the people sat down to eat and drink and they rose up to make merry") explains perhaps best the gradual and then complete dissolution of the Children of Israel at the pagan shrine.

> . . . Each act in the verse represents the increasing deterioration of their relationship with Torah and God. These stages serve as the prototype for understanding all future rebellions within the Jewish people.
>
> At first the verse says, *V'olo 'laht*, "and they offered burnt offerings." Every rebellion begins with what appears to be the right intentions. After all, a burnt-offering is totally consumed, with the owner receiving nothing in return. Given a little time, however, a change occurs, and now (they bring) . . . "peace offerings." A peace offering is consumed partially on the altar and partially by the owner. There is already a major element of self-indulgence. Shortly thereafter, the total reverse of the prior noble intentions begins to emerge. This is indicated in the Pasuk by . . . "to eat and drink." All values have been forgotten, all is profane. Finally, the bottom rung is reached and . . . "and they rose up to make merry."
>
> An understanding individual can see the parallel within our own times.

Weissman's *midrashic* collection gives one of the most complete treatises in one resource, including the view that

Aaron felt this was the preferable sin to proceeding over to idol worship in its entirety. At least, from this point of view, *teshuvah*, repentance, could occur.

> The greatness of the Generation of the Wilderness cannot be underestimated. After uttering ("We will do and we hear") at Har Sinai, they resembled angels rather than humans. They had regained the level of Adam before he sinned, and Hashem pronounced them free of the power of the Angel of Death.
> . . . If so, why did they stumble in the Sin of the Golden Calf? Why didn't Hashem protect them from sin, as He usually shields His *tzaddikim*?
> Hashem permitted the sin of the (calf) since it served as a sign of hope and encouragement to *K'lal Yisrael* for all future generations. The incident of the Golden Calf would prove that no matter how far a Jewish community strayed from the path of Torah, they would never be beyond *teshuva*. If after a sin as severe . . . B'nai Yisrael were reaccepted by Hashem, no community would ever be able to claim that they had fallen too low to return to Hashem. (Pp. 313f)

Weissman's collection also points out the failed attempt of Hur to stop the rebellion, and its tragic consequences, and that it was the women of Israel who refused to give up their gold jewelry and other objects for such a profane act. Thus, here is another reason that we may rejoice, in that it is through the women that Israel will be redeemed.

Nadich's selection follows the view of terrible sin, and that the same or similar retribution will be meted out to the generation's descendants in the same or similar circumstances in later generations. R. Eliezer and R. Joshua are discussing the destruction of the Temple in view of the verse from Isaiah 22:8, "And the covering of Judah was laid bare."

> R. Joshua explained the verse in this way: "In the place of justice, there was condemnation," that is, in the place where the Divine Attribute of Justice displayed itself in the story of the Golden Calf . . . there punishment was carried out, there the Lord smote

the people because they had made the Calf . . . there
they acted wickedly by making the Golden Calf and
prostrating themselves before it.

R. Eliezer then ties up the problem and its solution neatly,
referring back to the only thing the generation in the desert
could do, the only thing, ultimately, any of us can do in any
generation.

From the day the Temple was destroyed, sages began
to be like schoolteachers, the schoolteachers like
synagogue officials, the synagogue officials like the
ordinary run of people, the ordinary run of people
became feeble, and there is no one to seek compassion for them. On whom can we rely? On our Father
in heaven. (P. 30)

". . . The sin of the Golden Calf was for the most part
instigated by members of the mixed multitude who were
descendants of Amalek. Therefore, God commended that even
if they wish to become proselytes, they are not accepted.
Amalek has a spiritual fault that cannot be remedied" (*Torah
Anthology*, p. 14).

Finally, Fox (pp. 437–440) presents an equivocal view, and
one that, as is customary with his approach, is a literary
critical treatment.

. . . the Golden Calf story plays such an important
role in the . . . book of Exodus . . . It . . . provides
some insights into the complex relationships . . . it
focuses particular aspects of the Tabernacle idea . . .
and it makes clear the difficulties of the emerging
faith community. . . .

Everywhere there are fierce emotions: doubt,
anger, panic, pleading for mercy, courage, fear. And,
indeed, the entire enterprise of Exodus hangs in the
balance, as God wishes only to destroy the faithless
people (a rough parallel exists in Genesis 22, where
all that has previously been promised to Avraham is
threatened). Only after the stark emotions just mentioned have been cathartically absorbed, and the
covenant restored, can there be a return to the task

at hand—the building of an abode for the divine amid the very human community of Israel. . . . What we learn from this section is not only God's forgiving nature but something significant about Moshe: faced with a dictator's dream—the cloning of an entire nation from himself—he opts for staunchly defending the very people who have already caused him grief through their rebelling, and who will continually do so in the ensuing wanderings . . .

AN ADDITIONAL TALMUD TAIL (*Megillah* 25a–25b)

In the *Mishnah* we learn that certain parts of the text are permitted to be translated in the public reading, and certain parts of the text are not permitted to be translated. The story of Reuben in Genesis 35:22 ("While Israel stayed in that land, Reuben went and lay with Bilah, his father's concubine; and Israel found out. . . ."), for example, "is not permissible"; however, concerning the story of Tamar and Judah (Genesis 38): "It is permissible. The first account (Exodus 32:1–20) of the incident of the golden calf is both read and translated. The second (21–25) is read but not translated."

Gemarah: "You might think that [we should forbear] out of respect for Israel. Therefore we are told [that this is no objection]; on the contrary, it is agreeable to them (to recount) because it was followed by atonement."

A sardonic interrogatory retort follows: "And in our time they may atone?"

However, the *Mishnah* points out the second half should not be translated. It is a curious prohibition, because the *Gemarah* indicates the lesson to be learned: "It has been taught: A man should always be careful in working his answers because on the ground of the answer which Aaron made to Moses the unbelievers were able to deny [God], as it says, *And I cast it into the fire and this calf came forth.*"

. . . AND A *MIDRASH*

Leviticus (Emor 27:8–9): The argument is made by the Rabbis that it was not Israel who made the calf but the *avrav*, the riff-raff, those who were not fully connected: "... the nations of the world taunted Israel and said to them: 'You made the Golden Calf!' The Holy One, blessed be He, investigated their words and did not find any substance in them. For this reason the bullock was placed first among all the offerings."

12

CATTLE

CATTLE (Bull separate, which see number 27; overlap with Oxen, which see number 13)

Abimelech took sheep and cattle (oxen) and male and female slaves, and gave them to Abraham; and he restored his wife Sarah to him.

—Genesis 20:14

Bos taurus

CONCORDANCE

Genesis 21:27; 24:35; 32:5, 15; 33:13; 41:2–4; 18–20; 26–27; 47:17.
Exodus 9:3; 11:5; 20:24; 22:30.
Leviticus 22:19.
Numbers 19:2, 5–6, 9–10; 22:40, 31:9, 28, 30, 33, 38, 44; 32:1, 4, 16, 26; 35:3.
Deuteronomy 2:35; 3:7, 19; 5:14; 7:13–14; 13:16; 28:4, 11, 18, 51; 30:9; 32:14.
Joshua 1:14; 8:2, 27; 11:14; 21:2; 22:8.
Judges 6:5; 10:4; 14:18 (metaphorical, as Samson's wife).
1 Samuel 6:7, 10, 12, 14; 23:5; 30:20.
2 Samuel 17:29.
1 Kings 18:23, 25, 26, 33 (Elijah's test).
2 Kings 3:17.
Isaiah 7:21; 30:23; 46:1; 63:14.

Ezekiel 4:15; 34:17 (see numbers 7, 8), 20, 22.
Joel 1:18.
Amos 4:1 (*kine*, viz. Bashanites as cattle).
Jonah 4:11.
Psalms II–50:10; III–78:48; IV–104:14; V–148:10.
Job 21:10; 36:33.
Nehemia 9:27; 10:37.
1 Chronicles 5:21 (see numbers 3, 10, 14); 7:21.
2 Chronicles 14:14 (see also numbers 3, 14; 26:10, And he [Uzziah] . . .
    hewed out many cisterns, for he had much cattle . . . for he loved
    husbandry); 35:8–9 (see also number 13).

There is a fascinating comparison between the dream
interpretations of Yosef (Joseph) as a lad sent out to find his
brothers tending the sheep, and his dream interpretation to
Pharaoh, when called up from prison as an adult, dreams that
involve the cows. Something profound has happened to Joseph. He was designated the prince, the heir apparent (although later, that designate actually falls upon Judah) because
of something his father saw in him; but God is missing from his
earlier dream pronouncements. Before Pharaoh, Joseph declares it is God Who is making the interpretations.

In recognizing the cow dream and the grain dream as one,
Joseph establishes himself as a Wise Man, a Vizier, a Man of
God. Although not seen literally in the text, Pharaoh, of course,
had his magicians, courtiers, and dream interpreters try to
interpret, to no avail. Only this very powerful Hebrew slave
could give the answer (Fox, in his more literal translation,
never uses "grain," only "ears"; magicians are mentioned in
41:25—however, their own interpretations, the ones that Pharaoh discarded, are not mentioned).

From *Tanakh*, the New JPS translation:

> Once Joseph had a dream which he told to his
> brothers; and they hated him even more. He said to
> them, "Hear this dream which I have dreamed": . . .
> He dreamed another dream and told it to his broth-
> ers, saying, "Look, I have had another dream": . . .
> (Genesis 37:5–6, 9)
>
> And Joseph said to Pharaoh, "Pharaoh's dreams are
> one and the same: God has told Pharaoh what He is

about to do. The seven healthy cows are seven years,
and the seven healthy ears are seven years; it is the
same dream . . . It is just as I have told Pharaoh: God
has revealed to Pharaoh what He is about to do . . .
As for Pharaoh having had the same dream twice, it
means the matter has been determined by God, and
that God will soon carry it out." (Pp. 25–26, 28, 32)

Now when Joseph revealed himself to his brothers, and
then wished to notify his father that he was yet alive, according to the text, it was not until Jacob saw the wagons Joseph
sent that he believed his son was alive. There is a *Midrash*,
related perhaps best by *Likeuti Peshatim (Vayigash)*, that this
indeed represented a signal to Jacob; that is, prior to Jacob's
sending Joseph to seek his brothers, and the entire cycle
beginning, he had been studying with his son the Torah
passage of the Bloodguilt Heifer (Deuteronomy 21:1–9).

Joseph, instead of hitching oxen to the wagons, which
would have been customary, hitched instead strong, previously untrained heifers. This was the threefold visual message
from son to father: I am alive; I am become like unto Pharaoh;
I have not forgotten nor forsaken my Torah teaching.

They went up from Egypt and came to their father
Jacob in the land of Canaan. And they told him,
"Joseph is still alive; yes, he is ruler over the whole
land of Egypt." His heart went numb, for he did not
believe them. But when they recounted all that
Joseph had said to them, and when he saw the
wagons that Joseph had sent to transport him, the
spirit of their father Jacob revived. "Enough!" said
Israel. "My son Joseph is still alive! I must go and see
him before I die." (45:25–28)

The *Parshah* of the Unyoked Heifer, and the *mitzvah* of
absolving communities from guilt over a slain person discovered outside the community, occurs much later, of course,
than the incidents described in Genesis; however, the more
experienced student of Torah study recognizes one of the main
principles of Torah study—that linear time is suspended and,
therefore, presents no difficulty with Jacob's and Joseph's
study session. Perhaps, as well, this might give an insight into

that earlier mysterious phrase "So his brothers were wrought up at him, and (while, Fox) his father kept the matter in mind" (37:11).

The other line from a story I find curious is at the end of Jonah (4:10–11). Jonah's mission is at last complete, but now he seems contrite and pouting, in particular that the shady plant that grew up and kept the sun away has withered. Jonah exclaims in a hyperbolic fashion that he is so deeply grieved he wishes to die.

> Then the Lord said: "You cared about the plant, which you did not work for and which you did not grow, which appeared overnight and perished overnight. And should not I care about Nineveh, that great city, in which there are more than a hundred and twenty thousand persons who do not yet know their right hand from their left, and many beasts as well!" (Others: cattle, instead of beasts).

Ginsberg (IV) indicates that before the terrible decree is abolished due to the *teshuvah* of the Ninevites, as part of their repentance, and petitions, they separated the young of the cattle from the mothers and implored that for the sake of the beasts, for who would take care of these young, forgive them. The story presents a most interesting contrast to the Sodom and Gomorrah story (pp. 250–251).

Concerning the prohibition against carrying a certain distance on *Shabbat*, in *Shabbat* 76a, the following *Mishnah* indicates the rule applies, even when providing provender to animals, including one's cow.

> He who carries out a cow's mouthful of straw, a camel's mouthful of pea-stalks (*etzah*), a lamb's mouthful of ears of corn, a goat's mouthful of herbs, moist garlic or onion leaves to the size of a dried fig, (or) a goat's mouthful of dry (leaves), (is culpable). And they do not combine with each other. Because they are not alike in their standards.

How is this reconciled with the positive commandment to be kind to animals, in fact, to ensure one's animals are fed first? The *Tosefta* explains that this is not a cow's usual food, and it eats it only when nothing else is obtainable. Clearly, in any case, one should not allow his cow to be like the scrawny cow, but like the healthy cow that can leap up out of a river basin.

Finally, the first indication in the next entry, *Bava Kama*, uses the word *cattle*, but most translators regard it as *oxen*.

AN ADDITIONAL TALMUD TAIL (*Chullin* 59a)

The *Mishnah* recounts that "The characteristics of cattle and of wild animals are stated in the Torah." The implication, of course, is for *kashrut*, whether *shechting* for Temple sacrificial offerings or consumption under rabbinical supervision. The characteristics of the parted hoof and chewing the cud are, of course, well known. The *Gemarah* continues with a dental observance: "If an animal has no teeth [viz., the (absence of) the upper incisors and canines, a characteristic of herbivores and ruminants] one may be certain that it chews the cud and parts the hoof and it is therefore clean."

The *Gemarah* raises the question, Why not examine its hooves? That would, after all, seem the simplest thing to do. "We must suppose that its hoofs were cut off."

> And this accords with R. Chisda's statement, for R. Chisda said, If a man was walking in the desert and found an animal with its hoofs cut off, he should examine its mouth; if it has no upper teeth he may be certain that it is clean, otherwise he may be certain that it is unclean.

13

O X

OX
Hebrew *TSON*
Genesis 20:14

Bos primigenius. Latin, an ox, original.
The (now extinct) Aurochs.

I'm probably out on a limb here; but a (now generally accepted) zoological school of thought accepts these oxen as the progenitors of domesticated cattle. A herd was observed as recently as the late sixteenth century. Today, and over the last several centuries, of course, the term refers to bovine bulls that have been emasculated and are used for domestic purposes.

CONCORDANCE

Exodus 21:28–29 (When an ox gores), 32–33, 35–37; 22:1, 3, 8–9; 23:4, 12.
Leviticus 7:23; 9:4, 19; 17:3; 22:23; 27:26.
Numbers 7:3, 6–8, 17, 23, 29, 35, 47, 53, 59, 65, 71, 77, 83, 87–88; 18:17; 22:4; 23:22; 24:8.
Deuteronomy 5:14, 18; 14:4; 15:19; 17:1; 18:3; 22:1, 4, 10; 25:4 (muzzle); 28:31; 33:17.

Joshua 6:21; 7:24.

Judges 6:4.

1 Samuel 11:5, 7; 12:3; 14:32, 34; 15:3, 9, 14–15, 21; 22:19; 27:9.

2 Samuel 6:6, 13; 24:22, 24.

1 Kings 1:9, 19, 25; 5:3; 7:25, 29 (of brass, in Solomon's house); 8:5, 63; 19:19–21.

2 Kings 5:26; 16:17 (brazen ox).

Isaiah 1:3; 7:25; 11:7 (and the lion [number 16] shall eat straw like the ox); 22:13; 30:24; 32:20; 34:7; 65:25 (and the lion [number 16] shall eat straw like the ox); 66:3.

Jeremiah 5:23.

Ezekiel 1:10 (see numbers 16, 26, 88).

Amos 6:12.

Psalms I–8:8 (see number 3); 22:22 ("wild-ox"; but see number 91); IV–106:20; V–144:14.

Proverbs 7:22; 14:4; 15:17.

Job 1:3 (see numbers 3, 10, 14), 14 (see number 10); 6:5 (see number 10) (Doth the wild *ass* bray when he hath grass?/Or loweth the ox over his fodder?); 24:3 (see number 10) (They drive away the *ass* of the fatherless,/They take the widow's ox for a pledge); 39:9–10; 40:15 (see number 100); 42:12 (see numbers 3, 10, 14).

Daniel 4:22, 29–30; 5:21 (see also number 10).

Nehemia 5:18 (see also number 3) (Now that which was prepared for one day was one ox and six choice *sheep*).

1 Chronicles 12:41 (see also numbers 3, 10, 14); 13:9 (. . . Uzza put forth his hand to hold the ark; for the ox stumbled); 21:23.

2 Chronicles 4:4–5 (And under it [the "molten sea"] was the similitude of oxen . . . in two rows . . . stood upon twelve oxen . . .), 15; 5:6 (see also number 3); 29:33 (see also number 3); 31:6 (see also number 3) (And the children of Israel and Judah, that dwelt in the cities of Judah, they also brought in the tithe of oxen and *sheep*, . . .); 35:8–9 (see also number 12), 12.

In actuality, oxen and cattle are the same species. By human design, a male calf becomes either a mating bull or, castrated, a steer. Also by human design, a steer becomes either beef to market or trained to be an ox. Oxen are the fortunate ones. Like their human compatriots, they must work for their living, but, at least, it is a living. Oxen, like dogs, sheep, and horses, have been our symbiotic friends since before written history.

A well-meaning, hard-working ox can live a long time, and,

albeit it is an anthropmorphism, appears to take pride in his enormous strength and gentle demeanor.

An entire tractate of Talmud, *Bava Kama* (BK), "The First Gate," followed by *Bava Metziah* (BM), "The Middle Gate," and *Bava Batra* (BB), "The Third Gate," deals with compensation for loss, or "redress." To that end, the Talmud uses one of its most basic principles: To use a specific case to intuit for legal interpretation a general code that can be applied to cases, here, generally, in the matter of tort, or, in this case, property law. The specific case most often cited is the famous series of expressions from Exodus 21–22, "The ox that gored."

In addition, it is good sometimes to give pause, and to afford gratitude for the creatures that came along with us and put their trust in us, and have worked hard for us as we have developed what we term technological civilization.

BK Mishnaim 1–50 deal with the issue of the ox that gores, that falls in the pit, and the other Torah indications. I include a few brief entries as examples. I chose these because of the indication of the premise of law (specific to general), and for the somewhat charming story about R. Papa's ox that machinated.

Mishnah 34b:

> There are cases where there is liability for offenses committed by one's cattle [again, lit., ox], though there would be no liability should these offenses be committed by oneself . . . so also if an ox puts out the eye of the owner's slave or knocks out (his or her) tooth there is no liability, whereas if the owner himself has put out . . . he would be liable . . . So also where cattle has (sic) caused fire to be set to a barn on the day of *Shabbat* there is liability . . .

Gemarah:

> The case here supposed is one of an intelligent animal which, owing to an itching in its back, was anxious to burn the barn so that it might roll in the (hot) ashes. But how could we know (of such an intention)? (By saying that) after the barn had been

burnt, the animal actually rolled in the ashes. But could such a thing ever happen? Yes, as in the case of the ox which had been in the house of R. Papa, and which, having a severe toothache, went into the brewery where it removed the lid (that covered the beer) and drank beer until it became relieved (of the pain).

Mishnah 35a:

If an ox was pursuing another's ox which was (afterwards found to be injured) and the one plaintiff says, "It was your ox that did the damage," while the other pleads, "Not so, but it was injured by a rock (against which it had been rubbing itself)," the burden of proof lies on the claimant.

Rashi elucidates another circumstance of the law.

Rabbi Yochanan ben Zakai said: Hashem has much consideration for the honor of His creatures. When an ox—an animal that can walk by itself (i.e., cannot be carried)—has been stolen and sold or slaughtered, in which case the thief did not have to degrade himself by carrying it on his shoulders, he has to pay fivefold restitution. In the case of a lamb, however, which he had to carry on his shoulder, he has to pay only the fourfold, because he was forced to degrade himself by carrying it.

If the Torah expresses such concern and consideration for the sake of a thief who has violated a Torah precept, that it even diminishes this criminal's punishment due to his being possibly disgraced, imagine how much greater the Torah's deference must be in regard to those who exert themselves to *mitzvot*! We can imply further that the extra effort put forth by a Jew to fulfill the edicts of the Rabbis are recognized even more so. Obviously, an even greater reward must be in store for those who conscientiously remove themselves from the temptation to sin by the observance of appropriate precautions and limits. (*Likutei Peshatim, Mishpatim*)

Kahan's *Taryag* elucidates upon the first six chapters of the tractate, identifying that oxen (thus, any animal or property) that cause damages are classified into two categories: *tam*, an animal not yet proven, that is, a newly damaging animal; and *mu'ad*, a proven or habitually damaging animal.

> The first three times an animal causes damages it is considered a *tam*, and the owner is liable for only half of the damages, and only up to the value of the animal that did the damage.
>
> An animal that caused damages three times, and the owner was warned on all three occasions, is considered a *mu'ad*(;) however, in addition to losing his animal, the owner must pay "redemption money" (*KoPeR*) to the family of the victim killed by the animal. (P. 47)

To this, then, compare a brief excerpt from The Code of Hammurabi, lines 250–252 (Pritchard trans., Theophile J. Meek):

> If an ox, when it was walking along the street, gored a seignior to death, that case is not subject to claim./ If a seignior's ox was a gorer and his city council made it known to him that it was a gorer, but he did not pad its horns (or) tie up his ox, and that ox gored to death a member of the aristocracy, he shall give one-half mina of silver./ If it was a seignior's slave, he shall give one-third mina of silver. (Vol. 1, p. 165)

Also found in Pritchard is an excerpt from a treaty from a king of Assyria, Shamshi-Adad, to his vassal, Kuwari: ". . . From the time he took the hem of my garment, I never collected any silver, oxen, sheep, or grain from his land" (Vol. 11, p. 189).

In his discussion of "Dietetics," in Section VI, "Meat," Preuss derives a most interesting conceptualization in the differences between observing *mitzvot* in the desert community and the communities under the Commonwealths in the Land.

> During the wandering of the Jews in the desert, every slaughtering was an act of offering; that is, every ox,

lamb or goat that was to be slaughtered and was deemed fit therefore had to be brought as an offering in the Tabernacle, and the owner only received his portion. This rule in the desert was an expedient in order to prevent offerings to idols. This restriction was not lifted until after the conquest of Canaan and the dispersal throughout the land, whereby there were great distances between the masses of the people and the sanctuary in Jerusalem. (P. 556)

Preuss compares the passages from Leviticus 17:3–7 and Deuteronomy 12:20–21. The latter reference states:

When thou wilt say: "I will eat flesh," because thy soul desireth to eat flesh; thou mayest eat flesh after all the desire of thy soul. (If the place which the Lord thy God choose to put His name there be too far from thee) . . . thou shalt eat within thy gates after all the desire of thy soul.

AN ADDITIONAL TALMUD TAIL (*Chullin* 60a)

In the same *Mishnah* found at the end of the entry on Cattle, the *Gemarah* has very pragmatic advice, concerning what a potential purchaser should look for when considering an ox or a donkey: "Rab. Judah said, an ox has a large belly, large hoofs, a large head and a long tail; an ass has just the reverse."

14

CAMEL

CAMEL
Hebrew *GaMeL*

> *Then the servant took ten of his master's camels*
> *and set out, taking with him all the bounty of his*
> *master; and he made his way to Aramnaharaim,*
> *to the city of Nahor.*
> —Genesis 24:10–11, 14, 19, 20, 22, 30–32, 35, 44, 46, 61

Camelus dromedarius.
A dromedary: The Arabian or one-humped camel. A completely domesticated animal bred for travel and running (*dromeus* [Greek], a runner and *-arius* [Latin], pertaining to).

Its cousin, *C. bactrianus*, is two-humped and found only in northeastern provinces of Iran. Some say a few of these are still wild in desert regions of China and Mongolia.

This species may be a textual or literary anachronism. Dr. Freund suggests the camel may not have been domesticated until late in the monarchy period.

CONCORDANCE

Genesis 30:43; 31:17, 34; 32:7, 15; 37:25.
Exodus 9:3.

Leviticus 11:4.
Deuteronomy 14:7.
Judges 6:5; 7:12; 8:21, 26.
1 Samuel 15:3; 27:9; 30:17.
1 Kings 10:2.
2 Kings 8:9.
Isaiah 21:7 (riders on camels); 30:6; 60:6.
Jeremiah 2:23 (thou art a swift young camel).
Ezekiel 25:5 (and I will make Rabbah a pasture for camel).
Zechariah 14:15 (see also numbers 10, 15).
Job 1:3 (see numbers 3, 10, 13), 17 (in, "The Chaldeans . . . set upon the camel"); 42:12 (see number 3, 10, 13).
Ezra 2:67 (see also number 10).
Nehemiah 7:69.
1 Chronicles 5:21 (see numbers 3, 10, 12) (And they took away their *cattle* . . . camels . . . *sheep* . . . *asses* . . .); 12:41 (see numbers 3, 10, 18) (Moreover they . . . brought bread on *asses*, and on camels, and on *mules*, and on *oxen* . . . and *sheep* in abundance; For there was joy in Israel); 27:30 (see also number 10).
2 Chronicles 9:1 (And when the Queen of Sheba heard of the fame of Solomon, she came . . . [with] camels that bore spices and gold in abundance, and precious stones; . . .); 14:14 (see numbers 3, 12).

In spite of the previous description, the camel has been with us a long time. Perhaps more than any other creature, it is superbly adapted to its precise environment. It is thought by many to be one of the oldest mammals on the evolutionary scale. There are many reasons for this in the camel's evolved anatomy and physiology. Some more popularly held are misconceptions and will be dispelled here. My hope is to uncover some of the facts about this most mysterious animal, one seemingly at once ill-tempered and friendly, leisurely paced and swift, independent and able to be trained, obnoxious and sociable. The answer may lie in the fact of its superior attitude: camels seem to know that they can survive for long periods in places where other creatures, including women and men, cannot. They probably gaze down upon us and every other animal venturing into the harsh desert climate with disdain.

Camels cannot go without water. They cannot go without food. The hump in their back does not store water like a water tank tower seen in small towns in rural America, dispersing the precious liquid as the necessity arises. They do not have a fifth stomach that stores water, and then squeezes it back into their bloodstream, also as necessity dictates. They do not urinate a puddle and then lap it back up to refurbish their lost water. These are only a few of the myths that have arisen concerning the camel.

Some of the true behavioral developments of the camel, no less amazing, are: it can go for days and weeks on little water and little food; it can travel long distances with consistent gait over desert terrain; due to its stamina, it can, in long sprints or endurance challenges, run faster than a horse; it does have broad flat feet to enable it to traverse its terrain with a minimal expression of energy. In his landmark study, Yagil dispelled the misconceptions, and exposed these and other true behavioral insights.

There are several textual, midrashic, and talmudic commentaries concerning the camel. Whether the history is anachronistic or not, the patriarchs and matriarchs depended on this creature of the desert as their stories and lives unfolded. Some of the references use the camel as examples of property rights, in a sense, as was the ox. Finally, there are some fascinating nonbiblical stories about this animal that seems designed by a committee, but will always be one step ahead of us.

Clark indicates that the camel is one of the oldest known mammal species. ". . . They represent one of the most ancient of animal types still existing. Fossil remains of a type scarcely differing from the living one have been found in the Miocene of northern India. . . . (and) may be described as a living fossil saved from extinction by domestication" (p. 31). This would indicate, as Clark and Yagil both point out, that the camel has been part of our landscape for some thousands of years. Clark and Yagil also concur, along with other scientists, that the camel was born in America.

Yagil's study extended over the course of several years, although he didn't publish a complete summary of his findings until 1993.

> . . . I spent several weeks at the Negev Institute for Desert Research studying the effects of water deprivation on the kidney function of camels. The camels had gone without water for fourteen days. While I

had plenty of water to drink, I was nevertheless suffering from the heat and sweating profusely. Even though the camels had lost 50 gallons of body water, they gazed into the distance, serenely chewing their cuds, with contemptuous smiles at my discomfort. Only after I'd made shade for myself by stretching a sheet between four poles, was I able to finish my experiments. The camels appeared to be unaffected by the heat, but it has taken me years of research to find out why.

Before discussing his findings as to how and why camels are able to live so well in such a harsh climate, the author relates some of the known evolutionary details. These include: Their ancestors originated in North America 40 to 50 million years ago; about 3 million years ago, they migrated to other parts of the world, including the two-humped (fur-covered and somewhat larger) Bactrian in the cold life of the Gobi desert, and our animal, the one-humped Dromedary of the very hot, dry climate of the Near-East deserts; other relations include the llama, alpaca, and vicuna in the mountains of South America.

Yigal then proceeds to uncover, item by item, the anatomy and physiology of the camel that so superbly allows the species to be comfortable and superior in its environment.

—Its ability to relinquish strict homoiothermy and allow its body temperature to fluctuate according to the rise and fall of the environmental temperature. . . . the camel's internal temperature can range from 93° in the cool of the night to 106° in the heat of the day. Thus, the camel absorbs less heat from the air than do other animals.

—An adjustable metabolic rate: slower in summer than in winter (this is the reverse situation of other mammals).

—Dehydration slows the camel's metabolism further. There is a drop in thyroid function; thus, its respiratory rate slows, reducing water loss through the respiratory tract.

—The nose remains cool. Thus, every breath cools the blood flowing from the nose throughout the body. The brain in particular benefits from this process, through a finely defined network of blood vessels just beneath the organ called the carotid rate.

—The unique ability to circulate blood even after loss of body water.

—Conservation of bodily fluids and water, through:

—The facile expulsion of dry fecal matter.

—The recycling of water from the kidneys to the first of its four stomachs, and, from thence, back to the blood.

—When water is available, the ability to drink and rehydrate within a short period of time.

—The modification of its behavior, such as:

—Remaining in a recumbent position for long periods during the heat of the day.

—Urinating on its long legs (as the urine evaporates, the blood vessels therein are cooled).

—Nasal secretions which collect in a duct between the nose and the mouth evaporate to act as a coolant.

—The animal's size (as much as seven feet tall and weighting in at a thousand pounds; thus, it heats up much more slowly than a smaller animal). Also, a camel thus casts a large shadow on the ground, creating a cooler area beneath it. A herd will often crowd together, taking advantage of an even larger swath of cooled ground.

—Its distinguishing feature, the hump:

—The hump absorbs the most direct sunlight, exposing a smaller body area beneath it. Throughout the day, it will attempt to orient itself to cause its hump to face the sun.

—The hump is a concentration of body fat protecting the inner more vital organs.

–The hump conducts heat, thus transferring inner body heat quickly to the outside environment. The legs are particularly thin, again to allow heat transference to the hump, thence to the surrounding air.

Camels link the patriarchs and the matriarchs in the family history stories. Following Abraham's sojourn into Egypt, where his ruse to portray Sarah as his sister is uncovered by Pharaoh, Abraham and Sarah are perceived as very powerful figures and the king enhances Abraham's wealth with gifts of "sheep, oxen, donkeys, servants and maids, she-asses, and camels . . ." (Genesis 12:16, Fox 57).

Later, Eliezer, Abraham's servant, receives the fulfillment of his own annunciation of Isaac's selected wife, through the camel. "May it be that the maiden to whom I say: Pray lower your pitcher that I may drink, and she says: Drink, and I will also give your camels to drink—let her be the one that you have decided on for your servant, for Yitzhak . . ." (23:14, p. 101).

Although Jacob/Israel is more properly associated with sheep, and the expansion of his and Laban's flocks, still, when he escapes Laban to return to the Land, and Laban catches up to him, it is, in a fashion, the patriarchal link of the camel that allows his release:

> Now Rachel had taken the *terafim* and had put them in the basket-saddle of the camels, and had sat down upon them. Lavan felt all around the tent, but he did not find anything. She said to her father: Do not be upset in my lord's eyes that I am not able to rise in your presence, for the manner of women is upon me. So he searched, but he did not find the *terafim*. (31:34–35, p. 148)

Finally, albeit Joseph was sent to check on his brothers concerning the herding of the sheep, it was because of the link with the camel that he was able to escape death, and so began his own sojourn in Egypt, which would lead to this patriarchal family being forged into a nation:

> . . . They lifted up their eyes and saw: there was a caravan of Yishmaelites coming from Gil'ad, their camels carrying balm, balsam, and ladanum, traveling to take them down to Egypt. Now Yehuda said to his brothers: What gain is there if we kill our brother and cover up his blood? Come, let us sell him to the Yishmaelites—but let not our hand be upon him. . . . (37:25–27, p. 179)

It is interesting that the "rescuers" (although, ultimately, it is a band of Midianites who extricate Joseph from the pit) should be Ishmaelites. Ginsberg relates a little known *Midrash*, concerning Abraham's son—not Isaac, but his firstborn, Ishmael. Once again, it is the camel that is significant to the story and forms a patriarchal-familial link.

The story goes that, after some time of being separated from Ishmael, the father wished to see his son. And so he made preparation, saddling his camel, and proceeded over the terrain to where Ishmael lived with his wife. Now Hagar had chosen an Egyptian wife for her son, and this woman bore Ishmael four sons and a daughter; soon after the family returned to the wilderness. Ishmael became very wealthy, exceeding in sheep and cattle (the *Midrash* says on the account of his father).

> And some time after, Abraham said to Sarah, his wife, "I will go and see my son Ishmael; I yearn to look upon him, for I have not seen him for a long time." And Abraham rode upon one of his camels to the wilderness, to seek his son Ishmael, for he heard that he was dwelling in a tent in the wilderness with all belonging to him.

The image of Abraham jauntily riding along on his camel through the wilderness to see his son and his grandchildren conjures the image of the camel as the ship of the desert, able to go long distances at a swift and steady pace. He arrives at the tent. Ishmael's wife comes out to greet him. She is surly and does not invite him in, nor, in full contrast to Rebecca, Abraham's other daughter-in-law, proffers him or his camels water to drink. This, of course, is an unheard of rebuff, anathema amongst the Bedoin peoples of the deserts and wilderness. Abraham discovers Ishmael is away hunting game.

> . . . and she was sitting in the tent, and did not take any notice of Abraham. She did not even ask him who he was. But all the while she was beating her children in the tent, and she was cursing them, and she also cursed her husband, Ishmael, and spoke evil of him, and Abraham heard the words of Ishmael's wife to her children, and it was an evil thing in his eyes.

At this point, still mounted on the camel, Abraham calls out to the woman and transmits a message for his son. He informs her to tell him word for word when he arrives home.

> A very old man from the land of the Philistines came hither to seek thee, and his appearance was thus and so, and thus was his figure. I did not ask him who he was, and seeing thou wast not here, he spoke unto me, and said . . . When thou comest home, put away this tent-pin which thou hast placed here, and place another tent-pin in its stead.

Abraham departs. Ishmael returns. When he hears the message, he divorces his wife and sends her away. He journeys (probably on a camel) to the land of the Canaanites. He finds for himself a wife. At the end of three years, Abraham says, "I will go again and see Ishmael my son, for I have not seen him for a long time." Again there is the relation of the extensive journey on the camel; again Ishmael is not home, although, most significantly, this time his absence is due to his going out to feed the camels; the new wife, however, invites Abraham into the coolness of the tent, offers him water to drink and food to eat (and, we presume, water for the camel);

> And he finished his meal, and he blessed the Lord, and he said to Ishmael's wife: "When Ishmael comes home, say these words to him: 'A very old man from the land of the Philistines came hither, and asked after thee, and thou wast not here, and I brought him out bread and water, and he ate and drank, and his heart was merry. . . . The tent-pin which thou hast is very good, do not put it away from the tent.'"

When Ishmael returns home this time, his wife runs to meet him with joy and tells him the story. "Ishmael knew . . . that his wife had honored him, and he praised the Lord." Then Ishmael takes his wife and his children and his herds and journeys the long distance back to his father (we presume, of course, on camels). "And Ishmael and his children dwelt with Abraham many days in that land, and Abraham dwelt in the land of the Philistines a long time" (I, pp. 266–269).

In 92a, *Bava Batra*, the *Mishnah* relates the issue concerning if any person sells fruit to another person, "and (the buyer) sowed them and they did not grow . . . he is not responsible. R. Simeon b. Gamliel said: For garden seeds which are not eaten, he is responsible"; the *Gemarah*, 93a, derives the case using the instance of a mating camel.

> R. Aha said (In the case of a camel which covers [that is, is behind, i.e., seeking to mate]) among other camels, and a dead camel was found at its side, it is obvious the one killed the other. Now assuming that (the principles) of . . . confirmed legal status have the same force . . . one is to be (so) guided.

In *Makkot* 5a (and a similar case in *Yevamot* 116a), the credibility of witnesses in a case is questioned concerning the distances the witnesses would have had to travel in a prescribed time period. The matter is resolved, however, by the indication that if they traveled on swift camels, the distance of twenty parsangs could have been covered in one day.

Toperoff includes some of these talmudic references and other interesting ones as well. Unfortunately, he falls into the trap of accepting one of the myths, that camels have a fifth stomach that is used, in effect, as a water canteen. However, he includes a very sweet story concerning the burial of Maimonides.

> . . . a camel was involved in choosing the burial place for Maimonides. (The sage) lived and died in Egypt, but requested that his last remains be interred in the Holy Land. When the time for burial arrived, his body was placed on a camel and transported to the Land of Israel, and when it reached Tiberias, the animal stubbornly refused to go further. The authorities therefore had no alternative but to bury Maimonides in a plot of ground chosen by the camel. However, the grave was not in a deserted or isolated ground, but close to the sepulcher of Rabbi Johanan ben Zakkai. (Pp. 33–37)

It is Preuss, however, who relates perhaps the most famous of the talmudic references, from *Berachot* 55b: "R. Jonathan (said): 'A man is shown in a dream only what is suggested by his own thoughts; he never sees in a dream a date palm of gold or a camel going through the eye of a needle'" (p. 137).

On page 207, Preuss includes another interesting reference from *Berachot*. The discussion concerns the identification criteria determining priests unfit to serve in the Temple rituals. The hunchback is one of them.

> Since he is only unfit to serve in the Temple because of an unsightly appearance, this case probably refers to one who has a marked elevation of the flesh on his back, as the *Gemarah* also points out, "a hump in which there is no bone." Otherwise, *chatereth* [the word being defined here] is the usual expression for the camel's hump. (*Tosefta* 5:2, 43b; see also *Chullin* 9:2)

The final entry I include here from Preuss concerns the dietary laws, in particular, the law determining which animals may be consumed for meat and which may not.

> (Those permissible include): . . . three types of domesticated animals: cattle, sheep, and goats; and seven types of deer . . . : the hart, the gazelle, the roebuck, the wild goat, the pygarg, the antelope, and the mountain sheep. Common signs of clean animals are that they chew the cud and have completely split hoofs. Specifically excluded therefore are the camel, the rabbit (or badger), hare and the swine, which are obviously animals that were generally eaten by heathens. . . . (P. 500, referring to the *mitzvot* enumerated in Deuteronomy and Leviticus)

The Bahir is one of the oldest and most important of the mystical texts. Serving as a precursor to *The Zohar*, reportedly published by the Provence school of kabbalists about 1175 (Kaplan indicates probably 1176), its influence on Jewish mystics and mysticism has been profound. Kaplan says, "Some consider it the oldest kabbalistic text ever written." In Part One, the manner in which Eve was seduced, including through sexual intercourse by the wicked angel Samael in the transmogrified form of the Serpent, is related. This hearkens back to our earlier discussion of the serpent as a phallus symbol, as what Jung might call an archetype. Kaplan's translation and rendering is the most recent, and probably the best, choice for scholarship.

> . . . The wicked Samael made a bond with all the host on high against his Master. This was because the Blessed Holy One said [regarding man] (Genesis 1:26), "And let him rule over the fish of the sea and the flying things of the heaven."
>
> [Samael] said, "How can we cause him to sin and be exiled from before God?" He descended with all his host, and sought a suitable companion on earth. He finally found the serpent, which looked like a camel, and he rode on it. (P. 81)

Thus, in a fashion, we can extend our Genesis link with the camel back to the opening of the book.

Other biblical indications are found in W. Smith: "Not only was the camel important as a means of transportation, but it was also much used as a work animal. Its milk, along with butter and cheese, were important items in the Hebrew diet. Cloth was made from its hair. . . . Its hide was tanned for leather, and the dried dung was used as fuel and as an ingredient in roofing" (p. 8; and see Asimov, p. 7).

An Additional Talmud Tail (Niddah 13b–14a)

We learn that all camel riders may be considered wicked and are forbidden to eat *terumah* (the priestly portion); thus, a priest could not be a camel-rider.

The explanation is that the friction of riding could make them subject to erections and improper emissions.

15

HORSE

HORSE (Colt)
Hebrew *SUS* (soos)

> *So they brought their livestock to Joseph, and*
> *Joseph gave them bread in exchange for the horses,*
> *for the stocks of sheep and cattle, and the asses; thus*
> *he provided them with bread that year in exchange*
> *for all their livestock.*
>
> —Genesis 47:17

Equus caballus: Latin, Horse, Pack Horse. The domesticated most good friend of humanity, as the animal has evolved through natural selection and breeding.

Some zoologists contend that a true wild horse still exists in the Altai Mountains in Western Mongolia. It is a different species, however—*E. przewalskii* (sometimes known as Prjevalski's Horse, after N. M. Prjevalski, its modern observer, in c. 1875). If it still exists, it is rare.

E. caballus may have been domesticated as early as 10,000 B.C.E.

CONCORDANCE

Genesis 49:11, 7.
Exodus 9:3; 14:9, 23; 15:2, 21.

Deuteronomy 11:4; 20:1.

Joshua 11:6, 9.

1 Samuel 8:11 (of chariots).

2 Samuel 8:4; (10:18 [horsemen]).

1 Kings 5:6 (40,000 stalls of horses), 8; (9:1, 22 [horsemen]); 10:25, (26 [horsemen]), 28–29; 18:5; 20:1, 20–21, 25; 22:4.

2 Kings 2:11 (. . . there appeared a chariot of fire, and horses of fire . . .); 3:7; 5:9; 6:14–15, 17; 7:6–7, 10, 13–14; (9:17–19 [horsemen/back]); 9:33; 10:2; 11:16; (13:7 [horsemen]); 14:20; 18:23, (24 [horsemen]); 23:11.

Isaiah 2:7; 5:28; (21:7 horsemen), (19 horsemen); (22:6–7 horsemen); 31:1, 3; 36:8–9 (horsemen); 43:17; 63:13; 66:20.

Jeremiah (4:29 horsemen); 5:7; 6:23 (and they ride upon horses); 8:6, 16; 12:5; 17:25; 22:5; 46:4, 9; 50:11 (see number 6); 37, 42; 51:21 (and with thee will I shatter the horse and his rider), 27.

Ezekiel 23:6, 12, 23; 26:10–11; 27:14 (see number 10); 38:4, 15; 39:20.

Hosea 1:7; 14:4.

Joel 2:4.

Amos 2:15; 4:10; 6:12 (see number 13).

Micah 1:13 (bind the chariots to the swift *steeds*); 5:9.

Nahum 3:2 (. . . and prancing horses)–(3 horsemen).

Habakkuk 1:8 (see numbers 18, 47, 72); 3:15 (thou hast trodden the sea with thy horse).

Haggai 2:22.

Zechariah 1:8 (. . . and behold a man riding upon a red horse . . . and behind him there were horses); 6:2–3 ([vision of chariots with red, black, white, grizzled bay horses]), 6; 9:10; 10:5; 12:4; 10:15 (see also numbers 10, 13); 20 (. . . upon the bells of the horse).

Psalms I–20:8 (Some trust in . . . horses); 32:9 (see number 10); 33:17 (A horse is a vain thing for safety); III–76:7 (They are cast into a dead sleep, the riders also and the horse); V–147:10.

Proverbs 26:3 (see number 10).

Job 39:18–19.

Ecclesiastes 10:7 (I have seen servants upon horses . . .).

Esther 6:11 (Then took Haman the apparel and the horse, and arrayed Mordecai, and caused him to ride through the street of the city, and proclaimed before him: "Thus shall it be done unto the man whom the king delighteth to honor"); 8:10.

Ezra 2:66 (see also number 10).

Nehemiah 2:12, 14 ([as "Beast,"] and see number 95); 7:68 [authoritative codice] (see number 10).

1 Chronicles 18:4.

2 Chronicles 1:14 [as horsemen], 16 (And the horses which Solomon had were brought out of Egypt . . .)–17; 8:6, 9 [as horsemen]; 9:24 (see number 10)–25 (And Solomon has 4,000 stalls for horses and

chariots . . .), 28; 12:3 [as horsemen]; 16:8 [as horsemen]; 23:15 [as
horse gate—viz:] (. . . and they slew her [Athaliah]); 25:28.

Most of the Biblical references concerning the horse relate
to contexts of war or the bestowing of princely honor. Pharaoh's chariots hurtle after the Israelites at the Sea. Deborah
and Barak chase down the mountainside after an army of
horse-drawn chariots. Solomon stables his horses in a military
array. Mordecai rides the king's horse in a royal entry parade
honorific. Often the references in the concordance refer not
just to the horse, but to the horse and rider, the horsemen. In
fact, the image of the wild horse is the one that seems out of
sorts, and that of a man or woman on a horse is the one we are
more comfortable with.

The domestication of the horse has been with us for a long
time; the unit of horse and rider is part of our Jungian
archetype iconography. The animal itself has acculturated this
symbiotic atavism. "Old warhorses," or "old firehorses" received their nomenclatures because they were retired with
honors and put to pasture for the rest of their lives, usually in
close proximity to their active duty stations; thus, when the
bugler's call to arms sounded or the fire bell rang, they ran to
the edge of their enclosures, seemingly frustrated they could
not muster out on yet another campaign or errand of mercy.

In actuality, the horse has always contributed more to
civilization with us than simply going to battle. The horse has
been noble, loyal, courageous, helpful, and friendly. Horses
have plowed our fields, carried us and our children long
distances, pulled us out of trouble, given us affection, won and
lost money for us, and have quite simply always been there
when we needed them. There is a special bond between a man
and his horse, between a woman and her horse. They have
been here about as long as we have, and their evolutionary line
is more completely drawn through the layers of anthropological evidence.

There is a myth about horses that they are stupid and
difficult to train. Yet anyone who has been around horses for
any length of time knows these things: They are intelligent;
they are independent, yet loyal and willing to please; they do
not know how astonishingly strong they are; for all they do,
they expect to be well treated and they deserve to be.

I once served as a wrangler for a summer camp. I had been around horses for a good while and had learned to ride and take care of them at an early age. It has been a long time and I miss it. The horses came to recognize me and the others who took care of them. They knew when it was time to go to work. They learned which kids they liked to have ride them, and they let us, and the kids, know which ones they didn't. They decided at a certain time of the day that they had had enough, and expected to be fed and rubbed down. They came to like us and we them, and we were sorry, at the end of the summer, to see each other go. Obviously, I still remember them, every one.

Nonetheless, the biblical iconography of the war horse reflects the animal's immense impact on Near East history and history in general. Until the advent of modern vehicular warfare, the ultimate weapon was a man astride a powerful, valorous well-trained steed, or pulling a light chariot. In the late nineteenth century, what may have been the two most powerful forces in the world constantly clashed with each other in the American West—the light cavalries of the Indian nations and the United States. Although the end was inevitable (albeit its method was unconscionable) this clash of titans— men upon horses against men upon horses—went on for decades.

Perhaps because the horse is often associated in the Bible with armies, there do not exist as many midrashic or talmudic indications. We shall indicate a select few. Outside this context, the stories of horses and their owners are innumerable and reflect the great affection they and we feel for each other.

Tripett and others point out that the familiar relationship of horse and rider developed actually quite late, sometime between 3,500 and 1,700 B.C.E., probably in the Ukraine and Caucauses areas, thence appeared in the Near East. In the Near East, they seem to have replaced oxen and onagers as the preferred animal to pull war chariots and for riding. Horsemen and horsewomen will tell you that horses are never really broken or trained. They are skittish animals and rely on their speed to flee danger rather than their ability to fight, which, when cornered, is considerable. In fact, it is a rather unnatural behavior for a horse to accept a man or woman on its back; it is a herbivore, a herd animal, and subject to predation. Millions of years of evolution compel it to buck and fight exceedingly when a predator-like creature leaps upon its back. There are many stories throughout history about formerly loyal and trustworthy mounts that have bolted, thrown, and deserted their riders seemingly at little provocation.

> *I, the king, a hero from the (mother's) womb am I*
> *I, Shulgi, a mighty man from (the day) I was born am I . . .*
> *A princely donkey all set for the road am I,*
> *A horse that swings (his) tail on the highway am I,*
> *A noble donkey of Sumugan eager for the course am I,*
> *The wise scribe of Nidaba am I.*
> > *("The King of the Road," Sumerian Hymns,*
> > *Pritchard, Vol. II, p. 132)*

Both Tripitt and Toperoff are particularly engaged with the magnificent description of the horse in the Book of Job (39:19–25) which, again, inculcates certain war imagery. It is indeed poetry of a higher order, reflected even in English. Here is the JPS translation:

> *Do you give the horse his strength?*
> *Do you clothe his neck with a mane?*
> *Do you make him quiver like locusts,*
> *His majestic snorting [speaking] terror?*
> *He (or, They) paw(s) with force, he runs with vigor,*
> *Charging into battle.*
> *He scoffs at fear, he cannot be frightened,*
> *He does not recoil from the sword.*
> *A quiverful of arrows whizzes by him,*
> *And the flashing spear and the javelin,*
> *Trembling with excitement, he swallows the land,*
> *He does not turn aside at the blast of the trumpet.*
> *As the trumpet sounds, he says, "Aha!"*
> *From afar he smells the battle,*
> *The roaring and shouting of the officers.*
> > *(1398)*

The *Midrash* (*Rabbah* 21:5) refers to the event at the Sea, considering the loss of Pharaoh's horses and riders as the defeat of the Egyptian angel, Uzza, that rode above the Egyptians in battle. Sforno interprets the phrase as referring to Pharaoh himself (315). Toperoff mentions "The Horse Gate" of the Temple, "which was in the east section of Jerusalem overlooking the kidron. It opened into the southeast corner of the Temple and courts."

In Deuteronomy 17:16, the king that will be set over the Israelites is to be told: "Only: he is not to multiply horses for himself/and he is not to return the people to Egypt in order to multiply horses/ . . . And he is not to multiply wives for himself . . ." (Fox, pp. 930–931). Those following critical analysis will perceive at once the clear reference to Solomon and the dual reasoning for the division of empire.

Horses, among other domesticated animals, had meaning in Jewish folk literature also. Trachtenberg quotes from a thirteenth-century work, *Ets Chayim*. The excerpt is discussing omens, especially those in dreams to determine the interpretation of the dream. As we know, since the time of Joseph, Jewish dream interpretation has been considered most important: ". . . A white horse is a good omen; a red horse a bad, he will be hounded and pursued; a donkey, he may be confident of salvation . . ." (p. 239).

> There are three things that convey to man the idea of Paradise on earth: lying in the arms of a woman; being lost in the pages of a book; and being found upon the back of a horse. (Arab Proverb)

AN ADDITIONAL TALMUD TAIL (*Bava Batra* 73a–b)

A series of Tall Tales by the Rabbis is recounted in the *Gemarah*. Rabbah (others, Rabbah b. Bar Chana) relates his story concerning Lilith and her demonic offspring, Hormin. Rabbah claims to have seen the demon ". . . running on the parapet of the wall of Machusa, and a rider, galloping below on horseback could not overtake him."

Clearly, since a horse was the swiftest conveyance at the time, the demon was moving very fast indeed.

. . . And a *Midrash* (Genesis, *Vayera*, 52:5–7)

In the curious story of Abraham trotting out Sarah as his sister, first to Pharaoh, thence, (in text) and in our *Midrash*, to Abimelech, the horse and his rider is again used, this time as an analogy. Again, the horse is seen merely as utilitarian. The Rabbis expound upon Abimelech's virtue in not approaching Sarah.

> It is like the case of a warrior who was riding his horse at full speed, when seeing a child lying in the path, he reined in the horse so that the child was not hurt. Whom do all praise, the horse or the rider? Surely the rider!

Thus the credit is given to Abimelech and not to Abraham.

16

L I O N

LION
Hebrew 'aRiYEH

*Judah is a lion's whelp;/On prey, my son, have you
grown./ He crouches, lies down like a lion,/Like the
king of beasts—who dare rouse him?*
—Genesis 49:9

Panthera leo: Latin, panther, lion.
The king of beasts may have been somewhat larger then,
but it was the same animal—at that time, enjoying a wide
range, habitat, and a nearly unchallenged rule of the wild.

CONCORDANCE

Numbers 23:24; 24:8.
Deuteronomy 33:20, 22.
Judges 14:5, 8–9, 18.
1 Samuel 17:34, 36–37.
2 Samuel 1:23 (stronger than lion); 17:10; 23:20.
1 Kings 7:29 (of brass, in Solomon's house); 10:19–20 (next to Solomon's
    throne, of ivory and gold); 13:24-26 (and when he [the prophet] was
    gone, a lion . . . slew him), 28; 20:36.
2 Kings 17:25–26.
Isaiah 5:29; 11:6–7 [see numbers 7, 11, 12, 18]; 21:8; 30:6; 31:4; 35:9 (no lion
    shall be there); 38:13; 65:25 (see number 12).

Jeremiah 2:15 (the young lions have roared upon him [Israel]), 30; 5:6 (see numbers 18, 72); 12:8; 50:17 (Israel is a scattered sheep [number 3], the lions have driven him away), 44; 51:38.

Ezekiel 1:10 (see numbers 11, 15, 26, 92); 10:14 (see number 26); 19:2–3, 5–6; 41:19 (stone, in vision of resurrected Temple).

Hosea 5:14; 11:10 (they shall walk after the Lord, who shall roar like a lion); 13:7 (see number 72)–8.

Joel 1:6.

Amos 3:4, 8 (the lion hath roared/who will not fear?), 12; 5:19 (see numbers 2, 65).

Micah 5:7 (and the remnant of Jacob . . . as a lion among the beasts of the forest) (see number 3).

Nahum 2:12 (several) 14.

Zephaniah 3:3 (see number 18).

Zechariah 11:3.

Psalms I–17:12 (He [enemy] is like a lion that is eager to tear in pieces,/And like a young lion . . .); 22:14, 16 (see number 23), 22; 35:17; II–57:5; 58:7 (Break out the cheek-teeth of the young lion, O Lord); IV–91:13 (see number 2); 104:21.

Proverbs 19:12 (The king's wrath is as the roaring of a lion;/But his favor is as dew upon the grass); 22:13; 26:13: 28:1 (. . . But the righteous are secure as a young lion), 15 (see number 65); 30:30 (The lion, which is mightiest among beasts).

Job 4:10 (The lion roareth . . . yet the teeth of the young lion are broken)–11 (The old lion perisheth for lack of prey,/And the whelps of the lion [lioness] are scattered abroad); 10:16 (. . . Thou huntest me as a lion); 28:8; 38:39 (Wilt thou hunt the prey for the lion [lioness]?/Or satisfy the appetite of the young lion).

Song of Songs 4:8 (see number 72).

Lamentations 3:10 (see number 60) (He is unto me as a *bear* lying in wait,/As a lion in secret places).

Ecclesiastes 9:4 (see number 23) (. . . for a living *dog* is better than a dead lion).

Daniel 6:8, 17 (Then the king commanded, and they brought Daniel, and cast him into the den of lions), 20–23, 25, 28; 7:4 (see also number 26 [But see esp. number 88]).

1 Chronicles 11:22.

2 Chronicles 9:18–19 (And there were six steps to the throne . . . and two lions standing beside the arms. And twelve lions . . . on the one side and on the other upon the six steps . . .).

This magnificent creature in the wild has no predator. The animal is called the King of Beasts not without reason, albeit Brewer has informed me that no animal, including a lion, will disturb a hippopotamus, "the true king of beasts." Lions are sociable. They form family units called prides. Although it is not true that the males never hunt, it is true that the lioness organizes and leads the hunt strategy and is often responsible for the death blow. Lions are among those sociable predators that ensure their cubs have plenty to eat following the kill.

In the Bible, the lion in one fashion or another is associated with kings and kingship. This largely derives from Jacob's blessing of Judah as a lion and a lion's cub, as he doles out a sometimes good, a sometimes not so good blessing to his twelve sons from his deathbed in Egypt. From this point on, the lion seems to indicate the true scepter of Israel and Judah. Samson is attacked by a lion and kills it; so he casts away his leadership of the Jewish people, violating one after another his vows as a Nazir; later he returns to the battle spot and discovers bees formed a hive and produce honey in the lion's skeleton; Samson can have only a brief, sweet taste of what might have been. Later, Solomon's throne is associated with fourteen magnificent sculptured lions:

> The king also made a large throne of ivory, and he overlaid it with refined gold. Six steps led up to the throne, and the throne had a back with a rounded top and arms on either side of the seat. Two lions stood beside the arms, and twelve lions stood on the six steps, six on either side. No such throne was ever made for any other kingdom. (1 Kings 18–20, JPS, 538)

When Solomon's empire split in two following his death, Jeroboam built bull-places in the northern kingdom, at Shechem and Bethel (1 Kings 12:25–33, JPS, 543); these probably reflected not so much a return to idol worship as they did a statement by the northern kingdom, that these would be the Lord's footstool for his throne, clearly a non-lion icon, which would be associated with the southern kingdom of Judah.

Throughout history, and even today in some synagogues, the lion imagery is found on Torah ark covers and coverings, sometimes embroidered, sometimes in relief in faux gem sculpture. The heraldry of Judah, David, and Solomon is still recalled by this iconography, albeit minimalist, in synagogue and temple. Perhaps because of this close association with wise kings, the lion imagery and sculpture has also been associated with libraries and culture. The stone lions guarding the steps of the New York Public Library have names: Patience and Fortitude.

There are many non-Jewish, nonbiblical stories of course. The talmudic references often reflect the distinction between civilization and law and the wilderness or abeyance of law. Also, since the lion is regarded highly and regally, much of the extracanonical nontalmudic literature revolves quite favorably in truth and folk-tale. One prominent Jewish mystic even has his acrostic nomenclature in Hebrew.

The first of Heracles's labors involved killing the Nemean Lion, an enormous beast that ravaged the countryside, depopulating entire villages. This was the second lion Heracles set out to destroy. The first was the Cithaeron lion, near the kingdom of Thespis. The Nemean was much more powerful, in fact, thought to be invincible, for its hide was like thick armor; often the monster would simply ignore the javelins and arrows that fell harmless upon it. Heracles was compelled to perform these labors for King Eurystheus to repent his terrible deeds that he committed while he was in a period of madness. Ultimately, Heracles tracks and engages the lion in his lair. Following a battle royal between man and beast, the Greek demigod strangles the animal, thus freeing the countryside from terror. The comparison to the Samson story is too close to ignore and may include a rationale not overtly perceived in the biblical rendition. Heracles's carcass becomes a trophy-mantle-armor that he wears upon his back, the head as a crown. As we have stated, Graves remains the most scholarly and thorough approach to these myths.

Graves's approach to the derivation of the myth inculcates other biblical treatises as well. Ezekiel's magnificent vision of the strange moving chariot in the sky, replete with its animal iconography, is perhaps the most astonishing description in the Bible. Here is Graves's approach to the foundation of the Heracles-Nemean Lion myth:

> The sacred king's ritual combat with wild beasts formed a regular part of the coronation ritual in

> Greece, Asia Minor, Babylonia, and Syria; . . . in a
> four-seasoned year, they will have been . . . bull,
> lion, eagle, and seraph, as in Ezekiel's vision. (Vol. 2,
> pp. 97–106)

Once again, the difference in Ezekiel's vision from the pagan rituals, among others, was that the king's chariot-throne was that of the King of kings, and we, created in the King's image, must struggle with our spiritual wild beasts on a daily, not seasonal, basis.

> . . . the Chimaera . . . was a symbol of the Great
> Goddess's triparte Sacred Year—lion for spring, goat
> for summer, serpent for winter. . . . After the Ach-
> nean religious revolution which subordinated the
> goddess Hera to Zeus, the (iconography of the lion)
> became ambivalent. (Vol. 1, pp. 254–255)

Graves also points out that madness was the Greek excuse for child sacrifice, allowing the true boy-king to remain hidden until his surrogates received the dubious benefit of the ritual. Again, this sheds even more light on the Akedah, wherein the surrogate for the designated prince is an animal, not another child.

Another ancient myth, the epic trial of the Babylonian hero-demigod, Gilgamesh, reflects the concurrent stories and mythology common in the Near East, including the biblical stories; as always, of course, the biblical authors are concerned with establishing the justice and mercy attributes of God. The Sumerian, Babylonian, and Greek authors have quite their own agendas. David Ferry's poetic rendering of the poem attempts to capture as close as possible the metier of the original. Pritchard (Vol. 1, pp. 40–75) also contains the complete text, as far as the tablets we have allow:

> Tablets II and III
> Enkidu spoke these words to Gilgamesh
> "Huwawa's mouth is fire; his roar the floodwater;
> his breath is death. Enlil made him guardian of the
> Cedar Forest, to frighten off the mortal who would
> venture there. But who would venture there? Huwa-

wa's mouth is fire; his roar is the floodwater; he breathes and there is death. He hears the slightest sound somewhere in the Forest. Enlil made him terrifying guardian, whose mouth is fire, whose roar the floodwater. . . .

You who have fought with lions and with wolves, you know what danger is. Where is your courage? If I should fall, my fame will be secure. 'It was Gilgamesh who fought against Huwawa!'"

Tablet X

. . .

It is I who killed the lions in the passes. It is Gilgamesh, who killed the demon guardian, Huwawa the guardian of the Cedar Forest. (pp. 16–17; 55)

Shabbat 106b–107a
Mishnah

If a deer enters a house and one person shuts (the door) before it, he is culpable; if two shut it, they are exempt . . .

Gemarah

R. Jeremiah b. Abba said in Samuel's name: If one catches a lion on the *Shabbat* he is not culpable unless he entices it into its cage.

The halakhah here may involve the *Shabbat* violation by accident or design; or it may involve the principal of violating the *Shabbat* if one's life or another's life is in danger. Enticing a (trained) lion into its cage, however, would involve the lion trainer's regular weekly labors.

> *The blow of a whip leaves a bruise,*
> *But the blow of a tongue breaks the bones.*
> *Many have fallen by the edge of the sword,*
> *But not so many as have fallen by the tongue.*
> *Happy is the man who is protected from it, . . .*

Those who forsake the Lord will fall into it,
And it will burn at them and not be put out;
It will be sent upon them like a lion,
And ravage them like a leopard.
                              (Ecclesiasticus, p. 277)

Sforno provides particularly insightful *p'shat* commentary concerning Jacob's final blessings to his sons at the close of the Book of Genesis. Here is a partial indication of his interpretation concerning Judah as a lion, a lion's whelp or cub, a crouching lion.

> Though presently Judah is not yet a lion, for he is not yet a king, still he is like a young lion, ruling over his brothers, and ultimately will be king, nonetheless . . . (and Judah was) not prepared to kill (Joseph) in his anger, even though he (also) hated you . . . Thus is Judah perceived as a lion that does not strike, that merely crouches, but later "The scepter shall not depart from (him)." (Pp. 233–234)

In his opening paragraph, Preuss refers to a little-known *Midrash* on Psalms regarding a treatment that probably didn't seem so very strange to our ancestors: "As an internist, (the Jewish physician) prescribed warm animal milk for a patient with consumption, and cured a desperately ill Persian king with the milk of a lioness."

One of the Legends of the Rabbis concerns a time the emperor (probably Hadrian) inquired of R. Joshua ben Hananiah concerning the passage from Amos ("A lion has roared,/ Who can but fear?").

The emperor cannot understand since, in his logic, a horseman can kill a lion. The story is fascinating since it has elements that harken to both the Heracles and Samson stories, to Judah as a lion, which the Rabbis hoped would resurrect and destroy the evil empire, and to, perhaps, a recalling of the plagues, when, at the end, Pharaoh requested Moses and the Israelites pray for him at their sacrifices as well.

> Rabbi Joshua replied, "He has been compared not to the ordinary lion but to the lion of Be-Ilai." "It is my

will," declared the emperor, "that you show it to me."
He said, "That is impossible." "I affirm," the emperor
insisted, "that I will see it." Rabbi Joshua prayed and
the lion set out from its place. When it was four
hundred parasangs distant it roared once, and all the
pregnant women miscarried and the walls of Rome
fell. When it was three hundred parasangs distant it
roared again and the molar and incisor teeth of men
fell out. Even the emperor himself fell from his throne
to the ground. "I beg you," he implored of Rabbi
Joshua, "pray that it return to its place." He prayed,
and the animal returned to its place. (Nadich, p. 86)

Isaac ben Solomon Luria (1534–1572) is customarily referred to as *haAri*, the Lion, or, the Lion-Hearted one. Luria was
one of the major Safed mystics of the sixteenth and seventeenth centuries, studying with Moses Cordovero. The acro-
nym for his totem-like name comes from the Hebrew for "The
Angelic, or Divine Being Rabbi Isaac" (ha*E*(A)i *R*av *Y*(I)itschak).
Unlike other Safed mystics who emigrated from Iberia, Luria
was born in Jerusalem; he spent some years in Egypt, before
settling in Safed, and concentrating his studies on the *Zohar*,
the major Kabbalah text. Luria's main areas of interest were
the mystical concept of *Tsimtsum* and how to approach it.
Roughly, the term implies a withdrawing, in this case, of God,
for God's radiance and splendor is too magnificent to behold
("You cannot see my face, for no human can see me and live!"
Exodus 33:20, Fox, p. 452; but see also Exodus 24:10, "And they
saw the God of Israel . . . ," 391). Therefore, our acts of
sacrifice, *mitzvot*, deeds of Justice and Mercy, prayer, all
provide sparks that enable us to reach toward this splendifer-
ous magnificence that is hidden but may be revealed in these
spontaneous moments of ecstasy.

Know that before the emanations were emanated
and the creatures created, the simple supernal
light . . . filled all there was . . . It had no beginning
and no end. All was simple light in total sameness.
This is called the endless light. . . .
The purpose of (the) contraction was to bring to
light the source of judgment, in order to make it

possible thereafter for the attribute of judgment to
act in the worlds . . .

After this contraction . . . there was now available an area in which there could be the emanations,
the beings created, formed and made.

WAYS OF PRAYER

1. It is wrong for a person to pray in a state of depression,
   but . . . rather . . . in joy (for) the soul (to be able) to
   receive the higher illumination . . .
2. My teacher used to say that it is desirable for a person
   to consider himself the dwelling place and seat of
   the divine emanations, for man is made in the divine
   image. . . .
3. Know that there is no prayer . . . that does not engender
   a renewal of light and of divine influences. . . .
4. My teacher never raised his voice when reciting his
   prayers . . . Only on the Sabbath did he raise his voice
   slightly, in honor of the Sabbath.
5. My teacher used to recite the prayers from the prayer
   book and not orally. All parts quoted from the Bible he
   used to recite with the proper cantellation, and all parts
   quoted from the *Mishnah* he used to recite with a
   melody. (Bokser, pp. 142–145)

AN ADDITIONAL TALMUD TAIL (*Sanhedrin* 1, *Gemarah* 15b)

In this *Mishnah* an unusual *machlochet*, dispute: that an animal
may, or may not, be adjudicated by the courts. Indeed, it is
clear in a majority opinion—that of the sages and of R. Akiba—
that a wild animal accused of "criminal" conduct upon a
human has rights before the court. It is also clear, as according
to R. Eliezer, that it has no such rights and whoever slays it has
acquired perhaps a greater entrance into the world to come:
". . . The death sentence on the wolf or the lion . . . is to be
passed by 23. R. Eliezer says: Whoever is first to kill them
[without trial], acquires merit. R. Akiba, however, holds . . .
decided by 23. . . ."

In the *Gemarah*, R. Jochanan concurs with R. Eliezer. And what does he acquire? The possession of the animal skin, a very practical merit, indeed. It is understood here that one acquires this "merit" even in slaying the animal when it hadn't attacked or killed a human being, again, a view intolerant of our modern attempts and needs to preserve endangered predators and other species. Resh Lakish, however, proclaims the merit to be beyond the more earthly acquisition of possessions: "As soon as they killed someone, the Rabbis regarded them as sentenced [to death], in which case benefit from them is prohibited! When then does he acquire? He acquires [merit] in the sight of heaven."

Resh Lakish cites a *Baraitha* in defense of his position: ". . . It is all one whether . . . any . . . beast or animal . . . killed a man. [It is judged by 23] . . . whoever is first to kill them acquires merit in the sight of heaven."

And in a *Mishnah* in *Avodah Zorah*, we learn "one should not sell bears, lions or anything which may injure the public" to idolaters. A dispute in the *Gemarah* ensues between Rabbah b. 'Ulla and R. Ashi concerning the issue, "Were it not for fear of injury to the public would it (then) be permitted?" (16a–b).

17

D E E R

DEER (Doe, Fawn, Hart, Hind)
Hebrew *'AYLaH ('AYL)*

> *Naphtali is a hind let loose,/*
> *Which yields lovely fawns.*
>
> —Genesis 49:21

Dama dama: Latin, deer.

Fallow deer—a catch-all generic name for animals of this species or closely related. I have not yet found an antelope (Antilocapridae) outside Africa, Asia, or the Americas; but that may only be due to the encroachment of modern civilization. A hart may be thought of as a male, a hind as a female.

CONCORDANCE

Deuteronomy 12:15, 22; 14:5; 15:22.
1 Kings 5:3.
Isaiah 35:6 (then shall the lame man leap as a h[ind]).
Jeremiah 14:5. Deer 3:19 (and he maketh my feet like hart feet).
Psalms I–18:34 (who maketh my feet like hinds'); 29:9; II 42:2 (as the hart panteth after the water brooks).
Job 39:1 (see number 7) (Knowest thou the time when the wild *goats* of the rock bring forth?/Or canst thou mark when the hinds do calve?).

Song of Songs 2:7 (see number 42), 9 (and again), 17 (and again); 3:5 (and again) (I adjure you O daughters of Jerusalem,/By the gazelles, and by the harts of the field,/That ye awaken not, nor stir up love,/Until it please); 4:5; 7:4; 8:14.

Deer represent a large, diverse group of herbivores that seem to adapt very well to changing environmental and encroaching civilization conditions. Certain of the species may be considered among the largest of the world's herbivores. They are quite capable of defending themselves from predators, and two or more stags will turn to engage wolves or other predators in physical conflict. When this action occurs, a wise or experienced pack of wolves, more often than not, will break off the hunt, to secure a better chance of bringing down a weak or stray animal from the herd another day. Still, the main survival technique of deer is the speed of their flight. Deer are swift and graceful creatures, able to run considerable distance at high velocity, and to leap with facility over what appears at first glance to be insurmountable barriers. It is this characteristic of swiftness that is most extolled of the creature in the biblical text.

According to Putnam, deer seem to have developed as a north-temperate group of their ancestors, preferring a deep forest or woodlands habitat. This preference led to their marked degree of adaptation, in terms of plant diet; foreshortened digestive system (allowing rapid digestion for quick energy needed for the bursts of flight); a sophisticated system of olfactory, auditory, and visual communication; and a high order of adaptability. In fact, populations of the same groups, when separated for one reason or another, will seem to find a way to adapt each to their own new ecology (3–4). Deer will also venture out of their woodland habitats to raid refuse upon the fringes of human society; in some populations, they will even allow their human neighbors to approach them, before returning into the shadow of the woods' protection. In some societies, this relationship has developed into full domestication, such as the Lapp Reindeer.

The other most pronounced characteristic of deer is antlers. Only deer have antlers; not all deer possess antlers. If any other species of animal has a bony eruption upon its skull or brow, it is a horn, not an antler. If a subspecies has antlers,

it is most often the male that has them, although does may
have them as well. In most populations, the antlers brachiate,
sometimes stunningly so. Horned animals retain their protru-
sions throughout life. Deer shed their antlers every year, and
they are re-grown. In general, the new and usually more
complex antlers re-grow from the pedicle, circular surface
eruptions upon the head richly supplied in blood vessels. The
often dramatic appearance of antlers indicates that their
purpose is not merely defense, but social display, thus used in
mating behavior (p. 11).

Again, the admiration of the biblical writers for the hart or
the hind was in its swiftness and grace. In this was seen a
theological relationship (how swift one should be to perform
the acts of righteousness and lovingkindness), and one more
erotic, particularly idealized in the Song of Songs. Other
discussions relate to the animal's proper allowance in *kashrut*,
some of the rabbinical tales, and a mystical indication.

Toperoff (pp. 105–107) refers to two Psalms to demonstrate the allusion of swiftness of the animal, in this context, in
particular, David piously fleeing from his enemies, then, in a
magnificent water image, expressing religious fervor. In 18:32–
34: "Truly, who is a god except the Lord,/who is a rock but our
God?—/the God Who girded me with might,/ Who made my
way perfect;/ Who made my legs like a deer's,/ and let me
stand firm on the heights" (JPS, p. 1125). Toperoff's translation
is one truer to the biblical poetry: "Who makes my feet like
hinds"; and in 42:2, he also renders a wonderful translation
following his incisive comment: "In an amazing outburst of
religious fervor David exclaims, 'As the hart pants after the
water brooks, so pants my soul after Thee, O God.'" Interestingly, JPS exchanges the gender in its translation: "Like a hind
crying for water (lit., watercourses),/my soul cries for You, O
God;/ my soul thirsts for God, the living God." Toperoff
continues:

> . . . the *Yalkut* points out that the hind is the most
> pious of all animals. For when the animals thirst for
> water they gather round the hind who digs her horns
> deep into the earth and prays for water, and the
> Almighty in his (sic) abundant mercy causes the

water to rise from the depths of the earth, quenching
the thirst of the animals.

As we know, the hind would dig with her antlers, not her
horns, and it must be a subspecies or population wherein the
female with regularity grows them.

Still, it is in the Song of Songs that the most alluring and
haunting renditions related to deer are poetically inscribed.

> *His left hand was under my head,*
> *His right arm embraced me,*
> *I adjure you, O maidens of Jerusalem,*
> *By gazelles or by hinds of the field:*
> *Do not wake or rouse*
> *Love until it please!*
> *Hark! My beloved!*
> *There he comes,*
> *Leaping over mountains,*
> *Bounding over hills.*
> *My beloved is like a gazelle*
> *Or like a young stag.*
> *. . .*
> *Set out, my beloved,*
> *Swift as a gazelle*
> *Or a young stag,*
> *For the hills of spices!*
> *(JPS, pp. 1407–1408)*

The Torah forbids us to eat any land animal (or the
milk of that animal) that does not have two distinctive *simanim* (signs, indications) that attest to its
kashrus. The animal must both chew its cud (rumi-
nate) and have completely cloven hooves. Cows,
goats, sheep, deer, bison, gazelle, antelope, ibex,
addax, and giraffe are animals that have both of
these characteristics and are considered *beheimah
tehorah* ("clean"), kosher animals, and need not be
inspected individually . . . (note 4: In the opinion
of many authorities, one may not eat any animal
for which we have no tradition as to its permissibil-
ity, even though it possesses the proper *simanim*).
(Forst, pp. 33–34)

The magnificent antlers of a 14-, 16-, or 18-point stag gathered the imagination of the mystics. The brachiation of the rack, which, like a tree of life, branched and pointed ever upward toward the heavenly spheres, was seen as a manifestation of the *s'ferot*, the divine emanations, and the pathways we can attain through prayer, *mitzvot*, *tzedakah*, mercy, and justice. In *The Bahir*, that early mystical work, we are taught that the Torah was given with seven voices. "In each of them the Master of the universe revealed Himself to them, and they saw Him. It is thus written, 'And all the people saw the voices.'" *The Bahir* closes this unit with the Seventh Voice, again, from the passage from Song of Songs, as we indicated previously, in 2:7. Kaplan's translation from the mystical resource is somewhat different: "I bind you with an oath, O daughters of Jerusalem, with the hosts, or with the hinds of the field" (pp. 15–16).

AN ADDITIONAL TALMUD TAIL (*Shabbat* 105b–107a)

In a *Mishnah* allocating culpability for tearing in anger (or mourning), damaging in order to repair, bleaching, or wearing two threads together on *Shabbat*, we read a *Gemarah* that defines culpability in capturing a deer: "Our Rabbis taught: If one catches a deer that is blind or asleep, he is culpable; a deer that is lame, aged or sick, he is exempt."

It is Abaye who inquires of R. Joseph what all might be pondering: What is the difference? "The former try to escape; the latter do not try to escape."

Thus, the former might require the nonpermissible act of hunting and catching. Interestingly, R. Shosheth adds and distinguishes that even an animal sick with fever could fall into the category of attempting to escape while one sick from exhaustion obviously could make no such attempt and is acceptable.

This is immediately before the *Mishnah* describing culpability and exemption on the holy day if one shuts a door where a deer entered his house.

18

W O L F

WOLF
Hebrew *Zei'V*

> *Benjamin is a ravenous wolf,/*
> *In the morning he comsumes the foe,/*
> *And in the evening he divides the spoil.*
> —Genesis 49:27

Canis lupus lupus: Latin, dog, wolf.

The same intelligent pack creature from which, according to one school of thought, the dog selectively evolved. Despite mass slayings, encroachment of civilization, soil erosion, chemicals in their food chain, outright poisonings, and other environmental degradations, the noble animal continues to rebound every so often and still ranges throughout the world.

CONCORDANCE

Isaiah 11:6 (see number 3); 65:25 (see number 3).
Jeremiah 5:6 (see numbers 16, 72).
Habakkuk 1:8 (see numbers 15, 47, 72).
Zephaniah 3:3 (see number 16).

Wolves are faster than most people think. They have more endurance than most people think. They are not as large as most people think. In general, only one pair in the pack, not with full accuracy referred to as the alpha pair, mate and have pups. Wolves do bark, as well as howl and whine. They do have a high moral order, casting a member of the pack out if he or she disobeys the rules. The outcast may in time find another pack that will accept it. Females lead some packs, males lead others. They can bring down a large robust animal, but they prefer to attack the weak, lame, small, and young at the fringes of or separated from the herd. In a quite similar form, albeit larger, this magnificent creature may be as much as a million years old.

The social structure of a wolf pack is all-important to its survival. These all important behaviors—including breeding, hunting, feeding, grooming, territorial occupation, play behavior—are bound up in it. In general, three social structures cross lines across the pack: a hierarchy of males, a hierarchy of females, and a cross-gender social structure. Packs have been observed comprised of 30 or more individuals, albeit less than 25 is more common, and 8 to 12 or 15 appears to be typical.

Their social order seems at times practically human. There are differences, of course, but the similarities of the structure of their packs to human family-oriented societies may be a partial explanation of why their bred descendant, the dog, and we get along so well. Despite the myths that Western civilization has developed about them, in actuality, wolves and human beings get along quite well in the wild. Wolves, like men and women, are more interested in herbivore prey, not other predators. There are ancient oral tales of wolves and women or men hunting together and sharing the kill. The major precept of any oral legend remains: that there is at least an element of truth, and perhaps more, in it.

Indeed, Native peoples, especially in North America, felt a certain kinship to wolves. Many individuals of several nations invoked the animal for their totem. Innuit (Eskimo) and other northern nation stories recall those legends of hunters accompanied by wolves in the hunt, and sharing the kill; after all, present-day hunters do so with their dog companions. The similarities are striking.

Alas, Eurocentric and Middle Eastern cultures were not so symbiotic. All sorts of myths and outright lies grew up about the (pseudo-)viciousness of wolves, and their attacks on children and other people. In time, some of these stories evolved into demonology, giving birth to the myth of the werewolf, or were-people. A Jungian archetype balance to these stories was struck with the image of the wolf as a rescuing and nurturing creature, saving lost toddlers and children, giving them suck for nourishment, and teaching them to hunt and to survive. Sometimes the children are found; sometimes they are not. Feral children, when discovered, rarely retrieve communications and other human development skills.

What may have given rise to the unfortunate detrimental view is wolves' penchant for attacking the livestock of farmers, ranchers, and shepherds. Such prey is easy prey. Wolves are highly intelligent, adaptable, and can generally outwit a fence barrier or security measures. Since the husband-entrepreneur depends upon his or her stock for economic prosperity, it is easy to perceive how a symbiotic relationship could soon deteriorate into one of enmity. It is a conflict that continues and can be found in today's headlines.

Alas, the biblical text and the Rabbis later fell into this false assumption trap. Wolves are rarely admired in the textual and rabbinic literature and, in fact, are more often than not described in these false accusations of being ready to attack men, women, and children. Those who have studied the behavior of wolves in the latter days of the twentieth century know that this simply is not true (For a full treatment, see Lopez, especially pp. 1–92).

Again, there is little in the talmudic texts and all of the entries cast the creature in this unfortunate negative light. Rabbi Meir was known for collecting several animal fables, particularly concerning the sly fox that outwits human hunters and other competitive species. In *Sanhedrin* 39a, Rashi elucidates one of these stories: A fox induces a wolf to join the Jews in the preparation of their *Shabbat.* When he does so, he is beaten by them. He crawls back to the fox, demanding an explanation. The fox informs him he was beaten for the sake of his father. Next, the fox, apparently wanting some water from a well, induces the wolf to sit upon the counterbalance bucket and draw him up. Then, the fox leaves the wolf stuck in the well, in dire straits.

"And how am I to get out?" demanded the wolf.

"Ah," said the fox. "The righteous is delivered out of trouble and the wicked comes in his stead."

The allusion may be to the "father," viz, Babylon or Greece, and the contemporary wolf is clearly perceived as the evil, voracious empire, Rome; to the Rabbis, it appeared as though it would never disappear down any well of righteousness nor be replaced. The proof-text is from Proverbs 11:8.

In the *Midrash, Genesis Rabbah* (*Vayechi*), based on Jacob's blessing of Benjamin ("a wolf that raveneth"), the animal fares better. There is a complex argument and dispute between Rabbi Jose the Galilean, R. Akiba, and R. Judah. The dispute involves into which tribe the Temple was established and why. The opening of the argument establishes the righteousness of Mount Sinai in being chosen for the Revelation over all the other mountains; then, as these mountains ran to contend with one another, so later do the tribes run to contend with one another, each saying, "Let it be built in my territory." The argument turns more specific, in particular, regarding the tribes of Judah and Benjamin. Although the southern kingdom was called by the name of the larger tribe, there was always a consideration that the Temple Mount itself was upon the smaller tribal lands of Benjamin. In the *Midrash*, there is a series of proof-texts tossed back and forth, in particular between R. Judah and R. Simeon, based upon an earlier proof-text by R. Akiba:

> And thus you find that four hundred and eighty years previously the sons of Korah prophesied that it would be within Benjamin's portion, as it says, "My soul yearneth, yea even pineth for the courts of the Lord" (Psalms 84:3). And thus it says, "Lo, we heard of it as being in Ephrath; we found it in the field of the wood" (132:6).

R. Judah then takes his position: The Temple was built in Judah's territory, for it is written, "The Ephrathite of Bethlehem in Judah" (Samuel 17:12).

And so it would seem to be so. However, R. Simeon's retort

not only defeats R. Judah's position, it demonstrates that at least for once, the wolf is not seen altogether as a vicious destroyer, but as one that with righteousness defends its territory.

> It is in the territory of the son of the woman who died in Ephrath. And who died in Ephrath? Rachel. You might then think that it is in the portion of Joseph, seeing that he too was her son; therefore it states, "We found it in the field of the forest," which implies: In the portion of him who was likened to the beast of the forest. And who was so likened? Benjamin, as it is written, *Benjamin is a wolf that raveneth.*

Sforno takes another approach, in particular regarding the descendants of Benjamin—Saul, the first King of Israel, and Mordecai and Esther. Sforno perceives a wolf to attack prey ("ravens") at either dawn or twilight. Thus, Saul is perceived as the dawn of Jewish greatness, and Mordecai-Esther as the twilight of Jewish greatness. Sforno disarms in advance his commentators who would see the Second Temple period as "comparatively brief, and included many years of subjugation as well" (p. 241).

> Historically it has been hard to study wolves. The animals have long been elusive wilderness dwellers, primarily because humans have persecuted and exterminated them in most accessible regions. Furthermore, wolves generally live in low densities; one pack may have a territory of as much as 13,000 square kilometers (and) . . . travel long distances . . .
>
> The repopulation of the lower 48 states by wolves, which now seems well under way, will stand as one of the most remarkable conservation achievements of the 20th century. Society will have come full circle and corrected its grievous overreaction to its main mammalian competitor. . . .
>
> If these efforts are successful, and the wolf can be accepted as a regular member of our environment, rather than as a special saint or sinner, this will go a long way toward ensuring that the howl of the wolf will always be heard throughout the wild areas of the northern world. (Mech, pp. 7–8)

An Additional Talmud Tail (*Chullin* 9a–b)

In the first *Mishnah*, dealing with who may slaughter animals not consecrated, a question arises in the *Gemarah* and is put to R. Huna by R. Abba: "If a wolf came and carried away the intestines [of a slaughtered animal], what is the law?"

The question asked intends, how can we know if, even if discovered, the intestines were already perforated and thus the animal is *treif*—or, if the scavenger perforated "clean" intestines and the animal was permissible for consumption. A long disputation ensues, seemingly around R. Huna's remark, "We do not apprehend that it inserted [its teeth] in a perforation."

19

FROG

FROG
Hebrew *TS'F'ARD'ei*

> *If you refuse to let them go, then I will plague your
> whole country with frogs.*
>
> —Exodus 7:27

Rana esculanta

CONCORDANCE

Genesis 8:1–9; 11–13.
Psalms III–78:45 (see number 20); IV–105:30.

Frogs and toads belong to that class of animals known
as amphibians. In evolutionary science, amphibians are extremely significant for a number of reasons. They, or more
accurately, their ancestors, represent the evolutionary link
between sea animals and land creatures. Amphibians begin
their lives as sea creatures, much like fish, and, in the course
of their careers, metamorphose to an animal that can live on
land. Also, amphibians are perceived by biologists to be the
"canary in the tunnel," the herald, or early warning signal, that
our ecosystem may be breaking down all around us, for their

numbers are decreasing, and some species today are endangered. Their link between us, all animals, and the environment is not yet fully understood, but the strong shared suspicion is that it is of vital importance to the balance of life on earth.

Still, even today, in rural areas within any reasonable distance of lakes, ponds, creeks, and rivers, in early summer, one has to be careful walking at dusk and at night, for frogs and toads are criss-crossing the land. In such an area, practically every summer now for fourteen years, I have nearly stepped on or kicked a stone, only to suddenly stop and see the familiar shape frozen, or hop away into the grasses.

Frogs and toads occupy a wide range of environments throughout the world. There are many different species, some of them bizarre and poisonous. There are few differences between frogs and toads; in general, frogs are larger and present more mucous-covered smooth skins, whilst toads are smaller and exhibit dry skin. Frogs tend to remain on, within, or close to their watery home; toads may wander far afield and back again. Some biologists and pharmacologists suspect that divers of these animals, perhaps even a species as yet undetected, may hold the key to as yet undiscovered compound remedies for some of our most devastating diseases. It is yet another reason for us to redouble our efforts to attempt to rescue fragile ecosystems, especially in the temperate zones.

As one would expect, there are innumerable *Midrashim* and talmudic commentaries concerning the plagues visited upon Pharaoh and Egypt. Numerous stories and insights involve the frogs. One of the more well known concerns the end of the border dispute that had existed between Cush (Ethiopia) and Egypt for centuries. As the frogs grew in multitudinous numbers, a portion of them aligned themselves along this border; the demarcation now precise, the boundary dispute between the two nations came to an end. This story may hearken to another midrashic account that has Moses, upon his exile, and prior to meeting Yitro and Zipporah, rescue the Cushites from great danger; one of the versions of the story relates that, for a time, Moses was proclaimed King of Ethiopia. This may resonate with the later story in Numbers (12) concerning Moses' marriage to the Cushite woman and Aaron's and Miriam's futile protest.

There are several other interesting *Midrash* and *Gemarah* entries, not the least of which is a dispute between R. Akiba and R. Eleazar b. Azariah, who follows the *tannaim*.

The several *Midrashim* tend to follow the direction of Akiba, albeit they do so with an interesting opening of a giant maw:

> (In) a matter disputed by *tannaim*(,) R. Akiba said: There was one frog which filled the whole of Egypt (by breeding). But R. Eleazar b. Azariah said to him, "Akiba, what hast thou to do with *Haggadah*. Cease thy words and devote thyself to 'Leprosies,' *Neza'im* and 'Tents,' *Ohalot*. One frog croaked for the others, and they came." (*Sanhedrin* 67b)

Nezai'm and *Ohalot* are two tractates dealing with uncleanness of a corpse and leprosy. They are regarded as very difficult to study and to master; thus, R. Eleazar b. Azariah is attempting to indicate to Akiba that his extraordinary insights are more suited for dialectics than for homiletics (Note C 4, 5).

Ramban uses this dispute as a thesis-antithesis argument to develop his synthesis that these first two plagues (blood and frogs) "did not involve the creation of some new phenomenon out of nothing or some act of new formation." Thus, Pharaoh's magicians could repeat the act. What they could not do, Ramban explains, "is bestow a new nature upon the frog, that is, that one should give birth to so many" (pp. 87–88).

Again, the *Midrash* goes further.

> The second Plague was also brought by Aharon and not Moshe since it again entailed smiting the river, and it was not right for Moshe to smite the river which had protected his basket. . . . As soon as Aharon stretched out his hand, the Egyptians were amazed to behold a ghastly sight. Out of the river hopped a hideous supersized frog that began to march down the main road towards Pharaoh's palace. Hashem gave the Egyptians one last opportunity to repent before they would be invaded by additional frogs. The Egyptians brought weapons and sticks with which to kill the monstrous frog. Instead of

> falling dead, it opened its mouth wide, and spit out
> legions of baby frogs. It let out a shrill whistle, and
> at this sign, armies of frogs came tumbling out of
> the river, accompanied by other sea reptiles with
> huge mouths and teeth (Sforno states, "crocodiles").
> (Weissman, pp. 63–65)

The story continues at length, telling how the frogs pen-
etrate every aspect of Egypt, even the Egyptians' bodies. At
one point, they attain even greater mystical powers, demonstrating the ability to ooze through the marble and stone of the
king's palace. An analogy is made to the hornets that pierced
the rocks to attack the Canaanites, David's stone piercing the
helmet of Goliath, and the particular worm that was able to
split the rocks and precious stones for the building of the *Beit
Hamikdash.*

Another aspect of the story serves as a later lesson as well,
in the Book of Daniel, concerning the three who survived
Nebuchadnezzar's fiery furnace.

> Whenever an Egyptian woman heated her oven in
> order to bake bread, the frogs would hop into the
> dough and nibble at it. The woman therefore put it
> hurriedly into the oven. The frogs, though, clung to
> the dough, allowing themselves to be baked together
> with it. They cooled off the heat so that no bread was
> ever baked well.
> *When the emperor Nevuchadnetzar* (sic) *erected a
> statue in his honor and commanded his subjects to
> prostate themselves before it, Chananya, Mishael, and
> Azarya refused. They leapt into the ovens, sacrificing
> their lives for* kiddush Hashem. ". . . If the frogs were
> ready to sacrifice their lives for Hashem, we must
> certainly be prepared to do the same."*
> The Egyptians suffered severely from the Plague
> of Frogs. Not a single Egyptian could evade the
> frog-plague. . . . (Pp. 65–68)

In Daniel 3, the three Israelites are known by their Babylonian names, Shadrach, Meshach, and Abednego. Also, in the
text, the men are bound and hurled into the furnace. I count at

least four miracles that occur in the story: The Babylonians who brought them to the oven and hurled them in were then attacked by licks of the flame exiting the oven and killing them; the three Hebrews survived in the fiery oven unscathed; a fourth "man" was seen with them in the oven; following this event, and the exeunt omnes of the men, still unscathed, and the fourth "man" nowhere to be seen, King Nebuchadnezzar repents and proclaims God Most High. Soon after this, another miracle occurs; ". . . the Chaldean king . . . was killed, and Darius the Mede received the kingdom . . ." (5:30, 6:1).

> Then King Darius wrote to all peoples and nations of every language that inhabit the earth, "May your well being abound! I have hereby given an order that throughout my royal domain men must tremble in fear before the God of Daniel, for He is the living God Who endures forever; His kingdom is indestructible, and His dominion is to the end of time; He delivers and saves, and performs signs and wonders in heaven and on earth . . ." (6:26–28, JPS)

> The dead frogs did not disappear but were left lying all over Egypt. The Egyptians had to shovel them together. Since there were so many of them, each Egyptian collected at least four piles of frogs. The dead frogs were even more revolting than the live ones. They emitted a sickening stench which permeated the entire land. The Egyptians were thus repaid *midda-keneged-midda* (measure for measure) for having beaten the Jews mercilessly until a foul odor emanated from their mouths. (Weissman, p. 67)

Of course, the *b'nai Yisrael*, the children of Israel, were miraculously spared these calamities.

Toperoff points out versions of these stories and alludes to two additional most interesting anecdotes. It seems the frog is favored by the Rabbis not merely for these events and self-sacrificial service to God, but because the animal daily sings God's praises; even when croaking to each other to appear in Egypt, they continued their daily chorus. In one version, when David completes his compositions of the Psalms, a frog appears to engage in an *agon*, a contest pitting his songs against David's. Toperoff concludes his section with an incisive entry from *Niddah* 18a: ". . . even in the *Halakhah*, the frog in one sense is 'favored.' In Leviticus 11:29 there is mention of creeping things whose dead bodies defile by touch, but the frog . . . does not defile when it is dead" (pp. 83–85). One interpretation from *Tohorot* follows.

An Additional Talmud Tail (*Tohorot, Mishnah* 5:1, 4)

The tractate deals with that which is pure, clean, or impure, unclean, *tamei*. In the main, these concern ritual purifications, as indicated in the first sentence; for, in Leviticus 11, creeping things are considered unclean, and frogs are not.

> If in a public domain there was a [dead] creeping thing and a frog . . . R. Akiba ruled that he is unclean, but the sages rule that he is clean. *Mishnah* 4 details a complex set of rules concerning the preparation of the *Terumah*—basically, if he touches a dead creeping thing and a frog and then prepared the item and it was consumed, then he performed his ritual ablution (immersion) and prepared the item, the item is clean; the first, however, its remainder (and that of the second if he did not perform the ablution) are unclean.

Now, the understanding of *Mishnah* 4 depends on the understanding of *Mishnah* 1. The ellipsis details if he steps on it. The implication is, he looks back and does not know which he stepped on. The *Chachamim* favor the principle of leniency; R. Akiba favors the more strict interpretation. We *poskin* (i.e., prefer) the lenient fashion of the *Chachamim*.

Now, *Mishnah* 4 becomes an astonishing exercise in rabbinic logic and intuition. It could be explained as follows— hopefully to clarify a complex matter.

He walks along. He steps on something. He looks back. He prepares the ritual food. Since leniency is followed (i.e., he assumes it is the frog, not the lizard or shrimp thing; therefore, it is permissible for him to consume the food).

So far, fine. Now he goes to the *mikveh*. Upon exiting, he walks across and steps on it again. This time he cannot be lenient. One of the times the item likely was the lizard thing. Thus, both the remainder or the first and the second preparation are *tamei* for he must be in such a state.

20

LICE

LICE (Others Favor Gnat)
Hebrew *CHiNiM*

> *Then the Lord said to Moses, "Say to Aaron: Hold out your rod and strike the dust of the earth, and it shall turn to lice throughout the land of Egypt." "The gnat is our declared enemy"—Reaumur, in Figuier.*
> —Exodus 8:12–14.

Culex pipiens

CONCORDANCE

Psalms IV–105:31 (see number 19).

Another one of the plague creatures appearing only in one other context of the biblical text. The translations from one language to another are always difficult, and long periods of time and space (as well as sacred time and space) render it always somewhat uncertain that the correct term for the species is being indicated. In fact, Toperoff uses "lice," and defends his selection well: "Alternative translations . . . as 'gnats or mosquitoes' . . . but these insects hatch in water and not in the dust of the earth." Indeed, the text and the *Midrash* indicate that dust of the earth was struck and changed into these insects. The only problem is that gnats and mosquitoes take wing, while lice do not. It appears to be a toss-up. Toperoff allows that the word *kinnim* (as he transliterates it), is "of doubtful derivation" (pp. 141–142).

The *Midrash* favors the term *lice* and indicates that this time, the magicians could not mimic through their arts this plague. ". . . they admitted to Pharaoh, '. . . We are forced to admit that this plague results from the Finger of God'" (Weissman, pp. 68–69).

Ramban, however, favors the term *gnats* (at least, his own translators do). He engages Ibn Ezra in long debate concerning this term *Finger of God*, or *Finger of the Eternal.* Ibn Ezra takes the view, through a play on words, that it does not indicate the Egyptians' acquiescence to the Power of the Almighty, but to the evil spirits that inhabit Egypt. Ramban disagrees with this position, using the rabbinical proof that of the plagues so far, this is the only one wherein the natural state of the element (dust) was altered. Clearly, this is beyond any magician's artifice, whether the enactment be inhibited by evil spirits or nay (85–90).

The expression ". . . the finger of God" (Exodus 8:15) is a particularly noteworthy one, since it is also the expression used for God's inscription of the Tablets of the Pact (31:18).

In *Shabbat* 107b, there is an allusion that one who kills vermin on *Shabbat*, it is as though he slaughters larger animals on *Shabbat*.

An Additional Talmud Tail (*Avodah Zorah* 26b)

Although the *Mishnah* deals with whether a heathen can act as midwife to an Israelite woman (or suckle her child) and vice versa, the *Gemarah* uses various examples to differentiate when one may be considered a mere apostate or an actual *min*, which is a devout idol worshiper. Fleas and gnats and their (forbidden) consumption are used as one example. However, there is a dispute concerning even this example. R. Aha says if he eats to satisfy his appetite, he is merely an apostate; and to provoke the community—that is, purposefully for this reason, is a *min.*

"An objection was raised: If one eats a flea or a gnat he is an apostate. . . ." So the answer to this is: "Even in that case he may just be trying to see what a forbidden thing tastes like."

21

S WARMS OF I NSECTS

SWARMS OF INSECTS JPS renders "Swarms of Insects";
Fox, "Insects"; Others, "Fly"; (which see number 71)

> *For if you do not let My people go, I will let loose
> swarms of insects against you and your courtiers and
> your people and your houses; the houses of the
> Egyptians, and the very ground they stand on, shall
> be filled with swarms of insects
> [others, "wild beasts"].*
>
> —Exodus 8:17

22

LOCUST

LOCUST (includes Cricket, Grasshopper)
Hebrew *'ahRBehH*

> *For if you refuse to let my people go, tomorrow I*
> *will bring locusts on your territory.*
> —Exodus 10:4; 12–14, 19

Acridium (Oedipoda) migratorium.

The most destructive of the species and very common throughout the East and Africa. Figuier (pp. 301–302) relates:

> It is especially in warm climates that they become such fearful pests to agriculture. Wherever they alight, they change the most fertile country into an arid desert. They are seen coming in innumerable bands, which, from afar, have the appearance of stormy clouds, even hiding the sun. As far and as wide as the eye can reach the sky is black, and the soil is inundated with them. The noise of these millions of wings may be compared to the sound of a cataract. When this fearful army alights upon the ground, the branches of the trees break, and in a few hours, and over an extent of many leagues, all vegetation has disappeared, the wheat is gnawed to its very roots. The trees are stripped of their leaves. Everything has been destroyed, gnawed down, and

170

devoured. When nothing more is left, the terrible host rises, as if in obedience to some given signal, and takes its departure, leaving behind it despair and famine. It goes to look for fresh food—seeking whom, or rather in this case, what it may devour!

The author proceeds to relate how the swarms have changed the course of history through, as we know, the Exodus plague, and stopping more modern battles between armies poised for victory and defeat.

CONCORDANCE

Leviticus 11:22 (of these you may eat the following: locusts of every variety . . . crickets of every variety; and all variety of grasshoppers).
Judges 6:5; 7:12.
1 Kings 8:37.
Isaiah 33:4 (a locust leap . . .).
Jeremiah 46:23.
Joel 1:4 (see number 33 or 68); 2:25 (see again).
Amos 7:1.
Nahum 3:15, 17.
Psalms III–78:46 (see number 33 or 68); IV–105:34 (see number 33).
Proverbs 30:27 (The locusts have no king,/Yet go they forth all of them by bands).
Job 39:20.
2 Chronicles 6:28 (see also number 68) (If there be in the land . . . locust or *caterpillar* . . .); 7:13.

The *Midrash* presents an interesting twist on the affliction of the Egyptians from the plagues. At one point, the people of the afflicted land realize they now face starvation, and are glad to see a food source arrive. This may tie in with a very interesting Torah *Mitzvah* concerning *kashrut*, insects, and the locusts. Again, the *Midrash* quotation is taken from the selections by Weissman, pp. 84–86.

> The sight of clouds of locusts descending upon Egypt . . . cheered (the Egyptians). "These locusts will make delectable meals of locust preserves!" they rejoiced. "We will put them into barrels, salt them,

and eat them!" . . . The Pestilence had exterminated
their animals so that no meat could be obtained, and
the Plague of Hail had destroyed all fruit and vegetable supplies.

These locusts were not ordinary insects. They
were an army of wonder-insects, miraculously
equipped with special organs to wound and kill the
Egyptians. They possessed teeth like iron, horns
resembling those of oxen, claws like lions, wings like
eagles, and writhing backs like snakes . . . (and) literally insatiable.

Locusts, crickets, and grasshoppers are different species,
although their distinction is slight, other than locusts' strange
life cycle and swarming behavior. The Leviticus passage at
once dismisses the misconception that no insects are kosher.

Freund, however, states that, to the Ashkenazim, they are
not kosher, based on a series of p'shatim by Eastern European
rabbis; these rabbis felt that we could no longer identify the
particular species, so in a decision based on the fence around
the tree concept, all insect species were to be considered
treif. Israel points out that the Sephardim continue to regard
the species as kosher and consider certain cooked dishes of
them as a delicacy. Because the Holy Land is described as a
Land of Milk and Honey, honey, which is manufactured by
bees, is considered kosher by all.

The main discussion concerning the dispute over species
and kashrut is found in Mishnah 59a in Chullin. R. Israel is a
beekeeper.

The Mishnah in Chullin 8 states: "It is forbidden to cook all
flesh in milk except the flesh of fish and locusts." Forst
includes the (Ashkenazic) prohibition under the category of
SRTS (Sheretz)—"swarming insects and rodents."

. . . One type of insect, however, is permitted. The
Torah describes the features of certain species of
locust that are permitted; these are enumerated in
Shulchan Aruch. However, today we lack a definite
tradition about which species are allowed and therefore do not eat locust. Certain Sefardic (Yemenites,
mainly, according to Israel) communities follow a
tradition as to which locust is kosher. (Pp. 38–39)

Jose ben Joezer of Z(TS)eredah and Jose ben Johanan of Jerusalem received the tradition from Simon the Just and Antigonus. . . .

They called (ben Joezer) "Jose the Lenient" because he permitted three things that other authorities did not. He testified that the Ayal locust may be eaten, that the liquid flowing along the floor of the slaughtering place in the Temple is not susceptible to ritual uncleanliness, and that only he who actually touches a corpse becomes ritually unclean. (Nadich, I, pp. 187–188)

An Additional Talmud Tail (*Chullin* 59a, 65a)

It is in this *Mishnah* that we find the rabbinical excursus on the biblical allowance of the animal as kosher. The *Gemarah* differentiates and defines the permissible creature in a bit more detail.

It also includes two terms of subspecies, probably unknown to us today; Soncino (p. 351) indicates these as, "A species . . . born without leaping legs but (which) . . . grow in the course of time."

Mishnah:

> The characteristics . . . of locusts: all that have four legs, four wings, leaping legs, and wings covering the greater part of the body . . . R. Jose says, it must also bear the name, "locust."

Gemarah:

> Our Rabbis taught: If it has no [leaping legs] but will grow them later on, as in the case of the *zadral*, it is permitted. R. Eliezer b. R. Jose says, [the verse] . . . includes those that have none now but will grow them later on. What is the *zadral*?—Abaye answered, It is the *iskera*.

23

DOG

DOG
Hebrew *KeLeV*

> *But not a dog shall snarl at any of the Israelites, at man or beast—in order that you may know that the Lord makes a distinction between Egypt and Israel.*
>
> —Exodus 11:7

Canis familiaris: Latin, dog, domestic.

One of the most successful of all mammals, having thrown its symbiotic lot in with *Homo sapiens*. The destiny of these two species has been intertwined since at least 15,000 B.C.E. and, in some parts of the world, conceivably two or three times that long.

CONCORDANCE

Deuteronomy 23:19.

1 Samuel 17:43 (am I a dog's breath); 24:15 (. . . after a dead dog—David).

2 Samuel 3:8 (Am I a dog's head); 9:8; 16:9.

1 Kings 14:11; 16:4; 21:19, 23–24; 22:38 (. . . and the dog licked up his [Ahab's] blood).

2 Kings 8:13; 9:10 (and the dogs shall eat Jezebel . . .), 36.

Isaiah 13:22 ("wild-dog," [probably not a separate species]); 34:13; 56:10–11; 66:3.

Jeremiah 15:3.

Psalms 22:17 (see number 16), 21; 59:7, 15; 68:24 (That the tongue of thy dog may have its portion from thine enemies).

Proverbs 26:11, 17; 30:31 (the greyhound [number 96]).

Job 30:1.

Ecclesiastes 9:4 (see number 16).

As pets alone, in the United States alone, there are about 55 million of them, all shapes, sizes, colors, breeds. But they share common traits. They are pack animals. They regard us, their owners, as leaders of their pack. They crave attention. They shower us with nonjudgmental love. They are our best friends. They are intelligent. They are insatiably curious. They are adaptive. They may have a form of ESP. There are perhaps ten million more cats as pets today than dogs, to some extent because of the hectic lives most of us live, and cats do better as latchkey pets. But if you've ever had a dog, then both of you have been blessed. For it is the perfect example of nature's use of symbiosis; we need each other (Newman, Thomas).

Considering the "mutts" that compromise pure breeds, the particular number of breeds is in doubt, albeit over forty is a term commonly bandied about. There is considerable disagreement as to the origin of the species, involving those who follow they are domesticated from wolves, and those who follow there was always a unique ancestor with a proclivity to need interspecific companionship and give selfless beneficence. Thomas follows the former view, indicating how it returns in vogue practically in each generation. Shaler prefers the latter view, and states a most persuasive case, albeit it calls to us from an earlier generation.

> . . . it has been found impossible to educate captive wolves to the point where they show any affection for their masters, or (comfortable) in the arts of the household. . . . They are, in fact, indomitably fierce and utterly self-regarding. Moreover, . . . dogs show little or no tendency to revert to the form and habits of their brutal kindred, or to interbreed with them. . . . (P. 12)

Shaler continues to demonstrate how a long-ago lost ancestor may have given rise to the stalwart and loyal companion we know today. He and others contend the animal to be the first domesticated. He claims also that dogs, perhaps more than any animal, seem able to communicate their emotions, their feelings to us, and we to them. In this they are not only our friends, they are our teachers. As the Talmud might teach us, in its best-known technique of logic, that is the minor to the major, thus—if we can learn mutual love and respect with a dog, how much more should we do so with the other persons around us. Perhaps, then, it is not such a curious matter that the animal seems to prefer our company more than that of his or her brothers and sisters.

They herd our sheep. They hunt our game. They watch our homes. They give us unconditional love and only ask for a little of the same in return. There is only one problem—in one of her cruel tricks, nature has endowed them with only a fourteen- or fifteen-year life span, and it is hard, so very hard, when the inevitable time comes for us to say good-bye and, if we cared for them at all, to lay them gently into that sweet rest. Our hearts never fully heal at the profound loss, but oh, it was so worthwhile.

Alas, the Bible and rabbinic sources didn't often show a favorable eye toward the dog, perceiving the animal as a harbinger, a brute, a licker of blood, bad omens in dreams, and the like. This viewpoint came into a tragic, real focus during the Holocaust era, as the Nazis used their native shepherds and other dogs to set upon Jewish and other prisoners. In America, however, and especially in the postwar era, some of the most fortunate creatures in the world have been canine pets in Jewish homes. Not all views are unfavorable, however. And those who have known the joy of a canine friend have known true joy.

There is a larger issue here, and the dog's entry represents a particularly effective place to express it. The Rabbis saw animals as mere beasts, subject to impulses merely, a *Yesher Rah*, an "evil," that is, bestial, impulse; humans, however, had a *Yesher Rah* and a *Yesher Tov*, the evil and the good impulse. It is incumbent upon us to study Torah and to pray, so to learn to control the evil impulse and to enact the good impulse— this we do through observation of *mitzvot*, of the commandments or obligations. However, as to the viewpoint of the animals, this view has come under disputation.

Many zoologists today believe that the higher animals have far more resources, emotions, and moral choices than we have previously considered. Jane Goodall's landmark studies have presented one major exponent of this view. Regarding our good friend the dog, Thomas has been a major influence in this regard.

There are several references in the Talmud, of varying descriptions. I have chosen a select group here as representative of this aspect. The first one comes from *Berachot* 56b; it demonstrates an unusual aspect of dogs, that they could be perceived as messengers in a dream. The Rabbis have always concerned themselves with dream interpretation; after all, the biblical text is replete, and the story of Joseph, for example, is predicated upon accurate dream interpretation. The *Mishnah* involves the prayers one utters when one sees a place where a miracle for Israel has occurred, and the "vain" and worthwhile benedictions one should utter, as well as the proper way to enter the Temple Mount, and what benedictions to be said at that time. I chose this as the first talmudic entry, since its referent is directly related to the first *pasuk* in which the dog appears in Scripture: "If one sees a dog in his dream, he should rise early and say: *But against any of the children of Israel shall not a dog whet his tongue* before another verse occurs to him [such as] *Yea, the dogs are greedy*" (Isaiah 56:11).

The first verse comes immediately after one of the most powerful verses in the Bible. Moses is telling the Egyptians of the forthcoming terrible night of death of the firstborn. "And there shall be a loud cry in all the land of Egypt, such as has never been or will ever be again; but not a dog shall snarl at any of the Israelites, at man or beast—in order that you may know that the Lord makes a distinction between Egypt and Israel" (JPS; however, in a note on p. 100, the editors allow that others translate "move," or "whet." Apparently the Hebrew is very difficult).

(Indeed, Fox points this out in his note on p. 313. His translation, which seems to clarify the text somewhat for English readers, proceeds thus: "... But against all the Children of Israel, no dog shall even sharpen its tongue, against either man or beast, in order that you may know that YHWH makes a distinction between Egypt and Israel.")

Perhaps this is the reason that the Rabbis included this

aphorism in the *Gemarah*. It is another example of the *chol v'chomer* technique; if not even a dog . . . how much more so the Harbinger of Death. Indeed, this is the indication Fox gives in his note. Thus, if one sees a dog in his dream, she or he should say the *pasuk* in Exodus, to avoid misfortune, perchance even death that day. In this may be perceived the double-edged concept in which the Rabbis regarded dogs. The good thing is, they may be sent as messengers to warn us (many are known as watchdogs, for example, and bark with a clear message to us when danger approaches); the bad thing is, they may indicate the coming of something vicious, albeit perhaps just.

> Now, every Sabbath day (King David) would sit and study all day. On the day that his soul was to be at rest, the Angel of death stood before him but could not prevail against him, because learning did not cease from his mouth. . . . Now, there was a garden before his house, so the Angel of death went, ascended and soughed in the trees. [David] went out to see; as he was ascending the ladder, it broke under him. Thereupon he (ceased studying) and he had repose. Then Solomon went to Beth Hamidrash. My father is dead lying in the sun, and the dogs of my father's house are hungry; what shall I do? They sent back. Cut up a carcass and place it before the dogs, and as for thy father (only then) . . . carry him away. Did then not Solomon well say, *for a living dog is better than a dead lion.* (*Shabbat* 30b)

The lion, of course, is the king, the lion of Judah; in this can be inferred the same obligation that we have to feed our animals before we are fed, and even *Shabbat* obligations can be broken rather than allow an animal under our care to go hungry that day. In fact, the *Mishnah* opens with exclusions to the obligation not to extinguish the Sabbath lamp—"because he is afraid of Gentiles, robbers, or an evil spirit, or for the sake of an invalid, that he should sleep." The implication is more profound, however; for even a carcass may be cut up for the benefit of the living animals, and no impurities result. It is quite an amazing passage, and demonstrates, when all is said and done, the Torah's view toward kindness to animals.

The story of King David studying Torah unceasingly to avoid succumbing has several versions, including David's own rescue of a woman falling out of the tree, the king calling out or even leaping through the window to her rescue. The picture of the spry king is in sharp contrast to that presented in 1 Kings. "Our Rabbis taught: Three copulated in the ark, and they were all punished—the dog, the raven, and Ham. The dog was doomed to be tied . . ." (*Sanhedrin* 108b).

In *Midrash Rabbah* (*Vayikrah, Behar* 33:6) a discussion of idol worship leads the Rabbis to recall a disputation between Nebuchadnezzar and the three Isaraelites thrown into the fiery furnace (Shadrach, Meshach, and Abed-nego, Daniel 3:16). In a technique the Rabbis were all too familiar with, the king of the province or country attempts to use Torah verses out of context against the Jews. In these stories, the Jews always repartee with appropriate rhetoric to defeat the fallacy; alas, throughout the Middle Ages, it was not always the case. Here the discourse concerns the line in Deuteronomy 4:28, "And there ye shall serve gods the work of men's hands" (". . . should you act wickedly and make for yourselves a sculptured image in any likeness, causing the Lord your God displeasure and vexation [v. 25] . . . The Lord will scatter you among the peoples . . . [v.27] There you will serve man-made gods of wood and stone, that cannot see or hear or eat or smell," JPS). The three rhetors defeat the a priori argument by demonstrating that "gods" means "taxes."

> You are our *"King"* only as regards taxes . . . but in this matter of which you speak to us [i.e., that he is also to be their new god] you are just "Nebuchadnezzar" [sans the honorific "King"]). You and a dog are alike to us! O Nebuchadnezzar, bark . . . like a dog, swell . . . like a pitcher . . . chirp . . . like a cricket. . . . Thereupon he barked like a dog, swelled . . .

In *Kiddushin* 39b, we find one of the few mentions of Elisha ben Abuyah, the notorious apostate Rabbi who became known as Acher, the other one. Elisha was a brilliant student of R. Joshua's and, so far as we can tell, was R. Meier's teacher. Yet because of one or two incidents serving catalyst to a life-long crisis of faith, he not only shunned completely the tradition, he went over to the Roman side and gave every insight to the prefects as to how to destroy Judaism, or so the legend goes. The most popular story of the catalyst event involves him watching a young boy climb a tree to wave the mother bird away and take the eggs, as commanded in Deuteronomy 22:6, wherein one is promised long life; instead Elisha observed the lad fall to his death. This passage, however, offers an alternate incident.

> Now, what happened with Acher? . . . Others say, he saw the tongue of Chuzpith the Interpreter dragged along by a swine. "The mouth that uttered pearls licks the dust!" he exclaimed. [Thereupon] he went forth and sinned.

The *Midrash*'s version of the story, however, differs in terms of both the animal and the personage. It is found in *Shelach*. Again, it relates the story of the young man and the mother bird, with two variants—the first Jew desecrates the *Shabbat* and the *mitzvah* by taking the mother bird, and nothing happens to him; the second observes the *mitzvah*, is bitten by a snake on the way down, and dies.

> Others say that he became totally bewildered at the sight of R. Yehuda Hannachtom's tongue. This Sage had been slain and, while his corpse was lying on the ground, a dog nibbled off his tongue.
> "How is it possible that the tongue that studied so much Torah should be thus disgraced?" Elisha thought. "If this was the cruel end of this holy Sage, there is no hope for anyone else, because most people's sins are greater than were R. Yehuda Hanachtom's." (Weissman, p. 197)

The *Midrash* points out the traditional flaw in Elisha's reasoning, that he ignored the mystery in God's design, and our progression toward *Olam Habah*, the World to Come.

In either version of the story of the slain sage, the implication is a martydom, at the hands of the Romans. The Martyrology, of course, is read on the afternoon of Yom Kippur. This presents an odd quality to the story, however. The horrific deaths of the sages were one of the Roman institutions brought about through the treachery of Elisha. Was his shock at the dog's (or swine's) action truly the moment of his rejection, or is there creeping through the stories a hint of Elisha's regret of the terrible thing he had done?

Although fiction, a brilliant "biography" of Elisha ben Abuyah's lifelong crisis of faith, how he almost destroyed Judaism, and how the Rabbis rescued Judaism may be found in Rabbi Milton Steinberg's brilliant, disturbing, and landmark "novel," *Like a Driven Leaf*. At the end of the book, Meir is called out to Elisha's grave, which has just been struck by lightening and exposed. Confused, Elisha's pupil, in one final act of regard to his teacher, drapes his own cloak over the grave.

> Thunder rolled in the misty vault of the heavens. From the cemetery down the hill, from the grave at his feet and from out dead yesterdays ghosts came stealing. And he wept not alone for his master, but for himself as well, for a woman who rarely smiled, for sweet children who slept near by, for a people crushed and persecuted, for all the sons of men, their aches of the body and soul, and their dreams that die. (P. 477)

There are more scholarly treatises, of course; in these Elysha is given a lesser role, while Rufus, the cruel, uncompromising prefect in the novel treatment, is cast aside as insignificant. For example, Morrison, relying on the ancient histories, places the cruel edicts forbidding Jewish ritual observance at the feet of "jurists in Rome," Hadrian's general Severus, and Hadrian himself (see especially pp. 181–206 and those following). But the Jewish tradition that Elysha was the Benedict Arnold persists.

There is a charming reference in the Apocrypha that transcends the ancient world to our own time. Any number of us recall joyous times walking along the way and our good canine friends running up to greet us or simply tagging along after us, sniffing their own world, but also keeping a close tab on us, so as not to be left too far behind.

This small but significant reference is found in the Book of

Tobit (11:4), the tale that smacks a bit of Job, and a bit of the Prodigal Son story found in the New Testament. Tobias, Tobit's son, was feared lost and perished, and then at last returns home. And upon his return, that most faithful of all companions accompanies him: "So they went, and the dog went along after them" (Goodspeed, p. 124).

Trachtenberg recounts some old folk mythology, probably medieval, held about the dog.

> . . . Ritually unclean animals which see at night, such as dogs, cats and mice, have no vision at all until they are nine days old. . . . food remains in a dog's stomach for three days, so that it can go that long unfed. In our ignorance we may believe that dogs follow the scent of an animal upon the ground, but a "true investigation" revealed that it is not the odor but the breath of the animal upon the ground that the dog picks up; some bright hares are aware of this and outwit the dogs by keeping their snouts in the air as they race to their hiding-place. (P. 184)

Even Nadich, in recounting the Legends, and reviewing the rabbinic literature, misses the flaw in considering the dog as only recently domesticated. As we now know, the animal's domestication, or, more accurately, symbiotic relationship with us, goes back even beyond the known ancient world.

> . . . The dog was called "a wild beast" because in ancient times dogs were semi-wild and not fully domesticated. Two different dogs are mentioned in rabbinic literature—the ordinary dog, described by Rabbi Meir as a domestic animal, and the Cyprian dog, resembling a fox, called a wild animal. . . . (P. 178, n. 68)

Recalling again the first talmudic story, of King David's death, apparently the connection between dogs and lions circulated throughout the Middle East and occasionally is found in other cultures. In Jean M. Auel's *Clan of the Cave Bear* novel series, the stalwart heroine Ayla rides the grown lion she rescued as a cub (recalling the Androcles legends) while her domesticated half-wild wolf-dog dashes alongside. See especially *The Mammoth Hunters*, where the heroine has her wolf-turning-to-dog in the Lion Camp (pp. 548–550 are particularly interesting in terms of describing the thesis of the domestication of wolves into dogs). Again, as we have seen, it represents only one school of thought. A more academic view of the lion-dog connection is presented by Graves.

> Orthrus . . . who fathered the Chimaera, the Sphinx . . . , the Hydra . . . , and the Nemean Lion . . . on Echidne was Sirius, the Dog-star, which inaugurated the Athenian new year. He had two heads, like Janus, because the reformed year, at Athens, had two seasons. . . . Orthrus's son, the Lion, emblemizing (sic) the first half, and his daughter, the serpent, emblemizing the second. (P. 130, Vol. 1)

An Additional Talmud Tail (*Sanhedrin* 60b, 63b)

The *Mishnah* details the offenses of idol worship for which one could receive capitol punishment or lashes. This *Gemarah* is interesting in that it identifies the various animals the Assyrians and Babylonians worshiped as idols. In the case of the dog, Soncino points out that the text may be a variant, of *Nibchaz*, viz. NVCH, interpreted as "Bark," thus (The) "dog is perceived as the animal indicated."

> And the men of Babylon made Succoth-benoth. What is this?—a fowl . . . of Cuth made Nergal . . . — A cock. . . . of Chamath made Ashina . . . —a bald buck. . . . the Avites made Nibhaz and Tartak, . . . —a dog and an ass.

To indicate how far along was the people's worship of idols, the *Gemarah* continues with the story of Elijah the Righteous, who discovers an orphan, "Faint with hunger lying upon a dungheap." When Elijah attempts to teach the child the *Shema* prayer, the child tries to silence him as he was taught, brings forth his idol, embraces it and kisses it. Thereupon, "his stomach burst. His idol fell to the earth, and he upon it, thus fulfilling the verse (in Leviticus 26:30), 'And I shall cast your carcasses upon the carcasses of your idols.'"

Now, it may seem curious that Elijah didn't first attempt to take the child away from the terrible effluvia and cleanse and feed him—but it is important to keep in mind the story is, of course, also an allegory. Elijah's walk-about is intended purposefully to assist those afflicted and try to give them the means to help themselves. Saying the *Shema* protects one and that is why, after all, we recite it before we go to bed.

In *Avodah Zarah* 2, regarding the injunction that a woman should not find herself alone with cattle, R. Joseph learns in the *Gemarah*: "A widow should not rear dogs, nor accommodate a student as a guest." Clearly, this is concerning her own modesty's sake but a discussion arises since it is clear in the case of the student, but not so clear in the case of the dog (22b).

. . . AND A *MIDRASH*

Genesis Rabbah, *Veyeshev* 84:5: From the passage, "And Jacob dwelt in the land of his father's sojournings." R. Hunia said: "This may be compared to a man who saw a pack of dogs and being afraid of them he sat down among them. Thus, Jacob resides among the kings of Edom and with Esau, so as not to appear afraid, lest they pounce upon him."

24

Q U A I L

QUAIL
Hebrew *S(sh)'LaV*

*On the evening quail appeared and covered the
camp; in the morning there was a fall of dew about
the camp.*

—Exodus 16:13

Coturnix coturnix: Latin, a quail. Common quail.

As it inhabits a wide range through Europe and Asia, it needs to fly across the Mediterranean, a long, exhausting journey for any bird, but especially for one not a particularly efficient flier.

CONCORDANCE

Numbers 11:31–32.
Psalms IV–105:40 (They asked, and He brought quail).

The famous passage of the quails is set against the background of more grumbling by the Israelites in the desert, this time about not having enough flesh to eat. Moses scolds them, then indicates how they would soon have so much it will extrude through their nostrils, and the birds lying at their feet.

Although the animal is not mentioned by name, the implication is also clear in Psalms 78:26–30.

> He set the east wind moving in heaven and drove the south wind by His might. He rained meat on them like dust, winged birds like the sands of the sea, making them come down inside His camp. They ate till they were sated, He gave them what they craved. They had not yet wearied of what they craved, the food was still in their mouths when God's anger flared up at them. He slew their sturdiest, struck down the youth of Israel. (JPS, p. 1200)

Anyone who has eaten too much of a good thing can understand all that being struck down entails.

There is another implication here. Remember, Moses tracked through the desert extensively long before he returned as the deliverer from Egypt. He could easily have become familiar, as part of his desert-craft, of the long migration of the quails across the Mediterranean Sea, and the seasonal time of their exhausted arrival. This cycle still occurs today. (See *Encyclopedia Judaica*, Vol. 13, p. 1420.)

> The phenomenon repeats itself in spring and in fall when large flocks of quail pass over the Mediterranean Sea on the migration from northern countries to Africa in fall and on their return in spring. Weary from their lengthy flight, the flocks settle on the southern coast of the country (between Gaza and El-Arish) to be caught in nets spread out before they settle . . . Until the 1940s millions of quails were caught in this way at these seasons but their number has since decreased.

See also Josephus, *Antiquities*, 3:25: "(Flocks of quails from the Arabian gulf) came flying over this stretch of sea, and, alike wearied by their flight and withal accustomed more than other birds to skim the ground, settled in the Hebrews' camp."

AN ADDITIONAL TALMUD TAIL (*Sanhedrin* 17a)

The first *Mishnah* of *Sanhedrin* is a rather extensive delineation of where and under what circumstances the greater and lesser

Sanhedrins and courts would convene, when concerning capital sentences upon certain animals such as the ox, wolf, leopard, lion, bear, hyena, and serpent—in a way a curious list since an ox is neither wild nor a predator, allowing, of course, it deals with the one that gored.

The *Gemarah* proceeds after some time to evolve into a discussion of what it was that Eldad and Medad prophesied (Numbers 11:26). Among some opinions—Moses would die and Joshua would lead the people into the land. "Abba Hanim said on authority of R. Eliezer: They prophesied concerning the matter of the quails, [saying]: 'Arise, quail; arise quail.'"

25

WORMS

WORMS (Maggots in Other Translations)
Hebrew *To(V)La'*

*But they paid no attention to Moses; some of them
left of it until morning, and it became infested with
[worms; JPS, maggots: for a fuller treatment,
see number 75] and stank. And Moses was angry
with them.*

—Exodus 16:20, 24.

CONCORDANCE

Deuteronomy 28:39.
Isaiah 14:11; 66:24.
Jonah 4:7 (But the next day at dawn God provided a worm, which attacked
the plant so that it withered).
Job 7:5 (My flesh is clothed with worms and clods of dust); 17:14; 21:26;
(They lie down alike in the dust and the worms covereth them); 24:20;
25:6.

The main regard to the lowly but astonishingly important
worm in the Bible and rabbinic texts concerns disease-infested
food (and some proposed cures for ingesting them) and as a
metaphor. Although left out of the Concordance, since it does
not involve the animal directly, this metaphorical usage is
nowhere better expressed than in Isaiah 41:14: "Fear not, O
worm Jacob,/O men of (or maggots of) Israel;/ I will help you"
(JPS 703).

The law of hyssop . . . For what is it eaten?—[As a remedy] for worms. With what is it eaten?—With seven black dates. By what is [the disease of worms] caused?—Through [eating] barley-flour forty days old.

But one may eat *yo'ezer* (a certain plant, perhaps unknown to us today) . . . [As a remedy] for worms in the bowels. . . . through [eating] raw meat and [drinking] water on an empty stomach . . . (*Shabbat* 109b)

The *Mishnah* to this passage begins, "We may not eat Greek hyssop on the Sabbath, because it is not the food of healthy people."

. . . not only the earthworm, but any elongated crawling creature, such as the maggot, caterpillar, larva of an insect, and the like. Thus, in the account of the "worms" which appeared in the manna the terms evidently refer to caterpillars which feed on putrefying matter while the "worms" described as destroying vineyards and the gourd (in Jonah) were some variety of beetle or insect larvae, and the "worms" in Isaiah and Job . . . were maggots or larvae which feed on dead bodies. (Singer, Vol. 12, pp. 559–560)

In *Sanhedrin*, the *Mishnah* discusses the generation of the flood, which "has no portion in the future world, nor will they stand at the [last] judgment . . . (for) the Lord scattered them abroad from thence upon the face of all the earth . . ." The *Gemarah* provides a fascinating disputation between Eliezer (Abraham's servant) and Shem, Noah's eldest son. It is not only remarkable for the heritage of the Yeshiva of Shem (to which, by tradition, the patriarchs and matriarchs attended), but also for its explanation of the dietary habits of a most unique creature.

He replied, "[In truth] we had much trouble in the ark. The animals which are usually fed by day we fed by day; and those normally fed by night we fed by night. But my father did not know what was the food of the chameleon. One day he was sitting and cutting up a pomegranate, when a worm dropped out of it, which [the chameleon] consumed. From then onward he mashed up bran for it, and when it became wormy, it devoured it." (108b)

The Bible and talmudic texts are not the only ancient references to the distraction or the beneficence of worms. Pritchard presents an Akkadian or Hurrian healing invocation. Dental problems, then, like now, seem to reside in mysterious etiologies. This ANET is entitled, "A Cosmological Incantation: The Worm and the Toothache."

> After Anu [had created heaven],
> Heaven had created [the earth]
> The earth had created the rivers,
> The rivers had created the canals,
> The canals had created the marsh,
> (And) the marsh had created the worm—
> The worm went, weeping, before Shamash,
> His tears flowing before Ea:
> "What wilt thou give for my food?
> What wilt thou give me for my sucking?"
> "I shall give thee the ripe fig,
> (And) the apricot."
> "Of what use are they to me, the ripe fig
> And the apricot?
> Lift me up and among the teeth
> And the gums cause me to dwell!
> The blood of the tooth I will suck,
> And of the gum I will gnaw
> Its *roots*!"
> (There follows the instruction to the dentist.)
> Fix the pin and seize its foot.
> Because thou hast said this, O worm,
> May Ea smite thee with the might of his hand!
>   (Vol. 1, p. 74)

"One who cuts a worm while slicing a radish should cut away the cut surface of the radish. . . . The knife requires *ne'itzah* (being thrust in the ground to cleanse it from impropriety)" (Forst, p. 332).

One of the most remarkable creatures of all in Jewish

legends, rabbinical writings, and folklore is the Shamir, the small, hard-encased worm, apparently endowed with a powerful cutting edge on its underbelly. Moses and Aaron used it to etch the hard precious stones of the High Priest's breastplate, and Solomon used it to cut the stones for the building of the foundation of the *Beit Hamikdash*, the First Great Holy Temple in Jerusalem. The next animal in the line-up is the eagle, who makes a brief appearance here, thus soaring to a segue. The fullest treatment is given in Ginsberg, Vol. 1.

> The shamir was made at twilight on the sixth day of creation together with other extraordinary things. It is about as large as a barley corn, and it possesses the remarkable property of cutting the hardest of diamonds. For this reason it was used for the stones in the breastplate worn by the high priest. First the names of the twelve tribes were traced with ink on the stones to be set into the breastplate, then the shamir was passed over the lines, and thus they were graven. The wonderful circumstance was that the friction wore no particles from the stones. The shamir was also used for hewing into shape the stones from which the Temple was built, because the law prohibited iron tools to be used for the work in the Temple. The shamir may not be put in an iron vessel for safe-keeping, nor in any metal vessel, it would burst such a receptacle asunder. It is kept wrapped up in a woolen cloth, and this in turn is placed in a lead basket filled with barley bran. The shamir was guarded in Paradise until Solomon needed it. He sent the eagle thither to fetch the worm. With the destruction of the Temple the shamir vanished. (34)
>
> The *Shamir* (sic), now extinct, was a worm of great hardness, a barleycorn in size, which cleaves large stones when it crawls over them. . . . Our Sages . . . assign the following reason for (the iron tool) prohibition: "For iron was created to shorten man's days, while the altar was created to lengthen man's days: what shortens [life] may not rightly be lifted against what lengthens." And the Sages say again . . . "With the destruction of the Temple, the

Shamir worm ceased to exist." (*Pirke Avot* 5:9, Goldin, pp. 77–78)

The *Mishnah* lists the other "extraordinary things" created on the eve of *Shabbat* at twilight:

Ten things . . . the mouth of the earth, the mouth of the well, the mouth of the she-ass, the rainbow, the manna, the rod, the shamir, the letters, the writing, and the Tables [of stone]. Some add: The evil spirits, the sepulcher of Moses, and the ram of Abraham our father. Some add: The tongs made with the tongs.

The maw of the earth is that which swallowed up Korach, during the rebellion in the desert; the well is Miriam's well, which, by tradition, followed the Israelites for the years of their wanderings; the mouth of the donkey is Bilam's talking donkey, which saw the Angel of the Lord before he did; the Tables are the Tablets Moses brought down from Mount Sinai.

Why Tongs to draw out tongs? When tongs are withdrawn from a smith's fire, they have to be withdrawn by other tongs, for the heat is conducted to the handles and would severely burn the smith's hands. But there had to have been a first set in order to pull the second set out. (M. Schwartz)

In *Pesahim* 54a, following the *Mishnah* wherein one may light a lamp for the holiday period on the eve of the holiday (so to leave it burning throughout) ["Where it is the practice to light a lamp (at home) on erev Yom Kippur, one must light one, where not . . . not. One must light in Synagogues, Schoolhouses, dark alleys, and for the sake of invalids"]—the "ten things" and their additions are in a slightly different arrangement:

Well, ram, rainbow, writing, writing instruments, Tables, Sepulcher of Moses, the cave in which Moses and Elijah (beheld) the Glory of the Lord, opening of the ass's mouth, opening of the earth to swallow the rebels. R. Nehemiah said in his father's name: Also

fire and the mule. R. Josiah said in his father's name:
Also the ram and the *shamir* (sic).

See also: *Middot* 3, 4; *Sotah* 9, 12; and *Gittin* 68a. The *pasuk* in Exodus 20:22 is the one that prohibits the use of iron: "And if you make for me an altar of stones, do not build it of hewn stones; for by wielding your tool upon them you have profaned them." It is one of the 613 *mitzvot*. Taryag comments:

> It is forbidden to build an altar of stones which have been touched by (a) metal [instrument]. An altar built of such stones is unfit, and offerings may not be brought upon it. Stones used for the Altar had to be perfectly smooth. Also they had to be brought from the depths of the earth or from the sea where they could not have been touched by iron. The instrument used to paint [whiten] the Altar twice a year did not contain iron, so that no iron touch the Altar.

Apparently, there was a "mysterious" small implement used to hew some stones, which was not ironwork. Perhaps it was a special stone, like a diamond (which could be about the size of a barleycorn); and, following the destruction of the First Temple, it disappeared. For the building of the Second Temple, it was suspected for some time, and modern archaeology has verified, that many of these same stones were used in its construction.

Gesenius traces the root of S(H)MYR to "destroy, annihilate"; the breaking of stone could be seen. Gesenius also indicates "sharp," and "hard" or "firm," and includes the metaphorical sense as *adamant*, or *firm as a prophet's heart* (Ezekiel 3:9; Zachariah 7:12). He also references 1 Chronicles (24:24: "The remaining Levites . . . the sons of Micah: Shamir"). He does not indicate that it is the same root as "keep" or "guard" (Gesenius, pp. 1088–1089 [SH'MYR]; JPS, pp. 895–896, 1089, 1565; TO[V]RaH N'v[B]aY'YM CHTOO[V]v[B]'M SHin Tet).

In *Vayikra*, Leviticus, 16:13, the High Priest receives his instruction on entering the Holy of Holies of Yom Kippur. "He should place the incense on the fire before the Lord . . ." In the Second Temple period, there grew up a dispute between the

Sadducees and the Sages over whether this meant igniting the
fire pan outside the inner sanctum, or waiting and lighting it
within. Except for one instance, the High Priest followed the
way of the Sages, and all went well. However, there was once a
High Priest who was a Sadducee and followed his movement's
way.

> The sages relate that before long, this *Kohen Gadol*
> died. He was found in the garbage heap, with worms
> and maggots crawling out of his nose. They were
> crawling out of his nose because it was the first part
> of the body that had entered the Holy of Holies.
>   Some give another reason. He had sinned with
> the fragrance of the incense, so he was punished with
> his nose. (*Likutei Pishatim*, *Acharei Mot-Kedoshim*;
> see also *Yoma* 19a, b)

In one of his discourses, to "worm" his way out of a clear
indication that he has gone over to the Gentiles, Sabbatai
(T)Sevi's rhetoric used an analogy of the worms that burrow
into fruits. In Scholem's definitive work, the caliphate is
indicated by its closer transliterated form.

> . . . The messiah descended into the realm of the
> *qelippah* in order to destroy it from within. Only by
> feigning submission to the *qelippah* could he achieve
> his purpose of utterly destroying it. This stratagem
> or "holy ruse" can be compared to the action of a
> worm in a tree that appears healthy from outside
> but, when split open, is seen to be worm-eaten.
> Wherefore it is utterly impossible for any creature to
> comprehend the ways of his actions, and whoever
> says that he understands the ways of the messianic
> king is completely mistaken. (P. 802)

Although all animals and plants are vital for the biodiver-
sity and life of our planet, none is more important than the
seemingly lowly earthworm. Earthworms protect, rehabilitate,
and manufacture our soils; and they can do this out of the
effluvia and excrement of the other creatures, including ourselves. In this sense, the worm may be the last great hope of
our pollution-filled planet.

AN ADDITIONAL TALMUD TAIL (*Avodah Zorah* 42b–43b)

Mishnah:

> If one finds utensils upon which is the figure of the
> sun or moon or a dragon. He casts them into the salt
> sea. Rabban Simeon b. Gamaliel says: If it is upon
> (certain) utensils they are prohibited, but if upon
> common utensils they are permitted.

Soncino indicates this was a pendent attachment to a
utensil, probably, for the most part, the handles.

It is a rather astonishing *Mishnah*, and even more so in the
tract devoted to the prohibition of idol worship. In the
Mishnah, and in the *Gemarah*, we find graven images that are
permissible, even to the rendering of some of the heavenly
host—but only those in the lower of the seven realms; and
again, in keeping with the *Mishnah*, not when the utensils are
utilitarian. "This is to include the ministering angels! . . . But if
it is a matter of serving them, even a tiny worm is also
[prohibited]!"

26

EAGLE

EAGLE
Hebrew *NeSHaR*

> *You have seen what I did to the Egyptians, how I bore you on eagles' wings and brought you to Me.*
>
> —Exodus 19:4

Aquila chrysaltos: Aquila, Latin, an eagle; Khrusos, Greek, gold; Aetos, Greek, an eagle. The golden eagle.

Actually, the color is dark tawny to brown; but the adult does exhibit a golden crown and nape.

The most widespread of the large eagles, now rare in the Middle East—but they were more locally prolific in those days and what better magnificence to credit with carrying the Children of Israel upon its own wings. The size generally reaches the largest of the great eagles and vultures (excepting the condors).

CONCORDANCE

Deuteronomy 32:11.
2 Samuel 1:23 (swifter than eagles).
Jeremiah 49:16.
Ezekiel 1:10 (see numbers 13, 16, 88); 10:14 (see number 16); 17:3, 7.

Obadiah 1:4 (Though thou make thy nest as high as the eagle).

Psalms IV–103:5 (. . . thy youth is revered like the eagle).

Proverbs 23:5 (. . . For riches certainly make themselves wings,/Like an eagle that flieth toward heaven); 30:19 (see number 2).

Lamentations 4:19 (Our pursuers were swifter than the eagle of the heaven . . .).

Daniel 4:30 (. . . till his [i.e., Nebuchednezzar] hair was grown like eagle's feathers . . .); 7:4 (see number 16 [But see esp. number 88]).

Among the most lyrical and meaningful of biblical passages and metaphors is the image of the Israelites being borne out from Egypt on eagle's wings, as a mother raptor would carry her young in teaching them to fly. Eagles, vultures, condors, and other large raptors and carrion eaters soar higher and farther than any birds. It might have seemed to the ancients that they approached the very vault of heaven, and thus the simile has an even greater, higher, mystical concept. In recent years, in our own country, attempts to rescue and preserve the Bald Eagle and the Golden Eagle, symbols of our nation, have proven significantly successful. In spring and autumn, it is not uncommon to observe them along the Missouri and Platte River waterways, nesting, hunting, soaring. In truth they are magnificent creatures.

Encyclopedia Judaica (Vol. 6) points out a variant in the translation.

> Biblical passages . . . ascribe to the *nesher* characteristics that do not belong to the eagle, such as feeding on carcasses and having a bald head (?) and already R. Tam pointed out the mistake of regarding it as the eagle (*Tosefta* to *Chullin* 63a). The biblical (sic) *nesher* is the griffon vulture . . . although its traditional identification as an eagle was accepted by the sages of the Talmud who applied the word to the Roman eagle. (P. 338)

Toperoff (p. 59) also emphasizes this view, pointing out the traditionally held viewpoint that no bird flies higher than the griffon vulture. In actuality, ornithologists are in dispute, although outside the Middle East, condors are usually given the nod. Fox, however, translates as "eagle." "You yourselves

have seen/ what I did to Egypt,/ how I bore you on eagles'
wings and brought you to me" (p. 365).

The usurpation of this magnificent symbol of God lifting
the Israelites upon wings of glory by the Roman establishment
for its guidon emblem made it all the more difficult and ironic
to the Rabbis. *Sanhedrin* 12a describes an obvious reference to
members of the Great Assembly being detained and even captured by a Roman centurion or platoon. Apparently, through
their wits, they managed to escape. They were carrying
important items; "purple," no doubt for the fringes of daily and
prayer shawls.

> . . . Was not a message once sent to Raba, "A couple
> [of scholars] have arrived from Rakkath who had
> been captured by an eagle while in possession of
> articles manufactured at Luz, such as purple, yet
> through Divine mercy and their own merits they
> escaped safely.

Soncino points out that "Rakkath" was probably another
name for Tiberias.

In the ancient story of the warrior-king Gilgamesh, the
moment of his companion's death is among the most poignant
scenes in all of literature, and the great, soaring raptor is
appropriately indicated.

> Gilgamesh, weeping, mourned for Enkidu:
> "It is Enkidu, the companion, whom I weep for"
> . . .
> Gilgamesh touched the heart of the companion.
> There was nothing at all. Gilgamesh covered
> Enkidu's face with a veil like the veil of a bride.
> He hovered like an eagle over the body,
> Or as a lioness does over her brood.
>   (Ferry, pp. 44–45)

An Additional Talmud Tail (*Chullin* 59a, 61b)

The *Mishnah* recalls that the characteristics of mammals are
indicated in Torah, but those of birds are not. Of course, it has
not been difficult to discern that predators represent a large

forbidden category. In any event, the *Gemarah* uses the eagle as an example: ". . . The Divine Law . . . specified the eagle to teach you that you may not eat the eagle as it has none of the characteristics of cleanness, but whatsoever has one characteristic you may eat."

In 60b–61a, we learn these characteristics of the unclean and the clean: "The eagle . . . has neither an extra toe nor a crop, its gizzard cannot be peeled, it seizes prey and eats it . . . turtle doves . . . (have) an extra toe and a crop, its gizzard can be peeled, it does not seize prey and eat it . . ."

27

SEAL

SEAL (or Dugong [Sea Cow])
Hebrew *TaCHaSH*

> *tanned ram skins, [dolphin] [seal] [dugong] skins,*
> *and acacia wood;*
> —Exodus 25:5

The King James version lists *badgers*; however, the Masoretic Text's translation is, as indicated, "sealskins." JPS indicates "dolphin," but notes an alternate, "Dugong," indicating that the Hebrew is uncertain (123).

CONCORDANCE

Exodus 26:14; 35:7, 23; 36:19; 39:34.
Numbers 4:6, 10–12, 14.

The Masoretic Text prefers *seal*. The best guess, therefore, of these creatures found with perhaps the widest range of all mammals—North Pole to South Pole, East Pole to West Pole—is *Monachus albiventer*, the Mediterranean Seal. As its common name implies, its habitat lies in the Mediterranean Sea and its environs, although it has been known to extend its range into adjacent areas of the Atlantic Ocean. The animal feeds largely on fish, crustaceans, mollusks, and echinoderms. A curious, albeit well-rounded inclusion of their diet is grapes; and the creature reportedly ventures some distance inland to raid vineyards. If true, this odd behavior would render it susceptible to capture by enraptured men and women requiring the skins to include in the covering of a holy *Mishkan* (Tabernacle).

There is also reason to support the translation of dugong (*Halicon*), although these animals maintain a strictly marine existence. Still, they have been known to investigate estuaries of the Red Sea and so become ensnared in proximate shallow bays.

Their closest relative is the manatee, which they resemble, in size (about eight feet in length), in bulk considerable, and in color (brown to gray). The tails differ, the dugong's forming a crescent, the manatee's flowing round. The male has tusk-like incisors perhaps nine inches in length, directed down, like those of a walrus.

Fox avoids the problem altogether (or disputes it completely), preferring "tanned leather" skins.

28

B U L L

BULL (and see numbers 11, 12)

*This is what you shall do to them in consecrating
them to serve Me as priests. Take a young bull of the
herd and two rams without blemish;*

—Exodus 29:1

Bos taurus: Latin, bull. The domestic bovine, male.

CONCORDANCE

Genesis 24:5; 29:1, 3, 10–12, 14, 36.

Leviticus 1:5; 4:4–5, 8, 11, 14–16, 20-21; 8:2, 14, 17; 9:2; 16:3, 6, 11, 14–15, 18, 27; 23:18.

Numbers 7:15; 21, 27, 33, 39, 45, 51, 57, 63, 69, 75, 81, 87–88; 8:8; 15:8–9, 11, 24; 23:1–2, 4, 13, 29–30; 28:11, 14, 19–20, 28; 29:2, 8–9, 13–14, 17–18, 20–21, 23–24, 26–27, 29–30, 32–33, 36–37; 33:17.

Judges 6:25–26, 28.

1 Samuel 1:24–25.

Isaiah 1:11; 34:7.

Jeremiah 50:27 (Slay all her bulls); 52:20 (. . . and the twelve brazen bulls that were under the bases . . .)

Ezekiel 39:18 (see numbers 3, 7, 8); 43:19, 21–23, 25; 45:18, 22–24; 46:6–7, 11.

Hosea 12:12 (In Gilgal they sacrifice unto bulls); 14:3 (See we will render for bulls the offering of our lips). Psalms I–22:13 (Many bulls have encompassed me); II–50:9, 13 (see number 13); 51:21 (Then will they offer bulls upon thine altar [David's psalm of repentance]); 66:15 (see numbers 7, 8); 68:31 (see number 11); 69:32 (And it [praise] shall please the Lord better than a bull).

Job 21:10; 42:8 (see number 8).

Ezra 6:17 (see also numbers 3, 7, 8); 7:7 (See also numbers 3, 8); 8:35 (see also numbers 3, 7, 8).

1 Chronicles 15:26 (see number 8); 29:21 (see numbers 3, 8).

2 Chronicles 13:9 (see number 8); 29:21 (see numbers 3, 7, 8)–22 (see also number 8), 32 (see numbers 3, 8); 30:24 (see number 3); 35:7 (see also numbers 3, 7).

AN ADDITIONAL TALMUD TAIL (*Nazir* 5:1)

In what at first reading seems like one of the few cases in which Beth Shamai shows more leniency than Beth Hillel, the *Mishnah* indicates consecration: ". . . If someone says, 'The black bull that leaves my house first shall be sacred,' and a white one emerges B. Shammai declare it sacred, but B. Hillel say it is not sacred."

In actuality, however, upon closer study, we recognize that B. Hillel is more lenient, since both would be required for Temple offering under B. Shamai's ruling (that is, the hardship of requiring no substitution is abrogated by B. Hillel, and he can retain at least one of his bulls. Thus, vows in intent and word have to be the same or they are "mistaken," and thus invalid [see Leviticus 27:33]). As it happens, there are only six times when Hillel is more stringent than Shamai, including the consideration of the blood of animals that die naturally, and some laws of *shechita*, ritual slaughter; see also the opening four (some say five) *Mishnahs* of Eduyot.

An interpretation is customarily offered here as well, considering Jephtah's daughter (Judges 11); had Jephtah followed Hillel instead of Shamai, he could have offered a substitute and abrogated the sacrifice of his daughter.

. . . AND A *MIDRASH* (*Rabbah Leviticus, Emor* 28:8–9)

The question is raised, why was a (bullock) given the honor of the first offering? R. Levi explained that it was like the case of a false rumor concerning intimacy of a gentleman and a lady. Once the king found no substance in the rumor, he placed them at the head of the table for all to see the truth. "In the same way the nations of the world taunted Israel and said to them: You made the Golden Calf! 'The Holy One, Blessed be He, investigated their words and did not find any substance in them. For this reason the bullock was placed first among all the offerings.'" This may be an allusion to the tradition that it was the mixed multitude and not the Israelites who were responsible for the golden calf.

29

TURTLEDOVE

TURTLEDOVE (see Dove, Pigeon)
—Leviticus 1:14

Streptopelia turtur: S., Greek, a necklace; *turtur*, Latin, a turtle dove.

CONCORDANCE

Leviticus 5:7, 11.
Numbers 6:10.
Jeremiah 8:7 (see numbers 79, 81).
Song of Songs 2:12 (. . . and the voice of the turtle-dove is heard in our land . . .).

The same or similar animal as the dove, which Pinney calls the most important bird in the Bible (p. 150). The author meant, of course, concerning the story of Noah. However, that the turtledove as a symbol for peace throughout all time may have rendered his opinion stronger than even he suspected.

AN ADDITIONAL TALMUD TAIL (*Menahoth* 64b–65a)

This *Gemarah* discusses a case wherein three women brought three distinct pairs of doves to expiate their menses' *tamei* state. Mordecai, one of the members of the Sanhedrin, renders an opinion concerning the coincidence.

> Perhaps the one had been in danger by reason of her flux, the other . . . by reason of a sea journey, and the third . . . by an infection of the eye, and therefore all the doves are to be offered for burnt offerings.
> (See also *Chullin* 60b–61a, under *Eagle*.)

30

ROCK-BADGER

ROCK-BADGER (Eurasian Badger) (JPS, Daman; Fox, Hyrax)
Heb. *SHaPHaN*

> *The Daman (JPS, p. 168)—although it chews the cud, it has no true hoofs, you shall not eat; the camel—although it chews the cud, it has no true hoofs; it is unclean for you;*
>
> —Leviticus 11:5

Meles meles: Latin, a badger. It is the only member of the genus I find with a range including the Middle East.

CONCORDANCE

Deuteronomy 14:7.
Proverbs 30:26 (The rock-badgers are but a feeble folk,/Yet make they their houses in the crags).

Like many creatures, there are various names, based on variants of translation. Others render "coney," and "saphan"; the daman, hyrax, coney, and saphan are probably the same rodent/rabbit–like creature, and may be more accurate than a badger-like animal.

In the nineteenth century, it was not an altogether un-common practice for English-speaking gentlemen and gentle-women adventurers to take guided and unguided discovery tours of the Middle East, Egypt, and other parts of North Africa, often in attempts to uncover the truth of mysterious passages. In fact, much Egyptology, and Near East archaeology of significant origin was generated from these initial forays. Some are quite famous, resulting in magnificent discoveries cherished even today; others, albeit productive and no less perilous, are more obscure. In the early part of the century, a traveler named Bruce felt that he had unlocked the mystery of the animal he called the Ashkoko. Found in a rare book, *Calmet's Dictionary of the Holy Bible*, Bruce's description in-dicates that he may have located this elusive and multi-translated creature. Of course, in our own time of stressing each animal's biological niche, rare and elusive animals are much harder to find.

> This curious animal is found in Ethiopia, in the caverns of the rocks, or under the great stones in the Mountain . . . It is also frequent in the deep caverns of the rock in many places in Abyssinia. It does not burrow or make holes . . . nature having interdicted him this practice by furnishing him with feet, the toes of which are perfectly round, and of a soft, pulpy, tender substance . . .
>
> In place of holes, it seems to delight in less close, or more airy places, in the mouths of caves, or clefts in the rock, or where one projecting and being open before, affords a long retreat under it, without fear that this can ever be removed by the strength or operations of man.
>
> The Ashkoko are gregarious, and frequently sev-eral dozens of them sit upon the great stones at the mouths of caves and warm themselves in the sun, or even come out and enjoy the freshness of the sum-mer evening. They do not stand upright upon their feet, but seem to steal along as in fear, their belly being nearly close to the ground, advancing a few steps at a time, and then pausing. They have some-thing very mild, feeble like, and timid in their

deportment . . . I suppose he lives upon grain, fruit, and roots. He seemed too timid and backward in his own nature to feed upon living food, or to catch it by hunting.

The total length of this animal as he sits, from the point of his nose to his anus is 17½ inches. . . . His upper jaw is longer than his under . . .

He has no tail, and gives at first sight the idea of a rat, rather than of any other creature. His colour is a grey mixed with a reddish brown, perfectly like the wild or warren Rabbit. His belly is white, from the point of the lower jaw, to where his tail would begin, if he but had one. All over his body he has scattered hairs, strong and polished . . . His ears are round, not pointed; he makes no noise that ever I heard, but certainly chews the cud. ("Natural History," pp. 43–46)

As we can see, there is considerable evidence to indicate that this is the same or similar animal described in the Bible, especially from Proverbs. Bruce goes on to indicate that in Arabia and Syria, this animal is called Israel's Sheep, " . . . for what reason I know not unless it is chiefly from his frequenting the rocks of Horeb and Sinai . . ." and points out that the Abyssinian Christians and the Moslems will not eat its flesh, considering it unclean.

In 1 Enoch, the opening prefix called the "Animal Apocalypse" (often referred to by scholars as *An. Apoc.*) includes the animal, curiously alongside an odd category of creatures.

And they began to beget wild beasts and birds and there came from them species of every sort: lions, tigers, hyenas (var. wolf, bear), dogs, hyenas, wild boars, foxes, hyraxes, swine, falcons, eagles, kites, foqans-birds (sic), and ravens; and there was born in their midst a white bull.

The list is a simile of nations, following the allegorical designation of Israel as a white sheep. Most of these can be seen to be predator nations upon the chosen nation. Tiller explains the possible inclusion of the hyrax.

... Far from preying on sheep (the hyrax) eats vegetation only. The only justification for its inclusion in this list seems to be that, like the birds that follow, it is prominently included in the lists of unclean animals ... Since none of the other beasts in the list (except for the textually [sic] suspect swine) are mentioned in Leviticus 11 or Deuteronomy 14, it is likely that this animal was added by a scribe who mistook the significance of the list for a simple list of unclean animals modeled after Leviticus 11 and Deuteronomy 14.

If the swine and hyraxes were originally part of the list of animals ... then their function in the *An. Apoc.* would be primarily to stress the unclean nature of the animals listed. ... (Pp. 28–31)

AN ADDITIONAL TALMUD TAIL (*Chullin* 59a—see under numbers 31 and 95.)

31

HARE

HARE
Hebrew *'aRNeVeT*

The hare—although it chews the cud, it has no true hoofs; it is unclean for you;

—Leviticus 11:6

Lepus variabilis: European Varying Hare.

A common misconception is that hares and rabbits are the same species. Although related, they are not. The young of hares are born in "forms," shallow nests, fully clothed in fur, with their eyes open. After being suckled only a short time, they can fend for themselves. Rabbits bring forth their young sans fur, blind, helpless; thus, these creatures require deep burrows, or "warrens."

Hares resist fully domestication. *L. variabilis* is larger, with larger ears, than most hares and rabbits.

It is curious that no hare nor rabbit is native to the Middle East. This species is the closest proximate I have found. Perhaps its range was wider in ancient days; or, as is known to have happened in modern times, in other locales, as an opportunistic stowaway it was briefly introduced into the region by Mediterranean seafarers.

211

CONCORDANCE

Deuteronomy 14:7.

There is a legend that, at the writing of the Septuagint, God enhanced the wisdom of the elders-scribes so that each one wrote the same word in translation. On occasion, this translated word was incorporated so as not to offend the king. One of these was the Greek word for "hare," since the king's wife supposedly was known by this very word-name. Toperoff traces this legend to tractate *Megillah* 9b and goes a bit further. "In point of fact it was Ptolemy's father who was called hare" (p. 103).

In *Menachot* 39b, we learn that the fur of the hare was used for weaving.

AN ADDITIONAL TALMUD TAIL (*Chullin* 59a. For the *Mishnah*, see under *Eagle*.)

In the *Gemarah*, the animal is used to show that not all animals that chew the cud are permissible. ". . . the rock-badger and the hare chew the cud, nevertheless they have upper teeth and are unclean!"

32

S W I N E

SWINE
Hebrew *CHaZaR*

> *and the swine—although it has true hoofs, with the*
> *hoofs cleft through, it does not chew the cud; it is*
> *unclean for you.*
>
> —Leviticus 11:7

Sus scrofa: European wild boar. *S.*, Latin, a pig; *scrofa*, Latin, a breeding sow.

People of the distant premonarchy period would almost certainly have hunted wild boar. *S. scrofa* is the same as the domesticated common pig, from which it has been, through husbandry, derived.

Although called (the) European, its range in ancient days (and for a remnant even today) extends across the Euro-African-Asiatic landscape, including the islands of Sumatra, Java, Formosa (Taiwan), and Japan.

The "*treifest* of the *treif*": Jews and Moslems have always felt an aversion to the slaughter and consumption of swine, perhaps because of the stored meat's accessibility to trichinosis and other diseases, more likely due to its ritualistic command taboo: a *chok*, *chokim* being the category of Torah precepts reasonable to the Master of the Universe, but difficult for men and women to fathom a rationale; *chokim* are described in relationship with *mishpatim*, laws based upon a clear rationale in human society, such as crime (theft, murder), or torts (if an ox gores . . .). This is admittedly a simplistic explanation of the two categories of *mitzvot* but, for the understanding of the terms at this point, provides a convenient explanation

CONCORDANCE

Deuteronomy 14:8.
Isaiah 65:4 (that eat swine's flesh); 66:3, 17.

Toperoff derives the same rabbinical dicta from three talmudic sources in agreement (*Menachot* 64b, *Bava Kama* 7:7, and from the *Yerushalami, Shechalim* 47c): "Such is the abhorrence of swine that we are warned not even to mention it by name, and the Talmud refers to it as *davar acher*, another thing. It was not only forbidden to breed swine but also to keep them in flocks" (p. 194). Interestingly, Maimonides considered the animal to be *treif* not so much for the ritual negative commandment, but because of its inherent filth and resulting distemper in those who consume it. It appears he was commenting more as a physician than as a Rabbi.

Still, the Bible and the *Shulchan Aruch* are quite clear. Forst presents a succint distillation, pointing out some interesting contraindications.

> The Torah forbids us to eat any land animal . . . that does not have two distinctive *simanim* (signs, indications) that attest to its *kashrus*. The animal must both chew its cud (ruminate) and have completely cloven hooves. . . . A pig does not chew its cud although it has split hooves. A camel chews its cud but has no split hooves. . . . an animal possessing neither of the *simanim* (e.g., a donkey or horse) are therefore considered *beheimah temeiah*—("unclean") non-kosher animals. It has been noted that to this day no species have been discovered that has split hooves but does not chew its cud besides the pig. Similarly, except for the camel, shafan (var., saphan, viz., hyrax, rock-badger) and arneves (sic, ?) no

species has been discovered that chews its cud but
has no split hooves. (Pp. 33–34)

Thus, there are three categories: split hooves, but no cud
chewing; cud chewing, but no split hooves; neither cud chewing nor split hooves. Therefore, only animals that chew cud
and have split hooves are considered kosher, such as, of
course, the cow.

There is a fourth, little discussed category—or, rather, a
reversal of all doctrine. The question then becomes, when is a
pig kosher? This may seem like an oxymoron, but it is well to
remember that all the categories of *mitzvot*, whether biblical
or rabbinical, are designed for the survival of the individual
and of the nation. Thus, for example, if one were lost in the
woods for days, and a feral pig could be hunted, slaughtered,
and prepared, then one, rather than starving, not only may be
permitted to consume the meat, one is indeed obligated to do
so. Likewise, if one had a certain illness wherein, say, the
absence of an enzyme rendered her in a declining state toward
death, and the only food that allowed her to metabolize this
enzyme was pig, again, she would be obligated to consume it
and be restored to health. This raises an interesting question:
should she take it to the *shochet*, the ritual slaughterer, to
render it a kosher pig? (For an examination of this curious
matter, see Israel, exp. pp. 2–3: " . . . the *shochet* and the sick
[one] took the [slaughtered] pig to the rabbi and asked,
"Rabbi, is this pig kosher?" The rabbi looked at the animal's
lungs for some time and then declared, "It may be kosher, but
it is still a pig.") Nothing is mentioned, but we may presume
that the *shochet* used a unique knife and slaughtering-site.

Also, there is a question concerning the fitness of a
nonkosher animal for other uses. As it happens, there is no
problem. Even pigskin shoes may be worn for daily prayers.
Forst also points out that the favored opinion in the dispute
over aromas is that a kosher person may, indeed, take pleasure
from cooking aromas of unclean animals (say, for example, if
one were walking along the street past an open window at
dinner time); however, it should be pointed out that many
Jews who have kept kosher for some time find the cooking
aromas of pig repulsive.

All of this may help to answer a question that may confront the rabbis in the future.

> Research now being conducted at a number of centers may pave the way for transplanting pig organs into humans within a few years, said Duke University Medical Center scientist Jeffrey Platt, M.D., at a recent American Medical Association conference. . . . Researchers turned to swine as possible organ donors for several reasons, including their comparable size to humans and abundant supply. "Ninety million pigs are used for food each year; the number of pigs we need (for donor organs) is less than one-thousandth that number," Platt said. . . . The FDA recently approved trials of transgenic pig livers for use as a device to clean toxins from the blood of patients with liver failure . . . (Pig Organs)

The swine is regarded in *Sotah* 49b as the terrible unclean animal that began the downfall of the Second Temple. It is also seen as being compared to Rome itself. The events described occurred about 50 B.C.E., and surround the invitation of Pompey and the Romans to enter Jerusalem.

In the latter days of the Hasmonean dynasty, things had deteriorated to such an extent that two brothers engaged in civil war for the priestly or royal throne. Aristobulos fought from inside the Temple walls, attempting to keep the sanctification of the offerings; John Hyrkanos (2nd; variant, Hyrkanus) corrupted his power grabbing to such an extent he invited the Roman legions that were in Damascus to assist his side—of course, not without putting in the fix. This was the beginning of the long occupation by Rome. Now, when sheep for the two daily burnt-offerings were needed, the officiants would lower a basket of coins to those who were outside. They would proffer the two sheep, the basket would be raised, and the offering would be made. One day, following the advice of the Romans (some say a mysterious evil old man), they took the coins, but placed a pig in the basket. At once, the daily offerings ended.

This was the beginning of the end, which led to the destruction of the *Beit Hamikdash*. The old man was supposed to have been Greek; the Sages declared, "Cursed is the man

who knows Greek wisdom, and cursed is whoever raises a pig"
(see also *Taryag*, p. 116; and Morrison, pp. 3–92).
Mishnah 6:2:

> Rabbi Joshua ben Levi said: Every day a divine voice
> goes forth from Mount Horeb, proclaiming and say-
> ing: "Woe to mankind for their contempt of the
> Torah!" For whoever does not occupy himself with
> the study of the Torah is banned by God . . . as it is
> written (Proverbs 11: 22): "As a golden ring in the
> snout . . . of a swine, so is a fair woman without
> discretion." (*Pirke Avot*, 94)

AN ADDITIONAL TALMUD TAIL (*Becharot* 40a)

The tractate deals principally with the precepts relating to the
firstborn of humans and, in particular, bovine animals.

In this *Gemarah*, a first offering may be disqualified because its mouth resembles that of a swine. This may relate to
the principal of the appearance of the thing. Thus, for example,
one should not enter a *treif* restaurant even to request a glass
of water. There is nothing wrong with the glass of water;
however, another person may see one entering the nonkosher
restaurant, and not know the reason, and may wonder if Plony
(so and so) is consuming *treif* food. Here the verisimilitude to
a swine's appearance is rendered the same as if it were a
blemish. The *Mishnah* recounts a firstborn that was found with
a lower jaw larger than an upper jaw. "R. Simeon b. Gamaliel
asked the sages [for a ruling] and they said: This is a blemish."

33

GRASSHOPPER

GRASSHOPPER
Hebrew *ChaGaV(B)*; variant *SaLa'M*

> *of these you may eat the following: locusts of every*
> *variety; all varieties of bald locust; crickets of every*
> *variety; and all varieties of grasshopper.*
> —Leviticus 11:22

Locusta viridissima: the great green grasshopper.
The most common. Locusts, which take to the wing, also of
the family Orthoptera, were employed by the Lord as a plague
(see number 22). Grasshoppers, which hop in amazing fashion,
were seen as small and insignificant next to giants.

CONCORDANCE

Numbers 13:33 (We saw the Nephilim there . . . and we looked like grasshoppers to ourselves . . .);
Isaiah 40:22 (It is He Who is enthroned above . . . /So that its inhabitants
seem as grasshoppers);
Nahum 3:17.

Although, again, entomologists consider locusts and grasshoppers as variants of a species, the Talmud regards them as

separate species, probably due to their being so mentioned in the text. See especially *Shabbat* 152a, *Bava Metzia* 9:6, and *Pesachim* 48b. Toperoff includes an obscure but fascinating reference from *Yoma* 77b: "The spring of water oozing out of the Holy of Holies is of the thinness of the (grasshopper's [locust's?] antennae" (p. 100).

Crickets, another related species in the order Orthoptera, are also mentioned in the initial verse; indeed, the JPS note for this verse is: "*A number of these cannot be identified with certainty*" (p. 169).

AN ADDITIONAL TALMUD TAIL (*Ta'anith* 3:1, 19b)

The order of public fasts was observed unless an alarm was to be sounded in the case of disease or plague, or, in our *Mishnah*, if rain fell "for crops but not for trees, for trees and not for crops . . ."

The *Gemarah* indicates that even these insects were considered sufficient provocation. "In the case of locust the alarm is sounded no matter how small in number. R. Simeon b. Eleazar says: . . . also in the case of grasshoppers." R. Eleazar's reiteration may be one of those emphasis addendums, or it may be the Rabbis did not realize the animals were practically the same species (as may be the case in the *Midrash*).

. . . AND A MIDRASH (*Lamentations Rabbah* 34)

> . . . 700 species of clean fish, 800 of clean grasshoppers, and birds beyond number . . . went into exile with Israel to Babylon.

34

M O L E

MOLE (Note: JPS, p. 169, notes that "a number of these cannot be identified with certainty," referring to this list in 29 and 30.)
Hebrew *CHoLeD*

> *The following shall be unclean for you from among the things that swarm on the earth: the mole, . . .*
> —Leviticus 11:29.

Spalax ehrenberghi: a mole "rat"

"Surprisingly, for it is widespread in neighboring countries, the mole is not found in Bible lands and its ecological niche has been taken up by the Mole Rat . . . a very similar creature with eyes covered by skin and no external ears. It lives underground, making, like the mole, an extensive burrowing system with storage chambers, sleeping quarters and connecting passages" (France, 107).

CONCORDANCE

(some translations, Isaiah 2:20 [. . . men shall fling away/ To the moles and the bats/The idols of silver/ And . . . of gold]; viz., see France; however, see JPS (p. 621), which has an uncertain listing ("flying foxes"); Pinney,

127–128, clarifies some of the confusion with an excellent discussion concerning the difficulty in translations from biblical words that have no modern equivalent, especially when different words are used presumably for the same creature.

In fact, this list in 29 and 30 has received numerous translations. Preuss comments that, "According to Hoffmann, they are the weasel, the mouse, the toad, the hedgehog, the chameleon, the lizard, the skink and the mole" (p. 502). Fox translates: "the weasel, the mouse, and the great-lizard according to its kind; the gecko, the monitor and the lizard, the sand-lizard and the chameleon." Fox has no footnote indicating he is uncertain; however, as already indicated, JPS and others indicate their uncertainty. We follow here the list in JPS (p. 169).

Trachtenberg found in old German manuscripts a percussive aphrodisiac concerning moles. The majority of these "love potions" or "formulae," he points out, because they involved so much blood of forbidden animals, albeit nearly rampant in the neighboring Christian communities, rarely, if ever, entered the Jewish folk ways; however, a few, void of such impurities, managed to burrow into Jewish superstition as well.

> . . . Take a live mole, a male for a man, a female for a woman, and strike it on its right foot, "and it will bring you true love." This . . . is touted as "unequaled"! (Pp. 129–130)

An Additional Talmud Tail (*Kelim* 21:3)

The *Mishnah* details various implements in both shop work and trapping that, in the touching, could render one unfit for the Levitical service and appropriate purification ritual. One of these is a "mole-trap," which: ". . . is clean. R. Judah ruled: While it is set the separate parts are regarded as connected."

35

M O U S E

MOUSE
Hebrew *'aCHBaR*

> . . . *the mouse,* . . .
>
> —Leviticus 11:29

Mus musculus.

CONCORDANCE

1 Samuel 6:4–5 (gold), 11 (gold), 18 (gold)
Isaiah 66:17.

Mice seem to be creatures of paradox. On the one hand, they are pests, small vermin we feel repulsed by; on the other hand, in children's literature and in cartoons, they seem to appeal to our sensibilities of the rooting for the clever underdog. Indeed, a prodigious entertainment industry has grown up all around the divined character of one fictional, anthropomorphic mouse. Their cousin, the rat, is larger, carries the vectors that may harbor the more dangerous diseases, and is all the more obnoxious and malevolent to us.

Mice are tiny and largely defenseless. In fact, except for hiding within manufactured tunnels (and that not very well, as hidden animals go), they have basically one thing going for them: they multiply exceedingly. Without urban or rural predators, the mice population could explode within a relatively short period of time. It is another circumstance where our headlong destruction of predator habitat may ultimately result in an ecological disaster.

The various conflicting stories and legends concerning the mouse enjoy an ancient heritage. France (pp. 110–111) recounts such a legend going back to Noah's Ark. Noah, as we know, like God, felt compassion for all his creatures. Thus, when the cat chases the mouse into one of his holes, he tears a gash in his mouth. Noah sews stitches into the wound and the mouse's mouth heals into the peculiar shape we are familiar with.

Schochet (pp. 230–231) relates several variations of a mouse parable in which an individual is seeking a mate.

> The *Kalila wa-Dimna* version describes a female mouse which has been transformed into a beautiful maiden. The maiden declares: "I desire a very brave and valiant husband with whom none can compare for strength or power." A Nazarite approaches the sun in prayer, beseeching it to marry off the maiden to its master, but the sun refers him to the more powerful ruler of the clouds, who in turn sends him off to the lord of the winds, who refers him to the all-powerful mountain. But the mountain confesses that there exists a power stronger than it, capable of digging into and penetrating it—namely, the mouse. The Nazarite calls upon divine assistance and the maiden is transformed back into a she-mouse so that she can become the wife of the mountain-boring mouse.

The Talmud has several references to a mouse or mice. In *Avodah Zorah* 68b, the rabbis discuss a case in which a mouse fell into a casket of beer. Rav prohibited the beer from being fit for consumption. Again, it is the side of the creature that is vile and repugnant to us. In fact, in *Shabbat* 151b, a live infant may not need to be guarded against these animals, but even "Og, king of Bashan, dead, needs guarding from weasels and mice . . ." Those members of the *Chevra Kadusha*, the burial society, who watched overnight the deceased, knew well throughout their generations to keep a sharp eye out for mice and other rodents.

"If there are nine packages of *mazzah* and one of leaven, and a mouse comes and steals [a package], and we do not know whether it took *mazzah* or leaven, that is . . . forbidden" (*Pesachim* 9b).

". . . The belief in spontaneous generation was as firmly rooted among Jews as among non-Jews. Mice, worms, insects are often the children of dust and mud and filth; . . ." (Trachtenberg, p. 182).

AN ADDITIONAL TALMUD TAIL (*Chullin* 1; *Gemarah* 9a–b)

In this fascinating *Gemarah*, the animal serves as a catalyst into a *machlochet* (a dispute), concerning animals forbidden to be offered or eaten.

The *Mishnah* concerns who is qualified to perform *shechita* (ritual slaughtering). But the argument in the *Gemarah* elevates into the very question of ritual for ritual's sake or for the sake of life. R. Abba herein quotes from a *Baraita*, the previously known story or ruling from the *Tannaim* period.

> If one saw . . . a mouse nibbling at a (piece of fruit), one must apprehend that it was nibbling in a pre-existing hole, i.e., hole of a poisonous snake, "therefore the item is probably poisonous and dangerous to life."

The *machlochet* then begins.

> He replied: How can you compare what is forbidden ritually with what is forbidden on account of possible danger to life! In the later case, we are certainly more apprehensive. Said Raba: What difference is there? Whenever there arises a doubt concerning a prohibition based on danger to life the stricter view is preferred, and the same is the case with regard to a doubt in connection with ritual prohibition!

Abaye continues with the opposite viewpoint.

36

GECKO

GECKO (Unknown today but a related species may be:)
Hebrew *'aNaKaH*

> . . . the gecko . . .
>
> —Leviticus 11:30

Pachydactylus namaquensis; located mainly in southern
Africa.

The people may truly have known them in their earliest
desert days. All species are notorious for hitching rides on any
type of human conveyance, ship, caravan animals, tents, and
tabernacle appointments that are put up and taken down, and,
today, modern conveyances. They thrive in both desert environments and urban environments, due to the fact they are
excellent hunters of their prey, largely insects. They are about
three to four inches long, although the Levant species may
have been larger. Part of their stowaway migration advantage
is that they can be asexual—or, rather, one individual can
reproduce through parthenogenesis. Geckos are nocturnal and
insectivorous; they are remarkable climbers on any natural or
man-made surface, endowed as they are with sticky pads on
their toes. "They may forage for insects on trees, plants, and
buildings, requiring little more than a loose piece of bark or a
wall mirror to hide behind during the day" (Petren and Case).

This proclivity to hide or take temporary residence most

anywhere in the daytime while remaining quite still, may identify the species as the lizard in the story of Rabban Gamaliel the Elder. R. Gamaliel apparently knew his reptilian zoology well.

It happened once that such an animal was found in the slaughtering area of the Temple. It was one of the feast holidays. The officiants first proceed to the king and queen; now, they are not identified, but they probably represent the Roman emperor, Nero, perhaps, and his queen, or, more likely, Herod and Miramne. In any event, the king sends them to the queen who sends them to R. Gamaliel. It seems curious that the officiants did not at once proceed to R. Gamaliel; still, the story demonstrates that true knowledge and wisdom lie with the Rabbis and God, and not with earthly rulers. They proceed to the Rabban; he inquires of them if the area where the lizard was found was warm or cold.

> They replied, "Warm." He said, "Go, pour a glass of cold water upon it." They went, poured a glass of cold water upon the lizard, and it suddenly moved. Thus Rabban Gamaliel rendered the entire feast fit for eating (since it was not dead, and therefore, not *tamai*, unpure). (*Nadich*, 1, 238–239)

In the ongoing problem of translation of this list, even Gesenius indicates uncertainty, providing the possible translation of "ferret" or "shrew-mouse." Toperoff and other scholars choose not to deal with whatever animal may be identified.

37

LAND CROCODILE

LAND CROCODILE
Hebrew *KoaCH*

> . . . and the land crocodile . . .
> —Leviticus 11:30

Again, Fox, "Monitor," a tropical lizard of the genus *Veranus*. Since it has been known to give a "warning" of the approach of true crocodiles—possibly giving some evidence for its vulgar name—it may have become associated with the larger water reptiles.

AN ADDITIONAL TALMUD TAIL (See under *Snail*, number 92)

38

SAND LIZARD

SAND LIZARD
Hebrew *LT'a-aH*

> . . . *the sand lizard,* . . .
>
> —Leviticus 11:30

Gesenius: "a kind of lizard" (p. 538).

(Unknown today; possibly related to:) *Aporosaura anchietae*, largely found in southern Africa.

"Slowly it foraged along the bottom of the dune's steepest face, where food often collects. Stopping periodically, it pushed aside the sand with its broad, shovellike snout, searching for seeds from grasses and succulents, as well as for insects and other small arthropods" (Robinson).

Toperoff places all lizards into one category. Of the several talmudic and midrashic references he indicates, the most enlightening is the story of the rescued child and Moses at the well (*Rabbah* 1:39).

The *Midrash* compares Moses to the one who was bitten by a lizard and ran to place his feet in the water. At this point, the one bit observed a small child in the river who was drowning. The man rescues the child. The child says to his rescuer, "Had it not been for you I would have perished." But the man answers, "Not I have saved you, but the lizard who bit me and from which I escaped."

The daughters of Jethro greeted Moses. "Thanks for saving us from the hands of the shepherds." (But) Moses (answered), "The Egyptian whom I slew; he delivered you." Thereupon they said to their father, "An Egyptian (rescued us; from this you learn) [not Moses], but the Egyptian whom he slew." (P. 152)

39

CHAMELEON

CHAMELEON
Hebrew *TiNSHahMeT*

> . . . *and the chameleon.*
>
> —Leviticus 11:30

Interestingly, the Hebrew is derived from the same root as that for "soul," *N'SHahMahH*, as it is a breath from God, and the animal is likened to living on air. Most concur it is the chameleon (Gesenius, p. 675).

Chameleon vulgaris
Chameleons are native to the entire sea-to-sea range of the Mediterranean to Madagascar. This is the most common, and native to the entire region, from the Lebanon area to the west of Egypt. Species vary little, although there are a few distinctions. All share unique traits, including horns or vestigial horns, eyeballs that rotate independently within "turrets," peculiar threat displays, prehensile tails, asymmetrically bundled toes, a "baroque assemblage of crests, horns, helmets, flaps and frills," and, of course, their special ability to altar skin tone and color, almost at once (Martin).

The color change occurs through special adaptive cells beneath the first layer of skin, which sends chemicals, such as melanin, rushing to the outer layers. The adaptive-biochemical process is still not clear to zoological science. It is interesting that when two male chameleons approach each other and engage in intimidation behavior, they resort to puffing themselves up with air (an effective intimidation technique the creature uses against its own predators; in an entomological curiosity, it may give some credence to its Hebrew root), and engaging in a phantasmagorical display of color alteration, a sort of nonviolent, aesthetic battle for bragging rights.

I was once walking along the upper pathway at the University of Judaism in Los Angeles, when I caught sight of a small lizard on the walk. It was nearly as gray as the path. Its eyes—or, rather, its right eye, the one facing me (the animal rotates its eyes independently, but uses them in concert as a stereoscopic azimuth range detector when about to zap prey with its sticky tongue) rotated 180°, calculated my threat, and headed into some bush cover with leaves rust-red and green, into which combination of hues it promptly converted and was at once lost to my sight.

The Jew himself, the Jewess herself, have been throughout their exiled history compared to the chameleon in that they are able to adapt to the lands in which they find themselves.

AN ADDITIONAL TALMUD TAIL (*Sanhedrin* 11:3; *Gemarah* 108b)

Mishnah: "The generation of the flood has no portion in the . . . world (to come), nor will they stand at the [last] judgment . . ."

From this *Mishnah*, as we might expect, the floodgates are opened for all manner of stories concerning Parshah Noach (Noah). One of the most charming concerns directly the chameleon and demonstrates both the obligation to duty and the humane nature of B'nai Noach. Years later, Eliezar, Abraham's trusted servant, asks Shem, Noah's oldest son and Rav of a great yeshiva, how difficult it was to feed the animals. Shem recounts the story, much as anyone would recount a significant event in their past.

> . . . We had much trouble in the ark. . . . my father did not know . . . the food of the Chameleon. One day he was sitting and cutting up a pomegranate,

when a worm dropped out of it, which [the Chameleon] consumed. From then onward he mashed up bran for it, and when it became wormy, it devoured it.

(See also under number 99.)

40

HORNET

HORNET (but JPS, "Plague")
Hebrew *TSiRa'H*

> *The Lord your God will also send a hornet [others,
> 'plague'] against them, until those who are left in
> hiding perish before you.*
> —Deuteronomy 7:20 (but see Exodus 23:28)

Vespa crabro. The most common. Its most common nest is
the hollow of a decayed tree. ". . . The Lord . . . will send the
Hornet among them, until they . . . perish . . ." (their rot is
already in decay).

CONCORDANCE

Joshua 24:12.

The Jewish Encyclopedia relates one of the stories of the
evil of Sodom and Gomorrah. This one concerns a young
woman who felt sorry for a starving man and gave him some
bread. ". . . she was besmeared (sic) with honey and exposed
to the stings of hornets." However, in the Soncino translation
of this passage, the insects are bees. Still, whether bees or
hornets, we learn that this was the precipitating event that

prompted God to make his decision about Sodom and Gomorrah and enter into his dispute with Abraham.

> A certain maiden gave some bread to a poor man [hiding it] in a pitcher. On the matter becoming known, they daubed her with honey and placed her on the parapet of the wall, and the bees (hornets?) came and consumed her. Thus it is written, *And the Lord said, The cry of Sodom and Gomorrah, because it is great.* Whereon Rab Judah commented in Rab's name: On account of the maiden. (109b, JE, V6)

According to *Shabbat* 121b, unlike what is commonly thought, it is, in some cases, permissible to strike at vermin on *Shabbat*. Not only is the hornet mentioned herein, but our next animal, also quite unique and dangerous, the scorpion (41).

> Come and hear: For R. Abba, son of R. Hiyya b. Abba, and R. Zera were sitting in the anteroom of R. Jannai's academy, [when] something issued from between them (unclear—either a vermin appeared, or the question arose between them). [So] they asked R. Jannai: May one kill snakes and scorpions on the Sabbath?—Said he to them: I kill a hornet, how much more so snakes and scorpions?

AN ADDITIONAL TALMUD TALE *(Sotah, Mishnah* 7:1; *Gemarah* 36a)

The *Mishnah* delineates those prayers that may be said in any language, and those that can only be said in Hebrew, "the holy tongue." It also delineates how the people stood and conducted themselves for the blessings and the curses on Mount Gerizim and Ebal (Deuteronomy 17).

The *Gemarah* devolves into a discussion of Joshua's crossing of the River Jordan into Canaan.

> A Tanna taught: The hornet did not pass over . . . with them; but behold it is written (it would, in Exodus 28:28). R. Simeon b. Lakish: It stood by the bank of the Jordan and injected (propelled?) a virus [into the Caananites] which blinded their eyes above

and castrated them below, as it is said, "Yet destroyed I the Amorite . . . his fruit from above and his roots from beneath." (Amos 2:9)

R. Papa now uses a common technique in talmudic *pilpul* to resolve an issue—the additional item: "There were two hornets, one in the period of Moses and the other in the period of Joshua; the former did not pass over (Jordan) but the other did."

41

S C O R P I O N

SCORPION
Hebrew *'aKRaV(B)*

> *Who led you through the great and terrible*
> *wilderness with its* seraph *serpents and scorpions, a*
> *parched land with no water in it, who brought forth*
> *water for you from the flinty rock;*
> —Deuteronomy 8:15

Androctonus australis: which has a range extending into North Africa.

CONCORDANCE

1 Kings 12:11, 14.
Ezekiel 2:6.
2 Chronicles 10:11 (. . . I will chastise you with scorpions), 14.

Wiland has provided some basic facts about scorpions to "set the hysteria aside . . ." Here are a few, distilled into list form:

- Wasp stings are more dangerous and far more common.
- There are 1,500 known species; less than 2 percent are life-threatening.

- However, the toxicity of these few rates their venom 100,000 times greater than that of cyanide.
- They have been here, in largely unchanged form, for 450 million years, although they began in the sea and may have been the first arthropods to crawl upon and adapt to land.
- As if in heritage to their sea-borne origins, some species can survive underwater for two days.
- Some can be frozen for weeks, then, within a few hours of being thawed, resume normal activities.
- Some can withstand temperatures of 122 degrees F.
- Some can live indefinitely without water.
- Their metabolic efficiency is unsurpassed; some can survive without food for a year.
- Some can lift more than twenty times their body weight with a single pincer.
- Unlike other arachnids, they can live four to twenty-five years.
- Scorpions cannot "see"; they have photo cells instead of eyes to detect light; however, sensory hairs cover the animal's body and detect a disturbance in the surrounding air; sensory organs in their legs detect minute and larger tremors.
- They "hunt" by moving ten feet from their burrows in a straight line and waiting for something to come along; they are nocturnal. If no hapless nocturnal victim chances by, the creature scurries back home by first light. It will simply try it the same way the next night.
- Its prey is insects, spiders, and other scorpions.
- They are prey for owls, toads, mice, tarantulas, and other scorpions.
- The larger the size of the pincers, the less likely the tail-stinger is to be venomous, and vice versa; the most venomous is the bark scorpion, which lives in loose tree bark and woodpiles.

Again, from *Shabbat* 121b, concerning if one may kill certain things on the Sabbath Day:

> Mishnah: A dish may be inverted over a lamp, that
> the beams should not catch [fire], and over an

infant's excrement, and over a scorpion, that it should not bite.

Gemarah: R. Joshua b. Levi said: All [animals, etc.] that cause injury may be killed on the Sabbath. R. Joseph objected: Five may be killed on the Sabbath, and these are they: The Egyptian fly, the hornet of Nineveh, the scorpion of Adabene, the snake in Palestine, and a mad dog anywhere.

The dispute continues, R. Joseph tracing his defense to a *Baraita*.

In *Berachot* 32b-33a, the discussion concerns if one's attention may be diverted from his prayers. "Even if a snake is wound round his foot he should not break off. R. Shesheth said: This applies only in the case of a serpent, but if it is a scorpion, he breaks off." (A *machlochet*, a dispute, arises.)

From *'Eruvin* 56a, we learn that the Rabbis were also students of the zodiac and astrology: "Our Rabbis taught: If a town is to be squared the sides of the square must be made to correspond to the four directions of the world: . . . your guiding marks are the Great Bear in the North and the Scorpion in the South."

From *Berachot* 62a, we recognize the Rabbis were just as familiar with pragmatic, day-to-day, earthly activities: "R. Tanhum b. Hanilai said: Whoever behaves modestly in a privy is delivered from three things: from snakes, from scorpions, and from evil spirits."

It is interesting that serpents and scorpions appear so often together in the rabbinical tracts. Indeed, they are included as one of the ten miracles that were wrought in the *Beit Hamikdash*: ". . . never did serpent or scorpion injure anyone . . ." (*Yoma* 21a)

> . . . Human saliva, especially that of a fasting man, was believed to possess anti-demonic and anti-magical, that is, generally protective, powers. Galen tells of a man who undertook to kill a scorpion by means of an incantation which he repeated thrice. But at each repetition he spat on the scorpion. Galen claimed afterwards to have killed one by the same procedure without any incantation, and more quickly with the spittle of a fasting than of a full man.

> Maimonides wrote, in his capacity of physician,
> that the spittle of a fasting person is hostile to
> poisons. . . . (Trachtenberg, pp. 120–121)

Most are now familiar with the story of the scorpion and the frog. The animals came to the river's edge at the same time. The frog was at first wary, but the scorpion told him that he only wanted to go to the other side. He asked the frog if he could ride his back across, for the scorpion would surely drown if he attempted the crossing alone. The frog answered, "Surely, if I protect myself from you on land, I should fear you more in the river with you on my back, where you could easily sting me and I shall die." "Fool," answered the scorpion, "If I stung you in the middle of the river, then I too will surely die. Of what use would such an act be to me?" That seemed to make sense to the frog and so he agreed. They set out. When they were in the middle of the stream, the scorpion brought its tail-stinger over and stung the frog, killing him. Of course, the scorpion drowned as well. And why? Well . . . the incident occurred in the Middle East.

An Additional Talmud Tail (*Shabbat* 16:7)

An addition to the entry that "A dish may be inverted over lamp that (it) . . . should not catch [fire], and over a child's excrement, and over a scorpion, that it should not bite"—the *Mishnah* and commentaries warn against the act of trapping, which clearly is prohibited on *Shabbat.*

42

GAZELLE

GAZELLE   Hebrew *TSV(B)iY*

> *But whenever you desire, you may slaughter and
> eat meat in any of your settlements, according to the
> blessing that the Lord your God has granted you.
> The unclean and the clean alike may partake of it,
> as of the gazelle and the deer.*
>
> —Deuteronomy 12:15, 22

Gazella subgutturosa. Persian Gazelle. *sub*, L., below; *guttur*,
L., the throat; *-osus*, L. full of.

During mating season, the male's throat swells. In fact a
secondary vulgar nomenclature is Goitered Gazelle. It is the
only one with an extensive range, reaching from Persia to
across Suez. I also like the Persian insight. Babylonia was, of
course, of profound importance to Jewish history; I like the
throat-swelling as well. Not too far from the D 12 *parsha*,
wherein the people are called a stiff-necked people.

CONCORDANCE

Deuteronomy 14:5; 15:22.
1 Kings 5:3.
Isaiah 13:14.

Proverbs 6:5.

Song of Songs 2:7 (see number 17), 9 (and again) (My beloved is like a gazelle or a young hart), 17 (and again); 3:5 (and again).

AN ADDITIONAL TALMUD TAIL (*Chullin* 2:1; *Gemarah* 27b–28a)

This *Gemarah* employs rhetorical principles of metaphor and reversal.

> What does the verse, *Howbeit as the gazelle and as the hart is eaten* [*so shalt thou eat thereof*] (Deuteronomy 12:22) teach us? What do we learn from the gazelle and the hart? Indeed, "it comes as a teacher but turns out to be a pupil" (a proverbial saying).

Now the difficult explanation can be designed as a syllogism. Thus:

A. The matter of the gazelle and hart "teaches" how consecrated animals become unfit (e.g., with a blemish).
B. The halakhah (the way of law) in regard to animals unfit "throws light on the position concerning the gazelle and hart" (the pupil position).
C. Thus, the unfit animal and therefore the gazelle and hart [or: the gazelle and hart and therefore the unfit animal, i.e., unfit for consecration] must still be ritually slaughtered for consumption purposes.

Now, this is a *Baraita* attributed to R. Eleazarha-Kappar Beribbi, told by R. Isaac b. Phinehas. It is a very important *Baraita* in the protocol of kashrut *halakhah*.

The *Mishnah* explains the process of valid and invalid slaughter in regard to the cut of the organs of the throat, in effect, instructions for the *shochet*. "If a man cut [i.e., slaughtered] . . . the quarter part of each organ in the case of cattle, the slaughtering is valid."

(See also Soncino, pp. 143–144.)

43

R O E B U C K

ROEBUCK
Hebrew *YaCHMoo(V)R*

> *the deer, the gazelle, the roebuck, the wild goat, the*
> *ibex, the antelope, the mountain sheep,*
>
> —Deuteronomy 14:5

Capreolus capreolus. Roe Deer (European and Asia, east to China and Korea).

> One of the most extreme examples of how social systems may adapt to environmental circumstance, and indeed of how flexible individual species may be in terms of social organisation (sic), is offered by the European roe deer. . . . roe are relatively solitary, and are strongly territorial . . . Roe deer, however, are opportunists . . . While their feeding style confines them to relatively early successional (sic) environments, their small size and relatively modest food requirements in terms of actual bulk allow them to exploit a variety of potential niches. They may be found in small coppice woodlands in agricultural areas (and manage) to adapt to the totally agricultural landscapes . . . (Putman, pp. 67–68).

Such deer as "Roebucks" could not be native to desert climes, indicating the entry in Deuteronomy may be an anachronism from the period of the monarchy.

CONCORDANCE

2 Samuel 2:18.
1 Kings 5:3.

All of these animals, included in the large family of deer, are admired for their swiftness and communal sensitivity. They are included in the Deuteronomic passages to demonstrate herbivores that meet the category of those that may be eaten as meat.

44

WILD GOAT

WILD GOAT
Deuteronomy 14:5

Basically, the same species as the goat (number 7), from which the domesticated animal is in little doubt derived. However, it is mentioned here in a very significant context, concerning, again, that which is not abhorrent for consumption, and the "regular" goat is mentioned as well. JPS (p. 297) mentions that "a number of these creatures cannot be identified with certainty," although Fox (p. 915) translates the same or similar. Fox points out that this list of acceptably kosher animals is part of an entire Holiness Code section, which concludes with the concern of the community for those who depend upon the community ". . . the care one must take that the powerless members of society (sojourner, widow, orphan) are provided . . ."

In our modern, scientifically dependent era, *kashrut* has always been something of a mystery; perhaps herein is an insight to a clue—if one is concerned about the food one eats every time he or she sits down to eat, then how much more should one be concerned for those less fortunate who may have no food to eat.

The list and its context continues for the next two animals in the list; then the Torah proceeds to the forbidden animals for consumption, in particular the birds of prey.

44a

I BEX

It should be mentioned that the Ibex, *Capra ibex nubiana*, is mentioned in JPS, Fox, and other translations, although France, among others, points out its similarity to the wild goat. Again, this list of animals at D. 14:5 has plagued many translators. Some translations will also have in addition to, or in place of these, the Pygarg.

> The Ibex . . . sturdy body, strong legs and goat-like beard in the male. The adult . . . has magnificent horns sweeping high and wide over its back . . . The female's horns are shorter and more slender. It lives among the rocks on the mountain slopes and its flexible hooves enable it to get a purchase on the smallest protuberances so that whole herds of ibex have been reported as scaling apparently vertical rock faces. They are also very agile jumpers and can leap astonishing distances both vertically and horizontally if startled. For most of the year they live in segregated herds . . . In the autumn . . . they come together for mating . . . the ibex was long considered to have special therapeutic qualities . . . (P. 89)

44b

PYGARG

(Addax nasomaculatus), thus, also known as the Addax

A sort of "camel of antelopes," if you will, the animal is adapted for living in the desert. It can go for hours or even days without water. It has a long-haired beige-colored coat that turns white in the summer to reflect the glare and heat of the sun. "Its wide hooves are able to travel over the soft sands without sinking in" (France, p. 127).

45

A N T E L O P E

ANTELOPE
Hebrew *T'o(V)*
Deuteronomy 14:5

Tragelaphus strepsiceros (The only one proximate, in north-east Africa; perhaps its range was greater then.)

CONCORDANCE

Isaiah 51:20.

AN ADDITIONAL TALMUD TAIL (*Rosh Hoshanah* 3:3)

> The *shofar* used on Rosh Hoshanah was of an ante-
> lope's horn and straight and its mouth was overlaid
> with gold. There were two trumpets, one on each
> side of it. The *shofar* gave a long blast and the
> trumpets a short one . . . on (communal) fast days
> they used ([two] curved *shofars* of rams, the mouths
> of which were overlaid with silver. . . . R. Judah says

on Rosh Hoshanah the blast is made with a *shofar* of
rams and on jubilees with one of antelopes.

Now, the obvious question is, Why do we use curved rams'
horns today? They answer may lie with Maimonides's response about bending oneself to prayer and study. This
disagrees with the idea that the best form of doing a *mitzvah*
follows the antelope's horn—straight; however, R. Yehudah
thinks the more people bend their thoughts to the will of God,
the better they are. It is R. Yehudah's concept that Maimonides
agrees with.

46

MOUNTAIN SHEEP

MOUNTAIN SHEEP
Hebrew *ZaZaMeR*
Deuteronomy 14:5

47

(G R E A T) (B E A R D E D) V U L T U R E

(GREAT) (BEARDED) VULTURE
Hebrew *PeReS*

> *The following you may not eat: the eagle, the vulture, and the black vulture;*
>
> —Deuteronomy 14:12

Gypaetus barbatus. Bearded Vulture. *gups* (*gupos*), Greek, a vulture; *aetos,* Gr., an eagle; *barbatus,* L., bearded.

It has black feathers beneath its beak, forming a "beard." The creature has an extensive range, sightings having occurred in southern Europe, Northern Africa, the Pyrenees, and China.

CONCORDANCE

Deuteronomy 28:49.
Jeremiah 48:40; 49:22.
Habakkuk 1:8 (see numbers 17, 18, 72).
Proverbs 30:17 (see number 4) (. . . The *ravens* of the valley shall pick it out/And the young vulture shall eat it).
Job 39:27.

All of the several animals in the prohibitions list share the common element of being birds of prey. In fact, it may be deduced that all kosher animals are herbivores (although not all herbivores are kosher), and all carnivores, hunters, or carrion-eaters are not kosher. Still, the animals are admired for their bravery, their swiftness, their keen eyesight. The eagle (number 26), for example, is at the top of the admired list.

The eagle is the animal used in the soaring metaphor of Israel being carried out of Egypt on eagle's wings. The vulture was not so admired. Hunters seem to be admired; scavengers seem not to be. However, scavengers represent the largest birds that fly and can seem to glide for astonishingly long distances. Pilots at 30,000 feet have reported observing griffon vultures and condors, albeit such reports are few and far between and appear infused with hyperbole. Probably, they were seen between 15,000 to 20,000 feet while the plane was climbing to cruising altitude, nonetheless a respectable height.

According to Clark, the vulture is one of the land birds that frequently visits harbors (p. 417); since it is well seen in desert areas as well, this is another indication of its extraordinary range.

Cansdale points out that even today, seen at a great distance in the Middle East, it is difficult to discern whether the bird is an eagle or a vulture until the animal comes closer into view. Perhaps, he suggests, the Hebrew scribes had the same difficulty and the biblical allusions may be interchanged. Tristram, describing his travels and adventures in Palestine in 1863–1864, noted that "no landscape was ever without its circling vultures. There were breeding colonies . . . in the rocky gorges in and leading off the Jordan valley, some of which held hundreds of birds." Cansdale understates the tragedy we know all too well in our own time: "Those days are gone for ever." However, he points out that he was able to see some, and there are still areas of habitat for breeding. Sanitation regulations in Israel, however, have reduced the numbers of carcasses for scavengers. He also includes an ancient Hebrew proverb: "A vulture in Babylon can see a carcass in Palestine." The double entendre should be readily apparent: the admiration for the bird's lofty flying altitude and its unmatched keen eyesight—and, if one substitutes the defeated nation of Judah for Palestine, it becomes a lamentation, fraught with political and sardonic implications.

> ". . . the characteristics of birds are not stated, but the sages have said, every bird that seizes its prey is unclean" (*Chullin* 59a).

An Additional Talmud Tail (Bava Metziah 2:1; *Gemarah* 24b)

This *Gemarah* concerning a lost object not, as it turns out, ever really lost, confers ownership not only on one who finds the object, but also one who observes its being purloined and recovers it, a rather astonishing dicta; however, as we shall see, it makes perfect ethical sense under the auspices of the case cited.

First, the *Mishnah*:

> Some finds belong to the finder; others must be announced (to give the owner an opportunity to identify and claim it). The following articles belong to the finder: . . . pieces of meat . . .

Now the *Gemarah*. Notice how, in addition to the intuited ethics and legal code of the matter, the matter of *kashrut* must also be addressed. The implication is, that since the majority of residents in the area are Jews, the meat has such a probability of being kosher, it is considered to be kosher. This is a principle in *kashrut*, called *BiTu(V)L BRu(V)V*, nullification in a greater number.

> Once a vulture seized a piece of meat in the market and dropped it among the palm-trees belonging to Bar Marion. When the latter appeared before Abaye, (Abaye) said to him: Go and take it for yourself. Now the majority [in that case] consisted of Israelites, hence it must be concluded that the halakhah is in accordance (with a ruling by R. Simeon b. Eleazar) . . . and in regard to a vulture . . . it is like the tide of the sea (i.e., therefore the original owner has no hope of recovering the item).

The objection of Rab is now raised, for he stated that meat lost from sight is forbidden. After all, who could guarantee its *kashrut* under such a circumstance—it could be dealt with in a *treifa* manner or even *treif* meat substituted. But he has an excellent retort: "(Bar Marion) stood by and watched it (i.e., the entire event from the pick-up to the drop)."

In an interesting footnote Rashi states, "It is a bird we call in Old French 'u(V)ZLTo(V)R, which name comes from the root of 'enough, sufficiency.'"

48

OSPREY

OSPREY (Fox, JPS, "Black Vulture")
Hebrew *'aZNiyaH*
Deuteronomy 14:12

__Pandion haliaetus.__ Pandion was a mythical king of Athens. *haliaetus*, L., the osprey or sea-eagle.

Widespread in almost the entire northern hemisphere.

It migrates a significant distance south in winter.

Again, the biblical writers may have had some difficulty perceiving the differences between these magnificent raptors. Ornithologists and other zoologists today have little difficulty. In fact, the bird is rather striking.

> . . . predominantly white below with long gull-like wings and rather short barred tail. Above dark brown, except for the white crown of the head. The dark stripe across the sides of the face, crossing the yellow eye, is distinctive. (*Birds of Prey*, p. 34)

> But the true Osprey . . . in Bible lands today . . . unlikely to have changed greatly down the centuries since it only occasionally overwinters along the sea coasts. Because it lives on fish, it is usually associated with water and is therefore rather easier to spot

among the large birds of prey with its white head and underparts and its habit of flapping slowly . . . hovering high over the waves before suddenly swooping down to take a fish in its powerful talons. (France, pp. 114–115)

. . . This bird, in extent of wings, is nine or ten feet; it feeds principally on fish, by darting itself down on them. . . . they fasten their talons in the back of the fish, commonly salmon, which are . . . on the surface. (It has been reported that they can) take a young seal out of the water. . . . It always builds near . . . the sea, or inland lakes, where it finds its prey. (Calmet, NH 68)

49

GLEDE

GLEDE (JPS and Fox, Kite)
Hebrew *Ra'aH*

> *the kite (Glede),* . . .
> —Deuteronomy 14:13

Milvus migrans. (Common European Red Kite) *Milvus*, L., a bird of prey, a kite; *migro*, L., I move from place to place, from *migrans*, wandering. What better choice for this particular kite than a wandering bird, to be avoided by those wandering in the desert, and whose descendants would be doomed to wander? The bird is even today encountered almost throughout the warmer parts of the Old World. The plumage is very dark brown above and mixed brown below; yet its common name is Black Kite.

Fox and JPS, along with other modern translations, prefer "buzzard," or "kite"; but the glede, as found in older translations, is a different bird and seems every bit as good a choice.

50

FALCON

FALCON
Hebrew *'aZaH*

> . . . the falcon, . . .
>
> —Deuteronomy 14:13

Falco tinnunulus. Common Kestrel. *Falx, falcis*, L. a sickle; a reference to the genus's curved talons. *Tinnio, tinnulus*, L., to do with ringing or tinkling. Refers to the species' high-pitched call. It inhabits a wide range, in effect all of the northern hemisphere, as does the Peregrine, *F. peregrinnus*, which may be an even better choice, for, like the Jews themselves, the bird maintains its identity though it is a "wanderer (and) is known throughout the world except in the polar regions" (Gotsch, p. 103). Again, the translations are difficult, although, in this case, JPS (p. 297) and Fox (p. 219) concur.

CONCORDANCE

Job 28:7.

Very little talmudic or midrashic material exists concerning this magnificent creature. The *pasuk* from Job "The Falcon's eye has not gazed upon it" (JPS, p. 1377) discusses that

257

which is so precious and distant that not even a creature with this best of all eyesight can see it. The implication is that only a person of faith can see it. Like other raptors, the bird went through a terrible period of decline, but, as legislation in the Western democracies has reduced levels of pesticides, in particular, DDT, and with a little help from some human friends, the bird has made a rebound, to the benefit of us all.

"And they began to beget wild beasts and birds and there came from them species of every sort: . . . falcons . . ." (*An. Apoc.*, in Tiller, p. 269).

AN ADDITIONAL TALMUD TAIL (*Chullin* 3:1; *Gemarah* 53a)

This *Mishnah* delineates under which circumstances, upon inspection, cattle and fowl are to be determined as *treif*, unfit for consumption. The *Gemarah* covers a question about whether clawing by a falcon (or other "unclean" birds) is of consequence or not: "The following defects render . . . *trefah* . . . small fowl if clawed by a hawk, large fowl if clawed by a falcon."

51

KITE

KITE
Deuteronomy 14:13

__Milvus milvus.__ See number 49. The species may be the same. This specimen has red plumage, and is commonly known as the Red Kite. It enjoys a similar range as *M. migrans.*

CONCORDANCE

Isaiah 34:15.

Yet again, the Hebrew words in the list presented problems of identification for the writers and for the latter-day translators: Falcons, kites, gledes, buzzards. This raptor, however, is common to the region, and is included in all the modern translations. France concurs with this viewpoint (pp. 91–92). Toperoff omits the bird, as he does the others in this list.

The kite has two reputations, one expected, and another of a most interesting nature. This species is a scavenger (which might explain the confusion with the buzzard); however, it also has a habit of constructing and lining its nest with stray pieces of colorful cloth, from scraps of bournouses or kafayahs to tent strands. Thus, their nest takes on a colorful patchwork-quilt appearance of a pack-animal. One might be reminded of the importance of cloth in Jewish law, in particular regarding property rights.

> Two are holding on to a garment. This one says, "I found it," and this one says, "I found it." This one says "All of it is mine," and this one says, "All of it is mine." This one shall swear that he does not have in it less than half of it, and this one shall swear that he does not have in it less than half of it, and they shall divide [it].
>
> BACKGROUND: TL[Y]T, Garment. This is the specific term for the garment worn by men during the Mishnaic and Talmudic periods. This garment was essentially a large, square piece of cloth in which men would wrap themselves, using it as an outer garment. A TaL[Y]T might be woven in a geometric pattern for decoration, and occasionally decorations made of more expensive materials were added to it. . . . (Later it remained) used during prayer and various other religious ceremonies. (*Bava Metzia* 1, in Talmud, Steinsaltz, 7)

Steinsaltz points out that the *tallit*, this large outer-wear garment, was chosen as example by the Rabbis for several reasons: As an outer garment, it was often doffed while working, thus lying susceptible to theft or accidental discovery; its simple form permitted easy division into two complete pieces; if one were to hold onto the whole cloth the value of half could be easily calculated.

52

OSTRICH

OSTRICH
Hebrew *Ya'aNaH*

the ostrich, . . .
—(Leviticus 11:16) rep. Deuteronomy 14:15

Struthio camelus. *Struthio*, L., an ostrich; *camelus*, L., a camel. The only species alive today. However, in ancient days, the same and similar species roamed through much of Africa, the Middle East, and Arabia. It is true that it cannot fly; it is also true that running speeds of forty miles per hour have been clocked. It is not true that it hides its head in sand. However, if alerted to danger, it may lower its head to a plane along the ground, a behavior that probably gave rise to the myth. In the United States today, some farmers and ranchers have discovered a rejuvenation of prosperity raising the animal in addition to, or even instead of, cattle or sheep. Actually native of Africa, once introduced to Australia, it adapted in the wild, although today its habitat is restricted more to the south of the continent.

CONCORDANCE

Isaiah 13:21; 34:13; 43:20.
Jeremiah 50:39 (see number 72 [others, numbers 55, 75]).

Micah 1:8 (see number 74).

Job 30:29 (see number 74) (I am become a brother to *jackals,*/And a companion to ostriches); 39:13 (see number 53), (The wing of the ostrich beats joyously).

Lamentations 4:3, (. . . But my poor people has turned cruel, Like ostriches of the desert).

The animal is huge, some individuals attaining a height of eight feet, but most are in the seven-foot range, with a massive body, and extraordinarily powerful legs. Its wings, although useless for any possibility of flight, can serve as "sails," and "oars" to assist it in its characteristic loping gallop.

The continuation of the passage in Job (14–18) presents an interesting insight into divers misconceptions of this "primitive" bird; drawing a comparison to the naturalist truths reveals a primer on its behavior and rationale. Cansdale develops a similar methodology, in greater detail, and with further examination of several translations (pp. 190–193).

13. *The wing of the ostrich beats joyously*
    When it runs, as described.
    Are her pinions and plumage like the stork's?
    The feathers are white or most colorful, especially those of the male, and have been designed in fashion statements from early civilizations until today.

14. *She leaves her eggs on the ground,*
    Letting them warm in the dirt

15. *Forgetting they may be crushed underfoot,*
    Or trampled by a wild beast.
    The ostrich is also unusual in that it does not build a nest, but digs a shallow pit in the sand, with part of the eggs exposed. During the day, when the heat of the sun can sufficiently incubate the eggs, the hen goes off to feed and seek water. Unlike those of other birds, the eggs are huge in size, and the shells are thick and hard. Birds of prey and other carnivores have been observed attempting to crack the shells, but their size, thickness, and hardness prohibits the hunters and scavengers from securing a workable purchase with their beaks or fangs and they generally choose to give up the game and seek more promising prey.

16. *Her young are cruelly abandoned as if they/*
    were not hers;
    Her labor is in vain for lack of concern

When hatched, the chicks are well camouflaged, especially when lying low in times of approaching danger. The mother will use a protection device similar to the "broken wing" dissemblance of North American birds: her "escape" is to draw attention to her as prey and away from the nestlings. As the verse after the next one indicates, she is quite capable of leading a merry chase.

17. *For God deprived her of wisdom,*
    Gave her no share of understanding.

Almost as if hatched in Jurassic Park, the ostrich is a very old bird, with a huge body, and a minute brain. Farb claims that it is "a primitive bird that relies heavily on blind instinct, displaying little of the intelligence seen in more advanced birds . . . For all its great size, its brain is only the size of a walnut" (pp. 124–126).

18. *Else she would soar on high,*
    Scoffing at the horse and its rider.

In actuality, she has neither wingspread nor pinion feathers designed for flight, and besides she is too heavy to lift were she to have them. However, she is quite capable of outrunning horses. Greeks and Romans alike were astonished at the ostrich's ability to outdistance their light cavalry. Unfortunately, perhaps due to its lack of intelligence, the animal will typically run in a straight line, leaving it vulnerable to strategically designed capture.

Regarding *kashrut*, the Leviticus and Deuteronomy *pasuchim* are quite clear, even though the bird is largely an herbivore; nonetheless, odd items have been found in its belly, including man-made objects.

A further note of interest: the animal is quite capable of being tamed, and, once accustomed to its new environment, it appears to enjoy the company of humans. Such pets were apparently not uncommon sights in the open air bazaars and suks of various shopkeepers and peddlers. It appears to be true that it will eat almost anything, including shop cast-offs of the day. Podwal (p. 14) recounts an *Aggadah* of a case where an ostrich devoured a worshiper's pair of *tefillin*, the vellum-leather phylacteries with which the devout bind their arms and form a circlet about their heads during the morning services, other than *Shabbat* and Holy Days, and containing in two cube boxes the scrolls of the declaration of faith prayers. The story is examined in greater detail on following pages.

(See also France, pp. 117–118; and Moller-Christensen and Jorgensen, who indicate that the animal is not silent but has been known to bellow, like a protesting ox.)

Podwal continues with some interesting legends and historical presentations. ". . . its bodily structure and habits so resemble a camel that there are some who believe that it originated as a cross between a bird and a camel."

Apparently, in the mystical community of Safed, a custom developed to suspend the shell of an ostrich egg near the *Ner Tamid*, the light that burns eternally over the holy ark in every synagogue. This practice, for a time, extended to "over the tombs of the patriarchs in Hebron."

The rationale is attributed to an eighteenth-century rabbi, R. Jacob Emden. The practice was meant to intensify the devotion of prayer, to help the worshiper avoid being distracted. "For the ostrich hatches its young by staring intently at the egg. This demonstrates how powerful sustained observation and concentration are. And indeed, they befit prayer."

The use of nonkosher products in holy places presents no problem. Again, the Rabbis are clear that such by-products may be utilitarian, so long as they are not consumed. It should not be surprising that ostrich eggs were used for many purposes, considering their abundance at the time, their great size, and durability. Interestingly, on *Shabbat*, it is permissible to handle items that the ostrich may have handled or even eaten. There is a legend that Noah fed bits of glass to the ostrich in order to satiate its great hunger; again, ostriches do seem to eliminate little other than carrion (and, apparently, not always this) from their diets (Farb points out that the creature will swallow small stones, but this is to be used to aid its digestion in its gizzard). The halakhah is found in *Shabbat* 128a: "We may also handle fragments of glass because it is food for ostriches (which are) common (*Tosefta*—and they may be handled even if one has no ostriches)." (See also *Genesis Rabbah* 31:14.)

Ostrich eggs were also perceived as a medicament for women who were experiencing uninterrupted vaginal bleeding: ". . . take an ostrich egg, burn it and wrap the ashes in a linen rag in the summer or a cotton rag in the winter" (Preuss, p. 379).

> At Israel's Hai-Bar Yotvata nature reserve, an eighteen-square-mile protected area in the Negev Desert, scientists are trying to save a unique group of animals: species mentioned in the Bible that are now threatened with extinction. The reserve's goal is to breed the animals and return them to the wild. Among the species . . . (is) the Middle Eastern ostrich . . . which had disappeared from Syria and Saudi Arabia. (Olivares)

AN ADDITIONAL TALMUD TAIL (M.K. 3:5, *Gemarah* 26a)

Mishnah:

> None rend [their clothes] nor bare [their shoulder] nor provide a repast [for the mourners], save those [who are] near of kin to the dead; nor do they provide a repast save [seated] on an upright couch.

In the *Gemarah*, the tearing of mourners' raiment leads to a discussion concerning the tearing of a holy scroll is not such a far leap of faith. Herein we learn, according to R. Chelko, who cites R. Chuna, that one who witnesses such a tear is obligated to make a clean rent. Why a second? The text in Jeremiah is the reference (36:24): *Then the Word of the Lord came to Jeremiah that the king had burned the roll and the words which Baruch wrote at the mouth of Jeremiah.* Thus, the parchment roll, one, and the words of writing, two. Now a story is related when R. Abba and R. Chuna b. Chizya were studying together.

> R. Abba got up to . . . relieve himself. He took off his head-phylactery and put it on a pillow, when a young ostrich came and wanted to swallow it ("R. Chuna

seized the bird and held it by the throat." [R. Abba
said,] "If that had been swallowed I should now have
had to make two rents.").

Soncino points out that in the *Yerushalami* (3:7), the names
of the Rabbis are reversed (p. 167).

53

NIGHT-HAWK

NIGHT-HAWK
Hebrew *TaCHMaS*

> . . . *the nighthawk* . . .
> —Deuteronomy 14:15

Accipiter gentilis. The Goshawk. *Accipiter*, common hawk; *gentilis.*, L., noble.

Actually a Falcon, the most popular of the birds used in falconry. It inhabits an extraordinary range in the northern hemisphere, as does *Buteo lagopus*.

CONCORDANCE

Job 39:26 (as "Hawk").

France prefers *Caprimulgus europaeus*, the Nightjar, which:

> . . . winters in Africa, (and passes) through Bible lands in the summer. It is a nocturnal bird, which would give rise to suspicions that it was unclean in its habits, and spends the day lying along the branch of a tree, almost invisible because of its superb cryptic coloration of mottled brown. At night it hunts moths and beetles with its excellent vision from large

eyes and darting flight. (Pp. 113–114; see also Moller-Christensen, p. 282)

If a true goshawk, there is an interesting phenomenon associated with the process of maturing. Along with peregrines, the birds are vertically streaked in their first year and horizontally "barred" as adults. Further, eye color undergoes metamorphosis as the bird ages: from gray (chicks and yearlings) to yellow (end of first year) to orange (adult) to scarlet or deep red (as an elder) (*Birds of Prey*, pp. 110–111).

54

S EAGULL

SEAGULL
Hebrew *SHaCHaF*

> . . . *the sea gull* . . .
> —(Leviticus 11:16) Rep. Deuteronomy 14:15

Larus argentatus; *L. delawarensis* is more peculiar to the American continent.

Hertz and older translations use the English term Sea-Mew, but I have not yet located this designation in the literature. France and Toperoff exclude the bird from their lists. Moller-Christensen indicate that there is some support that the animal is a kind of owl (p. 282).

According to Cansdale, flocks winter along the Mediterranean coast and inland ponds, as well as along the Red Sea, thus crossing at least that part of the Negev close to the waters. "While we were staying at Eilat we saw many small parties fly in from over the Gulf and make their landfall; then they rested on buoys and hawsers just off the beach . . ." (p. 177).

Cansdale also points out what fishermen from time immemorial have felt about the seagull—only as a competitor. He also indicates the reason it may be included in the unclean list; not only does it fish exceedingly well, it is an opportunistic scavenger and will haunt harbors and ports for the castoffs of men and women.

I once observed them for a considerable length of time along Goat Island in Rhode Island. A walk about the circumference of the island (named for the unique wild goats that occupied it before humans eradicated or sent them away) revealed: anything of food value, as well as the spectacular diving acts described unerringly to capture fish. They seemed well-fed and healthy. The beach rocks appeared tidy.

55

(LITTLE) (GREAT)
(HORNED) OWL

(LITTLE) (GREAT) (HORNED) OWL

Hebrew *K(C)o(V)S, YaNSHoo(V)F, TiNSHaMeT*

the little owl, the great owl, and the white owl;
—(Leviticus 11:17–18) Rep. Deuteronomy 14:16

Bubo bubo. L., a horned owl. The Great Eagle-Owl, since, today, the Great Horned Owl denotes a bird native to the Americas. The Little Owl, *Athene noctua,* like *B. Bubo,* enjoys a European and Mediterranean range today, as it did in days of old.

CONCORDANCE

Isaiah 13:21; 34:11 [poss. 14, as *lilith*];
Psalms IV–102:7 (I am become as an owl of the waste-places).

Owls have held a certain fascination for humans throughout history. They are mysterious, swooping in unerring flight in the deepest dark of night. At a time when night was truly night and very dark indeed, the sound of a blood-curdling screech and the barely audible flap of wings could bring terror into any heart. Owls are unique among birds of prey, and among many animals in general, in that their eyes are fully set in front for binocular vision, more like carnivorous mammals and primates. Indeed, this curious aspect of their anatomy may be what has led to their anthropomorphic descriptions, such as being wise. It may also be what has led to some of the other myths.

Owls can be traced back as far as the Pliocene period, and their ancestors may have existed as far back as the Miocene. Among birds of prey, owls have a unique anatomical accommodation. The enormous eyes, suitable for nocturnal living and hunting, have been mentioned. The binocular sweep allows for a visual field of about 110°, with an overlapping sweep of about 65°; human binocular vision contrasts very well—180°/140°, in most cases. However, almost all owls can do something very few humans can do—an individual can rotate its head on its axis as much as 270°! Often overlooked is perhaps even a better developed hearing sense. Unlike other birds or raptors, the owl's ears are huge, set at opposite ends of its oversized skull, and placed asymmetrically; that is, one ear channel is lower than the other. The inner ear is engorged with an uncommon abundance of nerves and blood vessels. Researchers have discovered that owls can hunt prey by sound alone. Their body weight is slight compared to their wing spread, thus allowing for soundless flight, if they so desire to glide to prey, which most do. Although many raptors' beaks are curved, owls' describe a particularly sharp angle, allowing their binocular eyes even more of a visual field and affording a sharp penetrating death blow. Finally, their claws are covered by fur, to protect from prey with dangerous bites (Owls, pp. 30–38; see also Moller-Christensen and Jorgensen, pp. 158–161, and France, pp. 118–120 [although some of France's concordance listings are presented by Hebrew translators as "Ostriches"]).

In fact, English translation of the several Hebrew words have presented difficulties, as in virtually all cases with birds, especially raptors, and, in particular, those in the unclean (nonkosher) lists. Cansdale (p. 148) derives a chart comparing the vocabulary list, but omits *lilit(h)* that Toperoff (pp. 177–180) and Moller-Christensen and Jorgensen include. Toperoff perhaps derives the most trustworthy of the excurses. In any event, the word *lilith*, or *lilit*, would be most important, for it recalls the myth or *drash*, extracanonical story, of the first woman, she who was before Eve, who wished above all else to be equal, even superior to her man, and so was banished from the Garden.

In a moment of puritanical ethos, the Rabbis contend that the defining moment of her banishment was when Lilith demanded that she assume the superior position in sexual union, rather than the underneath, submissive one. Later, Lilith vows revenge upon Eve and her children; by the Middle Ages, she has evolved or metamorphosed into a demon of the night, a succubus, and a slayer of infants—perhaps an attempt to reckon with stillborns, and what we know today as Sudden Infant Death Syndrome (although there is growing evidence that many of these cases represent infanticide; see Okie).

Trachtenberg (pp. 36–37) traces the legend to the "Babylonian Lamassu, and the *lamiae* and *striga* of Greek and Roman folklore." Thus, as he indicates, it would be wrong to assume that the unwelcome night visitor was an invention of talmudic or posttalmudic Judaism. He then proceeds to recount a succint version of the story, with an interesting supposition I haven't found in the other sources: When once captured by the angels, she screams, "Let me be! . . . I was created only to weaken . . . boys during their first eight days . . . girls until their twentieth day." Clearly, for boys, the rite of the covenant of circumcision provides protection; the interesting item is that the author supposes there may have been an initiation rite for girls at twenty days, now lost.

Frankel (pp. 4–5) gives an excellent recounting of the legend, followed by the usual feminist cry for equality so well found in this resource. But the most succint and thorough recounting that I have found is in Hyman.

> After God created Adam, who was alone, He said, "It is not good for man to be alone" (Genesis 2:18). He then created a woman for Adam, from the earth, as He had created Adam himself, and called her Lilith. Adam and Lilith immediately began to fight . . . But they would not listen to one another. . . . Lilith . . . pronounced the Ineffable Name and flew away into the air. Adam stood in prayer before his

> Creator: "Sovereign of the universe!" he said, "the
> woman you gave me has run away." At once the Holy
> One blessed be He, sent these three angels (Sanvi,
> Sansanvi, and Semangelaf) to bring her back.
> Said the Holy One to Adam, "If she agrees to
> come back, fine. If not, she must permit one hundred
> of her children to die every day." The angels left God
> and pursued Lilith, whom they overtook in the midst
> of the sea, in the mighty waters wherein the Egyp-
> tians were destined to drown. They told her God's
> word, but she did not wish to return. (Pp. 8–9)

At this point, the rhetorical dispute between the angels and
Lilith ensues. In the end, she vows to take Eve's children, but
if the children wear an amulet with one of these angels' names
upon it, then she, Lilith, must let the child live. This latter
aspect, as Trachtenberg would be inclined to propose, indicates a strong folk-superstition attribution and not a theological teaching. As Hyman concludes, "When Lilith sees their
names, she remembers her oath and the child recovers."

In our own time, Lilith has evolved or metamorphosed yet
again; she is today considered a guidon of the strong, independent woman who is to be regarded equal in every opportune
fashion. To this end, Frankel's and Hyman's works are impressive and pronounced contributions to the midrashic canon.

In any event, it is easy to see how the early, demonic Lilith
could be derived from an owl: a silent predator of the night,
with a human-like face and tufted claws, with eyes that glow
red in the air if, in an instant seen, and, where it in silence
wings its night duty, somewhere out there death soon follows.

"All kinds of birds are a good sign in a dream, except the
owl, the horned owl and the bat" (*Berachot* 57b).

56

PELICAN

PELICAN
Hebrew *Ka'aT*

the pelican . . .
—(See Leviticus 11:18) Deuteronomy 14:17

Pelecanus onocrotalus, L, (a) (the) Pelican. European White Pelican.

Ungainly on land, graceful and extraordinarily competent in the air, on the waters, and describing its career in-between, as it dives to fish.

The name is too restrictive, since its range even today, albeit more so in ancient days, extends across Europe, the Middle East, Africa, India, and Malaysia, preferring, of course, the rivers, lakes, and coastal waters.

CONCORDANCE

Isaiah 34:11 ("Jackdaws," JPS, p. 688).
Zephaniah 2:14 ("Jackdaws," JPS, p. 1075; see numbers 55, 4).
Psalms IV–102:7 (I am like a pelican of the wilderness) ("Owl," JPS, p. 1227; see number 55).

Moller-Christensen and Jorgensen, among other ornithologists, proclaim the bird the largest of the aquatic birds. It is a curious-looking animal, and anyone who has seen one is at once taken with the size of its body, its wing spread (up to nine feet in some individuals), and its huge beak, with its characteristic pouch. It is so efficient a fisher that fishermen detest seeing the flocks arriving.

It is the Psalms entry that has captured the imagination of the biblical ornithologists; that is, why would a pelican be seen, and apparently often, in the wilderness? After all, it is a sea and coastline animal. The answer may come in a close reading of Farb (p. 91) and Cansdale (pp. 156–157). Apparently, in biblical times, Lake Huleh, which borders the desert area, was more of a swamp and served the birds for rest and restoration in their long flights from the Black Sea to the lakes of Uganda, and return. Indeed, Farb states it is so even today: "In the Bible the word 'wilderness' referred to any uninhabited place, such as a mountain or a desert or a marsh. Pelicans are often found living in the deserts of the Bible lands, so long as there is an inland lake within flying distance."

The pelican was a very important symbol to Christianity in the Middle Ages. Upon return to the nest, the mother will regurgitate some of its food for its young; the recent catch is still typically bloody; the parent opens its substantial beak wide for the young to eat out of the pouch; the lower part of the beak often taps its own chest, and it is not uncommon for blood to spill onto the white feathers. Since it was mistakenly thought the bird was piercing itself and drawing its own blood, and since it was always known to be a most competent fisher of fish, the symbolic attraction is at once evident.

AN ADDITIONAL TALMUD TAIL (*Mo'ed Katan* 3:5; *Gemarah* 25b)

The *Gemarah* details the funeral procession of *tzaddikim*, righteous men, on their final passage to the Holy Land, Rabbah b. R. Chuna and R. Hamnuna. After the cortege encounters a certain Arab and explains to him the honor of the march, "a certain child opened [his funerary oration] thus: A scion of ancient stock/from Babylon came/ With records of prowess in/Combat and fame/Twice numerous pelican and/bittern from far/Came for ravage and ruin in/Shinar/ . . . (God)/Welcomes the souls of the pure and right." Where "combat" refers to predominance in argument; "Shinar" refers to Babylon, in effect conquered by the exilarchs and Jews in God's intent who were seemingly initially conquered by earthly armies. Pelicans have long ranges but return to fish by the sea, while bitterns adapt well to hiding places in camouflage and adapt wherever they are.

57

CARRION-VULTURE

CARRION-VULTURE (JPS, Bustard)
Hebrew *RaChaMaH*

> . . . *the Bustard (Carrion-Vulture)* . . .
> —Deuteronomy 14:17

Unknown today; or may be a generic translation by the Masorites; but see JPS, "Bustard," or, in Leviticus 11:13, "Black Vulture." Also, refer to number 41.

AN ADDITIONAL TALMUD TAIL (See under number 47)

58

C O R M O R A N T

CORMORANT

Hebrew *SHaLaCH*

> . . . *and the cormorant;*
> —(See Leviticus 11:17) Deuteronomy 14:17

Phalacrocorax carbo. Great cormorant. *P.*, Greek, bald-headed; *carbo*, black (its plumage is a glossy blue-black).

The largest of the cormorants (up to forty inches). It enjoys a rather astonishing range—the North American Atlantic coast across the Atlantic and Mediterranean Oceans as far more than halfway across the world through India. Sightings have also occurred as far east and south as Japan, Australia, and New Zealand. It must have been at least as wide-ranging in ancient times. Its size and its range were why I chose it.

The bird has not been particularly admired throughout biblical nor modern history. Even today, Kelley reports the vitriol that the bird, which has rebounded with great success in the last few years, raises in human fishermen.

This excellent fisher is huge, about the size of a goose, and exhibits agile diving skills. It is dark-feathered, and has a long, narrow beak. When perched, it can have a somewhat sinister appearance, an aspect that perhaps led medieval commentators to equate it with Satan. "Mantegna's famous painting, *The Agony in the Garden,* has the dark shape of the cormorant perched high over the garden of Gethsemane and bleakly staring at the praying Christ" (France, pp. 44–45).

According to Zimmer, Steven Emslie, a paleontologist, may have discovered a solution to the mysterious red tides. A startling fossil find in Sarasota County, mostly long-dead skeletons of cormorants, may, through an analysis of their remains, provide a clue to the death-dealing algae, apparently abundant in ancient days. "Red tides are thought to have been the first plague visited on the Egyptians in the Bible, and they are becoming increasingly common these days . . . (However,) this particular species of algae has been (here) for at least 50 million years, essentially unchanged . . ."

59

STORK

STORK
Hebrew *CHaSiYDaH*

the stork . . .
—(See Leviticus 11:19) Deuteronomy 14:18.

Cicona cicona. **White Stork.** *C.*, *L.*, a stork.

The well-known and beloved bird that does not deliver babies, but does build its nest on the roofs of houses and issues its mating call by clacking its bill. In most habitats, it is protected, correctly admired for its ability to reduce the populations of vermin and snakes. It is widespread throughout Europe, Asia, India, and Japan today and in ancient days.

CONCORDANCE

Jeremiah 8:7 (Yea, the stork in heaven knoweth her appointed times ["seasons," JPS, p. 785]) (see numbers 29, 79, 81).
Psalms IV–104:17 (as for the stork, the fir-trees are her house).
Job 39:13 (see number 52).
Zechariah 5:9 (I . . . saw two women come soaring with the wind in their wings—. . . wings like those of a stork . . .)

Like the pelican, the stork is a magnificent bird of passage, using the thermals to glide over hot desert areas with water pathways in view. Unlike the pelican, the stork thrusts its substantial red bill out in front of it, much like a needle-nosed jet fighter plowing the airstream. In ancient days, flocks numbering thousands must have passed overhead en route in their migrations from northern Europe to Africa and return. Apparently, according to the Jeremiah entry, in those days, they stayed over at times.

Almost all birds are attentive parents; but in no species is this most manifest than in the doting and devoted stork. Some lay observers claim that adolescents, upon leaving the home nest to build their own, will choose a location nearby, and parent and child will continue to visit one another. Ornithologists and zoologists agree that the animal will attempt to maintain, return to, and rebuild its own nest year after year, in some cases building layers of nest up to three feet. It is this homebody and most admired parental trait of the bird that probably gave rise to the euphemism-myth of how babies are brought into the world (Moller-Christensen and Jorgensen, pp. 181–183; see also: Cansdale, pp. 157–158; Farb, pp. 115–116; and France, pp. 144–145).

Storks will eat frogs, snakes, small fish, insects, and other items when these are hard to find. Probably for this reason, it is placed in the unclean list. France recalls one of the legends concerning Moses in Ethiopia. When Moses first left Egypt, the text fails to cover all the years of his life. The legends fill in these years with the Ethiopian stories—that is, that he first sojourned to Ethiopia, there used his skills as a military man to lead the nation to victory, and become their king, before he felt the call to move on to the Sinai Desert: ". . . taught the people of Ethiopia, when besieging a city guarded by serpents, to train young storks to fly as hawks and then, having starved them for three days, to release them over the city, whereupon the storks killed all the serpents and the city was taken."

It was said of the stork that its keen eyesight allowed it to see all the land of Israel while flying above the land of Babylon. Thus, a legend grew that it was the stork who would look forward to the day of redemption—that is, from the diaspora in Babylon to redemption and return, and by extension, to that time in the future, in the world to come. . . . *"Pirkei Shirah* . . . asks: 'What does the stork say? . . . from Isaiah: 'Bid Jerusalem take heart, and proclaim unto her that her time of service is accomplished, that her guilt is paid off'" (Podwal, p. 10).

"The stork's compassion is reserved for its own kind" (Hasidic saying).

AN ADDITIONAL TALMUD TAIL *(Ketubot* 4:6; *Gemarah* 50a)

The *Mishnah* details under which circumstances sons and daughters inherit their father's estate, although it sounds more obtuse at the beginning: "A father is under no obligation to maintain his daughter. . . ."

The *Gemarah* evolves into a discussion about when a person is of age to encounter certain passages—prayer, study, fasting, and so forth. From there various treatments and cures for illnesses of these children-adults are mentioned.

> Abaye stated, Nurse told me: A child of six whom a scorpion has bitten on the day on which he has completed his sixth year does not survive (Rashi: unless the appropriate remedy is applied). What is his remedy?—The gall of a white stork in beer. This should be rubbed into the wound [and the patient] made to drink it.

Perhaps it is from this *Gemarah* that we learn out the age for a *Bar Mitzvah*—for Abaye also states, ". . . a child . . . of 13 [is prepared] for a full 24 hour fast, and in the case of a girl . . . the age of 12." If so, it is significant that a woman (almost) renders this decision, for Abaye received this *pshat* also from his stalwart and wise nurse. Soncino points out that Abaye's mother died while he was still an infant and his upbringing was entrusted to this nurse. (See also Preuss, p. 436.)

60

H E R O N

HERON
Hebrew *'aNaFaH*

>   . . . *any variety of heron* . . .
>   —(See Leviticus 11:19) Deuteronomy 14:18

Ardea goliath. Goliath Heron. *A. L.*, a heron.

Obviously a very large bird (up to, sometimes exceeding, five feet in height). Since its habitat is the eastern seaboard of Africa, including the Red Sea and its inlets, along with its Philistine sobriquet, it is a natural choice.

> The heron's neck, so prominent a feature, is remarkably flexible. The bird can twist its neck to look sideways and behind. When taking flight, the heron gradually retracts its neck into a tight curve. On short hops, however, it may not retract it at all. The neck is complemented by a spray of breast feathers that accentuates the great blue's beauty. This plumage is most noticeable when viewed in profile. (de Silva)

De Silva goes on to describe the animal's unique fishing technique. Using its long legs, it will stand in one spot for a long time—"almost seeming like a statue," Thoreau and others have remarked: then, when an unfortunate fish does happen by, it uses its long neck and scissors-like sharp bill to make a lightening strike, apparently so fast that observers watching cannot themselves see it.

France points out that during the age of falconry, herons were one of the prey and attempted to escape in speed flight from their pursuers, thus becoming known dubiously for cowardice. "A dish of herons was presented to Edward II— cowardly birds for the cowardly king who dared not invade France" (p. 80).

A story in *Midrash Rabbah* relates how one of the rabbis quelled a potentially disastrous situation and, with the parable of a heron, may have prevented a vast destruction of the people. It was in that period of time following the debacle of the war of 65–70. Regarding, then, the Roman Empire: "In the days of R. Joshua b. Chananiah the [Roman] State ordered the Temple to be rebuilt."

In actuality, historians indicate that the Sanhedrin went to the Prefect, and Rome perceived that if it placated the leaders of the people, it might at last have a peaceful province on its southern borders. Later, the Emperor was told that the province, when its Temple was rebuilt, would no longer pay tribute. Now the Emperor could not rescind his order. It was suggested to him that he simply change the site or change the dimensions, knowing they would revolt at one of these concepts.

> . . . Now the community [of Israel] was assembled in the plain of Beth Rimmon; when the [royal] dispatches arrived, they burst out weeping, and wanted to revolt against the [Roman] power. Thereupon they [the Sages] decided: Let a wise man go and pacify the congregation. Then let R. Joshua b. Chanania go, as he is a master of Scripture. So he went and harangued them: A wild lion killed [an animal], and a bone stuck in his throat. Thereupon he proclaimed: "I will reward anyone who removes it." An Egyptian heron, which has a long beak, came and pulled it out and demanded his reward. "Go," he replied, "you will be able to boast that you entered the lion's mouth in peace and came out in peace" [unscathed]. Even so, Let us be satisfied that we entered into dealings with this people in peace and have emerged in peace. (Genesis 64)

61

H O O P O E

HOOPOE
Hebrew *Doo(V)CHiYPHaT*

> ... the hoopoe ...
> —(See Leviticus 11:19) Deuteronomy 14:18

Upupa epops. L., Greek, a hoopoe.

A most distinctive-looking bird, with a feathery crown, in shape not unlike that of an erect top-feather of a native American Indian or Meso-American Indian chief, and exhibiting a strange loping-hopping gait. It was very widespread throughout the promised land in biblical times. Today it has been sighted as far north as Iceland, as far south as Madagascar, and as far east as Malaysia. Its range is much more vast than Aristotle thought at the time, believing it restricted to the mountainous areas (p. 17).

The hoopoe, or lapwing, its more well-known name throughout the world, is a most unusual bird. Although capable of skilled flight, it prefers to root on the ground through "good" items as well as "bad" ones. Although it is a fictional piece, Michener's description serves well, nearly as an ornithological treatise.

> For as long as men had existed upon the land of Israel they had been accompanied by a curious bird,

the hoopoe, who had given them more amusement
than any other living thing. He was a stubby creature,
about eight inches long, with a black and white body
and a pinkish head, and was remarkable in that he
walked more than he flew. He was always busy,
hurrying from one spot on the ground to another, like
a messenger responsible for an important mission
whose details he had forgotten. . . .

As long as man remembered, this comical bird
had been called the hoopoe because of its ugly,
short, sharp call. It could not sing like the lark,
neither could it mourn like the dove, and to the men
of Israel it evoked no poetry summarizing the earth
on which they lived. To the Egyptians the hoopoe
was sacred; to the Canaanites it was clever . . . To
the Hebrews the hoopoe epitomized family loyalty,
for young birds tended their parents . . . (P. 202)

Michener's fictional account is at least partly verifiable by
scholars. Cansdale (pp. 187–188), France (pp. 80–81), and
Toperoff (pp. 117–119) agree concerning the Egyptian Hoopoe
cult, and relate three fascinating stories concerning this truly
odd bird: All three of them concern one of the endless
Solomon-animal stories: How the Hoopoe got its feathered
crest; How the Hoopoe brought Solomon the Shamir; How the
Hoopoe brought Solomon's invitation to the Queen of Sheba.

Toperoff relates the feathered crest story in a most charming manner. One time when King Solomon wished to investigate the southern reaches of his empire, he took his flying
carpet. As he came to the desert areas, the sun began to beat
upon his head. He asked many birds to fly over him to give him
shelter. They all refused. Finally, a large flock of hoopoes came
by. They agreed to fly as shelter en mass, shielding Solomon
from the intolerable sun. As a reward, he invested them with a
feather crown (in a sardonic version, the crown is gold and
heavy, a true crown; but this makes them a target for hunters
and thieves, and Solomon is asked to change them).

In the Shamir story, the hoopoe discovers the Shamir in the
Garden of Eden. The bird soon realizes if it drops the living
rock-cutter onto rocks, that plants and vermin will spontane-
ously generate in those areas; thereupon, the hoopoe proceeds to eat them. This may be a response to its habit of taking

bugs and grubs out of the earth and depositing them on rocks where the victims cannot dig into the earth and escape; then the bird strikes the grub like a hammer upon an anvil. In any event, Solomon calls for assistance and the hoopoe brings him the Shamir to assist in building the Temple.

In the third story, when Solomon heard that the Queen of Sheba had heard of his wisdom and wished to visit him, it was the hoopoe he selected to carry his message of invitation. The Queen, of course, welcomed the tired little messenger, and began to organize her entourage and set out for the Kingdom of Israel (see also *Gitten* 68, where, in some translations, in particular the Soncino, the bird is rendered as a "woodpecker"; the two birds are both similar and dissimilar: the hoopoe spends much of its time on the ground, the woodpecker upon a tree; however, both birds exhibit a similar hammer-pounding movement of the head and beak upon their vermin prey, and it is this similarity that may have given rise especially to the Shamir tale).

Bialik weaves a much more complex tale, with the birds discovering that Sheba's realm is more extensive than that of Solomon's, the birds loyally but with increasing exhaustion serving thence as go-betweens between the great king and the great queen, until the monarchs agree to visit each other's kingdoms. Solomon conducts his diplomatic sojourn by flying upon his carpet; later, Sheba hers with a mighty entourage (pp. 156–189). In this version she is also known as Balkis; curiously, in this version, Solomon discovers how to acquire the Shamir by visiting Asmodeus, king of the demons. The Queen of Sheba's visit itself, the timbre of the visit, in which she is amazed, contradicting Bialik's version, and during which she asks the king difficult riddles that he answers correctly, and Sheba's return are recounted in 1 Kings 10. Afterward, before she takes her leave, she presents the king with gifts from her own lands: "She presented the king with one hundred and twenty talents of gold, and a large quantity of spices, and precious stones. Never again did such a vast quantity of spices arrive as that which the Queen of Sheba gave to King Solomon . . ."

Following the visit of the Queen of Sheba, there is a legend that Solomon, in his wisdom, foresaw the destruction in the future of his magnificent Temple and, upon her return, secretly entrusted the Queen of Sheba with the holiest of artifacts, including the ark itself, king and queen swearing the High Priest to their secret: "King Solomon, in turn, gave the queen of Sheba everything she wanted and asked for . . . Then she and her attendants left and returned to her own land."

This legend continues down to the present day, where, supposedly, the ark still resides in Ethiopia, in a hidden location, where it is taken out once a year for worshipers to dance around. Supposedly, visitors to this area have seen it or, at least, something that resembles it.

Midrash Rabbah relates a fourth story, more of an allegorical parable than a legend. The story is found in almost precisely the same version in Leviticus 22:4, *Achare Mot*, and Ecclesiastes 5:8f.

> R. Simeon b. Chalafta . . . possessed a garden in which was a sycamore trunk, and a hoopoe came and built its nest in it. R. Simeon arose and upset it. . . . He took a plank, placed it in front of the nest, struck a nail through it and fixed it. . . . the hoopoe . . . brought a certain herb, which it placed on the nail and destroyed it. . . . R. Simeon . . . exclaimed, "It is well that I should conceal this herb, lest thieves go and do this and destroy human beings."

Finally, Trachtenberg has traced a horrific love-potion popular amongst the Germanic tribes in the Middle Ages and (unfortunately) incorporated by some in the Jewish community.

> If a man will hang the tongue of the hoopoe at the right of his heart, he will vanquish every opponent, even the king himself; and if a woman will hang its left eye on her neck, her husband will love her, no matter how ugly she may be, and will never love another. (P. 130)

62

B AT

BAT
Hebrew 'aTaLeiF

> . . . and the bat.
> —(See Leviticus 11:19) Deuteronomy 14:18

Rhinopoma microphyllum. Egyptian Mouse-tailed Bat.

Rhino, having to do with the nose or nasal area, that is, the snout.

One of its favorite roosting places even today, and no doubt in ancient times, are the interior tunnels of the pyramids. Who can say that these nocturnal creatures did not provide mystery, diversion, and perhaps a winged flurry of hope to the Israelite slaves? After all, here was a creature who entered the king's tomb itself and, at night, whenever or wherever it wished, flew to freedom. With a diet largely of insects and some other carrion, it is forbidden under the Jewish dietary laws; nonetheless, its range extending throughout Egypt and the Arabian peninsula, it could have seemed to the Israelites to be accompanying them on their wanderings through the desert, a familiar old friend, perhaps, as they made their way to the promised land.

Allen (p. 331) describes in a stylistic fashion his search for one of these creatures in an ancient tomb.

(The Arab) led the way up the side of one of the lesser pyramids to the opening of the shaft that extended down at a steep angle into the blackness of the tomb of an ancient Pharaoh. I followed not less eagerly, armed with a collecting pistol, and presently found myself in the bowels of the earth, where a large rectangular chamber had been hewn from the solid rock below the base of the structure. Lighting a small candle-end, my guide pointed to the low ceiling, where I made out dimly a small gray form depending spider-like by all four feet from the rocky vault. The discharge of the pistol in the narrow quarters sounded with uncommon reverberation as a mouse-tailed bat . . . fell at our feet. I half expected the pyramid itself to collapse on top of us with the roar. Elated at this success my guide excitedly beckoned me on. Feeling our way, we descended a still lower flight of rock-hewn step and at once lost sight of the opening through which we had come. We were in complete darkness save for the flickering light of the small candle that made dancing shadows follow our footsteps with grotesque movements. A strange feeling of oppression came over me as we continued our descent down the narrow passage, a feeling that the walls might at any moment collapse behind us and hold us there forever. Yet, I recalled at once that since they had stood for four thousand years we might perhaps safely chance a few moments more. On we went, when presently a solid wall stopped further progress. But my guide had been there before and, feeling with one hand in a fissure of the rock, presently drew forth another of the same species of bat. I followed his example and felt a thrill of excitement as small sharp teeth closed on one of my finger tips. . . . Further search rewarded us with half a dozen of these extraordinary bats whose peculiarities rank them in a family by themselves.

CONCORDANCE

Deuteronomy 14:18.
Isaiah 2:20 (On that day, men shall fling away,/To . . . the bat,/The idols of silver/And the idols of gold . . .)

It is easy to see how Isaiah and the Israelites felt about the bats and the bat metaphor. Their behaviors are so foreign to us that perception and reality are combined to render them both fascinating and odious. They are particularly useful animals; without them, we might all be overrun by hordes of insects. Moller-Christensen and Jorgensen describe well this paradox, perhaps recalling how the ancients might also have felt.

> . . . in . . . the warm Dead Sea Valley . . . they can be seen flying all year round.
>
> The insect-eating small bats are found in old buildings in Jerusalem, in grottoes and caverns in Galilee, by the Sea of Galilee, and near the Dead Sea. . . . Incredible numbers of them can be found living in the same place, where their excrement forms thick layers at the bottom of their caves, giving off a most odious smell. (Pp. 16–18)

This material is known as guano and is used by many agricultural peoples around the world as a most efficacious fertilizer.

Cansdale, however, points out that fruit bats today may change the reputation of the bat from insect-killing ally to orchard-devouring pest.

> Its numbers were probably negligible in biblical times.
>
> Bats normally become active at dusk, having spent the day asleep hanging upside-down in their roosts. Their unusual appearance and habits have long made them the subject of strange beliefs, often with evil associations. (Pp. 135–136)

Another reason the bat may be in the list of unclean birds, seemingly an erroneous classification, is that it was considered to have magical properties and, therefore, was worshiped by the Egyptians. Indeed, throughout the centuries, bats have been associated with supernatural powers, as they swoop softly and unerringly in the darkest of nights. Bats are equipped with highly developed senses—sight, smell, hearing, and, in addition, a unique sonar-type sensory device called echolocation. This device can be used to seek out even the tiniest of insects on the wing as the bat whooshes through any natural or man-made barrier. Their populations are inestimable. In recent years, communities in the southwest areas of the United States have been protecting their habitats and have come to regard their ability to reduce significantly bothersome insect populations as very friendly indeed (see also France, pp. 20–21).

Again, from *Berachot* 57b: "All kinds of birds are a good sign in a dream, except the owl, the horned owl, and the bat."

AN ADDITIONAL TALMUD TAIL (*Betzah* 7a)

> Our Rabbis taught: All creatures which copulate during the day are born during the day . . . this refers to a fowl; "Those which copulate during the night are born during the night," this refers to the bat; "Those . . . by day and night give birth by day and night," this refers to man and whatever is like him.

63

Bee

BEE
Hebrew *DeVoRaH*

Then the Amorites . . . came out against you like
so many bees and chased you.
                    —Deuteronomy 1:44

Apis mellifera. The common honey bee.

"It is not rare to find 20,000 working bees in a hive . . . The opening of a . . . hive gives passage to 100 bees a minute, which makes . . . morning till . . . evening, 80,000 re-entrances, at 4 excursions for each bee . . ." (Figuier, pp. 319–320 [numerals mine, exchanges for spelled-out]).

CONCORDANCE

Judges 14:8.
Isaiah 7:18 (In that day, the Lord will whistle to . . . the bees in the land of Assyria).
Psalms 118:12.

Bees, like ants, have a highly engineered social structure, both in terms of behavior, and in terms of their constructed habitat. They are in-vitro biological engineers; at birth, each is born into its fated existence, all for the collective good of the hive. If we were to speak in anthropological terms, the entire order would seem to us Huxlian.

The biblical references indicate that bees, for a long time, were wild and fierce, and domestication appeared relatively late for the Israelites, perhaps not until the Babylonian exile. However, there is considerable evidence to support both the wild and dangerous swarms and a form of early domestication, perhaps by the Egyptians. Shaler points out that bees often search for new locations to build nests, perhaps due to overpopulation, in which a break-away group will attempt to live on its own; or two queens are "developed," and one will leave on her maiden (and only) flight, with her courtiers in tow. In all too many occurrences, this new swarm is doomed to wander to its death, unable to locate a suitable place.

The survival of bees and humans has evolved into a symbiotic relationship, for much of our food supply is dependent on the cross-pollination that bees provide for plants (pp. 190–193).

Pinney indicates that as late as the middle part of this century at least, there were still swarms of wild bees in the region.

> . . . The wild bees of this region are especially noted for their ferocity in attack. The virulence of their venom increases in warm weather. They build their hives and nests on precipitous rocks or in hollow trees hard for man or animals to reach. . . .
>
> Even today much of the honey of this region is collected from these wild bees . . . Some years ago the people of the region let a man down the face of the rocks by ropes. He wore protective clothing that completely shielded him from the attacks of the bees and gathered a large amount of honey. However, he was so intimidated by the great swarms of angry bees that he could not be persuaded to repeat the adventure. (Pp. 182–183)

The "dance" of the bees has been well described by Pinney and other entomologists. The larvae of bees are fed different nutrient concoctions; the result produces queens, workers (infertile females), drones (males), and fertile females that may become queens. Drones attend the queen and the fertile females. Workers tend to go out searching for nectar. When it is located, the bee returns to the "front door" of the hive. There she engages in a wiggle or waggle (or round) dance, sometimes described as a figure eight or infinity symbol. The dance largely indicates that nectar is discovered. If the flower is farther than 165 to 300 feet, the bee's dance will enhance the tail-wagging steps. The constant placing of the head informs her comrades of the distance of the flower. For color and consistency of the plant, she has brought with her a sample. Her fellow workers gather around her in a semicircle, watching the dance intently, and probably catching the scent of the sample; soon the squadron launches its sorties on its industrious mission to collect the necessary resource. Then the animals return to their hive and begin transmutation of the plant's product into honey, wax, and food for the colony.

Although the bee concordance lists only four appearances in the biblical text, honey appears over forty-five times and wax appears at least four (Pinney, Cansdale, pp. 244–246). Except for the entry in Judges, where Samson returns to the site of his defeat of the lion and discovers a hive of bees in the dried-out carcass, the three remaining references relate to the ferocity of the wild swarms.

However, it is the by-product of honey that particularly accompanies biblical and Jewish history. In the incident of the twelve spies (Numbers 13:27), the land is said to be a land flowing with milk and honey. This description repeats several times. The implication is that the land is so fertile it would readily yield grazing land for cattle, productive orchards, and great agrarian prosperity. From our own era of watching a desert and polluted land turned into a major agricultural economy, it is easy to see how this must have been the case, and why Canaan-Israel was such a desired territory throughout the generations.

If the Israelites did indeed wait to become apiculturists until influenced by the Babylonians, they caught up fast; ever since then, Jews have been among the best bee-keepers. The Talmud has several references to honey and its usage. *Berachot* 44b and *Bava Metzia* 38a relate its use for medicinal purposes. A passage quoted by most scholars includes a device as if torn from our own science and nature magazines—

controlling the population of the species through a form of eugenics: in this case, by rendering the bees who come in contact with mustard seed impotent (*Bava Batra* 80a); there was apparently in Babylon a mustard seed garden near a bee hive, and this was the observation of some of the bee keepers. *Berachot* 57b indicates that honey was to be considered as sweet as a sixtieth of manna itself (see also Toperoff, pp. 22–25; Newman pp. 135–136; Pinney; and Cansdale).

The issue of honey in terms of *kashrut* is an interesting one. The list of forbidden creatures, found throughout Leviticus 11, includes swarming things or flying insects. This would generally be seen to include the bee and its by-products that come from within the animal, which would seem to include honey. Certainly, honey of the wasp and the hornet is forbidden. There are three explanations. I once heard Rabbi Glickman answer this question with what Rashi might have said: so you see, the answer is simple—"They ate it" (meaning, of course, the generations in the desert and in the land). Again, the multiple listings of "a land flowing with milk and honey," a mantra that has even become part of our song repertoire, indicates that it was certainly acceptable. The rabbinical reason, found in a *Tosefta*, is as follows: ". . . the bee only gathers in its body and expels unchanged that which it sucks out of blossoms and leaves, and does not add anything from its own body" (unlike the other insects where the honey is a direct product of the body; *Berachot* 7b: see also Preuss, pp. 563–564; Forst, pp. 32–38).

Preuss enumerates some of the medicinal qualities or warnings:

> . . . it is not good to eat too much honey. He who eats one-quarter measure of honey at one time will have his stomach . . . torn out. . . . it serves as an extraordinarily efficacious nourishment for children. . . .
>
> Rancid honey was applied to the wounds of camels caused by the chafing of the saddle. Barley flour in honey was consumed for stomach pains . . . Wax was used for plasters.

Also, it is said to stimulate and satiate an appetite (see *Yoma* 83b, *Shabbat* 154b, *Gittin* 69b).

Another issue concerned why the substance was forbidden on the offering altar in the Temple. Some feel that it was because it was first cultivated by the heathen; but Preuss derives that it was known to sour or lead to souring of the offering itself.

Nonetheless, in the Middle Ages, mainly among the heathen, albeit Jews in surrounding communities were influenced, it was not unknown for sacrifices to occur for superstitious reasons. "One such prescription required that two white doves be slaughtered in a special manner, and their entrails mixed with old wine, pure incense, and clear honey, and the whole burned on the hearth; the smoke rising from this would induce a divinatory dream" (Trachtenberg, p. 131).

In one of the Hittite myths, Telepinus, the son of the Storm-god, in an adolescent fit of pique, runs off and cannot be found. The Storm-god must find his son, or the results could be catastrophic for an agrarian society. He sends giant and lesser gods, to no avail. Finally, one of his advisers suggests sending one of the smaller creatures, one who could fly here and there and is an excellent searcher.

> The Bee went away and searched . . . the streaming rivers and searched the murmuring springs. The honey (within) it gave out, [the wax within it] gave out. Then [it found] him in a meadow in the grove at Luhzina. It stung him on his hands and his feet. It brought him to his feet, it took wax and wiped his eyes (and) his feet, [it purified him] . . .
> (Trans. A. Goetze, in Pritchard 1, pp. 87–88)

> From the beginning good things have been created for the good,
> > Just as evils have been created for sinners.
> > The elements necessary for man's life
> > Are water and fire and iron and salt.
> > And wheat flour and milk and honey,
> > The blood of the grape and olive oil and clothing . . .
> (*Wisdom of Ben Sera*, 39:26, Goodspeed, 300)

"Five things are a sixtieth part of something else, namely, fire, honey, *Shabbat*, sleep, and a dream. Fire . . . of Gehinnom.

Honey . . . of manna. *Shabbat* . . . of the world to come. Sleep . . . death. A dream . . . of prophecy."

In the opening of *D'vorim*, Deuteronomy, *Midrash Rabbah* (6) provides several pointed similes: "Just as the honey of the bee is sweet and its sting sharp, so too are the words of the Torah . . ."

There is a beautiful play on words in the Hebrew. The opening of the book is *'eiLeH Had'VoRiM*, "These are the words . . ."; now DVR, depending on the voweling, can mean either "word" or "bee"; in fact, the name *D'VoRAH*, Deborah, comes from the same root as "bee." Deborah was a righteous judge in Israel who persuaded others to good deeds through her words, but a judge who could also use her sting. "Just as the bee reserves honey for its owner and for the stranger its sting, so to Israel the words of the Torah are the elixir of life, but to the other nations . . ."

Of course, the Rabbis did not mean that when the nations perform *mitzvot* it is poison to them; quite the contrary; here, however, the implication is when the nations use the words and teachings of Torah for evil purposes . . . "R. Judah b. R. Simon said in the name of R. Levi: Just as everything the bee gathers, it gathers for its owner, so too whatever merits and good deeds Israel accumulate, they accumulate for [the glory of] their Father in Heaven."

Toperoff provides succint reminders of two charming Jewish traditions concerning honey.

> . . . in the twelfth and thirteenth centuries . . . On Shavuot, which commemorates the giving of the Torah on Sinai, the Jewish child at the age of three was escorted to the synagogue to receive his first Hebrew lesson. . . . Each letter (on his slate) was smeared over with honey, and as soon as the child repeated after the rabbi the name of the letter, he was allowed to lick the honey covering the letter. . . . the Torah . . . became literally as sweet as honey.

The second custom is one with which almost all Jews are familiar. At the beginning of the spiritual new year, on the eve of Rosh Hoshana, one dips apples or bread into honey and eats it for wishes of a sweet year. Here is the blessing as rendered by the Bokser prayer book (p. 63): "May it be Thy will, O Lord our God and God of our fathers, to renew unto us the coming year in sweetness and in happiness."

An Additional Talmud Tail (*Betzeh* 5:1; *Gemarah* 36a)

Mishnah:

> One may let down fruit through a trap-door on a festival but not on a Sabbath, and cover up fruit with vessels on account of the rain; and likewise jars of wine and jars of oil; and [even] on a Sabbath one may place a vessel beneath the drops of rain.

The *Mishnah* here is discussing when letting down fruit into the bin may be considered carrying or servile work; however, sensibly, one may protect her or his house from water damage. *Gemarah*:

> Come and hear: one may spread a mat over a beehive on a Sabbath.

Such action is to protect the hive, in much the same way one protects his or her home from rain; albeit, if possible, it should not be moved. This now raises the question of whether the honey can be taken out on Sabbath. After all, it is there; yet the mat may be to protect the honey, not the bees—and besides, the ruling may differ in summer, when there is honey and in winter, when there is little or none.

The two honeycombs reserved for the bees' use must remain—and from this dicta R. Judah holds none can be taken; and, of course, one may not catch the bees themselves for he may be "trapping" them—certainly one of the thirty-nine forbidden tasks on *Shabbat*.

64

F O X

FOX

Hebrew *SHoo(V)'aL*

*S*amson went and caught three hundred foxes. He
took torches and, turning [the foxes] tail to tail, he
placed a torch between each pair of tails.

—Judges 15:4

Vulpes vulpes vulpes. L., a fox.

The most common of the species, commonly called the
European Red Fox. It inhabits North America, Europe, Africa,
Asia, and India. A better choice might be *Canis rueppelli*, or
Ruppell's Fox, observed and identified by its namesake be-
tween 1822 to 1827. The creature is native to North Africa and
the Middle East.

CONCORDANCE

Psalms 63:11 (They [enemies] shall be a portion for foxes).
Song of Songs 2:15 (Take us the fox, the little fox, that spoil the vine-
yards . . .).
Lamentations 5:18.

Foxes enjoy a reputation for being sly, clever, cunning.
Foxes tend to live solitary lives. They are small creatures, but,

when left undisturbed by human interference and encroachment, they are successful hunters and adaptable.

There are many fables about foxes, practically all showing
their cleverness and their facility with quick wit. Sometimes
this results in their triumph at the expense of a gull, sometimes
the trick backfires on them. Br'er Rabbit, Br'er Fox, and Br'er
Bear, and the story of the tar baby and the briar patch
represent good, well-known examples. In Judaism, too, the
main references follow this genre of stories, legends, parables,
and fables.

In *Sanhedrin* 39a, we are told by R. Jochanan: "R. Meir had
300 parables of foxes, and we have only three left." Rashi then
proceeds to tell these three stories (which really appear as
only two stories) as one.

The first concerns a story that appears frequently in
collections of parables concerning foxes, with fugues upon the
theme: A fox compels a wolf to attend a human affair where
there is food present, tricking him into thinking he will be
welcome. The wolf instead is beaten. When he returns to the
fox, the fox informs him it was his (the wolf's) father who was
to blame; aforetime the elder wolf had stolen food from these
affairs. The fox then persuades the wolf there is abundant food
at the bottom of a well "which had a beam across it from either
end of which hung a rope with a bucket attached."

The fox climbs down. He tells the wolf to follow. The wolf
scampers down. The counterbalance mechanism raises the
fox to leave the poor wolf below without sustenance. A parable
left out of this tale is one where the fox is to be drowned by the
Angel of Death and saves himself by pointing out to the angel
his reflection in the water—thus, that a fox has already died
that day. The angel releases him. He scoots away to safety.
Later, a drowning attempt is made upon him by a school of
fish, but he escapes, using the same machination. Here, the fox
uses a talmudic principle, a *chol v'chomer*: "If I was able to fool
the Angel of Death himself, how much more could I be
expected to fool lowly fish like you" (see also Podwal, p. 30;
France, pp. 60–62; Feliks, p. 37; Wiley, pp. 212–216); Schochet's
version provides the fox a Parthian shot: "And how am I to get
out?" demanded the wolf. "Ah," said the fox, "The righteous is
delivered out of trouble and the wicked cometh in his stead. Is
it not written, 'Just balances, just weights'?" (pp. 119–120).

Some scholars question the animal as being properly translated in the Judges entry. This is the famous story of Samson tying fire-brands to the foxes' tails and setting them through the fields of the Philistines. The Rabbis saw this as measure for measure punishment for a people with proclivities to idol offerings and human or child sacrifice. Since a fox is a solitary animal, these scholars argue that the more socially oriented jackal, which even resembles a fox, would be a better choice.

However, France argues that it is difficult to judge from our own time what was meant at that time; and Wiley draws a rational analysis, demonstrating that foxes were quite numerous at that time, and their lairs were not so far apart.

In *Pirke Avot* 4:20, R. Mattithiah ben Heresh said: "Be first in greeting every man, and be a tail to lions and not a head to foxes" (p. 66). Goldin's commentary derives from Maimonides:

> This Sage counsels his fellow Jews, who were subjugated to the Romans, to submit to their rule. In *Yerushalmi* (*Sanhedrin* 4, 8) an adverb the opposite of this one is recorded: "Be a head to foxes, and be not a tail to lions." Such was also the current proverb in Rome. According to Maimonides . . . "It is better for a person to be a disciple of someone who possesses more knowledge than he, than to be the master of someone who is inferior to him. The former will lead to his improvement, the latter to his deterioration."

Toperoff's commentary clears up any confusion concerning this interpretation.

> . . . in the ancient academy of learning, scholars sat in rows and when the head of the row was promoted all scholars moved forward. Therefore, the proverb . . . conveys the meaning that it is better to be placed at the tail of the first row than at the head of the second row. (Pp. 81–82)

A curious parable is found repeated in *Leviticus Rabbah* 22:4 and *Ecclesiastes Rabbah* 8. A certain man watches a series of animals revive dead comrades, placing a certain herb upon them. The man thinks to himself, "It is well for me to take this herb with which to revive the dead in the land of Israel."

> He . . . saw a dead fox lying in the road. . . . He placed the herb on it and revived it. He continued his journey . . . he saw a dead lion lying in the road. . . . He placed the herb on it and revived it. The lion sprang upon him and devoured him. That is what people say: "Do no good to an evil person and harm will not come to you; for if you do good to an evil person, you have done wrong."

> There is a saying among . . . (Iraqi) Jews in their Arabic dialect: "Till you prove who I am, there is time enough to strip off my skin."

Here follows the story upon which this saying is based.

> Once a fox was seen running away. (When asked why) he answered, "Hunters are chasing camels, killing them, and stripping off their skins."
> The people were amazed. "But you are a fox, not a camel . . ."
> The fox answered, "Till I prove who I am, there is time enough to strip off my skin." (*Folktales*, p. 65)

AN ADDITIONAL TALMUD TAIL (*Shabbat* 5:2; *Gemarah* 53a)

The *Mishnah* discusses the principle of items laid upon or attached to animals. It may appear that one may be readying them for work on the holy day or leading them to a place wherein they might begin work, obviously forbidden on the Sabbath Day. However, the principle of kindness to the animal (laying on of a cushion to keep it warm is also understood, an act not only permissible, but encouraged—it is presented in the *Gemarah*). Thus, for example: "An ass may go out with its cushion (or blanket) . . ."

One of the "objections" raised in the *Gemarah* is: "A horse must not be led out with a fox's tail." According to Rashi, the tail was suspended between the horse's eyes to ward off the evil eye. Nothing is indicated as to how the horse may have regarded this circumstance (Soncino, p. 242).

There is another consideration regarding the fox's tail tied to lead the horse. Peradventure it could fall off, and a person might come along and pick it up and, by mistake or negligence, carry the item past the required cubit limit. Therefore, it might, or might not, be considered to be a burden. One should err on the side of the circumstance never developing.

65

B E A R

BEAR
Hebrew *Do(V)V*

> *D*avid replied to Saul, "Your servant has been
> tending his father's sheep, and if a lion or a bear
> came and carried off an animal from the flock,"
> —1 Samuel 17:34, 36–37

Ursus arstos. *Ursus*, L., a bear; *arktos*, Gr., a bear.

Its wide-ranging habitat extends from Eurasia across Europe (where today remnants of forests and woods can be found) and North America.

CONCORDANCE

2 Samuel 17:8 (as a bear robbed of her whelps).
2 Kings 2:24.
Isaiah 11:7 (see numbers 12, 13, 16); 59:11.
Hosea 13:8.
Amos 5:19 (see numbers 2, 16).
Proverbs 28:15 (As a roaring *lion* [number 16], and a ravenous bear; /So is a wicked ruler over a poor people).
Job 9:9.
Lamentations 3:10 (see number 16).
Daniel 7:5.

Bears are large, powerful, swift, and agile animals, able to adapt to their particular environmental and habitat requirements. They range from the North Pole as polar bears, throughout the northern hemisphere as kodiaks and grizzlies, to the more common and numerous brown and black bears. They have several advantages in their size, power, and agility, as well as being able to stand for considerable lengths of time on their rear legs, thus affording them a long-range visual field, as well as occasionally employing their front paws for climbing and handling. Bears wisely attempt to avoid human beings. When there is encroachment, however, or, in particular, when a mother is afraid for the safety of her cubs, she will attack, viciously, without mercy. The incident in 2 Kings is an excellent example.

The brown bear can grow up to six feet and weigh in as cub at five hundred pounds. The bear is unique in that although it is a predator, it is an omnivore, and the construction of its teeth is also peculiar in that it allows for both prey and vegetables.

Bears eat roots, grass, berries, fruits, leaves, nuts, honey, and ants, and hunt deer, oxen, and horses. They seem particularly fond of sheep. For such a huge animal, it is a bit surprising that her young are so very small when born, even smaller than a pup or a kitten, and this may in some part explain her extreme protective instinct (Pinney, pp. 115–116; Moller-Christensen and Jorgensen, pp. 19–22; see also France, pp. 21–22).

When roused, their attacks are fierce, and few hunters or shepherds caught off guard come out the better for it. David was such an example of a shepherd able to protect his flock and was thus prepared for the battle with the giant Goliath.

There are several stories and fables concerning bears, and some deal with the mishnaic period. Feliks (p. 39) and Toperoff (pp. 17–19) recount the legend of Rabbi Chanina ben Dosa and the bears. R. Chanina ben Dosa appears frequently in the Talmud as one who has a certain control over dangerous animals. In this parable, R. ben Dosa was a goatherd. As we know from the story of David, shepherds and goatherds have to be particularly vigilant concerning wild beasts. Ben Dosa was told that his goats were doing crop damage. He stated, "If it should be so, then let bears devour them; but if it is not so, then, when my goats come home in the evening, let there be the bears on their horns." At evening the goats came with bears on their horns.

The stories of bears and the Rabbis continue beyond the mishnaic period, even into the time of the Enlightenment. Here is a version of the story of Rabbi Uri Strelisker and the bear.

R. Strelisker was traveling in the company of some of his *hasidim*. They were late, and, afraid they might not make it back to their village in time for *Shabbat* to begin, they determined to take a short cut through the woods. Suddenly their horses stopped. They looked up. A huge bear had come onto the path and was blocking their way, growling, and seemed about to attack both men and beast. R. Strelisker got out of the coach, walked up to the bear, and stared him in the eyes. After a while, the bear whimpered, stood down, and cowered back into the woods. The group continued on their way and arrived in time for a wonderful *Shabbat*. When the story was told over *Shabbat* lunch, his courtiers thought a miracle had occurred. R. Strelisker, however, merely quoted Genesis 9:2, "The fear and the dread of you shall be upon all the beasts of the earth and upon all the birds of the sky—everything with which the earth is astir . . ." (alternate version in Toperoff).

Another talmudic passage, *Berachot* 58b, demonstrates that the Rabbis were familiar with astronomy, astrology, and the zodiac. "Samuel contrasted two texts. It is written, *Who Maketh the Bear, Orion, and the Pleiades*." The quote is from Job. The Rabbis are discussing shooting stars. Samuel believes they are a comet. ". . . I am as familiar with the paths of heaven as with the streets of Nehardea, with the exception of the comet, about which I am ignorant. There is a tradition that it never passes through the constellations of Orion, for if it did, the world would be destroyed." Samuel then contrasts the passage from Job with one from Amos (5:8), which omits the Bear, obviously Ursa Major. The reconciliation is revealing: "Were it not for the heat of Orion the world could not endure the cold of Pleiades, and were it not for the cold of Pleiades the world could not endure the heat of Orion."

In *Genesis Rabbah* 87, Joseph's temptations in Egypt are given the simile of a bear. Once, in the matter of Potiphar's wife: "I will incite a bear against thee"; in the second, Joseph's vanity calls into question his manhood.

It may be illustrated by a man (Joseph) who sat in
the street, penciling his eyes, curling his hair and
lifting his heel, while he exclaimed, "I am indeed a
man." "If you are a man," the bystanders retorted,
"here is a bear; up and attack it!"

An Additional Talmud Tail (*Avodah Zorah* 1:7)

Regarding the nations, viz., idol worshipers—"One should not
sell them bears, lions, or anything which may injure the
public. . . ." From this we learn out that the nations are
regarded to have violent natures and Jews cannot sell them
weapons, since it is expected they will use them in a violent
fashion and will use them against human beings. These animals were used in so-called games of baiting, which were very
cruel to the animal, as well as terrible gore-causing gladiator
contests.

In *Gemarah Ta'anit*, which deals with fast days, we learn
that a decreed fast day was called Trajan's Day. The *Gemarah*
relates that when Trajan was about to execute two brothers,
he chided them that God did not rescue them as He did
Hananiah, Mishael, and Azariah (Daniel 3). Their retort is to
maintain *kiddush hashem*, the sanctification of the name:

(They) . . . righteous men . . . merited that a miracle
should be wrought for them, and Nebuchadnezzar
also was a king worthy for a miracle to be wrought
through him, but as for you, you are a common and
wicked man and are not worthy that a miracle be
wrought through you; and as for us, we have de-
served of the Omnipresent that we should die, and if
you will not kill us . . . the Omnipresent has, in His
world many bears and lions who can attack us and
kill us . . . (18b)

The men go on to predict the evil one's demise for his
doing the slaying—and, in fact, soon after the execution,
Trajan is assassinated. However, Soncino points out: "The
identification of the name with Trajan is disputed . . . (since
he) is known to have died a natural death."

The author indicates this may have been the emperor's

general, Lusius Quietus, who was in fact executed by Trajan (p. 89). There is a tradition that the day is called Yom Nicanor, and is disputed whether it was a day of joy or a fast day. Certainly, the day of Trajan's death would have been a day of joy for the Jews. Rashi indicates that the men were considered saints.

66

FLEA

FLEA

Hebrew *PaR'oSH*

Against whom has the king of Israel come out?
Whom are you pursuing? A dead dog? A single flea?
—1 Samuel 24:15

Pulex irritans

CONCORDANCE

1 Samuel 26:20.

I think it is about fifteen years ago, that the whole population of Paris could see the following wonders exhibited on the Place de la Bourse for sixty centimes. They were the learned fleas. I have seen and examined them with entomological eyes, assisted by a glass.

Thirty fleas went through military exercise, and stood upon their hind legs, armed with pikes, formed of very small splinters of wood.

Two fleas were harnessed to and drew a golden carriage with four wheels and a postillion. A third flea was seated on the coachbox, and held a splinter

of wood for a whip. Two other fleas drew a cannon on
its carriage; this little trinket was admirably finished,
not a screw or a nut was wanting. These and other
wonders were performed on polished glass. The flea
horses were fastened by a gold chain attached to the
thighs of their hind legs, which I was told was never
taken off. They had lived thus for two years and a
half, not one having died during the period. To be
fed, they were placed on a man's arm, which they
sucked. When they were unwilling to draw the cannon of the carriage, the man took a burning coal, and
on it being moved about near them, they were at
once roused, and recommenced the performances.
(Baron Walckenaer, *Histoire Naturelle des Insectes
Apteres*, c. 1840 [see Figuier, p. 28]).

Figuier also reports a rather uncommon trait among these
creatures in the insect world: "The mother disgorges into the
mouths of the larvae the blood with which she is filled." The
author also indicates that if a lion (number 16) were to leap
with the analogous leaping ability of the flea, she could leap
nearly a mile.

Fleas are parasites. Although they can live off detritus and
effluvia, their life-cycle cycles best when they have landed or
laid eggs upon a furry or, as all too many of us unfortunately
know, occasionally a smooth-skinned, mammal. Pinney accords a clear entomological description of the animal.

The Order *Siphonaptera* contains only the fleas. . . .
their mouth parts are formed into piercing and
sucking tubes. The body is laterally compressed, the
head is distinct but the thorax is composed of three
hinged segments. The limbs progress in length, size,
and strength backward (allowing for their prodigious
leaping ability) as well as by normal running and
crawling. Fleas are all of very small size.
    Fleas pass through a complete metamorphosis.
The eggs are laid in the nests of the animals the adult
parasitizes . . . There is a resting pupal stage— . . .
(188)

France picks up the cycle description.

The female flea lays several hundred eggs at a time . . . on the host, and these develop after a week or two into white, worm-like larvae, having neither heads nor eyes, but simply biting jaws which enable them to live . . . Adult fleas need a stimulus of some kind to enable them to emerge from the cocoon, and this is provided by a vibration or movement from the body of a living animal. . . . if they happen to be situated on an animal which has died, they can remain in cocoon until a living animal comes along on which they (hop upon and) feed . . . (Pp. 58–59)

Fleas have been throughout history, and continue today to be, major vectors of bacterium and viruses that have devastated human urban populations. Garrett has drawn a most unnerving picture of the ways in which these vermin vectors allow the microbes, our predators, to invade and decimate our systems and populations.

Sometime around 1346 the Black Death began on the steppes of Mongolia; infected fleas infested millions of rodents which, in turn, raided human dwellings in search of food. . . . The disease made its way rapidly across Asia, carried by fleas that hid in the pelts of fur traders, the blankets and clothing of travelers, and the fur of rodents that stowed away aboard caravans and barges criss-crossing the continent. Rumors of the Asian scourge preceded its arrival in Europe, and it was said that India, China, and Asia Minor were literally covered with dead bodies. The Chinese populations plummeted from 123 million in 1200 to 65 million in 1393 . . .

It reached the prosperous European trading port of Messina, Sicily, in the fall of 1347 aboard an Italian ship returning from the Crimea . . . Rats from the plagued ship joined the abundant local rodent population. Ailing men from the ship passed the bacteria on to the Messina citizenry directly, exhaling lethal microbes with their dying gasps.

As the plague made its way across Europe and North Africa, . . . outright slaughter of tens of thousands of Jews and alleged devil worshipers were staged. The city of Strasbourg alone savagely slew

16,000 of the Jewish residents, blaming them for spreading the Black Death. . . .

The terrorized European population did everything save what might have spared them: ridding their cities of rodents and fleas. The cities fell not only because of rat infestations but also due to both human population density and hygienic conditions. Bathing was thought to be dangerous (allowing) . . . fertile ground for flea and lice infestation. . . .

The daily death rates were staggering . . . one-third of Europe's total human population (20 to 30 million) . . . between 1346 and 1350. (Pp. 236–239; see also DeFoe; see also Gottfried, esp. pp. 33–76, wherein the author traces both the historicity and the flea physiology that led to two pandemics, one in the sixth century, and the other, as we know, in the fourteenth, and especially pp. 52–53, wherein is discussed the old canard against the Jews.)

Garrett, throughout her magnificent, landmark work, presents a wake-up call for us, regarding the loss of predator habitat that keeps vector populations in check and may soon no longer be able to do so.

. . . a divergence of opinion between R. Acha and Rabina, one says that [he who eats forbidden food] to satisfy his appetite, is an apostate, but [he who does it] to provoke is a *min* (an actual idol-worshiper); while the other says that even [one who does it] to provoke is merely an apostate.

An objection was raised: If one eats a flea or a gnat he is an apostate.

Even in that case he may be trying to see what a forbidden thing tastes like. (*Avodah Zorah* 26a–b)

67

PARTRIDGE

PARTRIDGE
Hebrew *Ko(V)Rei'*

> *Oh let my blood not fall to the ground, away from the presence of the Lord! For the king of Israel has come out to seek a single flea—as if he were hunting a partridge in the hills.*
>
> —1 Samuel 26:20

Perdix perdix: L., a partridge. Common (or, grey) partridge. But France prefers *Ammoperdix heyi*, the sand or desert partridge, which, interestingly enough, may not be a true partridge.

CONCORDANCE

Jeremiah 17:11 (Like a partridge hatching what she did not lay, so is one who amasses wealth by unjust means . . .)

The partridge is a unique bird in that it doesn't seem to want to fly very much. It isn't a bad flyer at all; in fact, it can take off with rapidity and assume cruising altitude in a relatively short time. But it seems to prefer to rummage among the bushes and grubs on the ground. In fact, one of the references is an allusion to the way in which the bird hunts for insects along mountain pathways. The second reference carries the allusion that the hen does not care for her eggs very well. Apparently, clutches of eggs are too large for one hen to cover. This seems rather odd, and the idea grew that hens share a nest, but only one sits the eggs, and that not too well. France has uncovered some zoological evidence for this biblical and long-standing view.

> . . . (An ornithologist) found as many as 30 eggs in the nest of a Desert Partridge and suggests that this is because often two hen partridges will lay close together and then one will drive off the other and attempt to sit on the whole clutch herself. Because she is too small to incubate such a large number, which, according to the habits of birds, she constantly moves around, none of the eggs reaches the required temperature to develop the foetus (sic) to its final stage and she abandons them all before they hatch. (Pp. 121–123)

Thus, the allusion to one who receives ill-gotten gains, but is unable to derive any benefit from them.

The issue of *kashrut* is an interesting one, and one that has disputations with a fascinating resolution. Feliks, and Toperoff's apparent derivative entry from Feliks, both mention the *Mishnah* where, supposedly, the bird is given a *hechsher* for being kosher. Here is the passage from Feliks, later repeated by Toperoff: "The *Mishnah* includes it among the ritually clean birds and observes that the male also hatches the eggs." The note to the inclusion lists *Chullin* 12:2, *Chullin* 140b, and *Tosephot* on *Chullin* 63a beginning with the word *Netz* (57; Toperoff, pp. 189–190; see also Schochet, p. 98).

The problem lies with the fact that, according to the *Shulchan Aruch*, this simply isn't true or, perhaps more accurately, not quite true. A more trustworthy authority is Forst. In both text and notes, referring to *Yoreh De'Ah*, Forst both presents and clarifies the dilemma. Italics are mine for emphasis.

. . . However, since we lack the experience to apply these rules, we are permitted to eat only those birds traditionally accepted as kosher. All variations of the domestic chicken are accepted as kosher. Similarly, common domestic ducks, geese and doves are considered kosher. Many Sefardic communities have a tradition that the quail is a kosher fowl. With the appearance of turkeys, Poskim questioned whether a reliable tradition exists about their kashrus (sic). Common custom today accepts turkeys as kosher fowl. *There is no definitive tradition about the status of a pheasant, peacock, guinea hen, partridge, swan, or certain species of wild ducks, geese, pigeons and doves, therefore they should not be eaten. The eggs of any non-kosher fowl are also forbidden to be eaten.* (Pp. 35–36, Yoreh De'ah 82:2)

However, in his note, Forst points out that even in Yoreh De'Ah, there are conflicting traditions. In 82:4, the *Shulchan Aruch* rules that "one who finds himself in a community that has a tradition of eating a (partridge, for example) may eat that species although he plans to eventually return to his own community which has no such tradition." Now the peculiar aspect of this *halakhah* is that it violates a standard *halakhah* that, in ritual *mitzvot*, one is bound by his or her own tradition or community's tradition, even when traveling to another community. The observance of two-day Yom Tovim by diaspora Jews while in Israel (Israelis observe one day) is an example. The resolution is a paradoxical syllogism and the logic, albeit pure, is convoluted and a bit difficult to follow, but, in essence: there is no definitive tradition to treat these fowl as nonkosher; one should simply "traditionally" err on that side of the decision fence—or, in other words, the "tradition" of *not* eating these fowl is due to the *lack* of a definitive tradition.

"For migraine one should take a partridge and slaughter it over the side of the head where there is pain, taking care that the blood does not blind him" (*Gittin* 68b; see also Preuss, following Lewysohn, p. 265).

"A proud man's heart is like a decoy partridge in a cage, And like a spy he looks for your downfall; . . ." (Ben Sirach, 11:30, Goodspeed 245).

AN ADDITIONAL TALMUD TAIL (*Chullin* 12:1)

A fascinating *Mishnah* in that it delineates the *halakhah* regarding the letting go—or waving away—the mother bird from the nest (Deuteronomy 22:6–7).

> The law of letting (the mother) go from the nest is in force both within the Holy Land and outside it, both during the existence of the Temple and after it, in respect of unconsecrated birds but not consecrated birds . . . as to a cock partridge, R. Eliezer says one is bound to let it go; but the sages say one is not bound. (See also Jeremiah 17:11 and 12:2.)

68

CATERPILLAR

CATERPILLAR
Hebrew *YaTSaR* (?)

> *So too, if there is a famine in the land, if there is*
> *pestilence, blight, mildew, locusts or caterpillars,*
> *or if an enemy oppresses them in any of the*
> *settlements of the land.*
>
> —1 Kings 8:37

Charaxes jasius:
   As larva, when they emerge from the egg, caterpillars are long and cylindrical. Later they enter the pupa, forming about themselves a chrysalis or cocoon; from this stage, a magnificent metamorphosis emerges, the most beautiful and graceful insect of all, perhaps, the butterfly or moth. Caterpillars have twelve segments or rings, some of which later transform into the wings; the head; three segments, upon which form the legs, constituting the thorax; the remainder, the abdomen.
   Caterpillars are typically voracious, devouring leaves and bushes in what seems a frenzy of consumption. They are themselves ripe pickings for insect predators—birds, bats, and carnivorous-hunter insects.
   I selected this species since Figuier (p. 190) points out, it "is found along the whole of the Mediterranean coast." In its larva stage, then, the creature is green, flat, with four yellow

horns bordered with red. Its main diet is a common shrub. As a butterfly, its color is varying hues of brown or brownish-yellow; its lower wings divide, terminating in two points, the points being black, twinged with white fringe. The image of the *tallit* is also too compelling to let slip by.

The silkworm, by the way, is not a worm but a caterpillar that gives way to a huge moth (*bombyx mori*). Although first cultivated in China, by the time of the Crusades there were large silkworm and silk-producing houses in the Mediterranean region, especially in Tuscany and Lombard. Several of these houses were Jewish businesses. The Moslem conquest of North Africa and Spain in the latter Middle Ages may have been largely responsible for this relocation of an industry.

CONCORDANCE

Isaiah 33:4.
Joel 1:4 (as "hopper"; uncertain, possibly another stage of the locust, which see).
Psalms III–78:46 [JPS, "grubs"] (see number 22).
Ecclesiastes 12:5.
2 Chronicles 6:28 (see also number 22).

In the Bible, the caterpillar is mentioned along with the locust. Thus, it was seen as a very destructive animal. It still is in our own time; however, our recognition of its transmutation into the beautiful butterfly tempers this view. France's discussion indicates the nonromantic view of the ancients (pp. 34–35).

> *The last, the very last,*
> *So richly, brightly, dazzlingly yellow.*
> *Perhaps if the sun's tears would sing*
>   *against a white stone . . .*
> *Such, such a yellow*
> *Is carried lightly 'way up high.*
> *It went away I'm sure because it wished to*
>   *kiss the world good-bye.*
> *For seven weeks I've lived in here,*
> *Penned up inside this ghetto.*

But I have found what I love here.
The dandelions call to me
And the white chestnut branches in the court.
Only I never saw another butterfly.
That butterfly was the last one.
Butterflies don't live in here,
    in the ghetto. (Friedmann)

An Additional Talmud Tail (*Sanhedrin* 10:1; *Gemarah* 94b–95a)

In this *Gemarah*, which references Isaiah 33:4, "And your spoil shall be gathered like the gathering of a (the) caterpillar," the Rabbis allow that "spoil," in this case, wealth taken by Sennacherab when he conquered the northern kingdom, and that left behind is therefore available to the Judeans, using the crawling animal as metaphor to this right. "When (Israel) . . . abandoned all hope of the return thereof; hence other Jews may take it" (Soncino, p. 638).

How is this so? "The possessions of Israel (may fall) . . . into the hands of heathens" and thus become "clean" on the occasion when they are "gathered" by the Judeans.

The *Mishnah* is the rather famous *Mishnah* of inclusion which opens, "All Israel have a portion in the world to come, for it is written 'Thy people are all righteous; they shall inherit the land for ever . . . that I may be glorified.'" The *Gemarah* connection can now be explained—it is not merely the lands and what lie upon them in this world that is to be gathered by the Jews, but that in *'Olam Habah*, the World to Come.

69

APE

APE
Hebrew *Ko(V)F*

*℘or the king had a Tarshish fleet on the sea, along
with Hiram's fleet. Once every three years, the
Tarshish fleet came in, bearing gold and silver, ivory,
apes, and peacocks.*

—1 Kings 10:22

<u>CONCORDANCE</u>

2 Chronicles 9:21 (see number 70).

About thirty years ago, the renowned zoologist Desmond
Morris wrote: "There are 193 living species of monkeys and
apes" (p. 8). Since that time, zoologists and anthropologists
may have discovered another species, although there is ongoing debate as to whether the Bonobo is a "new" species or a
race of chimpanzee. The term *ape* in the Bible is misleading.
Feliks (p. 49); Pinney (pp. 124–125), and France (p. 13) allude
or state that the Hebrew term is probably a catch-all for any
simian or nonhuman primate. In zoology and anthropology,
apes are considered to be gorillas, orangutans, chimpanzees,
and gibbons; therefore, the other intelligent simians are considered to be monkeys (typically apes are larger, more powerful, take to the ground [often in the case of gorillas and
chimpanzees] and have no tails). Ape behavior often is parallel

or similar to that of humans, whether the creatures are in human company or not. Researchers in the wild, such as Jane Goodall, have, over the years, found this to be so true as, at times, to be remarkable.

Goodall's chimpanzees exhibited craft at tool making, experienced family disputes, cherished their loved ones, were depressed and distraught at the loss of one, hunted meat and gathered flora, watched sunsets for no other apparent reason than aesthetic; also, reflecting tragedies and disasters humans have known all too well over the centuries, tribes would disband and engage each other in war over territory, females, and children.

In fact, modern science recognizes that there is less than 2 percent difference in the DNA of chimpanzees and humans. Their behavior, and the genetic analyses, hold profound implications for our own species and its survival.

Perhaps, then, the animals discussed as gifts to King Solomon were monkeys, although Pinney points out that the Egyptians, at the time of Israelite enslavement or sojourn, kept baboons, an unusual simian that walks more like a dog than a monkey or ape and is blessed and cursed by a complex social structure relying on an intense hierarchy struggle. "This baboon was considered sacred to the god Thoth. The male . . . was revered primarily in the temples, while the . . . female was often kept as a house pet. . . . That these creatures were highly prized by their owners is evident from the fact that quite often they were mummified and buried with great honors . . ." (pp. 124–125). Pinney claims that the species of monkey that was brought to Solomon from the east were Indian rhesus, wanderoo, or langur.

Feliks concurs, claiming that "In all probability they were a mixed lot, and almost certainly they were the tailed variety since these exist in India as well as in Africa. We often come across them in ancient drawings" (p. 49).

France points out that "Monkeys . . . are represented, with long tails, on Assyrian monuments; they were also worshipped in Egypt and are seen on the wall paintings of Egyptian tombs" (p. 13).

A proof answer to a dispute in *Bava Kama* 80a tends to demonstrate that the Rabbis and folk of at least the *mishnaic* period were familiar with "apes," although, again, these were probably smaller and more manageable monkeys. All these animals, as any pet owner knows, will quickly learn to prowl beneath a child's seat at table.

> Just as the Sages said it is not right to breed small cattle, so also they have said it is not right to breed small beasts. R. Ishmael said: It is however allowed to breed village dogs, cats, apes . . . as these help to keep the house clean.

On the other hand, two entries from the *Midrash* show the Rabbis holding monkeys and apes in disdain; however, by its discourse, the diatribe demonstrates that there were those who kept and raised these creatures for other than utilitarian purposes.

> For instance, they who rear monkeys, cats, porcupines, chimpanzees, and sea dogs (?), of what use are they? It is either a bite or a sting (one gets from them). (*Ecclesiastes Rabbah* 6:11)
>
> Four things changed in the days of Enoch: The mountains became [barren] rocks, the dead began to feel [the worms], men's faces became ape-like, and they became vulnerable to demons . . . (*Genesis Rabbah* 23:6)

AN ADDITIONAL TALMUD TAIL (*Yadaim* 1:5)

The inherent context of this *Mishnah* indicates a *machlochet*, a dispute, between *tannaim*, regarding whether, in the case of the ritual of the washing of the hands, the ritual (water being poured over a *kohen*'s, a priest's, hands) is valid even if not accomplished by human hands. Another *tanna* takes a dissenting view. Further investigation may reveal a story about whether this was ever done or seen—with a *kohen* in a traveling circus or carnival, perhaps: ". . . All are fit to pour water over the hands, even a deaf-mute, an imbecile, or a minor . . . An Ape may pour (however) . . . R. Jose declares . . . invalid."

. . . AND A *MIDRASH*

Ecclesiastes Rabbah 1:2 can be held up as a mirror to Jacque's speech of the seven ages of man in Shakespeare's *As You Like It*. The *Midrash*, with the opening exception, uses vivid animal imagery all through.

> At a year old he is like a king seated in a canopied litter, fondled and kissed by all. At two and three he is like a pig sticking his hands in the gutter. At ten he skips like a kid. At twenty he is like a neighing horse, adorning his person and longing for a wife. Having married, he is like a (donkey). When he has begotten children he grows brazen like a dog to supply their food and wants. When he has become old, he is [bent] like an ape.

70

PEACOCK

PEACOCK
Hebrew *TooKiYiYM*

> *. . . and peacocks.*
>
> —1 Kings 10:22

Pavo Cristatus: *Pavo*, L. a peacock. *Cristatus*, L., crested.

CONCORDANCE

2 Chronicles 9:21 (see number 69) (For the king had ships . . . bringing . . . *apes* and peacocks).

It is a bit surprising that the Rabbis found no allusion to Noah's rainbow in the gorgeous and unique spread of feathers that pea fowl exhibit. Anyone who has seen them fan their feathers is always taken aback by the astonishing beauty of it all. The creatures generally are tame and will often, seemingly for human visitors as well as for their hens, express their spreading glory. It is as if they know the uncommon aesthetic with which they have been blessed. Toperoff points out that the Rabbis felt the animal "boasts of 365 different colors and it was created from a drop of the white (of an egg)"; (p. 191).

I have not been able to track to the original source, but

Pinney and France concur that "Alexander the Great so prized the beauty of these birds that he forbade his soldiers to kill any of them" (p. 155; France, pp. 124–125). This would tend to indicate the populace in the Second Temple period were as familiar with this unusual bird as were their ancestors who lived in Solomon's days.

The peacock is a member of the same family as the partridge and, therefore, falls under the same curious *halakhah* as that bird (again, Forst, p. 35). However, in *Shabbat* 130a, in the *Mishnah* discussing allowances on *Shabbat*, there is a fascinating entry that puts into question the *kashrut* of eating fowl with milk.

> . . . In the locality of R. Jose the Galilean they used to eat flesh of fowl with milk. Levi visited the home of Joseph the fowler [and] was offered the head of a peacock in milk, [which] he did not eat. . . . R. Jose the Galilean said: . . . Now since . . . it is stated, "in its mother's milk," hence a fowl is excluded, since it has no mother's milk.

71

F L Y

FLY
Hebrew *ZV(B)u(oo)V(B)*

> *On that day, the Lord will whistle to the flies at the*
> *ends of the water channels of Egypt and to the bees*
> *in the land of Assyria;*
>
> —Isaiah 7:18

Musca bovina: Latin, ox fly; or *M. carnifex.*

Both pests attack the nostrils, eyes, and wounds of oxen and other animals. The dastardly insect has in general a dark metallic green color, a silvery forehead, the wings hyaline. However, for Ecclesiastes 10, see *M. domestica*, the common house fly, our reviled and inevitable companion, to which the following quotation applies.

"Their fecundity, the rapidity with which one generation succeeds another, and their great voracity . . . are such . . . that three flies, with the generations which spring from them (undetected and uninterrupted), could eat up a dead horse as quickly as a lion could" (Figuier, p. 34). (See number 14 for *horse* and number 16 for *lion.*)

Psalms III–78:45 (see numbers 19, 21); IV–105:31 (see number 21).
Ecclesiastes 10:1 (Dead flies make the ointment of the perfumer fetid and putrid . . .)

Bats, birds, amphibians, and "higher" insects can thank heaven for these fecund creatures that we hold in revulsion, else the higher animals, and therefore we, as well, could not survive. As we indicate in our morning prayers, it is with wisdom that Hashem has designed the order of the world.

We have already covered the well-known story of the fly and Titus; a quick reiteration: At the end of the Judean Wars, on Tisha b'Av, Titus entered the smoldering ruins of our once magnificent *Beit Hamikdash*. He entered the inner court. He stopped before the curtain of the *Kadosh Kadoshim*. He pierced the curtain with his sword. The curtain bled. "Behold, I have slain the god of the Israelites," he proclaimed. When he entered the Holy of Holies, desecrating it, he found only an empty space and a fly buzzing around. He tried to swat the fly but failed. Soon he exited. He commanded that the accouterments of the Temple, the wealth that was left, be transported to Rome. But the fly also accompanied him. As his ship crossed the sea, the fly flew up his nose. For the rest of his days, the fly remained there, tormenting him with its scratches and bites. Neither physician nor magician could provide him relief or cure.

In time, the emperor discovered that if he sat next to the blacksmith's striking of the anvil down in the village, the compression would cause the animal to cease its attacks and provide for him temporary relief. But always when he returned to the palace, the fly resumed its tormenting affliction. (Again, some say the animal was a gnat; refer to *Gittin* 57b.)

Another version of the story relates that as his hours by the smithy's shop increased, he grew increasingly deaf, but more open to the needs of his poorer citizens, whom he now was able to observe daily.

If, as we have learned out from Talmud, every creature has a purpose, it is at those times in our lives when we seem continuously frustrated from the persistence of the pest, it might be difficult to discern the value of this creature. However, we have already alluded to some of it in our discussion of their larvae stage, the maggot. Even as adults, the innumerable animals clear away much filth and carrion. Nonetheless, the folk wisdom that they carry disease appears to have increasing scientific evidence. In the Middle East especially, with the climate so conducive to their procreation, many of the age-old scourges could probably be traced to the fly as vector of the microbes. That the animals are such astonishingly good fliers places no limit on their range of operations, and this also contributes to the problem. It is another case where we must be careful not to harm the ecology or directly inflict harm upon the various predators of these insects, especially songbirds and bats. (See especially, "Houseflies.")

"Flies are so pertinacious that successful Egyptian generals were rewarded with golden collars bearing colossal silhouettes of the tiny animals—a wry tribute to their stubbornness in returning again and again to the same spot for food in spite of being shooed away" (Pinney, pp. 186–187).

However, in *Shabbat* 121b, we learn that the Egyptian fly is considered so much of a pest that it is permissible to kill it, even on the holy day, while a fascinating *Gemarah* is found at 83b:

> R. Ahedbuz b. Ammi asked: What of an idol less than an olive in size? R. Joseph demurred to this: In respect of what [does he ask]? . . . let it be no more than the fly . . . of Baal Ekron, for it was taught: And they made Baal-berith their god: This refers to the fly-god of Baal Ekron.

In mystical Judaism, the fly is perceived as one of the evil demonic hordes, sent from the lower depths to torment the sons and daughters of Adam and Eve on earth. This concept may derive from the passage in 2 Kings 1:1–4:

> After Ahab's death, Moab rebelled against Israel. Ahaziah fell through the lattice in his upper chamber at Samaria and was injured. So he sent messengers, whom he instructed: "Go inquire of Baal-zebub, the god of Ekron, whether I shall recover from this

injury." But an angel of the Lord said to Elijah the Tishbite, "Go and confront the messengers of the king of Samaria and say to them, "Is there no god in Israel that you go to inquire of Baal-zebub, the god of Ekron? Assuredly, thus said the Lord: You shall not rise from the bed you are lying on, but you shall die." And Elijah went.

This term is where we derive master/lord of the flies. Apparently, one of the pagan deities was the fly. Thus, the mystical indication is even more revealing, as one who succumbs to idol worship would be perceived as one succumbing to Satan himself. In any event, it was clear to the ancients and to the Rabbis, that at Ekron they worshiped the fly as a god, and Zebub refers to this animal. In later generations, Baalzebub became associated with demonic forces, "the Lord of the Flies." In Christian mystical or supernatural thought, Beezelbub takes on these demonic dimensions. In Jewish folklore as well, hordes of flies are perceived as Satan's minions, his messengers sent upon earth to torment humans.

In the last chapters of Genesis, the magnificent story of Joseph is told. One of the items seemingly omitted from the story is what was the crime of the two men for whom Joseph interprets their dreams while in prison. One of the legends concerns how a mere fly helped to propel Joseph to the height of Egypt and began the process that eventually resulted in the formation of the nation of Israel. Simply put—the cup-bearer allowed a fly to be discovered in Pharoah's cup of wine. Also, Haman attempted to destroy the Jewish people through a mere fly. His calumny attempted to persuade King Ahasuerus that the Jews would drink from their cups even if a fly ventured upon it, but they would not drink from the king's cup. This is obviously a reference to those who maintain a strict *kashrut* which could be misinterpreted as arrogance by those who do not understand the *halakhah* (see Toperoff, pp. 73–75, and *Megillah* 13a–b).

Ten miracles were wrought for our fathers in the Temple; no woman miscarried from the scent of the holy meat; the holy meat never turned putrid; no fly was seen in the slaughter house; no unclean accident ever happened to the High Priest on the Day of Atonement; the rain never quenched the fire on the woodpile on the altar; no wind prevailed over the column of smoke . . . never was a defect found in the *omer*, or in the two loaves, or in the showbread, [the people] stood pressed together, yet bowed themselves at ease; never did serpent or scorpion do harm in Jerusalem; and no man ever said to his fellow: "The place is too crowded for me that I should lodge in Jerusalem." (*Pirke Avot* 5:8; Goldin 76)

AN ADDITIONAL TALMUD TAIL (*Niddah* 2:5; *Gemarah* 16b–17a)

The *Mishnah* concerns when a woman needs to test her menstrual flow upon a cloth or, in actuality, two cloths to ensure she is prepared to receive her husband in intercourse.

The *Gemarah* follows R. Simeon b. Yochai. Among others he despised and stated the Holy One, blessed be He, despises, is "The man who has intercourse in the presence of any living creature." The discussion concerns whether lower creatures or servants were meant; herein we learn that while Abaye was performing the holy rite with his wife, he "drove away the flies."

72

LEOPARD

LEOPARD
Hebrew *NaMeiR*

> *The wolf shall dwell with the lamb,/The leopard lie*
> *down with the kid;/The calf, the beast of prey, and*
> *the fatling together,/With a little boy to herd them.*
> —Isaiah 11:6 (see 7)

Panthera pardus: L., a panther.

The two words describe the same species and are interchangeable. "Panther" generally is employed for the darker or black variety, "leopard" for the lighter or spotted variation. At one time this magnificent feline roamed unchallenged through a wide range, including virtually all of Africa and Asia, save the severest desert areas.

CONCORDANCE

Jeremiah 5:6 (see numbers 16, 18) (a leopard watcheth over their cities); 13:23 (Can . . . change . . . the leopard his spots?).
Hosea 13:7 (see number 16).
Habakkuk 1:8 (see numbers 15, 18, 57).
Song of Songs 4:8 (see number 16).
Daniel 7:6 (but see number 88).

Leopards, or panthers, are extremely powerful and swift predators. Were it not for the incursion of humans and destruction of their habitat, they would probably be today among the most successful of creatures, as indeed once they were. Feliks states: "The leopard is the strongest of all the predatory beasts present in Israel. . . . (Even today one) sallies forth at times, from the Lebanon into Northern Israel, (and) seizes an animal and withdraws" (p. 33). This, as recently as thirty-six years ago.

Clark claims that it is not uncommon to discover individuals seven to eight feet in length, with a tail exceeding three feet in length. The animal is usually "Much dreaded by the natives of all the regions in which it occurs." Also significant is that, unlike the "true" cats, the tiger, lion, jaguar, and leopard have pupils in their eyes that are circular and not vertically slit (pp. 187–188).

France distills some interesting legends that grew up about the seemingly unlimited power and finesse of this magnificent animal. The story about Judah is particularly interesting in two ways, since he is typically associated with a lion; sometimes, however, the imagery in the Bible and in lore appears to interchange lion and leopard—and it resonates more like a children's story that we seem to have heard or read somewhere before.

> . . . The dying Judah, boasting of the gifts which the Lord had bestowed on him, told how he had seized a Leopard which had attacked his dog at Hebron, and flung it by the tail down to the coast.
>
> Enemies were . . . crushed "as a leopard crunches the skull of a kid."
>
> On the steps of the throne of Solomon, (crouched) golden leopards which, by the operation of machinery, would growl at the approach of a visitor. (Pp. 94–96)

The name Nimrod may have been derived from the Hebrew for the animal's name. There are innumerable legends concerning Nimrod as a great hunter, but also as a fantastic being; Nimrod in ancient lore may have been perceived as a wild leopard-man-king, someone who gained his rule by stealth and by power, there being created a myth of his animal-morphism, a wereleopard. Also, as typically perceived as an evil king, and one who wished to challenge God by building the Tower of Babel, he could be perceived as how evil ones never change their true spots, a lesson that world leaders of democratic countries even today could learn well (see Pinney, pp. 114–115).

Schochet alludes to trials that were held against animals who committed "crimes" against human beings. The leopard, along with the wolf, lion, bear, panther, and serpent, was included in this list (p. 141). The complete judicial considerations are found in *Sanhedrin*, which see further on.

There are several entries in the *Mishnah* and in the Gemarah concerning leopards. Some of them deal with the legal status of damages, termed *mu'ad* (if an animal in one's care, or upon one's lands, or under one's ownership attacks three times, and thus is known to attack, the person is liable for all damages) and *tam* (if such an animal under the same circumstances has been known to attack two or less times, the person is liable only for half the damages), and capital crimes wherein an animal must forfeit its life. First, however, there is a metaphorical allusion found in *Pirke Avot*.

> Rabbi Judah ben Tema said: Be strong as the leopard, light as the eagle, swift as the deer, and brave as the lion, to do the will of your Father Who is in heaven. He used to say the arrogant are for Gehenna, and the shame-faced for the Garden of Eden.
>
> May it be Thy will, O Eternal our God and the God of our fathers, that the Temple be built speedily in our days, and grant us a portion in Thy Torah. (5:24)

Goldin's note regarding R. Tema indicates "It has not been definitely established who his teacher was or in what century he lived . . . (probably) at the end of the second century c.e." Goldin also states, "In Mahzor Vitry, the Mishnaic Tractate Abot ends here. The Mishnahs that follow were then obviously added later from other sources." Thus, the prayer that immediately follows our *Mishnah* was likely a closing prayer following completion of study (88).

In Bava Kama, the *Mishnah* following 15b seems quite difficult; however, the *Gemarah* 16a tends to clear up the matter.

> *Mishnah*: There are five cases of *Tam* and five cases of *Mu'ad*. Animal is *Mu'ad* neither to gore, nor to collide, nor to bite, nor to fall down, nor to kick. Tooth . . . Foot is *Mu'ad* to break [things] in the course of walking; ox . . . and man; so also the wolf, the lion, the bear, the leopard, the . . . [panther] and the snake . . .
>
> *Gemarah*: . . . The reply was: Rabina said: The *Mishnah* is incomplete and its reading should be as follows: There are five cases of *Tam*; all the five of them may eventually become *Mu'ad*—(thus, not only in these cases the ox, but) the wolf, the lion, the bear, the leopard and the snake.

Kiddushin 4, gives the categories of the classes that went up from Babylon. In addition to priests, Levites, and Israelites, there are also included *mamzerim* and others with questionable genealogies. *Mishnah* 14 in *Shabbat* discusses the prohibitions against wounding animals on the holy day. *Gemarah* 107b uses the allusion in the (unfortunate) passage in Jeremiah that mentions Ethiopian skin changing color as well as a leopard changing its spots. There then follows a wordplay in which wound marks is substituted for the word that ordinarily means spots. And, finally, *Mishnah* 1 in *Sanhedrin* returns the discussion to the culpability of animals committing capital crimes against humanity, and which court should be appointed to adjudicate the case.

> The death sentence on the wolf or the lion or the bear or the leopard or the hyena or the serpent is to be passed by twenty-three (judges). R. Eliezer says: Whoever is first to kill them [without trial] acquires merit. R. Akiba, however, holds that their death is to be decided by twenty-three.

An Additional Talmud Tail (*Kiddushin* 4:1; *Gemarah* 70a)

The *Mishnah* lists ten categories of people—including Kohanim, Leviim, Yisraelim, converts, freed slaves, freed Jews, Gibbonites, and *mamzerim*, then which of these can marry the other. The *Gemarah* uses the seemingly promiscuous habits of the animal to criticize the behavior of many Israelites, in particular, those who produce *mamzerim*: "R. Abbahu said: 'The Lord said, "I said Israel should be as precious to me as the Cherub, whereas they made themselves like the leopard."'"

However, the verse is turned upside down, in a charming, generous fashion. "Others state ' . . . Though they have made themselves like the leopard, yet they are as precious to me as a cherub.'"

73

CAT

CAT ("beasts," JPS, p. 644)
Hebrew *TSiYiM;* modern, and common, *CHaTooL*
("wild-cat"; alternate translation, the generic "beast")

> *But beasts (wild-cats?) shall lie down there,/*
> *And the houses be filled with owls.*
>
> —Isaiah 13:21

Felis silvestris: Feles, L. a cat; *silvestris,* L., a wood. There was a species closely related to the domestic cat, also known as *F. ocreata (F. catus,* or *F. domestica)* that inhabited Europe and Western Asia. Even today, isolated reports, particularly in Scotland, report sightings of the animal. Prides of *F. catus* or *F. domestica* run wild throughout the Middle East today, the more fortunate having adapted to fend for themselves.

CONCORDANCE

Genesis 34:14.
Jeremiah 50:39 (see numbers 52, 85). Again, in all entries, "Wild-Cat."

All the biblical animal scholars concur that the domesticated cat appears not once in the biblical canon and do not include the animal in their lists. Clearly, in Israel, at least, the cat had not yet been domesticated as the faithful pet we know her to be today.

But scholars also concur that she or he most likely received pet domestication in Egypt, probably after the Exodus period. And there the animal from which domestication evolved was known. It was a large yellow animal, not altogether unlike the male tabby we know today. Bodenheimer states: "The Libyan wild cat . . . and the jungle cat were the wild ancestors of the domestic cat in Egypt . . . where their mummies . . . are often found . . ."

The animal was known in Sumeria and Assyria as well. Landsberger's translation of *The (C)Har-ra—(C)Hubullu* places the creature in Lines 108–115. Bodenheimer comments: ". . . Landsberger thinks it to be a domestic cat. This is, however, improbable, perhaps it is (the) wild cat. The Sumerian epitheta of this list are: predatory, large, horned, yellow cat" (pp. 44; 107–109).

Deerkoski concurs.

> . . . Historical evidence indicates that the animal (the Egyptians) domesticated was the African wildcat, a large amber-colored tabby. This species had a friendly disposition and proved its usefulness to man by controlling the rodents that destroyed the grain supplies. . . . The cat and its nocturnal lifestyle must have both awed and frightened the people. Not only could the cat see in the darkness that humans found so terrifying, but its eyes even appeared to light up at night.

(See also Busch and Silver, who recount a remarkable discovery of two feline mummies in as recent a dig as 1990 [pp. 13–17].)

In the modern American myth of Batman, the hero's nemesis who later changes her evil ways and fights for justice alongside the caped crusader is Catwoman. She may be an atavism for an old mythic metamorphosis, growing out of magical powers of a witch and her familiar, which was usually a cat. Schochet (p. 222) recounts the story in a brief retelling. Here is a more complete version, with the citation, in Trachtenberg:

> . . . We read in thirteenth-century works of witches . . .
> who assume animal forms to carry out their nefari-
> ous designs. A story in *Sefer (C)Hasidim* is a replica
> of dozens found in non-Jewish works: a man was
> attacked by a cat which he fought off; the next day a
> woman appeared, badly wounded, and asked him for
> bread and salt to save her life. In 1456 the German,
> Johann Hartlieb, told a similar tale of a cat which
> attacked a child and was driven off and stabbed by
> the child's father; a woman was later found with a
> wound in the same place. Jacob Sprenger related as
> a recent occurrence in a town in the diocese of
> Strasbourg, that a laborer, attacked by three enor-
> mous cats, beat them off with a stick, and was
> subsequently arrested on a charge of brutally beat-
> ing three ladies of the best families in town. (Pp.
> 13–14)

Cats appear in the Talmud, presumably our more friendly
and more familiar (in the true sense) variety; wherein: *Bava
Kama* 80a, they are permitted and encouraged, for they keep
houses clean (not only in terms of food crumbs, but chasing
and keeping out vermin); 80b, where their breeding is discussed, especially as involves a black cat and a white cat; 15b,
regarding liability for its damages; *Shabbat* 51a, where the
animal may go without a muzzle on the holy day; modesty is its
virtue heralded in Eruvin 100b. Of course, the cat has always
been admired for its fastidiousness.

Goldin recounts the story of R. Judah ha-Nasi, walking one
day in the market, when a calf being chased by its slaughterers
runs up to him and lows for the Rabbi to rescue it. R. Judah
fires off a *pasuk* concerning the appropriate purpose for which
the hapless creature was born and returns the bereft animal to
its doom. The story may recall the more enlightened action of
Moses in the *Midrash* wherein he rescues the lamb and, at that
moment, is declared fit to lead the people. R. Judah at his
moment acted not like his teacher and suffered the consequences.

> For this utterance, the Rabbi was punished with
> great bodily suffering for many years.

One day R. Judah noticed that his servant was sweeping out a litter of new-born kittens. The Rabbi interfered and said: "Let them be, for it is written, 'And His tender mercies are over all His works.'"" It was then said in heaven: From that time on the Rabbi was relieved of his affliction. (P. 53)

When the Almighty allotted the means of living, he asked the cat, "From whom do you want to receive your daily bread . . . ?"
The cat answered wholeheartedly, "Give me my daily bread from an absent-minded woman who leaves the kitchen door open." (Folktales, p. 64)

The famous poem-ditty that completes the Passover *Seder*, "Chad Gadyah," is well known to practically every Jew. Some scholars feel it is a metaphor for the nations (Judah-Babylon-Persia-Greece-Rome-Christendom . . .), which ultimately will end in retribution for God and Israel.

"And a cat came and devoured the kid, which my father bought for two zizim . . ."

AN ADDITIONAL TALMUD TAIL *(Shabbat* 7:3; *Gemarah* 75b–76a)

The *Mishnah* deals with the principle of what may be put away or not put away on *Shabbat*: ". . . Whatever is fit to put away . . . is [generally] put away . . . (if) one carries it out on (*Shabbat*), he is liable . . . whatever is not fit to put away and . . . [generally] put away . . . only he that put it away is liable."

The *Gemarah* states: "The blood of menstruation is put away for a cat."

74

FERRET

FERRET

Isaiah 13:21 (which some translations, but highly improbable, and JPS prefers the vague "beasts"; also, the often presented Leviticus 11:29–30 listing is replaced by JPS for "Gecko," a type of lizard, along with chameleon [p. 169]). Pinney concurs: ". . . popularly known as the wall lizard. The gecko makes a low, mourning sound . . . There also was a popular folk legend that a gecko would cause leprosy if it crawled across one's body. The gecko (unlike the ferret) was commonly found throughout the Holy Land" (pp. 177–178). Tristram felt that the gecko was the proper animal as well. See Forward.

**Vormella peregusna:** Mottled or marbled polecat.

It is the only ferret I find native to southeast Europe and western Asia. Its range extends east as far as the Gobi Desert. (For a fuller treatment of gecko, see number 36.)

75

JACKAL

JACKAL

Hebrew *'iYiM*; also, *TaN* (somewhat interchangeable with "dragon," which might indicate a certain feeling about the creature.)

> *And jackals shall abide in its castles/And
> dragons in the palaces of pleasure/Her hour is close
> at hand;/Her days will not be long.*
> —Isaiah 13:22

Canus aureus: *aureus*, L., golden.

At that time, under the monarchies, its range probably extended through southeast Europe, northern Africa and the Middle East, and as far southeast as Malaysia.

CONCORDANCE

Isaiah 34:13; 35:7; 43:20.
Jeremiah 9:10 (I will turn Jerusalem into rubble,/ Into dens for jackals . . .); 10:22; 14:6; 49:33 (And Hazor shall be a dwelling-place of jackals, a desolation for ever . . .); 51:37.
Micah 1:8 (see number 52).
Malachi 1:3 (and gave his heritage to the jackals).
Psalms II–44:20 (Though thou hast crushed us into a place of jackals).
Job 30:29 (see number 52).

There are few rabbinical commentaries concerning the jackal. This seems a bit odd, since, according to France, it is generally regarded the most prolific of the predator/scavengers of the Middle East. Indeed, it seems one of the most adaptable of animals, produces large numbers of pups, and is apparently not yet an endangered species (pp. 89-91). *Encyclopedia Judaica* concurs: ". . . the most prevalent beast of prey in Erez Israel. Being omnivorous, it is encountered most commonly near inhabited areas . . . (and) prays on small animals." The howls of packs sometimes pierce the northern night air in the land (9:1190).

There was a common perception, which seems to have been verified by veterinary science, that jackals and dogs can interbreed, which raises interesting questions, again, concerning the ancient dog. Since the wild animals are susceptible to rabies and can communicate rabies to humans, this matter has been an ancient problem that continues.

Preuss points out that, in the Persian faiths, bodies were left for "burial," to enable the jackals to dispose of them, thus ensuring the holiness of earth and fire. This clearly was in conflict with Jewish practice, which considers the body itself a holy vessel and inviolate, to be buried in undisturbed ground (p. 519).

Toperoff explains that, in fact, Jewish families would check frequently and cover their loved ones' graves with large stones, to ensure that the jackals did not disturb the graves or the bodies (pp. 133–134). Perhaps he was referring to the *Mishnah* in *Nazir*, which see next.

An Additional Talmud Tail (*Nazir* 7:3)

The tractate, of course, deals with the laws and principles regarding the vow of the Nazarite (found in Numbers 6:1–22).

> . . . for [defilement caused by] . . . the *golel* (covering stone) or *dofech* (side stones) of a tomb . . . the Nazarite is not required to poll (cut his hair). He must, however, be sprinkled on the third and seventh [days] . . .

According to Rabbenu Tam, *golel* and *dofech* signified the tombstone and side stones of a grave—to prevent jackals from disturbing the corpse. These were large, heavy stones, perhaps similar, on a smaller scale, to ashlars.

76

MAGGOT

MAGGOT (see number 91)
Hebrew *To(V)La'*

> *Your pomp is brought down to Sheol,/And the strains of your lutes!/Worms are to be your bed,/Maggots your blanket!*
>
> —Isaiah 14:11

Ulcus Verminosum

CONCORDANCE

Job 25:6 (But some translations render number 25 at Exodus 16:20 as worms, which see).

The biblical animal scholars tend to overlook or ignore the maggot. However, JPS is clear in the two entries indicated. It is true that it is a disgusting creature, but one that is most necessary to nature. Indeed, the world would probably be overrun with decaying corpses were it not for the efficient cleaning machine that is the maggot. The creature's profligacy is its own survival technique, as well as the fact that it is capable of transforming decayed and rotting organic material into disposable and recyclable waste material.

In actuality, maggots are larvae of certain flies and other similar insects. Thus, they would appear to the unscientific eye as a host of worms. As we shall see, this is apparently how the ancient world thought of them. They are prodigious consumers of decaying flesh; then, they metamorphose into flies and depart the scene, having accomplished their necessary tasks. In fact, they are known to heal wounds that frustrate treatments of even advanced medical science. Physicians and surgeons are once again rediscovering that the seemingly despicable vermin may literally be a life saver. Zimmer discusses such a case.

Again, there is little rabbinical commentary. In *Sotah* 35a, we learn that the ten spies that brought up the evil reports about the land (Numbers 13–14) were suddenly afflicted with maggots growing out of their tongues and crawling down to infest their navels.

Zimmer, quoting a doctor Petro and Wells, indicates that the "disgust factor" inhibits physicians, nurses, and patients from using the entomological treatment until it is too late; then the practitioners are faced with one of those paradoxical situations one sometimes finds in medicine: The wound heals, but the patient dies.

It must have been too late for Antiochus, or he was simply too far gone. Preuss expounds on the passage in 2 Maccabees, explaining that the "worms" in the passage, by description and etiology, must have been maggots (pp. 183–184).

> Now about that time it happened that Antiochus returned in disorder from the region of Persia. . . . "I will make Jerusalem the common graveyard of the Jews, when I get there."
> But the . . . God of Israel, struck him down with an incurable but unseen blow, for he had hardly uttered the words when he was seized with an incurable pain in his bowls and sharp internal pains . . . was flat on the ground and . . . worms swarmed from the impious creature's body, and while he was still alive in anguish and pain, his flesh fell off, and because of the stench the whole army turned from his corruption in disgust. (9:1–11; Goodspeed, pp. 470–471)

The same or similar story is told concerning Herod's manner of death in Acts 12:23 (NIV/KJV, p. 1370).

An Additional Talmud Tail (*Parah* 9:2)

In discussing the validity or invalidation of the vessel containing the water mixture of the red cow, if an insect or "creeping things" fall into it, the contents may (if the animal "burst asunder") became invalid, but otherwise, it may be considered permissible. However, it is most interesting that "a maggot or a . . . weevil . . . causes no invalidity, because it contains no moisture."

R. Simeon and R. Eliezar b. Jacob concur in this ruling.

In other words, it was thought, even if a maggot should "burst asunder," there would be no entrails moisture for its explosion to contaminate the holy mixture. Perhaps the Rabbis were somewhat observant and cognizant of the creature's mysterious metamorphosing cycle after all.

77

DRAGON

DRAGON
Isaiah 27:1

Refer to Appendix A, "Mythological and Supernatural Creatures."

CONCORDANCE

Genesis 51:9.
Jeremiah 51:34.
Ezekiel 29:3.

78

BITTERN

BITTERN
Hebrew *KiPoD*
Isaiah 14:23, but uncertain; 34:11

Botaurus stellaris: Boo, L., cry, roar, referring to the loud call characteristic of bitterns. *Stellaris*, starry. The plumage has spots.

Bitterns may be the loudest of all birds. The male's call reportedly extends a distance of nearly three miles and resembles a foghorn. Bitterns are members of Ciconiformes, and thus resemble somewhat herons, storks, flamingos, and egrets.

CONCORDANCE

Zephaniah 2:14 (JPS, "Jackdaw," and see numbers 4, 55).

Schochet points out that the few times the bittern is mentioned, it is in an allusion regarding a sense of feeling desolate (p. 43). Pinney concurs, and expounds the possible reason: ". . . Most bitterns inhabit marshes, where it is easy for them to hide. Bitterns are remarkably proficient at camouflaging themselves. In situations of danger, they use their plumage to duplicate the color and shape of swamp vegetation. They actually seem to disappear before the observer's eyes" (pp. 141–142). Thus, their need to be hidden and alone serves the metaphor. Bitterns have shorter legs than Herons, but use the same technique of fishing with their long, facile necks and sharp bills. (See also France, p. 28, and *Encyclopedia Judaica*, 4:1062.)

AN ADDITIONAL TALMUD TAIL (See under number 56, pelican)

79

SWIFT

SWIFT

Hebrew *'ahGoo(V)R*

> ♪ *piped like a swift or . . . (continued below)*
> —Isaiah 38:14

Swifts are generally considered any swiftly (of course) flying insect-eating bird of the family *Apodidae*, characterized typically with long wings and a superficial resemblance to a Swallow; others translate it as Crane; but see Gesenius (p. 723), where "note of crane not suitable" adjective of (with) Soo(V)S [also in text, as K'SooS 'GooR], "twittering" (i.e., more like a swift or similar bird).

80

S WALLOW

SWALLOW
Hebrew *'TSahFTSeiF* (text, S'Noo(V)NiT, Dict)

> . . . *a swallow,/I moaned like a dove,/As my eyes,*
> *all worn, looked to heaven:/"My Lord, I am in*
> *straits;/Be my surety!"*
>
> —Isaiah 38:14

Hirundo rustica: L, a Swallow; rural.

Nothing romantic here—quite simply one of the most successful of all birds or animals enjoying practically a world-wide habitat. Swallows seem equally at home in rough areas or adapting to the environment of humans.

CONCORDANCE

Jeremiah 8:7;
Psalms III–84:4 (Yea, the sparrow [94] hath found a house, and the swallow a nest for herself);
Proverbs 26:2.

AN ADDITIONAL TALMUD TAIL (*Shabbat, Gemarah* 77b)

Our Rabbis taught: There are five instances of fear
[cast] by the weak over the strong: The fear of the
(plague); (a gnat) over the lion; . . . mosquito over
the elephant (it enters its trunk and torments it); . . .
The spider upon the scorpion (it enters its ear); . . .
the swallow upon the the eagle (it creeps under its
wings and hinders the larger bird from swooping
down); Rashi (adds): . . . The (stickleback) upon Leviathan.

81

CRANE

CRANE (JPS, "Swift," p. 696; but MiLo(v)N/, "Crane," p. 71)
Hebrew '*aGoo(V)R*
Isaiah 38:14

Grus grus: L. Crane.

A common bird, widespread throughout the world. All cranes have an unusually long trachea, allowing them to produce a loud call, especially the males. *G. Americana*, the Whooping Crane, in particular produces a trumpet-like or trombone-like sound, hence its common nomenclature. Gotsch, in 1981, mentions whoopers as nearly extinct, with a total number of fifty individuals. However, by 1994, conservationist and wildlife intervention had raised this number to close to two hundred. Today they can be seen roosting on the Platte River during their annual migration, usually early to mid-April. Their cousin, *G. grus*, is no longer so visible in the Middle East.

CONCORDANCE

Jeremiah 8:7 (see numbers 60, 78).

Again, cranes are admired for their voices and their migratory promptness in the text. An alternative to the heron story in the *Midrash*, concerning the rescue of the Jews by the telling of the story of sticking its beak in the lion's mouth to pull out an offending object, is told placing the crane in the allegory. (See Pinney, pp. 159–160; Schochet 121; and *Jewish Encyclopedia* 5:1059–1060.)

AN ADDITIONAL TALMUD TAIL (*Kiddushin* 2:1; *Gemarah* 44a [Supra 43b])

In this complex and rather remarkable passage, the animal is used as a simile to try to bring empathy for (another interpretation: criticism of) the disputant whose opinion was not at the moment accepted, but who may have been correct after all. To understand this brief allusion, it is important to understand the *Mishnah*.

> A man can betroth [a woman] through himself or through his agent. A woman may be betrothed through herself or through her agent. A man may give his daughter in betrothal when [she is] a *Na'arah* [12 years of age but not yet 13] himself or through an agent.

In 43b, R. Jochanan disputes Resh Lakesh's argument that the situation is the same as in a *get*, a Jewish divorce; that is, that either she or her father can accept the documentation in either case.

"R. Jochanan maintained . . . but as for *kiddushin* (betrothal), all agree that her father [alone can accept . . . on her behalf] but not she herself."

Later, R. Assi encounters R. Zera; neither one, it turns out, went to the *Beth Midrash* that day. However, R. Zera heard it from R. Abin: ". . . and he told me that the entire band [of disciples agreed with R. Jochanan; and . . . Resh Lakish cried like a crane (i.e., 'vehemently protested,' Soncino, p. 221)."

82

M O T H

MOTH
Hebrew *'aSH*
Isaiah 50:9

Galleria cerella: Beehive or wax galleria.

Most moths, in larva, pupa, and adult insect phase, occupy arboreal plants and are peculiar to a regional ecology. This species, perhaps the most widespread, is found commonly to abundantly in all countries or regions with bee (number 63) populations. Even in the monarchial period, due to an extent to the edifices being built, trees were not as common as in the still extant forests of Europe. In addition, Isaiah's comment is, "The moth shall eat them up." This reference could be to the creature's usurpation of life and territory. True, any moth or its caterpillar stage will consume leaves and wool; however, *G. cerella* hides during the day about the beehive, surreptitiously enters the hive at night, devours the wax, then twines its thread round the honeycomb, strangling or smothering the larvae. Although the bees attack with fury, it seems to be able to develop the wax or its twine for its defense and the defense of its eggs, laid in the honeycomb. In more ways than one, it resembles a true daughter of the Middle East.

Isaiah 51:8.

Job 13:28 (Though I am like . . . a garment that is moth-eaten).

The day belongs to the butterfly, but the night is the moth's. Moths are much more complex creatures with far more survival attributes than butterflies. In an interesting example of parallel development and adaptation in nature, moths and butterflies evolved at separate times, moths about 100 million years ago, butterflies somewhat later. Due to the astonishing beauty of the butterfly, moths tend to get the bum rap. However, they are far more numerous, far more diverse, and exhibit behaviors of much more unique qualities.

According to Conniff, "There are more species of moths in the world than all the species of mammals, birds, fish and reptiles put together—12,000 in North America alone. . . . moths are important pollinators . . . some plants might eventually go extinct without them. As caterpillars, they are the primary food of songbirds."

> Moth behavior . . . is much more interesting than people generally believe. Some moths, for example, practice virgin birth. In other species, the females are sexually promiscuous and seek out toxic males as a way to improve the health of their offspring (the poisonous scent keeping moth predators at bay). One moth caterpillar eats only horns, another moth pierces grapes for their juice. Yet another survives on a diet of tears, fanning out below a cow's eye . . . One . . . can pierce skin and suck blood. One spits cyanide.

The numbers and varieties of the species continues, and as many as 1,200 varieties, each with different behavior patterns, have been found in a common residential backyard. There are species that can escape bats, by listening to their echo radar and flying away at oblique angles, or, if the bat is heard to be too close, fold up its wings about its body, and plunge into the soil.

The biblical references, however, follow none of these

fascinating species differentiation; rather, they associate the animal with its most common known quality: the destruction of household items. This is the literary allusion in the text.

In the *Mishnah* before *Shabbat* 90a, it is discussed which items may not be carried on the holy day: ". . . Long pepper . . . various kinds of perfume (and) . . . metal . . . (pieces) of the altar stones or the altar earth. Moth-eaten scrolls or their moth-eaten mantles . . . [he is culpable] because they are stored away in order to be 'hidden.'"

There is an interesting *Midrash* in Deuteronomy Rabbah 2 concerning Moses' being forbidden to enter the land. All the joy that he longed for to enter the land, has decayed "as a moth enters garments and makes them decay."
Toperoff includes an interesting story of the rabbis.

> Rabbi Bunam was asked by the Lubliner Rabbi for a remedy to stop the hair from falling out of his . . . (streimel). Rabbi Bunam answered: "If all the moth-eaten hair is combed away the remainder will not fall out, otherwise the good (fur) . . . will also fall prey to the moths."

The Lubliner replied that Bunam should remember his lesson when he becomes a leader in Israel (p. 168).

An Additional Talmud Tail (*Shabbat* 9:6)

"[If one carries out] . . . moth-eaten scrolls or their moth-eaten mantles . . . [he is culpable], because they are stored away to be [buried (because it is a sacred object)] . . ."
In this *Mishnah*, we learn that the insect or its larvae was apparently a problem in the synagogues and study halls—and one could not take care of the problem on *Shabbat* due to the prohibition of carrying beyond the confines on the Holy Day.

83

BASILISK

BASILISK Some translations (but JPS, adder, which see Snake or Serpent, number 2; also see dragon, number 76) Isaiah 59:5

Refer to Appendix A, "Mythological and Supernatural Creatures."

CONCORDANCE

Jeremiah 8:17.

84

SPIDER

SPIDER
Hebrew *'KaViYSH*

> *They hatch adder's eggs/And weave spider*
> *webs;/He who eats of those eggs will die,/And if one*
> *is crushed, it hatches out a viper.*
>
> —Isaiah 59:5

Arachnida araneida theridion.

CONCORDANCE

Proverbs 30:28 (The spider thou canst take with the hands/Yet is she in
  kings' palaces [JPS 1336: You can catch the spider in your hand,/ . . . ,
  and, alt., "lizard"])
Psalms 140:4 (They sharpen their tongues like serpents;/spider's poison is
  on their lips.)
Job 8:14 (. . . whose trust is a spider's web . . .).

The common misconception that spiders and insects are
alike or the same order of animals may still prevail in some
quarters. Insects have a three-part segmented body, spiders
two; insects have six legs, spiders eight; insects have multi-
faceted eyes, spiders have eight eyes. As diverse as insects

obviously are, spiders exhibit even more diversity, but not as notable. Clark found documentation supporting a species in residence at the 18,000-foot mark of Mount Everest; since no other species exists in such a harsh climate, the specter of cannibalism looms as the creature's survival technique.

Conversely, a species exists at the lowest point on earth. The animal survives practically at every biological niche in between. Some animals are as small as mites; others can reach body size of three to four inches across, with a leg "spread" more than this again.

Most are web builders, waiting patiently for a hapless insect to be caught in the sticky silk. Some leap upon prey. Others build trap-doors and wait for the unsuspecting victim to chance by. Others spit a paralyzing toxin. All are agile, and many can skitter across water, and raise their bodies above pesticide layered upon a plane. In fact, often, after a building is sprayed, spiders, unaffected, will emerge to seek a new food supply. There are spiders that "balloon," spreading their silk to the winds and hitching a ride aloft. Clark claims one researcher found a spider floating along in her silk parachute close to 15,000 feet.

The web spinners spin their gossamer but sturdy threads from a glutinous substance in their abdomen, through a number of orifices, called, appropriately enough, spinnerets. They spin at once several, which at a certain distance from the animal unites into one silken thread. Thence the wind may capture it and take it to some remote spot, to which object it immediately adheres; following, or even before the wind defines its parameter, the spider directs the threads into the same or similar design its mother had devised in her lifetime.

Curious also, is that, in most species, the female is very much larger than the male and torments him mightily, even, on occasion, maiming him, albeit the concept that the spider devours her mate in the act of copulation is a bit hyperbolic and occurs, if at all, rarely (pp. 145–148; see also Pinney, pp. 191–192; McCook, pp. 182–196; Nardi, pp. 3–4; Fisher, pp. 253–259).

We are probably much too quick to destroy spiders, which should be regarded, for the most part, as our good friends, in their turn destroying hordes of vermin that would otherwise infest our habitats.

* * *

Trachtenberg uncovered an old "sovereign" remedy, one that may be practiced in some parts of the world yet today. ". . . poultices for open wounds were made of spiders' webs" (p. 203).

Wiland reports more modern, perhaps more scientific medical remedies.

In *Sanhedrin* 99b R. Assi draws an allusion to a spider's web, perceived in the analogy as progressing from a relatively unstable to a most strong tether: "Temptation at first is like a spider's thread, but eventually like a cart rope."

There are stories that resonate so strongly with us, we feel that they are textual, part of the canon. The story of Abraham as a child with the idols, in which he proves to his father that idols are mere wood and stone is so well known, so much a part of our Jewish education, many are convinced the story is found in Genesis. In actuality, it is found in legends and *Midrash*. So it is with the story of King David and the spider that saved his life. It is so well known many are certain it appears in 1 or 2 Samuel. In actuality, it also is found in legends and the *Midrash*. Now, in the text, to be sure, David hides in a cave and approaches Saul in his camp; indeed, the two stories appear to represent two strands of the same legend, wherein the proto-king receives his rescue by the grace of God and returns to taunt his pursuer (1 Samuel 24–27). The Spider (and Scorpion) story is related by Podwal (p. 28), by Toperoff (pp. 225–227), and many others. Toperoff's recounting includes the nemesis animal as a hornet; Podwal omits it. The definitive version, in its entirety, is Bialik's.

> One day while David sat in his garden he saw a scorpion devouring a spider. And he said, "O God, why hast Thou created these things for naught? The scorpion destroyeth honey but never maketh it; and the spider spinneth the whole year through, yet will its webs never make a garment. What profit is there in them or what pleasure?"

At this point God reproves David, telling him a day will come when he will require both creatures. Indeed, not long after:

. . . King . . . Saul sought to take away his life. And
David hid himself in a cave in the wilderness. And
God ordained for him a spider, and it wove its web
over the mouth of the cave and blocked it up. And
Saul and his men passed by. . . .

"See a spider's web, unbroken, is over the mouth
of the cave; had any man entered thither the spider's
web would be torn to shreds. The cave is surely
empty."

And the men turned aside and did not enter into
the cave. And David, lying at the far end of the cave,
heard all their words.

Later, when David skulks into Saul's camp, he is caught by
the warrior Abner's massive thighs, as the man rolls over in
slumber, just as David is sneaking through that area. A scorpion stings the man's legs, he moves them in response, and
David is freed. Note: Psalms 142 is a prayer "of David, while he
was in the cave" (JPS, 1277).

". . . Bachya ibn Pakuda writes in his *Duties of the Heart*
that 'as the cobweb obstructs the light of the sun, so does
passion the light of reason'" (in Toperoff).

AN ADDITIONAL TALMUD TAIL (See under Swallow, number 80)

85

HYENA

HYENA (so JPS in a compromising fashion [p. 796]; but Toperoff, "speckled bird of prey" [p. 131]; Gesenius also renders *Ha'ayit* as speckled or striped coloring, and *tsavooah* as a bird of prey [pp. 743, 841]; still, the dictionary renders *tsavooah* as "Hyena")
Hebrew *(Hah'ahYiT) TSahVoo[V]'ah*

> *My own people acts toward Me/Like a bird of prey [or a hyena];/ . . . (p. 796).*
> —Jeremiah 12:9

Hyaena hyaena: one of three species, this one the striped hyena, and the only one whose range encompasses the Middle East, thus for both reasons its choice. Its stripes are brown or black across a grayish brown coat. It has a distinct mane. Its head-to-tail length is about 45 inches, with a tail of about 15 inches, and a shoulder height of about 45 inches, and it can weigh in as much as 120 pounds. An interesting need characteristic is that it must always be within 6 miles or less of fresh water. Although it is popularly thought of as merely a scavenger, in actuality, it is a most effective diurnal or nocturnal hunter, both as a solitary tracker or, and especially effective, in group strategies. It fears no creature, especially when in its group setting, and has been known to bring down animals commonly thought of as prey for lions or tigers. More often than lions and tigers have been documented, hyenas have turned their carnivorous viciousness on humans (Estes).

"By virtue of their size and abundance, . . . hyenas . . . are, perhaps, the most significant terrestrial carnivore on the planet" (Spotted Hyena).

Mishnah 8:3 leads to a *Gemarah* (83b–84a) that presents the animal, or, at least, a part of it, as being useful for (apparently, a type of sympathetic) medicinal purpose. The issue here concerns a case when one may eat prohibited food. In certain cases, such as one's life being threatened otherwise, one should not hesitate to consume prohibited foods. The case presented here seems, at first glance, to be a little odd.

> *Mishnah*: "If one is seized by a ravenous hunger, he may be given to eat even unclean things until his eyes are enlightened. If one was bit by a mad dog, he may not . . . eat the lobe of its liver. But Matthia b. Cheresh permits it . . ."

In the *Gemarah*, after identifying the symptoms to diagnose an unfortunate dog as mad, the Rabbis discuss what curative treatments are available if one is bitten or even merely comes in contact with the dangerous creature. Besides the sympathetic cures alluded to earlier, both folk and modern medicine recognize that drinking copious fluids is typically a warranted prescription. It is also interesting to note here that the name expressed is that of a mother's child, not a father's.

> . . . Abaye said: Let him take the skin of a male hyena, and write upon it: I, Plony and Plony, the son of that and that woman, write . . . *Kanti, Kanti, Klores*, God, God, Lord of Hosts, amen, amen, selah. Then, let him strip off his clothes, and bury them in a grave [at cross-roads], for twelve months of a year. Then he should take them out and burn them in an oven, and scatter the ashes. During these twelve months, he drinks water . . . out of a copper tube, lest he see the shadow of the demon. . . . (*Yoma*).

A̲n̲ A̲dditional̲ T̲almud̲ T̲ail̲ (*Sanhedrin* 1)

. . . The death sentence on the wolf or the lion or the bear or the leopard or the hyena or the serpent is to be passed (by a court of) 23 (judges). R. Eliezer says: Whoever is first to kill them [without trial], acquires merit; R. Akiba, however, holds that their death is to be decided by 23. . . . The Great Sanhedrin consisted of 71 members; the small Sanhedrin of 23. . . . what must be the population of a town to make it eligible for a [small] Sanhedrin?—120. R. Nehemia says: 230, so that each member should be a ruler of [at least] 10.

86

GADFLY

GADFLY

Hebrew *KeReTS* (But JPS, alternate "Butcher," p. 865; *MNiLo(V)N/*, *"Z'Voo(V)V Soo(V)SiMN*, 'horse-fly,'" mod., p. 127)

> *Egypt is a handsome heifer—/A gadfly from the north is coming, coming!*
> —Jeremiah 46:20 (see number 6)

Oestrus bovis: **Bot-fly.**

The three animals that follow in this "series" are largely archaic translations. JPS translates "locust, grub," or, simply, "worm," especially for Palmer-worm and canker-worm, albeit it maintains this creature, the gad-fly. It is another indication both of the difficulty of translating the Hebrew to attempt to understand what the ancients had in mind, and how translations often reflect the cultural mores of the time and place in which they occur. Palmer-worm is especially interesting, since, as France indicates, the term may have a derivation to the Palmers, who entered Jerusalem during what must have been the holiday of Succot, when each person gathered up his or her palm frond, that is, *lulav*, as, indeed, Jews around the world continue to do so today. In any event, there is probable validity in perceiving these creatures as some larvae or pupae stage of the locust or grasshopper (which see for scientific nomenclature), certainly destructive creatures all.

Returning to this gad-fly, then, there are three species in the genus that attack domesticated animals: The horse-fly (*O. gasterophilus equi*); the sheep-fly (*Cephalemyia ovis*); and *O. bovis*.

The life-cycles of these insects (or, more accurately, parasitic worms that metamorphose into insects) is nothing less than disgusting and astonishing. *O. equi*, especially, is remarkable and horrific.

The animal deposits its eggs on the hairs of the horse. The horse licks itself. The eggs that survive mastication and esopageal muscle-throe attach as larvae to the interior membrane of the stomach. Later, they traverse the entire alimentary canal embedded in excretory material, and erupt with the excrement out of the anus. They fall to the ground. Here, the larvae openings become permanent. The now completed insect crawls away into the ground. If not trammeled under hoof, it soon takes to the air.

Nonetheless, our major concern in this reference is *O. bovis*. As we shall see, the Egyptian reference is no accident. The following extensive quote is taken from Figuer, p. 60f.

> As soon as the cattle are attacked, they may be seen, their heads and necks extended, their tails trembling, and held in a line with the body, to rush to the nearest river or pond, while such as are not attacked disperse. It is asserted that the buzzing alone . . . terrifies a bullock to such an extent as to render it unmanageable. As for the insect, it . . . deposit(s) its eggs under the skin of our large ruminants. . . . The mother insect makes a certain number of little wounds in the skin of the beast, each of which receives an egg, which the heat of the animal serves to bring forth. It is a natural parallel to the artificial way which the ancient Egyptians invented of hatching the eggs of domestic fowls, and which has been imitated badly enough in our day.
>
> Directly the larva of the Bot-fly is out of the egg and lodged between the skin and the flesh of its host, the bullock, it finds itself in a place perfectly suitable to its existence. In this happy condition the larva increases in growth, and eventually becomes a fly in its turn. Those parts of the animal's body in which

the larvae are lodged are easily to be recognised (sic), as above each larva may be seen an elevation, a sort of tumour (sic), termed a bot—a bump . . . (like) the bump caused on a man's head by a severe blow.

Again, these creatures appear to be true denizens of the evil spirit of the Middle East; and yet, from the Middle East has emerged so much concept of good as well. It is, as it has always been, a great mystery.

87

CANKER-WORM

CANKER-WORM (But see also numbers 25, 76)
Hebrew *YeLeK*; but JPS, "Locust Swarm," p. 883; *MiLo(V)N/* also
YLK, 43
Jeremiah 51:14, 27

CONCORDANCE

Joel 1:4; 2:25 (JPS, "Grubs").
Nahum 3:15–16 (JPS, "Grubs").
Psalms I–22:7.

AN ADDITIONAL TALMUD TAIL (See under number 25 for all worms)

88

EZEKIEL'S VISION

(Ezekiel's Vision, Winged and Wheeled Creature[s]) Ezekiel 1, 2 (nearly all verses)

Refer to Appendix A, "Mythological and Supernatural Creatures."

CONCORDANCE

Genesis 10 (nearly all verses). (See 11, 13, 16, 26).
(Daniel 7:3–25 [similar vision of Belshazzar]).

89

PALMER-WORM

PALMER-WORM

Hebrew *GaZaM*; JPS, "Cutter, Grub, Hopper, . . . probably designate stages in the development of the locust" (p. 1005).

What the cutter has left, the locust has devoured:
And what the grub has left, the hopper has devoured.
　　　　　　　　　　　　　—Joel 1:4 (See number 25)

CONCORDANCE

Joel 2:25.
Amos 4:9.
Jonah 4:7.

Again, France indicates the allusion to the Palmer, but, naturally, from his perspective, from the Christian viewpoint, which is also in the Prologue to Chaucer's *The Canterbury Tales*: "And palmeres for to seeken strange strandes." Following, a more Jewish viewpoint is indicated.

> . . . there was a palmerworm written of in English as early as 1560; it was a hairy caterpillar of a migratory or wandering habit, destructive to vegetation. The name comes from the palmer, or pilgrim from the Holy Land who would carry, as a sign that he has completed his pilgrimage, a palm leaf to excite the admiration and envy of others. (P. 121; see also Cansdale, pp. 238–240, who tracks through a schol-

arly methodology the various translations and derivations.)

Nadich recounts the story of how the *halakhah* came about that each person would perform the *mitzvah* of *lulav* by having one in the home.

> In earlier days when the first day of Sukhot fell on a Sabbath, the men would bring their palm branches on the even of the Sabbath to the Temple Mount, and the officials would take them and place them in order on top of the portico. The older people put theirs in a special chamber. They were all taught to say, "Whoever gets possession of my *lulav*, let it be his as my gift." On the next day they would arrive early and the officials would throw down the *lulavim* and the people would snatch them. In so doing they would sometimes injure each other. When the Court saw that the situation was dangerous they decreed that each person should use the *lulav* in his home. (Pp. 137–138; refer to *Sukkah* 3, 4, and 45a)

The *Gemarah* does not indicate whether the *halakhah* prohibiting carrying on *Shabbat* was in effect during Temple times; the indication here may be an anachronism more appropriate to talmudic and posttalmudic synagogue observance. Nadich alludes to this in his Note on p. 156. It is customary even today for an observant man to visit the synagogue on Friday with any necessary holy object, such as his *tallit*, and deposit it in a certain cubby, so it will be there for him when he appears on the day of prayer, and he will not have to carry it outside the confines of the synagogue.

AN ADDITIONAL TALMUD TAIL (*Avodah Zorah* 2:3; *Gemarah* 28a–b)

Mishnah: "We may allow them (idol-worshippers) to heal us . . . (but there is a dispute from the curious indication) . . . but not personal healing . . .

The *Gemarah* says that treating an open wound is so vital the Sabbath may (must?) be profaned. One of the treatments does not sound especially sanitary—but it may be referring to maggots, which we know can heal difficult wounds, metamorphose into flies, and buzz off: "Said Samuel . . . What is the remedy—For stopping the bleeding, cress with vinegar; for bringing on [flesh], scraped root of cynodon and the paring of the bramble, or worms from a dunghill."

90

"A GREAT FISH"

"A GREAT FISH"
Jonah 2:1 (and f)
(See Leviathan, in Appendix A).

Refer to Appendix A, "Mythological and Supernatural Creatures."

CONCORDANCE

Psalms V–148:7 (ye sea-monsters [or at number 93, which see]).

91

WILD-OX

WILD-OX

Hebrew *ReiM* (?)

Psalms I–22:22 (but see number 13)

CONCORDANCE

Psalms 29:6 (see number 11);
Psalms IV–92:11.

As alluded to earlier in the various bovine entries, there existed up until the Middle Ages a few herds of the original animal, the once-proud and fierce Aurochs.

92

S N A I L

SNAIL
Hebrew *TeMeS*; *MiLO(V)N/*, *CHiLaZo(V)N/* p. 248

> *like a snail that melts away as it moves;/like a*
> *woman's stillbirth, may they never see the sun!*
> —Psalms II–58:9

Murex trunculus, M. brandaris
JPS, as indicated, indicates that the Hebrew meaning is uncertain.

Yet almost all translators have a similar rendition. The image is the smooth trail of slime a snail or a slug leaves behind as it traverses the ground. It was apparently thought by the ancients that a part of the animal was being lost in the ooze and that it would eventually fade away, leaving aught but its shell. The discovery of a beautiful empty shell would have contributed to this erroneous naturalist view. Today we know that a slug is a snail that has either lost or has not yet grown a shell, and the slime is manufactured by the animal to assist it in progressing on its one foot.

Clark indicates that these land mollusks "occur practically everywhere and except for the insects and the spiders are the most numerous in kind of all the larger invertebrate types." Nearly all inhabit damp or humid places and venture outside when the weather is wet or even more humid, usually at night.

A few are subterranean and there are blind animals that burrow in caves. Interestingly, a few species can burrow into rock, which raises the idea that the concept of the Shamir may have developed from the snail and not the worm. France and Podwal develop this thought as well. Clark continues:

> Taken in the broad sense of gastropod mollusks as a whole the snails have the greatest range of any animal type, with the possible exception of nematodes or protozoans. They live from above the snow line in the Himalayas at an altitude of 16,400 feet down to at least 15,900 feet, or a little more than three miles beneath the surface of the sea. They are found in desert regions where the temperature at noon is 122° Fahrenheit and in hot springs with the same temperature. One fresh-water snail lives . . . where the . . . winter temperature is 30° below 0. Many fresh-water snails can be frozen in the ice without damage . . .
>
> Land snails vary in size from minute to a length of 7½ inches . . . (P. 153)

The snail was an animal that occupied considerable attention of those in biblical times and the Rabbis as well. France gives some succint indications, in particular mentioning how the animal was an example of how all things have a purpose in God's plan. Also, ". . . Lupton . . . advised that 'The two horns of a snail born upon a man will pluck away carnal or fleshly lust from the bearer thereof'" (pp. 138–140).

The purposes alluded to are many, but the particular reference that France indicates may be found in *Shabbat* 77b. The Rabbis are discussing that, indeed, all things have a purpose; in this instance, Rab Judah, in Rab's name, indicates the creature's curative powers: "Of all that the Holy One blessed be He, created in His world(:) He did not create a single thing without purpose. [Thus] He created the snail as a remedy for a scab . . ." Regarding divination or the ability to perceive omens, Trachtenberg indicates that "The snail, or the mole, which is noticed burrowing in a house and casting up the earth behind, is proclaiming that an adulterous act is soon to be committed there" (p. 211).

Even more enlightening is the use of the animal to close a

proof regarding resurrection and eternal life, the use of *Shehe-let*, and the inclusion of *tekhelet.*

In *Sanhedrin* 91a, "A sectarian [*min*, viz, a heathen] said to R. Ammi: 'Ye maintain that the dead will revive. But they turn to dust, and can dust come to life?'" R. Ammi retorts using a specific case to enhance a general concept. ". . . go up to the mountains, where thou wilt see but one snail, whilst by to-morrow the rain has descended and it is covered with snails." We should point out that when the Rabbis give argument to heathens, and not to their students or colleagues, we are never quite sure if they are holding back, sometimes referred to as the twig and the branch ("This heathen you whisked away with a twig, but for us what is the thick branch?"). The *Gemarah* gives no indication here if that is the case or not.

Podwal gives the clearest description of how the creature was associated with the *Shehelet.*

> . . . the aromatic spice . . . said to have been derived from the shell of a snail found in the Red Sea, which emits a pleasant odor when burned. *Shehelet* was one of the ingredients that . . . composed the holy incense burned as an offering in the Tabernacle and later in the Temple. This fragrant offering is recalled in the ceremony of *Havdalah*, performed at the conclusion of the Sabbath and festivals . . . (P. 12)

By far, though, the most attention given to this interesting animal is through the derivation of the *tekhelet*, the single blue (or purple) cord that dangled upon the fringe of the *tallit*, or four-corned garment, worn on a daily basis by the devout. Although the pious still engage in the practice, the *tekhelet* cord coloration has been considered lost and arcane for centuries. The requirement is a textual one, found in Numbers 15:38–39.

> Speak unto the children of Israel, and say unto them that they make them a fringe in the borders of their garments, throughout their generations, and that they put upon the fringes of the borders a thread of blue purple; And it shall be unto you for a fringe that ye may see it, and remember all the commandments

of the Eternal, and do them; and that ye search not
after your own heart, and your own eyes, after which
ye use to go a whoring. (Silbermann tr., p. 76)

Rashi is not so specific as to call the animal required to
produce the dye a snail; however, "It is the blue dye of
(obtained from) the blood of the Chalazon (a kind of shell-
fish)." Most other scholars, however, regard the creature that
produced the substance to manufacture the blue-purple dye as
the snail. By the Talmud and by the *halakhah,* of course, the
blue-purple cord has not been used since tannaic times (some
say since Temple times), since the skill of extracting the dye,
indeed even the identity of the particular species, has supposedly been lost. Today, however, some prayer shawls are
colored redux with a single blue or blue-purple fringe at the
corners.

The *Encyclopedia Judaica* article is especially well drawn
and even identifies the possible species in this very entry.

The color of *tekhelet* was between green and blue
and . . . "resembles the sea, the sea resembles grass,
and grass resembles the heavens." . . . (it) was usually dyed on wool . . . The color was fast and with-
stood oxidization. . . . The best dye was obtained
when extracted from live snails . . . and to make it
fast various materials were added . . .

The article then describes how, in the mishnaic period, a
substitute from a plant, indigo, was used, and a dispute arose
if this were permissible. A *baraita* (the original source, from
which argument and precept are derived) concluded that
"There is no way of testing the *tekhelet* . . . and it should be
brought from an expert." As late as the *amora* period Abbaye
claimed that a Sage taught him the dyeing method. Nonetheless, by the end of the talmudic period, the fringes were, and
came down to us as, only white.

Gershon Hanokh Leiner, the Hasidic rabbi of Radzin,
proposed . . . that the precept . . . be reintroduced.
He came to the conclusion that *tekhelet* had been
extracted from the cuttlefish . . . which has a gland

in its body that secretes a blue-black dye, and his
suggestion was adopted by his followers. . . .

The article then proceeds toward the zoological, deriving
from the species indicated the probable source of the color.

> . . . in whose bodies is a gland containing a clear
> liquid, which when it comes into contact with the air
> becomes greenish; . . . after the addition of various
> chemicals, receives its purple color, the "royal
> purple" of literature. The Phoenicians in particular
> specialized in it. . . . Around . . . the site of ancient
> Ugarit large quantities of shells of the purple snail
> have been found. . . . A modern investigator ex-
> tracted 1.4 grams of the purple dye from 12,000 such
> snails, thus explaining the high cost of the *tekhelet*.
> Isaac Herzog . . . reached the conclusion that it was
> extracted from the snails *Janthina pallida* and *J.
> bicolor* that are found a considerable distance from
> the shore and only reach it at long intervals. This in
> his opinion explains the statement that the *tekhelet*
> comes up once in 70 years.

The article cites many of the talmudic sources, especially
Men. 39a–43a; the legend that the animal appears once every
70 years can be found in 44a. *Megillah* 6a tells the tradition that
it was members of the tribe of Zebulun that were responsible
for gathering the animal and extracting the substance. See also
Sotah 46b and the talmudic references indicated further on
(Vol. 15, p. 914; also Vol. 16, p. 1188).

One of the *Shabbat* prohibitions is indicated in *Shabbat* 75a,
that of crushing the animal for the dye, although the Soncino
translation refers to the animal as a "purple fish." The place for
the manufacture of the dye is given in *Sanhedrin* 12a: "A couple
[of scholars] have arrived from Rakkath who had been captured by an eagle while in possession of articles manufactured
at Luz, such as purple . . ." From our earlier reading of this
Gemarah, we know the "eagle" was Rome and that "through
Divine mercy and their own merits they escaped safely."
Midrash Rabbah 17:5 is where the *pshat* occurs that the blue
thread is no longer needed: ". . . It is a religious duty to get
white wool and a blue thread and make the fringes. When does

this rule apply? When the thread is real blue. Now, however, we possess only white, for the blue has been (divinely) hidden."

Finally, the second *Mishnah* in the opening tract of the Talmud, *Berachot*, derives when one may begin the morning prayers: "From what time may one recite the *Shema* in the morning? From the time that one can distinguish between blue and white. R. Eliezer says: Between blue and green." See also the Milgram commentary to the JPS Torah, which tends to follow the *Encyclopedia Judaica* inclusions.

AN ADDITIONAL TALMUD TAIL (*Chagigah* 1:5; *Gemarah* 11a–b)

In regard to laws concerning Levitical "uncleanness" (Fox, better, "charged state") in particular to the touching of a dead creeping creature, there apparently must be a minimum of size involved. "The Sages fixed the measure at the size of a lentil, for a snail is at first the size of a lentil" (Danby translates not "snail" but "land crocodile," Soncino N5, p. 58).

93

LEVIATHAN

LEVIATHAN
Psalms III–74:14 (but see Isaiah 27:1)

Refer to Appendix A, "Mythological and Supernatural Creatures."

CONCORDANCE

Psalms IV-104:26; V–148:7 (Ye sea-monsters).
Job 3:8 (Let them curse [the night] that curse the day,/Who are ready to rouse up leviathan); 7:12 (Am I a . . . sea-monster . . .); 40:25 (Canst thou draw out leviathan with a fish-hook?).

94

S PARROW

SPARROW
Hebrew *TSiPo(V)R*; mod., "bird"; sparrow, *D'Ro(V)R*, same as "Swallow," *MiLo(V)N*

> *E̋ven the sparrow has found a home,/*
> *and the swallow a nest for herself/in which to set her*
> *young,/near Your altar, O Lord of hosts,/*
> *my king and my God.*
> —Psalms III–84:4 (see number 74)

Passer domesticus domesticus:
Very widespread throughout Eurasia, later introduced by *Homo Sapiens* to the Americas and the Australian subcontinent. The common house sparrow.

CONCORDANCE

Psalms IV–102:8 (I am become . . . /Like a sparrow that is above upon the housetop).
Proverbs 26:2 (see number 80).

Pinney traces the animal as being at the top of the line of bird evolution; yet Norell et al. report a recent fossil find in Mongolia that may track its ancestor as a link between flying dinosaurs and birds (with a provocative alternative proposal): "Could flight have arisen twice in the history of birds? . . . (This) discovery . . . shows that the boundary between modern birds and their typically dinosaurian ancestors is a diffuse one and that the path of early bird evolution is a circuitous one." Still, Pinney insists that the bird's delicate nest building, the form at times resembling a tent, as well as other factors, places it high up on the ladder (pp. 171–172).

A curious article proposes that "in the ways between a man and a maid," humans are more like birds than fellow mammals.

> The importance of male support probably explains the evolution of monogamy. . . . male sparrows do not take two wives because the first wife objects when they try and, being perhaps aggressive . . . succeeds in driving the interloper off. . . . (Sparrows and other) birds are nearly all monogamous whereas mammals are nearly all polygamous, a phenomenon often explained by the observation that birds of both sexes can feed their young at the nest . . . so women have an incentive to monopolize men and use them as assistant food providers.

The suppositions here may be suspect in terms of flawed rhetoric and absence of additional scientific investigation, and there may be a bit of whimsy involved, but "we do believe birds of a feather do flock together" ("Birds and Be").

It is a common twittering bird practically as familiar as the robin or swallow, a charming, vivacious, ubiquitous, sometimes annoying, playful animal. One might not suspect the several legends and stories about it, at times seeming to invest it with certain shape-shifting or metamorphosing powers. Perhaps the fact that in some areas at some times of the year it seems to be everywhere may have contributed to these concepts.

Here is the entry from France: "According to Jewish lore the sparrow, molded in gold, stands on the throne of Solomon and, through an ingenious piece of machinery, would chirp as the king set his foot on the first of the steps leading up to it." (pp. 140–142).

Solomon, who, by legend, discerned how to talk to the

animals, may have used this device (in lore, of course) as a medium or, in more practical terms, as a message to his courtiers and supplicants concerning his decisions.

One of the more enchanting and inspiring legends concerning the sparrow, and all the other animals as well, is their uniquely designed prayer service. According to this legend, every day the animals lift up their voices in prayer, each with its own peculiar voice and character reflected in the prayer. Thus, some fish, for example, chant, "The voice of the Lord is upon the waters"; the sparrow, being a chirping song-bird, twitters in a melodic hymn (sometimes in duet with another bird), "Yea, the sparrow hath found a house and the swallow a nest for herself, where she may lay her young: Thine altars, O Lord of Hosts, My king and my God" (*Schochet* 134–135). Many of these are extracted from Psalms and other biblical entries.

The gnostic gospel writers included the animal, recalling it as one offered for sacrifices. Until the so-called X manuscript, the original *baraita*, is discovered, we can never be certain what the original strand of the story intended. In Matthew 10:29–31 and Luke 12:6–7 two versions of the same Christian "commandment" are indicated.

> Matthew: Are not two sparrows sold for a farthing? And one of them shall fall on the ground without your Father. But the very hairs of your head are all numbered. Fear ye not, therefore, ye are of more value than many sparrows.
>
> Luke: Are not five sparrows sold for two farthings, and not one of them is forgotten before God? But even the very hairs of your head are all numbered. Fear not therefore; ye are of more value than many sparrows. (KJV–NIV, pp. 1212; 1294)

The stalwart little sparrow also allows us to bring to a denouement our earlier story of Titus and the gnat (others, fly) that flew up his nose, and excepting the brief time he received relief sitting next to the smithy's anvil, was tormented for the rest of his life. In *Gittin* 56b the story is related virtually in its entirety, with a most revealing ending, one that is not usually recounted in the telling of the legend. (See also *Midrash Rabbah* 10:7 and Preuss, pp. 204–205.)

. . . R. Phineas b. Aruba said: I was in company with the notables of Rome, and when he died they split open his skull and found there . . . a sparrow two (pounds) in weight. Abaye said: We have it on record that its beak was of brass and its claws of iron. When he died he said: Burn me and scatter my ashes over the seven seas so that the God of the Jews should not find me and bring me to trial.

95

CONEY

CONEY

Psalms IV-104:18 (JPS, Rock-Badger [which see number 30]).
Also a.k.a. Rock-Rabbit, Hyrax, Daman.

AN ADDITIONAL TALMUD TAIL (*Chullin* 59a. See also under
numbers 30 and 31.)

". . . The Rock-Rabbit and the hare chew the cud, nevertheless
they have upper teeth and are unclean!"

96

ANT

ANT
Hebrew *N'MaLaH*

Lazybones, go to the ant;/Study its ways and learn.
—Proverbs 6:6

Polyergus rufescens: (Russet ants); France prefers *Atta Barbara* and *A. Structor*, since they are native to the region *and* they are among those species that, indeed, store up food, as is recounted in Aesop's fable of "The Ant and The Grasshopper" (p. 12).

The habits and behaviors of ants are, upon mere observation, or scientific inquiry, to strike the observer or scientist alike with astonishment. They communicate, care with seeming compassion for each other, appear to treat their females with disdain, plot and engage in complex military stratagems, herd and exploit other species, design and construct sophisticated architectural "walled" cities—so as to make human beings wonder just how far they have come from the lower orders. Ants are resolute, resourceful, adaptable, innumerable, exhibit a cunning that can almost be described as intelligence, and may very well be on, in, and about the planet long after *Homo sapiens* has departed.

Because of a description by Frances Huber (presented by Figuier on p. 391), a description of an event not unlike

countless similar events in biblical history and the Middle
East, I have chosen *P. rufescens.* The reader should also
investigate *Formica nigra* (the ashy-black ant) and *F. rufa* (the
red ant), the two most common.

As I was walking . . . between four and five in the
afternoon, I saw at my feet a legion of largish (sic)
russet ants crossing the road. They were marching in
a body with rapidity, their troop occupied a space of
from eight to ten feet long by three or four inches
wide; in a few minutes they had entirely evacuated
the road; they penetrated through a very thick
hedge, and went into a meadow, whither I followed
them. They wound their way along the turf, without
straying, and their column remained always continuous, in spite of the obstacles which they had to
surmount. Very soon they arrived near a nest of
ashy-black ants, the dome of which rose among the
grass, at twenty paces from the hedge. A few ants of
this species were at the door of their habitation. As
soon as they descried the army which was approaching, they threw themselves on those which were at
the head of the cohort. The alarm spread at the same
instant in the interior of the nest, and their companions rushed out in crowds from all the subterranean
passages. The russet ants, the body of whose army
was only two paces distant, hastened to arrive at the
foot of the nest; the whole troop precipitated itself
forward at the same time, and knocked the ashy-
black ants head over heels, who, after a short but
very smart combat, retired to the extremity of the
habitation. The russet ants clambered up the sides of
the hillock, flocked to the summit, and introduced
themselves in great numbers into the first avenues;
other groups worked with their teeth, making a
lateral aperture. In this they succeeded, and the rest
of the army penetrated through the breach into the
besieged city. They did not make a long stay there; in
three or four minutes the russet ants came out again
in haste, by the same adits, carrying each one in its
mouth a pupa or larva belonging to the conquered.
They again took exactly the same road by which they

had come, and followed each other in a straggling manner . . .

The author continues to describe how the vanquished managed successfully to muster a daring rescue mission and to recover at least a remnant of their progeny, the majority being turned into, for want of a better term, slaves for the victorious invaders.

CONCORDANCE

Proverbs 30:25 (The ants are a people not strong,/Yet they provide their food in the summer; JPS: Ants are a folk without power . . . , pp. 1293, 1336).

Not all species store food away, as is popularly thought, but, as indicated, some species native to the Middle East apparently do, and it is these that must have captured the imagination of the biblical writers.

The animal, like all insects, is quite old, durable, adaptable to most climate and ecological conditions, and largely unchanged for millions of years. According to Staedter, "biogeologist Stephen Hasiotis . . . found a fossilized ant nest that's 160 million years old."

Pinney points out that to the ancient Hebrews (and we might say, to the Rabbis, as well), the ant embodied two particular attributes, observed clearly in both biblical entries: wisdom and industry. "It must have been a common enough experience for the Hebrews to see ants carrying bits of grain, leaves, and other matter to their nest. The ants' work never seemed to cease . . ." (p. 184). These attributes are reflected in the various stories concerning King Solomon and in various observations by the Rabbis, who appear almost as naturalist investigators.

Again, Solomon, acknowledged as the wisest man on earth, learned to talk to the animals. Along with the bear, bat, bee, hoopoe, and other animals, the king had an experience with an ant. Once the king and forty thousand of his soldiers happened on a bivouac to find themselves in the valley of the ants (some say it occurred when Solomon was abroad on one of his solitary sojourns, the places being revealed only to the king). At the approach of the men, Solomon overheard the queen issue orders to her colony to withdraw lest they be trammeled. Solomon ordered his company to halt. He approached the queen ant. There then ensues a conversation between the queen ant and King Solomon. The ant tricks Solomon into holding her up in his hand so she may better address him. Solomon and the ant engage in an *agon*, a rhetorical dispute over which ruler is the more powerful in the world. The ant-rhetor wins the contest by pointing out that her tiny creatures had preceded humanity in the order of creation; as well, as Solomon, chastened, returns her to the ground, again at her request, she retorts with this parthian shot: "Were I not greater than you, you would not have complied with my demand" (Podwal, p. 2; see also Toperoff, pp. 5–10).

In a homiletic taught through a study session between Rabbi Eliezer, a student of Rabbi Joshua, the student asks the teacher the meaning of the wisdom (Proverbs) verse. R. Joshua replies: "My son, the ant has neither king, nor overseer, nor ruler to make her wise, rather her wisdom comes from within her. God (rebukes humanity) and said, 'And you wicked ones, should you not have learned from her? But you held on to your laziness and your foolishness and failed to repent'" (*Nadich*, p. 101).

It is interesting that the Rabbis could, like the biblical writer, ignore the naturalistic fact, and Solomon legend that validates it, that the animal does, indeed, have a "wise" ruler. Rabbi Joshua was a first century *tanna* and recalled all too vividly the destruction of the *Beit Hamikdash*. This great debacle and tragedy may have been what he had in mind in his rebuke.

The flawed concept of the ants lacking a queen (or king) may have been abetted by a socio-zoological experiment conducted by Rabbi Simeon. Coming across a large anthill, he spread his coat over it, presumably to block out the sun. Soon one ant, apparently a scout, appeared from under the canopy. R. Simeon marked it in some way for identification purposes. The creature re-entered the colony. Apparently he was to inform his compatriots that it was safe to emerge since there was now shade over the top of the anthill. Now, however, R.

Simeon removed his coat from over the anthill. Many ants soon emerged, believing it was safe to come out. At once, feeling exposed to the sun's rays, they turned upon the hapless individual responsible for the compromised intelligence and executed him. From this, R. Simeon drew the conclusion that the ants lacked a king (Schochet, pp. 106–107).

The author also points out that in another experiment, R. Simeon deduced the animals enjoyed a highly developed olfactory sense. Further, "In a rather imaginative development, we read . . . of the use of large ants as surgical clamps!" The ants would be allowed to bite into the required areas of the surgical incision, then their bodies would be severed, with their mandibles remaining attached as the clamps until the procedure was over.

> R. Simeon b. Halafta said: Once it happened that an ant dropped one grain of wheat and all the ants came and sniffed at it and yet not one of them took it, until the one to whom it belonged came and took it. Consider her wisdom and all her praiseworthiness inasmuch as she has not learnt [her ways] from any creature. She has no judge or officer over her . . . Then you, for whom I have appointed judges and officers—how much more should you hearken unto them . . . (*Midrash Rabbah* 5:1–3)

Finally, in a rather pessimistic *Midrash*, the all too true nature of humanity is commented upon. "It was a sufficient humiliation for man that he had to learn from the ant; had he learnt and acted accordingly he would have been sufficiently humbled but he did not learn from the wise ant" (*Yalkut Shimoni*, Joshua 24:22; see also Toperoff, p. 8).

AN ADDITIONAL TALMUD TAIL (See also *Ketubot* 75a; *Yevamoth* 118b; *K'mish* 7:4) Pesach 2:1; *Gemarah* 24a–b

The *Mishnah* deals with the time one is permitted to eat [leaven], feed it to domestic animals, and sell it to a Gentile—thus, when one may receive benefit of it, and when one may not. The *Gemarah* denotes a series of lashes for various infringements, quotes Abaye: "If he ate . . . an ant, he is flagellated five times; . . ."

In *Mo'ed Katan* 6b–7a, we learn of a way to destroy ants' nests, apparently permissible during the mo'ed period. "Rabban Simeon b. Gamliel says: Earth is fetched from one hole and put into another and they strangle each other." That is (and as ancient observation, it is not altogether unlike that of Huber's serendipitous Thoreauesque naturalistic latter-day experience), "The ants of the two nests (do) not (know) . . . each other and thus engage in battle to the death." (See also Soncino N1, p. 33.)

97

"HORSELEECH"

"HORSELEECH" (Or, simply, Leech, JPS, 1335)
Hebrew 'aLoo(V)KaH

> *⊘he leech has two daughters, "Give!" and "Give!"/*
> *Three things are insatiable;/*
> *Four never say, "Enough!"*
> —Proverbs 30:15.

Haemopsis sanguisuga
This species is one of the aquatic versions found in the Middle East; the water relationship will become evident.

It is a very curious passage in Proverbs, and the scholars of biblical animals spend some time attempting to deduce it, more time, apparently, than drew the attention of the Rabbis. A clue may lie in the zoological fact that several species of this specialized segmented worm can attach themselves at both the posterior and anterior ends, thus the emphasis in the repetition; also, simply adding blood to the end of each redundant command clarifies what may be intended here— the animal (or a selfish, voracious person) takes only blood and gives nothing in return.

Yet throughout history, the leech has been used, to be later validated scientifically or perceived as utterly flawed, for medicinal purposes. That is, the "art" of bloodletting using leeches may have done more harm than good—indeed, in some cases, contributing to the hasty demise of the patient—

but it may have had some beneficial effects as well. Recent evidence suggests that those who give blood on occasion will tend to experience up to 30 percent less chance of heart attacks. This admittedly is not a totally valid analogy, but it does present an interesting new way of looking at an ancient technique. Further, the use of leeches as treatments of wounds and stubborn blood clots has been returning in recent years. The Rabbis also were concerned with preventative and curative medicinal usages involving this creature.

The scholars tend to agree that the species indicated was particularly dangerous in that it would take up residence in watering buckets and pipes. When an unfortunate horse or human chanced to drink from such a source without checking or being particularly careful, the animal would attach itself to the nasal and oral mucosa. Apparently, many a horse owner had to become a skilled veterinarian in terms of removing this segmented parasite with as minimal damage and suffering to his discomfited horse as was possible (Clark, p. 81; Pinney, p. 195; France, p. 85; Toperoff, pp. 129–130).

As with any animal that cannot be seen or discerned very well until it is almost too late, or that seems to have certain powers of an almost magical nature, myths and legends grew up about it in ancient times and in the Middle Ages. Trachtenberg reports such a myth, the underlying truth that may have given it birth not boding well for an unfortunate bovine: "Cows whose udders are unprotected while they are at pasture are likely to be milked by a species of leach" [sic] (p. 184).

It is *Avodah Zorah* 12b to which the scholars must have been referring (Toperoff accords this as one of his references) to the caveat of drinking from a certain water pipe or standing bucket of drinking water.

> One should not place one's mouth at a waterpipe (sic) and drink because it is dangerous. (They asked) Wherein lies the danger? They swallowing of a (leech was the answer. Also) . . . one should not drink water from rivers or from pools directly with his mouth or with (his) hand; he who does so (will find) his blood . . . upon his head. . . . If a person has swallowed one, one may warm water even on the Sabbath for him . . . (and) he should drink vinegar.

See also Preuss, who points out as well that another
remedy for this malady was thought to be swallowing certain
types of bugs; or, to heat the bugs on hot coals near the patient
so he may "inhale the fumes; then the leech will surely emerge"
(pp. 199–200). Preuss also refers to the remedies elucidated in
Gittin 69b for ailments of the spleen, typically translated as
"water worms": "Take seven . . . (leeches) and dry them in the
shade and every day drink two or three in wine" (p. 188).

"'All raw vegetables make the complexion pale,' R. Isaac
said: That is, in the first meal taken after blood-letting"
(*Berachot* 44b).

Finally, Toperoff has uncovered a most interesting interpretation of the redundancy in the biblical entry.

> Mar-Ukba interprets the words "Give, Give" (as) . . .
> the voice of these two who cry from Gehenna, calling
> to this world "Bring, Bring!" And who are they?—
> (idol-worshipers) which continuously lure(s) the
> unwary to (their) erroneous teaching and the gov-
> ernment (which constantly imposes new taxes and
> duties). (See also *Avodah Zorah* 17a)

AN ADDITIONAL TALMUD TAIL (*Avodah Zorah* 1:4)

The *Mishnah* denotes when one may conduct business within
or without a city, depending upon where the idolatry occurs.
The *Gemarah* is the one mentioned previously wherein one
should not place "one's mouth on the water-pipe to drink
therefrom for fear of danger . . . (being) the swallowing of the
leech." Now although it is not permissible to kindle a fire on
Shabbat, that the principle of saving a life comes first is
indicted, as included previously.

> . . . R. Chanina said: For one who swallows a leech it
> is permissible to (kindle a fire) and get water heated
> on the Sabbath.
>
> There was actually a case of one swallowing a
> leech, when R. Nehemiah declared it permissible to
> get water heated for him on the Sabbath.
>
> "Meanwhile," said R. Hana son of R. Joshua, "Let
> him sip vinegar."

98

GREYHOUND

GREYHOUND (Refer to number 23)

CONCORDANCE

Proverbs 30:31.

Toperoff omits it; the other scholars dismiss it as a poor translation. JPS includes it but indicates the meaning of the Hebrew is, indeed, difficult to discern. See especially France: ". . . some early commentators have thought the reference must be to the warhorse (sic), ornamented about the loins with girth and buckles . . . (or) the wild ass of Abyssinia . . ." (p. 73).

99

PHOENIX

PHOENIX

I thought I would end my days with my family,/
And be as long-lived as the phoenix.
                                    —Job 29:18.

(Refer to Appendix A, "Mythological and Supernatural Creatures.")

100

BEHEMOTH

BEHEMOTH
Hebrew *B'HeiMaH*

> *Take now behemoth, whom I made as I did you;/*
> *He eats grass, like the cattle.*
> —Job 40:15 (See number 15)

(Refer to Appendix A, "Mythological and Supernatural Creatures.")

CONCORDANCE

(Nehemiah 2:12, 14 [but, on a pragmatic level, obviously a reference to numbers 14 or 15, which see]).

APPENDICES

MYTHICAL AND
FANTASTICAL CREATURES

The animals discussed herein are the stuff of legends or devout belief, but of which no zoologist has yet been able to observe or to discover a fossil. They include numbers: 77, Dragon; 83, Basilisk; 90, Jonah's Great Fish; 93, Leviathan; 99, Phoenix; 100, Behemoth. Also briefly discussed is number 88, Ezekiel's amazing vision of the Throne of God, and, as well, divers creatures not mentioned in the text. These supernatural creatures will not be considered in this order; rather, in the order, according to the commentaries, of their creation.

In this, I have relied heavily upon Ginzberg (and Szold), in particular, Volume 1, pages 26–46. Of course, Ginzberg has extruded his study from the various midrashic (especially *Rabbah*) and talmudic sources.

Leviathan: On the fifth day God created the fish out of fire and water. This huge sea-dwelling animal rules the seas and all sea-creatures. "So enormous is leviathan that to quench his thirst he needs all the water that flows from the Jordan into the sea." He is so formidable that even behemoth shies from going near him, especially if he is still thirsty. But besides this, "he is wonderfully made . . ." His fins radiate light so bright, even the sun seems a secondary light; his eyes are so luminous that he dares open them only a small crack at a time, lest all ocean life

405

would be destroyed at once from his laser-like beams. Still, like all animals, leviathan's life will someday end. At that time, the flesh of his body will serve as the food for the pious in the World to Come. Meanwhile, a tiny fish, the stickleback, is so elusive the larger animal can never grab it; by alternatively cleaning its flesh and jaws of barnacles and sea effluent and by tormenting it this way and that way, it keeps the huge sea-monster in check.

AN ADDITIONAL TALMUD TAIL (*Bava Batra* 5:1; *Gemarah* 74a–b)

From this *Mishnah* concerning the rights of selling a ship or a boat (under some situations it may include the crew and stores, under others it may not) the Rabbis in the *Gemarah* begin spinning fantastic tales. Whether believable-believed or not, they obviously serve some metaphorical purpose regarding the power and hopeful end to the power of that evil empire, Rome.

> R. Safra related: Once we traveled on board a ship and we saw a fish that raised its head out of the sea. It had horns on which was engraven: "I am a minor creature of the sea, I am 300 parsangs [in length] and I am [now] going into the mouth of Leviathan."

Leviathan, or one of his gargantuan emissary-sycophants, was commonly thought by the Rabbis to be the great fish that swallowed Jonah and taught him Torah for the time of his innards entombment.

Ziz: Albeit not mentioned in the text, still the amazing ziz hovers over Jewish legend. Birds were also created on the fifth day, and the colossus set over them was this odd winged-giant appearing somewhat like an enormous vulture.

> It once happened that travelers on a vessel noticed a bird. As he stood in the water, it merely covered his feet, and his head knocked against the sky. The onlookers thought the water could have any depth at that point, and they prepared to take a bath there. A

heavenly voice warned them: "Alight not here! Once a carpenter's axe slipped from his hand at this spot, and it took it seven years to touch bottom."

Of course, this was the ziz. "His wings are so huge that unfurled they darken the sun. They protect the earth against the storms of the south . . ." (see Podwall).

Behemoth: Land animals were created on the sixth day, and this monster presides over them. This creature is so huge that if there were male and female and they propagated, the world would be overrun in two generations. He requires the produce of a thousand mountains for his daily food intake. It was necessary to afford him his own river for his drink, and this flows out of Paradise, called the stream of Yubal. Like leviathan and ziz, behemoth is destined to be offered on a plate to the righteous as they enter the heavenly dining areas.

An Additional Talmud Tail (*Bava Batra* 74b)

. . . Behemoth on a thousand hills were created male and female, and had they mated with one another they (with their progeny, Soncino, N9, p. 246) would have destroyed the whole world. What did the Holy One, blessed be He, do? He castrated the male and . . . the female . . . preserved it for the righteous for the world to come . . .

Others not mentioned in the text include the *reem* and *adne sadeh*. The *reem* exists as a couple, male and female; but, for the world's protection, the pair can only find each other after seventy years, nearly the time of their deaths. Thus, it is ensured that in each seventy- year cycle only one pair exists. "A traveler who once saw a *reem* one day old described its height to be four parasangs . . . Its horns . . . one hundred ells."

The *adne sadeh* appears like a human being, but "he is fastened to the ground by means of a navel-string, upon which his life depends. . . . This animal keeps himself alive with what is produced by the soil around about him as far as his tether permits him to crawl. He is also called, the 'man of the mountain.'" There are some who believe this may be the first Adam, or a precursor of Adam, and Ginzberg employs this name as well.

The "Barnacle-goose is grown to a tree by its bill." It seems to be a nexus of sorts of creation, since it is difficult to tell whether it is animal or vegetable.

Phoenix: "Among the birds the phoenix is the most wonderful." In the Jewish version of the legend, the phoenix was the only animal to refuse the seductive offering of the fruit of the tree by Eve. Therefore he was accorded eternal life—or, more accurately, a resurrected life. "When he has lived a thousand years, his body shrinks, and the feathers drop from it, until he is as small as an egg. This is the nucleus of the new bird."

The phoenix has also a strong connection to the sun, spreading his huge wings and intercepting much of the dangerous rays so that humanity might survive. "His food consists of the manna of heaven and the dew of the earth." The descriptions of the bird recall a haunting similarity to Ezekiel's chariot-vision (which see further on).

In some versions, the animal stays too long near the sun, crashes to earth in a conflagration, and later rises from its ashes to live again. In any event, it is another in many versions of the Near-Eastern resurrection cycle-myth.

AN ADDITIONAL TALMUD TAIL (*Sanhedrin* 11:3; *Gemarah* 108b)

This is the same *Gemarah* mentioned under number 39, which see. We recall Eliezar asking Shem about the difficulty in feeding the animals on board the ark. Here we see an unassuming side to the bird that dies and is resurrected, almost recalling the old joke of the holiest of men who goes before the Supreme Judge upon his death and wants only, every day, a somewhat fresh bagel and a "glass te," a glass of tea.

> As for the Phoenix, my father discovered it laying in the hold of the ark. "Dost thou require no food?" he asked it. "I saw that thou wast busy," it replied, "So I

said to myself, I will give thee no trouble." "May it be (God's) will that thou shouldst not perish," he exclaimed; as it is written [Job 29:18].

Like the Jews, the phoenix never fully perishes and, even in seeming death-throes, still it survives, to emerge even stronger than before.

. . . AND A *MIDRASH*

In *Genesis Rabbah* 19:4–5, we learn that the woman (Eve) offered the fruit to the cattle, the other animals, and the birds. "All obeyed her and ate thereof, except (the phoenix)." A *machlochet*, a dispute, ensues between students of R. Jamai and R. Judah b. R. Simeon as to how its resurrection syndrome and immortality occur: They both maintain it lives a thousand years and R. Jamai maintains it then burns up and R. Judah b. R. Simeon that its "body is consumed and its wings drop off"; but in both instances, ". . . as much as an egg is left, whereupon it grows new limbs and lives again."

Dragon: The animal is not discussed as one marvelous at creation. It might have been a later addition to the mythos pantheon. It is an oddity that all cultures have stories about dragons. Are these residual collective memories from the days when large lizards roamed the land? Are they resonances of some deep human internal conflict? Were they in actuality real, and did the very physiology that allowed them to produce flame consume them, upon their deaths, in conflagration endings, eradicating all fossil evidence? Paul and Karin Johnsgard have developed a clever zoological study, if presented with a bit of whimsy.

The authors first point out it is erroneous to consider that the animals had four legs and two wings. Like any flying animal (and it was never easy for dragons to fly, and certainly neither far nor high) the creature had two legs and two wings.

Three major categories are identified: lake dragons; flying dragons; flightless dragons. ". . . all species generate flammable gas, and . . . able to ignite this gas when it is threatened." It does so by allowing undigested food to decompose in one of its three stomachs, thus producing methane gas. Upon being startled or threatened, it belches the odoriferous substance through its oral cavity; then, gnashing its teeth together, it thus produces a spark, which ignites the methane gas (pp. 1–3, and f).

AN ADDITIONAL TALMUD TAIL (*Avodah Zorah* 3:3)

"If one finds utensils upon which is the figure of the sun or moon or a dragon, he casts them into the Salt (Dead) Sea. Rabban Simeon b. Gamaliel says: If it is upon precious utensils they are prohibited, but if upon common utensils they are permitted."

See also *Ketubot* 49b, wherein, however, there is a dispute over whether the term is a dragon or a type of bird (*Yarod* or *T'niem*).

> R. Elai stated in the name of Resh Lakish who had it from R. Judah b. Chanina: At Usha it was ordained that a man must maintain his sons and daughters while they are young . . . when people came before Rab. Judah he used to tell them: A *Yarod* bears progeny and throws them upon [the mercy] of the townspeople.

R. Judah's case is that in which a father fails to provide for his offspring and he indicates only a huge or terrible beast would do that. Usha was the site of the reinstitution of the Sanhedrin following the end of the Bar Kochba revolt. It is considered extremely important as it basically continued the continuity of the *taanaim* and *mishnaic* periods.

. . . AND A MIDRASH (*Esther Rabbah* 8:5–6) (also found in Apochrypha 9)

In this story Mordecai recounts a dream to Esther, in which the two beasts fighting for dominance (will come to) represent himself and Haman, where the parting waters represent Esther.

In the second year of King Ahasuerus he saw, and behold there was a great and mighty quaking and confusion upon the earth, and fear and trembling came upon all its inhabitants. And behold two dragons raised a cry against one another and prepared for battle, and all the nations of the earth fled at their voice(s). . . . Then behold a small stream of water passed between these two dragons and parted them and put a stop to their fighting . . .

Mordecai kept in mind the dream . . . and when Haman vexed him he said to Esther . . . "Here is the dream I related to you in your childhood. Now rise and pray for mercy from God and come before the king and supplicate for your people and your kindred."

Basilisk: ". . . a fiendish-looking . . . monster (resembling a horned lizard) with malignant powers. It was said to exist in inaccessible regions. . . ." There is a tradition that it was a pet of the king of demons, Asmodeous, and a willing partner in his dastardly deeds.

Zoological scientific observation and investigation have overtaken the mythology. A few years ago, the creature was found—a new species of lizard, and was named for the mythological monster. However, *Basiliscus basiliscus* is neither son nor daughter of the Middle East. It is found throughout the American tropics, from Jalisco and Veracruz in Mexico, southward to Columbia and Ecuador. "A conspicuous crest extends from the back of the head of the adult male and there is a high crest down the center of the back." Some individuals attain a length in excess of thirty inches.

It does, however, have a biblical connection, albeit not with the *Tanach*. The creature can walk on water, crossing rivers and other streams upon the surface without sinking. Thus, as we might suppose, it has been dubbed, "The Jesus Lizard." Thomas A. McMahon, a biomechanist, studied this unique ability. His team "found that most of the lizard's support comes from a well-timed foot stroke. With each step, the basilisk slaps the water and strokes its foot down, creating an air-filled cavity, then moves into the next step" (*Science News*). (See also Shine and "It Takes More . . .")

*   *   *

(Jonah's) "Great Fish": By tradition, it is leviathan, which see. There are several traditions concerning the time Jonah spent in the belly, not the least of which being that Leviathan taught him the entire Torah and the end of days; since Jonah, upon proceeding to perform his mission in Nineveh, now knew that eventually the ancestors of this city would destroy the city of his co-religionists and send them to exile in Babylon, the reason for his anger at his loss of protection at the end of the book is clearer.

Ezekiel's Majestic Vision: Opening the book of soaring poetry is this phantasmagoria by this mysterious prophet. I have heard rabbis say one should not study these verses until he (or she) has completed his study of Talmud. The implication is clear; when does the day ever come that one can state he has completed his study of *Mishnah* or *Gemarah*? It is one of the passages in the Bible indicating profound mystical search and attainment; the kabbalists refer to it as the *Merkavah*, the chariot, or the holy chariot, and Ezekiel is perceived as one who has completed his journey through the *s'ferot* to the *keter*, to the Crown. Here are the verses from JPS, pp. 893–894:

> In the thirtieth year, on the fifth day of the fourth month, when I was in the community of exiles by the Chebar Canal, the heavens opened and I saw visions of God . . . I looked, and lo, a stormy wind came sweeping out of the north—a huge cloud and flashing fire, surrounded by a radiance; and in the center of it, in the center of the fire, a gleam as of amber. In the center of it were also the figures of four creatures. And this was their appearance.
> They had the figures of human beings. However, each had four faces, and each of them had four wings; the legs of each were [fused into] a single rigid leg, and the feet of each were like a single calf's hoof; and their sparkle was like the luster of burnished bronze. They had human hands below their wings. The four of them had their faces and their wings on their four sides . . .

> Each of them had a human face [at the front];
> each of the four had the face of a lion on the
> right; . . . an ox on the left; . . . an eagle [at the
> back]. (Chapter 1)

The description continues for a total of twenty-eight
p'suchim, verses, in even more fantastical outlines. There are
wheels alongside, descending in an even larger wheel; a
curiosity of these curious passages is found in 20 and 21—"the
spirit of the creatures was in the wheels." In Verses 26–28,
however, we find the most amazing passage in perhaps all of
the sacred text—what may be no less than the description of
God Almighty, or at least, how the Prophet was allowed to
perceive the One that day:

> Above the expanse over the heads was the sem-
> blance of a throne, in appearance like sapphire; and
> on top, upon this semblance of a throne, there was
> the semblance of a human form. . . . the appearance
> of the semblance of the Presence of the Lord. . . .

Throughout history, rationalists, especially in the late
nineteenth and twentieth centuries, have attempted to demonstrate that this is hallucination by a troubled individual.
Hillmer is the latest to demonstrate effectively that "Ezekiel
had visions of God. He did not hallucinate." So the kabbalists
and those of faith have known it to be so.

Freehof has developed a scholarly excursus on the entire
book. In a brilliant fashion, he develops a synthesis between
the misgivings of the Rabbis and the misgivings of modern and
contemporary scholars. The argument is too detailed and too
lengthy to delve into for the parameters of this study, but, in
summary, it concerns whether the book is by the actual
Prophet, or a pseudepigrapha for later political requirements.

The sources are all indicated; refer especially to *Shabbat*
13b, wherein Hannaniah ben Hezekiah attempts to reconcile
the laws of Temple officiating diverging with those in Leviticus;
see also *Chagigah* 13a–b, wherein a lad who has not yet
studied sufficiently studies this text and loses his life, thus
indicating the rabbinical dicta on the dangers of studying
ma'aseh merkavah, Ezekiel's chariot.

The kabbalists too were careful to indicate that this was not in actuality God, nor even a vision of God; rather, it was one person's vision of God. However, any person can have such a vision "by becoming a vehicle or chariot . . . to the divine, this being a (very high) level." One attains this lofty state through study and prayer. "The concept of prayer is basically that of attachment to God. Engaging in the *Merkavah*, the mystical experience, however, is an even higher level of attachment. It refers to a vision of the Godly . . ." (Bahir, p. 133).

Well, then, what of the animal imagery? Man-Lion-Ox-Eagle: a tetrahedron of four powerful creatures, one of which is superior on earth, one of which is superior in the heavens, one of which is superior in the forests and wild places, and one of which is a domesticated beast. Together, "moving as one," this awesome tetrarchy guides the chariot; however, human beings on earth can achieve the divine emanations by traversing the divine pathways. Ultimately, of course, these are not animals at all, but an anthropomorphism of how one brilliant prophet, and we in turn, may begin to catch a glimpse of truth and of the heavenly spheres. Like the animals we share this planet with, and for whom we are ultimately responsible, what is left is a great mystery, penetrated best, as our fathers and mothers well knew, through faith.

An Additional Talmud Tail (*Chagigah* 2:1; *Gemarah* 13b)

There is a great expounding on the *Merkava*, the *Chasmal*, the Chariot, and its mystery in this tractate, especially this *Mishnah*. I chose this jewel out of many as it refers to the *pasuk*, "Now as I beheld the living creatures, behold one wheel at the bottom hard by the living creatures [JPS, p. 894: . . . one wheel on the ground next to each of the four-faced creatures]" (1:15). Ezekiel's (and Isaiah's, 6:1f, as well) magnificent vision of the heavenly host and of God's throne, in its utter glory of mysticism, is accepted and expounded further by the Rabbis.

> R. Eleazar said: [It is/may be] a certain angel, who stands on the earth and his head reaches unto the living creatures. In a *Baraita* it is taught: His name is

Sandalfon; he is higher than his fellows by a [distance of] 500 years' journey, and he stands behind the chariot and wreathes crowns for his maker. ("Wreathes crowns"—"Offers up prayers for the righteous," Soncino, N1, p. 79.)

THE SPECIES LIST
AT A GLANCE

The Order of Their
First Appearance in the Text,
Repeated
This Time Accompanied
by Their Total Number of References
in the Books of *Tanach* (The Hebrew Holy Scriptures)

Note: Number counting in either the empirical sense or the mystical (i.e., *gematria*), of items in Holy Writ is always fraught with difficulties and dangers imaginable and unimaginable. For example, the 613 *mitzvot* located b'Torah are not always easy to locate empirically, but there is no question of the number's acceptance as accurate. In this study, we are dealing with numbers in the thousands. Although I have relied heavily upon the JPS version of the Masoretic text, there may still be textual variations. More likely, although I have re-checked, it is possible that a reference has been overlooked or a number count here or there is not perfect. Still, these are the numbers that have come up. If anyone else wishes to count the animals, I welcome your corrections. I ask only that you double-check, and emerge at least as confident in your tally as I am in mine.

1. Humanity. *Homo sapiens*. Genesis 1:26.

   Again, some fundamentalist theologians will not permit this species to be considered as an animal; some theologians and nearly all more secular scholars will perceive it as not only permissible, but responsible. This resource will consider the argument moot. But we will present his and her stories, although we shall not emphasize them.

   At least three thousand different *men* appear in the text, although many names repeat; Azariah (1 Kings 4:2), for example, shares his name in this precise spelling alone with twenty-seven other men (the last in Daniel 1:6). Personages such as Elisha (1 Kings 19:16) are, of course, unique. Also, in uncountable legions, a vast unnamed host tends flocks, emerges from slavery in Egypt, engages in war as armies, and so on.

   Some of the more familiar or more eminent names, in alphabetical order, are: Aaron, Abel, Abner, Abraham; Absalom; Adam; Amos; Barak; Cain; Daniel; David; Eli; Elijah; Elisha; Enoch; Esau; Ezekiel; Ezra; Gideon; Goliath; Ham; Hezekiah; Isaac; Isaiah; Jacob; Jephthah; Jeremiah; Jereboam; Joab; Job; Jonah; Joshua; Josiah; Lot; Melchezedek; Methuselah; Moses; Naaman; Nehemiah; Nimrod; Noah; Pharaoh; Samson; Samuel; Solomon; Zaccariah; Nehemiah; Nimrod; Noah; Pharaoh; Samson; Samuel; Solomon; Zaccariah; and TS(Z)eddikiah.

   And the twelve sons/tribes of Israel: Reuben; Simeon; Levi; Judah; Zebulun; Issachar; Dan; Gad; Asher; Naphtali; Joseph (Ephraim and Manasseh); and Benjamin.

   At least two hundred different *women* are named, but perhaps as many again are unnamed. Once more, a vast uncountable host, particularly in the story of the escape from Egypt ("And Miriam the prophetess, the sister of Aaron, took a timbrel in her hand; and all the women went out after her with timbrels and with dances. And Miriam sang unto them . . . " [Exodus 15:20–21]).

   Some of the more familiar or eminent are: Eve, Sarah, Rebecca, Leah, Rachel, Tamar, J(Y)ochevet, the Daughters of Zelophehad (Mahlah, Tirzah, Hoglah, Milcah, Noah), Debra [Devorah, Deborah] (same name, two different women), Delilah, Hanah, Abishag, Michael, Jezebelle, Bath-Sheba, Ruth, and Esther.

2. Serpent. *Elaphe logissima.* Genesis 3:1. *33 listings*
3. Sheep. *Ovis aries.* Genesis 4:2. *273*
4. Raven. *Corvus corax.* Genesis 8:7. *8*
5. Dove. *Oena capensis.* Genesis 8:8. *21*
6. Heifer (See numbers 11, 12, 28). *Bos taurus.* Genesis 15:9. *11*
7. Goat. *Capra aegagrus.* Genesis 15:9. *142*
8. Ram. (See number 3). *O. aries.* Genesis 15:9. *145 (O. aries,* Sheep + Ram = *418)*
9. Pigeon. *Columbia livia.* Genesis 15:9. *11*
10. Ass. *Equus asinus.* Genesis 16:12. *145*
11. Calf (See numbers 6, 12, 28). *B. taurus.* Genesis 18:7. *40*
12. Cattle (See numbers 6, 11, 28). *B. taurus.* Genesis 20:14. *95*
13. Ox. *Bos primigenius.* Genesis 20:14. *141* (includes similitudes in buildings.)
14. Camel. *Camelus dromedarius.* Genesis 24:10. *49*
15. Horse. *Equus caballus.* Genesis 47:17. *135*
16. Lion. *Panthera leo.* Genesis 49:9. *99* (including similitudes in buildings.)
17. Deer. *Dama dama.* Genesis 49:21. *20*
18. Wolf. *Canis lupus lupus.* Genesis 49:27. *6*
19. Frog. *Rana Esculanta.* Exodus 7:12. *13*
20. Gnat. *Culex pipiens.* Exodus 8:12. *4*
21. Fly as "swarms of insects"; but refer to number 71
22. Locust. *Acridium migratorium.* Exodus 10:4. *19*
23. Dog. *Canis familiaris.* Exodus 11:7. *33*
24. Quail. *Coturnix coturnix.* Exodus 16:13. *4*
25. Worms. (See Maggots for taxonomy, number 76). Exodus 16:20. *9*
26. Eagle. *Aquila hryaetos.* Exodus 19:4. *15*
27. Seal. *Monachus albiventer.* Exodus 25:5. *11*
28. Bull. *B. taurus.* Exodus 29:1. *130 (B taurus:* Calf + Heifer + Cattle + Bull = *267)*
29. Turtle-Dove. *Streptopelia turtur.* Leviticus 1:14. *6*
30. Rock-Badger. *Meles meles.* Leviticus 11:5. *3*
31. Hare. *Lepus variabilis.* Leviticus 11:6. *2*
32. Swine. *Sus scrofa.* Leviticus 11:7. *5*
33. Grasshopper. *Locusta viridissima.* Leviticus 11:22. *3*

34. Mole. *Spalex Ehrenberghi*. Leviticus 11:29. *2*
35. Mouse. *Mus musculus*. Leviticus 11:29. *5*
36. Gecko. *Pachydactylus namaquensis*. Leviticus 11:30.
37. Land Crocodile. *Vernus* (*V. Monitor?*). Leviticus 11:30.
38. Sand Lizard. (poss. *Aporosaura Anchiaetae*.) Leviticus 11:30.
39. Chameleon. *Chameleon vulgaris*. Leviticus 11:30.
40. Hornet. *Vespa crabro*. Deuteronomy 7:20. *2*
41. Scorpion. *Androctonus australis*. Deuteronomy 8:15. *6*
42. Gazelle. *Gazella subgutturosa*. Deuteronomy 12:5. *11*
43. Roebuck. *Capreolus capreolus*. Deuteronomy 14:5. *3*
44. Wild Goat. Same as number 7, which see.
44a. Ibex. *Capra ibex nubiana*. Deuteronomy 14:5.
44b. Pygarg. *Addax nasomaculatus*. Deuteronomy 14:5.
45. Antelope. *Tragelaphus strepsiceros*. Deuteronomy 14:5. *2*
46. Mountain Sheep. Deuteronomy 14:5, 47.
47. Vulture. *Gypaetus barbatus*. Deuteronomy 14:12. *7*
48. Osprey. *Pandion haliaetus*. Deuteronomy 14:12.
49. Glede. *Milvus milvus*. Deuteronomy 14:13.
50. Falcon. *Falco tinnuculus/peregrinnus*. Deuteronomy 14:13. *2*
51. Kite. *Milvus migrans*. Deuteronomy 14:13. *2*
52. Ostrich. *Struthio camelus*. Deuteronomy 14:15. *9*
53. Night-Hawk. *Accipiter gentilis*. Deuteronomy 14:15. *2*
54. Sea Gull. *Larus argentatus*. Deuteronomy 14:15.
55. Owl. *Bubo bubo*. Deuteronomy 14:16. *3*
56. Pelican. *Pelecanus onocrotalus*. Deuteronomy 14:17. *4*
57. Carrion-Vulture. Unknown today. Deuteronomy 14:17.
58. Cormorant. *Phalacrocorax carbo*. Deuteronomy 14:17.
59. Stork. *Cicona cicona*. Deuteronomy 14:18. *4*
60. Heron. *Ardea goliath*. Deuteronomy 14:18.
61. Hoopoe. *Upupa epops*. Deuteronomy 14:18.
62. Bat. *Rhinopoma microphyllum*. Deuteronomy 14:18. *2*
63. Bee. *Apis mellifica*. Judges 14:8. *2*
64. Fox. *Vulpes vulpes vulpes*. Judges 15:4. *5*
65. Bear. *Ursus arctos*. 1 Samuel 17:34. *12*
66. Flea. *Pulex irritans*. 1 Samuel 24:15. *2*
67. Partridge. *Perdix perdix*. 1 Samuel 26:20. *4*
68. Caterpillar. *Charaxes jasues*. 1 Kings 8:37. *7*
69. Ape. (unknown) 1 Kings 10:22. *2*
70. Peacock. *Pavo cristatus*. 1 Kings 10:22. *2*

71. Fly. *Musca bovina/carnifex*. Isaiah 7:18. (poss. *4*)
72. Leopard. *Panthera pardus*. Isaiah 11:6. *7*
73. Cat. *Felis silvestris/catus/domestica*. Isaiah 13:21. *2*
74. Ferret. *Vormela peregusha*. Isaiah 13:21.
75. Jackel. *Canus aereus*. Isaiah 13:21.
76. Maggot. *Ulcus verminosum*. Isaiah 14:11.
77. Dragon. *Neodraco pluvialis*. Isaiah 27:1. *4*
78. Bittern. *Botaurus stellaris*. Isaiah 34:11. *2*
79. Swift (See Swallow, number 80 and Crane, number 81).
80. Swallow. *Hirundo rustica*. Isaiah 38:14. *4*
81. Crane. *Grus grus*. Isaiah 50:9. *2*
82. Moth. *Galleria cerella*. Isaiah 50:9. *2*
83. Basilisk. *Basilicus basilicus*. Isaiah 59:5. *2*
84. Spider. *Arachnida araneida theridion*. Isaiah 59:5.
85. Hyena. *H. Hyaena*. (poss. Jeremiah 12:9).
86. Gadfly. *Oestrus bovis*. Jeremiah 46:20.
87. Canker-Worm. Jeremiah 51:14.
88. (Ezekiel's Fantastic Vision.) Ezekiel 1:2 . . . (Nearly all verses in Chapters 1 and 2—not to be counted as animal species in this survey; also same or similar in numerous verses in Daniel 7.)
89. Palmer-Worm. Joel 1:4. *4*
90. (Jonah's "Great Fish.") By mystical thought, Leviathan, which see. Also referred to in Psalms V 148:7.
91. Wild-Ox. *Aurochs*. See Ox, domesticated. Psalms I 22:22. *3*
92. Snail. *Murex trunculus/M. brandaris*. Psalms II 58:9.
93. (Leviathan). No species given. (poss. *L. leviathanus*). *6*
94. Sparrow. *Passer domesticus*. Psalms III 84:4. *3*
95. Coney. See at number 30. Psalms IV 104:18.
96. Ant. *Polyergas rufescens/Formica nigra/rufa*. Proverbs 6:6. *2*
97. "Horseleech"; Leech. *Haemopsis sanguisuga*. Proverbs 30:15.
98. (Greyhound: Refer to number 23). Proverbs 30:31.
99. (Phoenix. No species given; poss. *P. Phoenixus*). Job 29:18.
100. (Behemoth. No species given; poss. *B. gargantuans*). Job 40:15. *2*

THE SPECIES LISTED BY MOST NAMED FIRST TO LEAST NAMED LAST

1. Sheep (273) + Ram (145) (*Ovis aeries*) = *418*
2. Cattle (98) + Calf (40) + Heifer (11) + Bull (130) (*Bos taurus*) = *276*
3. Donkeys, Ass = *145*
4. Goat = *142*
5. Horse = *135*
6. Ox = *127*
7. Lion = *99*
8. Camel = *49*
9. Serpent, Dog = *33*
10. Dove = *21*
11. Deer = *20*
12. Locust = *19*
13. Eagle = *15*
14. Frog, Jackal = *13*
15. Bear = *12*
16. Pigeon, Seal, Gazelle = *11*
17. Worm, Ostrich = *9*
18. Raven = *8*
19. Vulture, Caterpillar, Leopard = *7*
20. Wolf, Scorpion = *6*

21. Swine, Fox, Mouse = *5*
22. Gnat, Quail, Turtle-Dove, Pelican, Stork, Swallow, Fly, (Dragon), "Palmer-Worm" = *4*
23. Rock-Badger, Roebuck, Owl, Sparrow = *3*
24. Hare, Grasshopper, Hornet, Antelope, Kite, Night-Hawk, Bat, Bee, Flea, Partridge, Ape, Peacock, Cat, Bittern, Crane, Moth, (Basilisk), Turtle, Ant, (Behemoth) = *2*
25. The remainder, numbering in the aggregate 18, are mentioned but once.

TORAH AND *TANACH* LISTINGS

Some *Gematria*

The Torah references the number of newly cited species (first number shown) and the total number of species (second number shown) as:

Genesis:	18	124
Exodus:	9	124
Leviticus:	4	101
Numbers:	1	291
Deuteronomy:	23	65

giving a total of species listing as *55* (new/first) and *705* (total) = *TeSHaH*, which could be translated as "You will make or do or create"; perhaps, we cannot fulfill the *mitzvot* of Torah very well without regard to our animal friends.

The total number in the listings is *1,840* (sans *H. Sapiens* and some fantastical creatures).

SELECTED BIBLIOGRAPHY

A

Aid to Bible Understanding: Containing Historical, Geographical, Religious and Social Facts Concerning Bible Persons, Peoples, Places, Plant and Animal Life, Activities, and So Forth. New York: Watchtower Bible and Tract Society, 1971.

Allen, Glouer Morill. *Bats.* New York: Dover Publications, Inc., 1962 (1939).

Amato, I. "Scorpion Toxin Tells An Evolutionary Tale." *Science News* 139:6 (February 9, 1991): 85–86.

Angell, Tony. *Ravens Crows Magpies and Jays.* Forward by J. F. Lansdowne. Seattle: University of Washington Press, 1978.

Aristotle. *Historia Animalium,* tr. A. L. Peck. Cambridge: Harvard University Press, 1965.

Asimov, Isaac. *Animals of the Bible,* il. Howard Berelson. New York: Doubleday & Company, 1978.

Auel, Jean M. *The Mammoth Hunters.* Earth's Children Series (see also *Clan of the Cave Bear* and *The Valley of the Horses,* which previously published, and a fourth planned). Toronto: Bantam, 1986.

Austad, Steven N., and Randy Thornhill. "This Bug's for You." Phot. Mark W. Moffett. *Natural History* (December, 1991): 44–50.

Ausubel, Nathan. *A Treasury of Jewish Folklore.* New York: Crown Publishers, 1948.

————. *A Treasure of Jewish Humor.* Garden City: Doubleday & Company, Inc., 1951.

B

The Babylonian Talmud. All volumes. Tr. into English under ed. Rabbi Dr. I. Epstein. London: The Soncino Press, 1938.
Barnstone, Willis, ed. (and Introduction[s?]). *The Other Bible: Jewish Pseudepigrapha; Christian Apocrypha; Gnostic Scriptures.* San Francisco: Harper & Row, 1984.
"Basilisk." *Encyclopedia Americana.* http://ea.grolier.com/cgi-bin/build-pageartbaseid=0036590-00.
Begley, Sharon. "Beauty in the Beast: A Second Look (at Spotted Hyenas)." Phot. Mitsuaki Iwago. *International Wildlife* 28:2 (March–April, 1998): 30–38. Also @ EbscoHost IN 235727.
Bialik, Hayyim Nahman. *And It Came to Pass: Legends and Stories about King David and King Solomon.* Prev. *And It Came to Pass on a Certain Day*, 1934. Tr. Herbert Danby. Woodcuts, Howard Simon. New York: Hebrew Publishing Company, 1938.
"Birds and Be." *The Economist* 324:7773 (August 22, 1992): 72–73.
Birds of Prey. Cons. Ed. Ian Newton. New York: Facts on File, 1990.
Bodenheimer, F. S. *Animal and Man in Bible Lands.* Leiden: E. J. Brill, 1960.
Bokser, Ben Zion. Tr. and arr. *The High Holy Day Prayer Book: Rosh Hashanah and Yom Kippur.* New York: Hebrew Publishing Company, 1959.
————. *The Jewish Mystical Tradition.* Northvale, NJ: Jason Aronson Inc., 1993.
"A Book of Lists." Picks and Pans. *People* 43:3 (January 23, 1995): 31.
Bradbury, Margaret. *The Shepherd's Guidebook.* Emmaus: Rodale Press, 1977.
Brand, Stewart (and ed.). *The Essential Whole Earth Catalog.* Garden City: Doubleday & Company, 1986.
Brewer, Gary. Personal interview. Omaha, Nebraska, July, 1996. G. Brewer is a recognized naturalist.

Brown, Francis, S. R. Driver, and Charles A. Briggs. As tr. by Edward Robinson. *A Hebrew and English Lexicon of the Old Testament*. Based on the Lexicon of William Gesenius. Oxford: Clarendon Press, 1972.

Busch, Heather, and Burton Silver. *Why Cats Paint: A Theory of Feline Aesthetics*. Berkeley: Ten Speed Press, 1994.

Buxbaum, Yitzhak. *The Life and Teachings of Hillel*. Northvale, NJ: Jason Aronson, Inc., 1994.

C

Calmet's Dictionary of the Holy Bible: Historical, Critical, Geographical, and Etymological. V. Fragments 501–650, with "The Natural History." London: Charles Taylor, 1823.

Cansdale, George. *All the Animals of the Bible Lands*. Grand Rapids: Zondervan Publishing House, 1970.

Chekhov, Anton. *The Seagull*. In *Five Major Plays by Anton Chekhov*, tr. and int. Ronald Hingley. Toronto: Bantam Books, 1977.

Clark, Austin. *Animals Alive*. New York: D. Van Nostrand Company, Inc., 1948.

Conniff, Richard. "When it Comes to Moths, Nature Pulls Out All the Stops." *Smithsonian* 26:11 (February, 1996): 68 and 79f.

Culi, R. Yaakov. *The Torah Anthology*, tr. R. Aryeh Kaplan. New York: Marznaim Publishing Corporation, 1979.

D

Dane, Joseph. "The Syntaxis Recepta of Chaucer's Prologue to The Miller's Tale." *English Language Notes* 31:4 (June, 1994): 11f.

de Silva, Ian. "A Feathered Friend Stands Tall." *World and I* 11:4 (April, 1996): 192–196.

Deeskoski, Bernadette. "Pussycat, Queen of the Nile." *Hopscotch* 6:5 (March, 1995): 44.

DeFoe, Daniel. *History of the Plague in London*. c. 1670. ed. L. DuPont Style. New York: American Book Company, 1894.

———*A Journal of the Plague Year*. Oxford: Blackwell, 1928 (orig. pub. c. 1670).

Dewey, Jennifer Owings. "Locusts on My Windshield." *Highlights for Children* 51:9 (September, 1996): 30–31.

"Dromedaries in Distress," il. Charles Peale. "Outlook: Eye on the 90's." *U.S. News and World Report* 109:24 (December 17, 1990): 36.

E

Encyclopaedia Judaica. Jerusalem: Encyclopaedia Judaica, 1972.

Estes, Clarissa Pinkola. *Women Who Run with the Wolves: Myths and Stories of the Wild Woman Archetype*. New York: Ballantine Books, 1992.

Estes, Richard. "Hyena." *Encyclopedia Americana*. http://ea.grolier.com/cgi-bin/build-pageartbaseid=0210740-00.

F

Fackelmann, Kathy. "Loafing at the Landfill." *Science News* 145:16 (April 16, 1994): 252–254.

Farb, Peter. *The Land, Wildlife, and Peoples of the Bible*. New York: Harper and Row, 1967.

Feliks, Juhuda. *The Animal World of the Bible*. Tel-Aviv: Sinai, 1962.

Ferry, David. *Gilgamesh: A New Rendering in English Verse*. New York: Farrar, Straus & Giroux, 1992.

Fighier, Louis. *The Insect World*. New York: D. Appleton and Company, 1872.

Fisher, Jonathan. *Scripture Animals*. Princeton: The Pyne Press, 1845.

Flake, Carol. "Over the Hump." *Texas Monthly* 23:2 (February, 1995): 36–41.

Folger, Tim. "The First Masterpieces." *Discover* 17:1 (January, 1996).

Folktales of Israel, ed. Dov Noy and Dan Ben-Amos. Tr. Gene Beharan. Chicago: The University of Chicago Press, 1963.

Forst, Binyomin, Rabbi. *The Laws of Kashrus: A Comprehensive Exposition of Their Underlying Concepts and Applications*, ed. R. Nosson Scherman and R. Meir Zlotowitz. ArtScroll Hallachah Series. Brooklyn: Mesorah Publications, 1993.

Fox, Everett. *The Schocken Bible:* Vol. 1, *The Five Books of Moses: Genesis, Exodus, Leviticus, Numbers, Deuteronomy: A New Translation with Introductions, Commentary, and Notes*. New York: Schocken Books, 1995.

France, Peter. *An Encyclopedia of Bible Animals.* phot. Eric and David Hosking. London: Croom Helm, 1986.

Frankel, Ellen. *The Five Books of Miriam.* New York: G. P. Putnam's Sons, 1996.

Freehof, Solomon Bennett. *Book of Ezekiel.* New York: Union of American Hebrew Congregations, 1978.

Freund, Richard. Personal interview(s), the last March 2, 1997, Omaha, Nebraska. Dr. Freund is Professor of Jewish Studies at the University of Nebraska at Omaha, and Co-Director of the Beit Saida Archaeology site.

Friedman, Joseph, Rabbi. Several lessons and conversations. Omaha, Nebraska, 1992–1994.

Friedmann, Pavel. "The Butterfly." April 6, 1942. *I Never Saw Another Butterfly: Children's Drawings and Poems From Terezin Concentration Camp 1942–1944,* ed. Hana Volav-kovd. Foreword, Chaim Potok. Afterword, Vaclov Havel. New York: Schocken Books, 2nd ed., 1993, p. 39.

Friedman, Richard Elliot. *Who Wrote the Bible?* New York: Harper & Row, 1987.

G

Garrett, Laurie. *The Coming Plague: Newly Emerging Diseases in a World Out of Balance.* New York: Farrar, Straus and Giroux, 1994.

Gellman, Marc. *Does God Have a Big Toe?*, il. Oscar de Meja. New York: Harper Collins, 1989.

Ginsberg, Louis. *The Legends of the Jews,* tr. Henrietta Szold. Philadelphia: The Jewish Publication Society of America, 1909.

Glickman, Irving P., Rabbi. Chicago: Vaad.

Goldin, Hyman E. *The Jewish Woman and Her Home,* il. Nota Koslowsky. New York: Hebrew Publishing Company, 1941.

Golding, William. *Lord of the Flies.* Jackson Heights: Aconian Press, 1954.

"Good Heavens, How Pigs Have Changed!" *Countryside and Small Stock Journal* 79:4 (July–August, 1995): 45.

Goodall, Jane van Lawick. *In the Shadow of Man.* Boston: Houghton Mifflin Company, 1971.

Goodspeed, Edgar J. *The Apocrypha: An American Translation,* int., Moses Hadas. New York: Vintage Books, 1959.

Goodwin, Derek. *Pigeons and Doves of the World.* 2nd ed. Il., Robert Gillmor. Ithaca: Comstock Publishing Association, 1970.
Gotch, Arthur Frederick. *Mammals: Their Latin Names Explained.* Poole: Blandford Press Ltd., 1979.
———. *Birds: Their Latin Names Explained.* Poole: Blandford Press Ltd., 1981.
———. *Reptiles: Their Latin Names Explained.* Poole: Blandford Press Ltd., 1986.
Gottfried, Robert S. *The Black Death: Natural and Human Disaster in Medieval Europe.* New York: The Free Press, 1983.
Graves, Robert. *The Greek Myths.* 2 Volumes. Harmondsworth: Penguin Books, 1979.
Greenstein, Edward L. "Biblical Law." *Back to the Sources,* ed. Barry W. Holtz. New York: Summit Books, 1984.

H

Hebrew-English Edition of the Babylonian Talmud, tr., notes, indices Maurice Simon, ed. Rabbi Dr. I. Epstein. London: The Soncino Press, 1983.
Heidel, Alexander. *The Babylonian Genesis: The Story of Creation.* Phoenix Books, 1951.
Hillmer, Mark. "Ezekiel, Minor Prophets, Lamentations and Ecclesiastes." *The Niv/KJV* (which see) *Reference Edition.* Notes and Commentary. Grand Rapids: Zondervan Bible Publishers, 1983.
The Holy Scriptures: *According to the Masoretic Text.* Philadelphia: The Jewish Publication Society of America, 1962.
"Houseflies May Transmit Ulcer Bug." *Cancer Weekly Plus,* ed. Sandra W. Key and Michelle Marble (June 9, 1997): 16–17.
Hyman, Naomi Mara. *Biblical Women in the Midrash.* Northvale, NJ: Jason Aronson, Inc., 1997.

I

The Interpreter's Bible. 12 Vols. New York: Abingdon Press (Abingdon-Cokesbury), 1951–1957.
Israel, Richard, Rabbi. Personal interview. Omaha, March 2, 1997.
"It Takes More than Faith." Breakthroughs: Animals. *Discover* 17:5 (May, 1996): 20–21.

J

(The) Jewish Encyclopedia. Isidore Singer, Managing Editor. New York: Funk and Wagnalls Company, 1916.

Johnsgard, Paul, and Karin J. *Dragons and Unicorns: A Natural History.* New York: St. Martin's Press, 1982.

The JPS Torah Commentary. Comment. by Jacob Milgram. Philadelphia: The Jewish Publication Society, 1990.

K

Kahan, A. Y., Rabbi. *The Taryag Mitzvos 613.* Brooklyn: Keser Torah Publications, 1987.

Kaplan, Aryeh, Hakana, Nehunia ben. tr. and comm. *The Bahir.* Northvale, NJ: Jason Aronson, Inc., 1995.

Kelley, Ken. "Cormorants: Voracious Competitor or Bit Player?" *National Fisherman* 76:12 (April, 1996): 46–47.

Kipling, Rudyard. "How the Camel Got His Hump." *Just So Stories.* In John Beecroft: *Kipling: A Selection of His Stories and Poems*, il. Richard M. Powers. Garden City: Doubleday and Company, 1956.

Klinkenborg, Verlyn. "If It Weren't for the Ox, We Wouldn't Be Where We Are." *Smithsonian* 24:6 (September, 1993): 82–91.

Koehl, Carla, and Lucy Howard. "Pigeons Pilfered for Pies?" Periscope. *Newsweek* 127:12 (March 18, 1996): 6.

Komroff, Manuel, ed. *The History of Herodotus*, tr. George Rawlinson. New York: Tudor Publishing Company, 1928.

Kook, Avraham Yitzhak HaCohen, Rabbi. *Orot* (p. 14). In: Moshe Sokolev. *The Pursuit of Peace.* New York: CAJE (The Coalition for the Advancement of Jewish Education). Pamphlet. October, 1993.

Kramer, Samuel Noah. *History Begins at Sumer.* Garden City: Doubleday Anchor Books, 1959.

Kruuk, Hans. *The Spotted Hyena: A Study of Predation and Social Behavior.* Chicago: The University of Chicago Press, 1972.

L

Lawrence, R.D. *In Praise of Wolves.* New York: Henry Holt and Company, 1986.

Lewittes, Mordecai, ed. *Likutei Peshatim (The Student Bible)*, il. Audrey Namowitz. Sheet Music, Julius Grossman. New York: Hebrew Publishing Company, 1950.

————. *Likutei Peshatim*, ed. Rabbi Ben-Zion Rand. Skokie: Hebrew Theological College. Date unknown.

Lockyer, Herbert. *All the Men of the Bible.* Grand Rapids: Zondervan Books, 1958.

————. *All the Women of the Bible.* Grand Rapids: Zondervan Books, 1960.

Lopez, Barry Holstun. *Of Wolves and Men.* New York: Charles Scribner's Sons, 1978.

M

Mammal Species of the World: A Taxonomic and Geographic Reference, Don E. Wilson and DeeAnn M. Reeder, eds. 2nd edition. Smithsonian Institute Press, 1993.

Martin, James. "The Engaging Habits of Chameleons Suggest Mirth More Than Menace." *Smithsonian* 21:3 (June 1990): 44f.

Mattison, Chris. *Snakes of the World.* New York: Facts on File Publications, 1986.

McCarthy, Pat. Earthwised: "Dinner at Ding Darling." *Children's Digest* 45:7 (October–November 1995): 44–47.

McCook, Henry Christopher. *Nature's Craftsmen.* New York: Harper and Brothers Publishers, 1907.

Mech, David L. "The Howlings" (inset, "The Wired Wolf"). *Earthwatch* 13:6 (November–December, 1994): 24f.

Michener, James A. *The Source.* New York: Random House, 1965.

Midrash Rabbah, tr. under ed. of Rabbi Dr. H. Freedman and Maurice Simon. London: Soncino Press, 1939.

The Mishnah: Oral Teachings of Judaism, selected and trans. Eugene J. Lipman. New York: W. W. Norton and Company, 1970.

Moller-Christensen, V., and K. E. Jordt Jorgensen. *Encyclopedia of Bible Creatures*, ed. M. Theodore Heinecken, trans. Arne Unhejm. Philadelphia: Fortress Press, 1965.

Montifiore, C. G., and H. Loewe. *A Rabbinic Anthology.* London: Macmillan and Company, Ltd., 1938.

Morris, Desmond. *The Naked Ape: A Zoologist's Study of the Human Animal.* New York: McGraw-Hill Book Company, 1967.

Morrison, W. D. *The Jews under Roman Rule.* New York: G. P. Putnam's Sons, 1899.

N

Nadich, Judah. *The Legends of the Rabbis.* 2 Vols. Northvale, NJ: Jason Aronson, 1994.

Nardi, James B. *Close Encounters with Insects and Spiders.* Ames: Iowa State University Press, 1988.

The Natural Moment: "Falling Into a Rut." *Natural History* 104:1 (January, 1995): 78.

Newman, Cathy. "Nature's Masterwork: Cats." *National Geographic* 191:6 (June, 1997): 55–85.

The NIV/KJV Parallel Bible. Grand Rapids: Zondervan Bible Publishers, 1985.

Norell, Mark, Luis Chiappe, and James Clark. "New Limb on the Avian Family Tree." *Natural History* 102:9 (September, 1993): 38–42.

Nowak, Ronald M. *Walker's Mammals of the World.* 5th ed. Johns Hopkins University Press, 1991.

O

Okie, Susan. "SIDS Theory Criticized in Book." Omaha *World-Herald.* October 13, 1997, 32:4 (also *The Washington Post*).

Olivares, Javier. "A New 'Noah's Ark.' " Notes on the Sciences. *World Press Review* 41:7 (July, 1994): 44.

Owls of the World: Their Evolution, Structure and Ecology, ed. John A. Burton, il. John Rignall. Glasgow: Eurobook, 1984.

Oxford Complete Wordfinder, ed. Frank Abate. Pleasantville: Reader's Digest, 1996.

P

Parmelee, Alice. *A Guide to the New Testament.* Wilton: Morehouse-Barlow Company, Inc., 1980.

———. *A Guide to the Old Testament and the Apocrypha.* Wilton: Morehouse-Barlow Company, Inc., 1979.

Passover Hagadah. Deluxe Edition. Kraft General Goods, Inc., 1996.

Pedrini, Lura Nancy, and Duilio T. *Serpent Imagery and Symbolism.* New Haven: College and University Press, 1966.

"The Pelican Man's Bird Sanctuary." *Sarasota Magazine* 19:3 (March, 1997): 236.

The Pentateuch and Haftorahs, *Hebrew Text, English Translation and Commentary,* ed. Dr. J. H. Hertz, C. H. 2nd Ed. London: Soncino Press, 5721/1961.

Petren, Kenneth, and Ted J. Case. "Gecko Power Play in the Pacific," phot. Mike Severns. *Natural History* 103:9 (September, 1994): 52f.

"Pig Organs Could Reduce Need for Human Donors." *Executive Health's Good Health Report* 32:3 (December, 1995): 2.

Pinney, Roy. *The Animals in the Bible.* Philadelphia: Chilton Books, 1964.

Podwal, Mark. *A Jewish Bestiary.* Philadelphia: The Jewish Publication Society of America, 1984.

Pirke Avot (Chapters, but tr. as) *Ethics of the Fathers,* tr. and annot. Hyman Goldin. New York: Hebrew Publication Company, 1962.

Preuss, Julius. *Biblical and Talmudic Medicine* (1911), tr. and ed. Fred Rosner. Northvale, NJ: Jason Aronson, Inc., 1993.

Pritchard, James B. ed. The Ancient *Near East: An Anthology* (V. 11, *A New Anthology) of Texts and Pictures.* Princeton University Press, VI, 1973; VII, 1975.

"Probing Animal Intelligence." *Earthwatch* (January–February, 1996): 6, 13.

Putman, Rory. *The Natural History of Deer.* Ithaca: Comstock Publishing Press, 1988.

R

Raphael, Simcha Paull. *Jewish Views of the Afterlife.* Northvale, NJ: Jason Aronson, Inc., 1996.

Ramban (Nachmanides). *Commentary on the Torah,* tr. and annot. Charles B. Chael. New York: Shilo Publishing House, Inc., 1973.

"A Review of the Namaqua Gecko, *Pachydactylus Namaquensis* (Reptilia: Gekkonidae) from Southern Africa, with the Description of Two New Species." *South African Journal of Zoology* (April, 1996).

Robinson, Michael D. "Death and Dancing on the Sun-Baked Dunes of Namibia." *Natural History* 102:8 (August, 1993): 28–31.

Rosstein, Maishe. "A Modern Midrash of an Ancient Tale." Unpublished manuscript, 1997. Used by permission of the author.

S

Schochet, Elijah Judah. *Animal Life in Jewish Traditions: Attitudes and Relationships.* New York: Ktav Publishing House, Inc., 1984.

Scholem, Gershom. *Shabbatai (T) Sevi: The Mystical Messiah 1626–1676,* tr. and annot. Hyman Goldin. New York: Hebrew Publishing Company, 1962.

Schwartz, Mordecai. Shiur on *Ethics of the Fathers.* Beth Israel Synagogue. Omaha, Nebraska, June 7, 1997.

Sforno, Ovadiah ben Yaacov (generally known as "The Sforno"). *Commentary on the Torah.* Vol. 1 *B'reishis and Shemos,* tr. and notes by R. Raphinel Pelcovitz, ed. R. Nosson Scherman and R. Meir Zlotowitz. *The Artscroll Mesorah Series.* Brooklyn: Mesorah Publications, Ltd., 1987.

Shaler, Nathaniel Southgate. *Domesticated Animals.* New York: Charles Scribner's Sons, 1907.

Shakespeare, William. *The Complete Works of William Shakespeare.* Vol. 1. Garden City: Nelsen Doubleday, Inc.

Shilleto, A. R., Reverend, Revisor. *The Works of Flavius Josephus.* Vol. 5, *The Jewish War,* tr. F. Whiston, notes by C. W. Wilson. London: George Bell and Sons, 1890.

Shine, Jerry. "Walking on Water," ed. Dawn Stover. Nature: Newsfronts. *Popular Science* 247:1 (July, 1995): 26–29.

Silbermann, Rabbi A. M., and Rev. M. Rosenbaum., tr. and annot. *Chumash with Targum Onkelos, Haftorah and Rashi's Commentary.* 5 Vols. of the Pentateuch. Jerusalem: The Silbermann Family, 1934.

Simpson, George Gaylord. *Horses.* New York: Oxford University Press, 1951.

Smith, Willard S. *Animals, Birds and Plants of the Bible.* Abingdon: Church Art, Inc., 1971.

Smith, W. Robertson, and the Rev. T. K. Cheyne. *The Prophets of Israel and Their Place in History: To the Close of the Eighth Century.* London: Adam and Charles Black, 1897.

Sophocles. *Oedipus Rex,* tr. and ed. by L. R. Lind. *Ten Greek Plays in Contemporary Translations.* Boston: Houghton Mifflin, 1957.

Speiser, E. A. "Introduction," tr., and notes. *The Anchor Bible: Genesis.* Garden City: Doubleday and Company, Inc., 1964.

"The Spotted *Hyena* from Aristotle to the Lion King: Reputation Is Everything." *Social Research* 62:3 (Fall 1995): 501f. Also @ EbscoHost IN 9601260766.

Staedter, Tracy. "Jurassic Ants." Paleontology. *Earth* 6:1 (April 1, 1997): 20.

Steinberg, Milton. *As a Driven Leaf*, Forward by Chaim Potok. Behrman House, 1939 (1996).

Stephenson, Carl. "Leiningen Versus the Ants." *The Penguin Book of Horror Stories*, ed. J. A. Cuddon. Manchester: Penguin Books, 1984.

T

The Talmud. *The Steinsaltz Edition*, trans., and ed., commentary Adin Steinsaltz. New York: Random House. The Israel Institute to Talmudic Publications, 1989.

Talmud Bavli: The Artscroll Series, ed. Schottenstein. Brooklyn: Mesorah Publications, 1993.

"Teacher Knows His Beeswax." Midlands News. Omaha *World-Herald.* 2:7B, 1.

Telushkin, Joseph, Rabbi. *Jewish Literacy: The Most Important Things to Know about the Jewish Religion, Its People, and Its History.* New York: William Morrow and Company, Inc., 1991.

"Third Group of Rare Ferrets Released to Wild." *Internal Wildlife* 24:1 (January/February, 1994): 27f.

Thomas, Elizabeth Marshall. *The Hidden Life of Dogs.* Boston: Houghton Mifflin Company, 1993.

Tiller, Patrick. *A Commentary on the Animal Apocolypse of I. Enoch.* Atlanta: Scholars Press, 1993.

Tanakh: The Holy Scriptures. *The New JPS Translation According to the Traditional Hebrew Text.* Philadelphia: The Jewish Publication Society, 1985.

"Tools from the Stone Age." *Alberta Report.* "Albertans." *Western Report* 23:3 (January 1, 1996): 25f.

"Tools of the Trade." *Natural History* 104:3 (March, 1995): 48–49.

Toperoff, Shlomo Pesach. *The Animal Kingdom in Jewish Thought.* Northvale, NJ: Jason Aronson Inc., 1995.

The Torah: *A Modern Commentary*, ed. W. Gunther Plaut. New York: Union of American Hebrew Congregations, 1981.

Trachtenberg, Joshua. *Jewish Magic and Superstition: A Study in Folk Relgion*. New York: Atheneum, 1970.

Trippett, Frank. *The Emergence of Man: The First Horsemen*. New York: Time-Life Books, 1974.

Tristram, H. B. *Natural History of the Bible: A Review of the Physical Geography, Geology, and Meteorology of the Holy Land*. New York: American Tract Society, 1867.

Twain, Mark. "The Diary of Adam and Eve." *The Complete Short Stories of Mark Twain*, ed. Charles Neider. Garden City: Doubleday and Company Inc., 1957, pp. 272–294.

W

"A Walk on the Wild Side." Technology. *Science News* 149:1 (January 6, 1996): 15–16.

Wijesniha, Sanjiva. "New Help for Hearts." *World Press Review*. Section: "Notes on the Sciences." 40:8 (August, 1993): 45.

Wikramanayake, Eric. "Everyone Knows the Dragon Is Only A Mythical Beast." *Smithsonian Magazine* 28:1 (April 1997): 74f.

Wiland, Lawrence. "Little Devils." Animalia. *Backpacker* 23:145 (October, 1995): 18–22.

Wiley, Lulu Ramsey. *Bible Animals*. New York: Vantage Press, 1957.

Y

Yagil, Reuven. "From Its Blood to Its Hump, the Camel Adapts to the Desert." "Special: Beating the Heat." *Natural History* 102:8 (August, 1993): 30–34.

Youatt, William. *The Horse*, with "An Essay on the Ass and the Mule," by J. S. Skinner. New York: George A. Leavitt, 1843.

Z

Zimmer, Carl. "Death in the Pliocene." Paleontology. *Discover* 16:1 (January, 1995): 85–86f.

———. "The Healing Power of Maggots." *Discover* 14:8 (August, 1993): 17.

INDEX